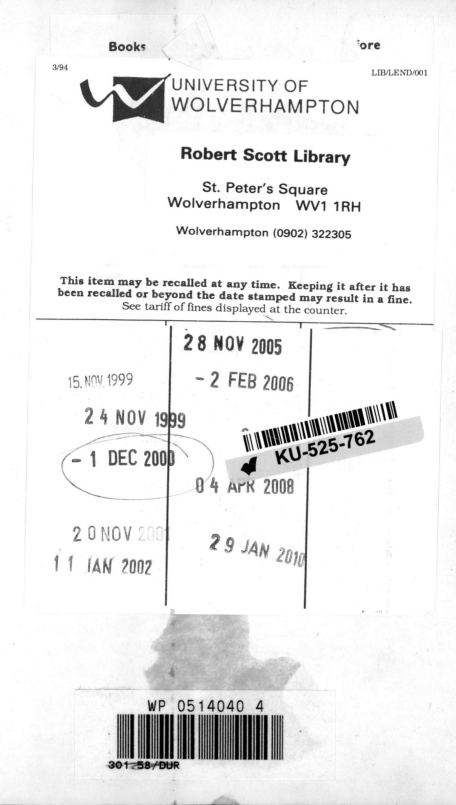

Durkheim on religion

Durkheim on religion

A selection of readings
with bibliographies

W. S. F. Pickering

New translations by Jacqueline Redding and W. S. F. Pickering

Routledge & Kegan Paul
LONDON AND BOSTON

First published in 1975
by Routledge & Kegan Ltd
Broadway House, 68–74 Carter Lane,
London EC4V 5EL and
9 Park Street,
Boston, Mass. 02108, USA
Set in Photon Times
and printed in Great Britain at
the Alden Press, Oxford

ISBN 0 7100 8108 1

Contents

Acknowledgments

The development of this book has been greatly facilitated by the encouragement, help and guidance that have been so freely given by many people. Of the names that could be mentioned that of Steven Lukes stands out most prominently and I should like to thank him in particular for his kindness and great generosity exhibited in a multitude of ways, not least in allowing us to use his bibliographical index system. Gratitude is extended to others who have helped in one fashion or another, especially to Rodney Needham, Herminio Martins, Elisabeth Labrousse, Andrew Fairbairn, D. H. Killingley and Nora Kofman; and in connection with compiling notes on Gaston Richard, Professors Château and Moreau of the University of Bordeaux, and Mme Y. D. Miroglio. Mrs Jacqueline Redding has been largely responsible for the translations which bear our joint names. We wish to make it clear that the deficiencies of this volume can be in no way laid at the feet of those who have been kind enough to offer advice and help. We also want to thank Mrs A. Rule for her patience and diligence in the arduous task of typing the script.

I wish to record my gratitude to the Research Committee of the University of Newcastle upon Tyne, which in the late 1960s awarded me two grants in order that some of the early translations could be carried out.

Finally, and by no means least, I wish to thank very sincerely the Warden and Fellows of St Antony's College, Oxford, for allowing me to reside in the college during the academic year, 1972–3, and thereby providing congenial and stimulating conditions for undertaking research which is in part embodied in this book.

W.S.F.P.

The translations

The English translations which we have made and which appear in this book are of works of Durkheim and others which have not been translated before, or if they have been translated, are in some way deficient.

In carrying out our task we offer a fairly literal rendering of the French, provided it presents acceptable English. The reason for having such an aim is simple. In philosophical and sociological works, exactness of translation is more important than style: we hope, however, that we have not sacrificed too much of the second for the sake of the first. Those who have translated Durkheim know that a number of problems have to be faced: long sentences; the repetition of words and phrases, both technical and non-technical; and the tendency of Durkheim at certain times to be rhetorical. Faced with these problems we have taken the risk of making small changes, as in punctuation, which we trust will help rather than hinder the reader reaching the heart of what Durkheim had to say. As is common practice, we have retained the French for certain words which defy translation, for example, *conscience*, *représentation*, together with their associated adjectives. For the meaning of these and other terms the reader is referred to Lukes's book (1973:4–16). We have on occasions used different words to translate the one French word according to context, such as *laïque* which is translated by secular in one instance, by lay in another. According to current usage we have translated *sociologie religieuse* as the sociology of religion, not religious sociology. It was decided to use the more traditional English term, though it might be argued that in one or two contexts, *sociologie religieuse* might imply a sociology based on religion. Where Durkheim quotes in French from books originally written in English, we have used the words of the English text. All the footnotes in the original text are reproduced at the end of each document, and in a few cases annotated. References to English translations have also been inserted. Any additions to the original footnotes are followed by the initials W.S.F.P. Unless otherwise stated, the translations are made from first editions.

Where original translations of Durkheim's works have appeared to be satisfactory, we have used such translations, for there is no good reason to carry out further translation for its own sake. We wish to thank those responsible for permission to use the translations, in particular to S. and J. Lukes for allowing us to use their translation of 'L'Individualisme et les intellectuels'.

On the shoulders of Jacqueline Redding has fallen the bulk of the work involved in translation. However, we both take responsibility for those deficiencies which we are sure still remain.

J.R.
W.S.F.P.

Notation

The shorthand sign for the name of a book is the date which follows the author's name. The title of the book, its publisher, date, and so on, can be found under the author's name in the Durkheim and Richard bibliographies at the end of the book. The numbers which follow the date refer to the pages in the book. It should be noted that where English translations exist, the (first) number refers to the pages in the original text. The corresponding pages in the translation are given in a second number which follows the sign / and has a prefix t. E.g. Durkheim 1897a:149/t.152 means Durkheim's *Suicide*, first edition 1897, p. 149, which corresponds to the English translation by Spaulding and Simpson published in 1951, p. 152.

Where several editions of a French text exist in which there are significant changes, for example, Durkheim's *De la Division du travail social*, the first date refers to the first edition, the second, where given, to a relevant later edition, followed by the page number of the later edition—1893b/1902b:200 means p. 200 of the 1902 edition of *De la Division du travail social*, first published in 1893.

Some of the references to English translations relate to translations made in this book.

In adding references to English translations of books mentioned by Durkheim and other authors in their texts and notes, we have adopted a more traditional and self-explanatory system.

Abbreviations

AJS	American Journal of Sociology
AS	L'Année sociologique
ASR	American Sociological Review
ASRel	Archives de sociologie des religions
BJS	British Journal of Sociology
BSFP	Bulletin de la Société Française de Philosophie
EJS	European Journal of Sociology (Archives européennes de sociologie)
MF	Mercure de France
PR	Philosophical Review
RB	Revue bleue
RHPR	Revue d'histoire et de philosophie religieuses
RIS	Revue internationale de sociologie
RMM	Revue de métaphysique et de morale
RNS	Revue néo-scolastique
RP	Revue philosophique de la France et de l'étranger

Introduction

I

This book was planned and actually started a considerable time before the appearance of Steven Lukes's *Émile Durkheim: his Life and Work* early in 1973. The publication of such an important and superb intellectual biography had the effect of making my own limited beginnings and plans in writing about Durkheim's analysis of religion seem somewhat questionable. In the light of the thoroughness and careful documentation of Lukes's book, what more could now be said about Durkheim? And particularly, what more about his sociology of religion, which is so extensively treated? My efforts were in part undermined because Lukes pointed to several books and articles which referred to religion and which until now were not generally known in this country. Some of these works Jacqueline Redding and I had already translated into English. Also, a few months prior to the release of *Émile Durkheim: his Life and Work*, Anthony Giddens of Cambridge University published his *Émile Durkheim, Selected Writings* (1972), in which sections of certain of the books and articles just alluded to became available to the English-reading public through his translation.

However, despite the effervescence—if one might adopt a Durkheimian expression—of interest in the great French sociologist, and through the encouragement of Lukes, who had just written so much on the subject, as well as that of others, it seemed worth while pressing on with the original plan of presenting selected translations of Durkheim's work on religion, together with bibliographies and an accompanying commentary. It was hoped then and it is still hoped that the project will be valuable and in no way a pale reflection of these recently published books.

The first part of the scheme is embodied in this volume: the commentary will appear as a separate book in the near future. That publication should proceed in this order seems right because it is on the whole better to present some of the documents and the bibliographies before offering a critical review of Durkheim's work on religion. And surely the man himself would be pleased to see the starting point is to be the 'facts'.

No attempt is made in this introduction to interpret Durkheim's religious thought or even to describe it. In this sense the introduction makes no contribution to academic studies. Such contribution as I have to offer will appear in the succeeding book. What is presented here is an attempt both to justify publishing a volume of translations of Durkheim's sociology of religion and to show the principles on which the selection of readings has been made. Readers who want a general description of Durkheim's religious thought are advised to consult the bibliography, and at the risk of repetition it might be said that Lukes's treatment of the subject is probably the most comprehensive yet to appear.

II

Interest in Durkheim's life and work has probably never been as widespread as it is at the moment, both within the sociological world and beyond it. This has partly come about because of the great development of the sociological world itself since the time of Durkheim who died in 1917, and particularly because in England and the United States, since the end of World War II, there has been a considerable growth in the teaching of sociology in universities. The interest has also arisen through a recent gathering of clouds of uncertainty about the path sociology should take in the future. Driven by a rejection of sophisticated theory on the one hand

and crude empiricism on the other, many are turning to the writings of the founding fathers for enlightenment and inspiration.

Repeatedly one hears it said that the three men who contributed more than any others to sociology in the nineteenth century were Durkheim, Weber and Marx. If some may doubt the presence of Marx within the trinity and would prefer to see Simmel, Pareto or Spencer as the substitute, the fact remains that no one can dethrone Durkheim from being one of its members. The continual publication of his works in their original language, the ever-growing number of translations into various languages, and a very recent upsurge in books written by English-speaking academics—for example, those of LaCapra (1972), Wallwork (1972), Lukes (1973), Clark (1973), Bellah (1973)—are but the external signs of a renewed awareness of his place at the zenith of the sociological world at the end of the last century, if not the first half of the present century. There is no need to extol in detail the contributions this Alsatian Jew made to sociology—this man who in 1887 held one of the first academic teaching posts in sociology in France at Bordeaux, although first under the guise of education, who became a professor in 1896 and then taught in Paris in 1902. The story and the nature of his greatness have been told often enough, and now in a more recent book we have it before our eyes in large letters.

However, there is one point that ought to be emphasized, since it has direct bearing on this volume: the prominence that Durkheim gave to religion. From the time he went to the École Normale Supérieure, and even before, Durkheim showed an extraordinary interest in religion that persisted, and indeed grew, with the passing of years until his death in 1917. To an outsider such an interest would seem incompatible with his convinced rationalist and anti-clerical outlook. But the fact remains that in a very great deal that he wrote—and this is certainly true for most of his books—there appeared constant references to religion, which though framed in a scientific mould were often more in praise than condemnation. Indeed, towards the end of his career, and it was a career that was snuffed out at the height of its powers when he was fifty-nine years old, religious issues were of burning importance. The demonstration of this fact is in the publication of his most definitive, and some would add his finest and most original book, *Les Formes élémentaires de la vie religieuse. Le système totémique en Australie*, published in 1912. With carefully stated assumptions, Durkheim set

out to explain by sociological means the phenomenon of religion.
Although he used material gathered from primitive peoples—the
primary source, Australian aborigines; North American Indians
his secondary—the findings were held to be applicable to religion in
general. None the less, while it is true that Durkheim tried to
understand religion on scientific grounds by reference to social
phenomena, even society itself, the obverse is also true, that is, he
used religion to explain society. Such was the importance it assumed
before his eyes.

The sociological study of religion owes Durkheim an enormous
debt which it has not always acknowledged. From the time he
founded the journal. *L'Année sociologique*, in 1896, he began to
exert a powerful influence on all those around him who wished to
study religion within the terms of reference of sociology. But
because his ideas became so readily accepted and developed, his
creative ability has not been as widely recognized as it should have
been. All too frequently it has been taken for granted. In a recent
book, *Ecstatic Religion* (1971:11), I. M. Lewis, professor of
anthropology at the London School of Economics, has written:
'Except in such specialized areas of interest as witchcraft, initiation
rites, or pollution behaviour, the subject [of the sociology of
religion] remains as a whole very much where it was left by
Durkheim and Weber.' Lewis admits this is a harsh judgment but a
true one. And if the point is taken, it might legitimately be asked,
why has no further progress been made? It is a question too vast to
try to answer here but in the case of Durkheim (and indeed of
Weber) no answer can be offered until a thorough analysis has been
made of what Durkheim set out to do, the methods he employed,
and the conclusions he drew from substantive material.

Those who have but a limited acquaintance with Durkheim's
religious thought are usually those who have read *Les Formes
élémentaires*, in part or in whole in the English translation, or who
have gained knowledge of the book from the lectures of others. They
might also recall a relevant chapter or so in the earlier book, *Le
Suicide*, which appeared in 1897. To some degree this is
understandable since *The Elementary Forms* is not only a superb
piece of writing and forms the peak of Durkheim's study of religion,
but it was also the first of his books to be translated into English, in
fact by an American classical scholar, J. W. Swain, in 1915. But as
has just been noted, Durkheim's interest in religion is evident in his

very early writings, and therefore any comprehensive appreciation of his religious thought must take into account his early references and generalizations about religion, as well as those which appeared at the summit of his thought. No one climbs a mountain starting at the peak!

Despite Durkheim's wrestling with religious issues, it is most surprising that commentators, especially his disciples such as Mauss, Davy, Halbwachs, Fauconnet, and so on, have given very little space to the subject compared with other issues. Halbwachs's *Les Origines du sentiment religieux* (1925) is but a résumé of *Les Formes élémentaires* for popular consumption: indeed it is reminiscent of a tract. Georges Davy, friend and admirer, in the many articles that he wrote on Durkheim after his death—and he seems to have assumed the role of an official interpreter of the master—gives relatively little space to his thought on religion. It might be suggested that one writer was an exception, namely Marcel Mauss, his nephew, who from the early days of *L'Année sociologique*, often in collaboration with Durkheim himself, wrote many monographs and reviews on religious topics. Aided by Hubert and Hertz, Mauss became the foremost authority on religion in the Durkheim school. However, his most fruitful period on the subject of religion was up to the time of World War I rather than after it. It is true he lectured on religious sciences at the Hautes Études and at the Sorbonne but his creative work seems to have been in another direction, for example, exchange-theory as in the *Essai sur le don*. R. Bastide wrote a systematic treatise on the sociology of religion based on Durkheim's ideas entitled *Éléments de sociologie religieuse*: it appeared in 1935 but in the event did not prove to be an important book. Of course it could be argued that Durkheim's work on religion was extended by ethnographers and anthropologists in, say, the Institut d'Ethnologie and the Musée de l'Homme, and by the historians of early civilizations. One calls to mind such scholars as Lévy-Bruhl, Granet, Rivet, and of course Mauss himself (see Lévi-Strauss, 1945). But by and large there was not a great interest amongst scholars in expounding Durkheim's theories of religion as such. Apart from the flourish of reviews in 1912 and the years that immediately followed, direct references to Durkheim's work on religion in the 1920s and 1930s become meagre indeed, particularly in France where one would have expected a contrary state of affairs. This is no occasion to elaborate the point, to document it or to try to account for it, but simply to state that when Durkheim died widespread interest in religion amongst his disciples died with him. At least it might be observed that within his followers, neglect of his ideas on religion seems to have arisen because of overriding interests in other fields opened up by his sociology, and by comparison many more references were made to basic issues raised by *De la Division du travail social* (1893b), *Les Règles de la méthode sociologique* (1895a), *Le Suicide* (1897a), and essays reproduced posthumously in *Sociologie et philosophie* (1924a). Interest centred on the sociology of the family, the sociology of law, the sociology of knowledge (admittedly a very important element in *Les Formes élémentaires*), the relation of psychology to sociology, methodology, etc. It is possible to argue that the position was not quite as bare in the English-speaking world since, through the work of the British social anthropologist Radcliffe-Brown, Durkheim's works began to be introduced to students in a comprehensive way from the 1930s onwards. Radcliffe-Brown both accepted and developed some of the ideas of Durkheim on religion. Generally speaking, it cannot be denied that Durkheim's theories through the process of general diffusion became very important in the development of anthropological and sociological studies in religion. However, if one examines the whole gamut of his writings and the subjects he analysed, his ideas, and those on religion which were so crucial to his thought, have not been accorded by commentators the attention given to other aspects of his work. This book and the one which is planned to follow is an attempt to help redress the situation.

III

The primary consideration in selecting extracts from Durkheim's works which incidentally deal with or are devoted to religion was to choose items from the entire period of his academic life. Such an aim has the advantage of showing, however inadequately, the development of his thinking on religion. A further principle of selection was to focus on items which although important in themselves had not been translated into English: for example, his early approach to a systematic study of religion which appeared in an article in volume II of *L'Année sociologique* entitled 'De la Définition des phénomènes religieux' (1899a[ii]). Moreover, it was thought desirable to present something of Durkheim's ideas on modern religion—ideas which are evident in *Les Formes élémentaires*. He did not write scientifically or extensively on the subject, although he was ready enough to talk about it. (See 1898c, 1919b: also 1909a and 1913b not translated.)

A formidable task was encountered in choosing sections from Durkheim's *magnum opus, Les Formes élémentaires de la vie religieuse*. In one sense, any selection of parts is destined to failure. A piecemeal reading of this great book cannot but be unsatisfactory: it is a work that has to be read in its entirety. However, in such a volume as the present one, only travesty and failure would result if no extensive reference were made to it. Inevitably one has to take the plunge and it was decided that the points of entry would be those in the early, middle and late chapters which portray Durkheim's methods and findings which have application to religion as a whole. In short, his detailed analysis of the social and religious life of the Arunta has been excluded, and attention has been focused on the generalizations he deduced from such analysis. Sadly the chapters towards the end of the book on ritual and sacrifice have also been excluded because of the close intertwining of ethnographic material and the generalizations that Durkheim deduces. With rather more decisiveness, sections of the sociology of knowledge have been excluded, important though they are. Durkheim's sociology of knowledge requires a separate volume; and to introduce such a topic here, together with his earlier writings on the sociology of knowledge, would be to completely miss the focal point of this book. Therefore, where well-defined sections on the sociology of knowledge appear in the chapters which have been selected, such sections have been omitted. Nevertheless, a certain small portion has been retained which shows at a very elementary level how, in Durkheim's eyes, religion has contributed to the development of concepts. It should also be noted that sections in the opening chapters of *Les Formes élémentaires* which correspond to sections in the earlier essay, 'De la Définition des phénomènes religieux', have been omitted in order to avoid repetition. For a very brief summary of the book, the reader is referred to that which Durkheim wrote together with Mauss in a review in *L'Année sociologique* which is included here (see 1913a[ii] [12]).

After some deliberation it was decided to incorporate one or two critical reviews of the many that appeared at the time of the publication of *Les Formes élémentaires*, as well as criticisms that

were published subsequently. Of the early reviews, that of
Goldenweiser (1915) is outstanding because of its wide approach
and, in the light of continual reflection, the soundness of its
criticisms. In recent times that of Stanner (1967), which is an
analysis of one or two of Durkheim's ideas, notably the concept of
the sacred and profane, has received wide acclaim. This, together
with Goldenweiser's review, has been included as well as that of van
Gennep (1913). This last review is of interest because it comes from
a well-known, respected and creative anthropologist who was never
given an academic post in France. The review has not been
translated before and neither has a much longer, general and more
searching attack made by Gaston Richard in 1923. Richard's work
in sociology is virtually unknown in England. He was an early
collaborator with Durkheim: later he turned against him. A key
issue, but not the only one, that caused Richard to oppose his former
master was Durkheim's approach to religion. A short account of
Richard's life and work is given at the end of the book.

From the outset, another type of principle dominated the selection
of extracts. As stated already, there scarcely exists a book by
Durkheim which does not mention religion. Some of the references
are short but none the less of great importance, as for example those
in *De la Division du travail social* (1893b). But in compiling a book
such as this it seemed totally wrong to reproduce by themselves
short paragraphs or even sentences. Thus presented, they would be
given in a vacuum, against many kinds of contexts, and their overall
number would be very great. There would be the temptation to
group together extracts which had a common subject and this
would give rise to a string of maxims and sayings, hardly doing
justice to Durkheim's scholarship. As far as possible all the extracts
offered here are complete articles, chapters, or sections of chapters.
When there has been an omission in a chapter, a very brief summary
of the missing section is put in its place.

If no reference were made to those works by Durkheim which
raise religious ideas because the ideas are encapsulated in a few
sentences or paragraphs, the object of the book would not be
achieved. To forestall such a deficiency, it seemed appropriate to
provide notes on all the writings of Durkheim which make a
significant reference to religion, but which for reasons, including
those just stated, have not been mentioned in the readings. The notes
are given in a separate section and it is hoped that for those not well

acquainted with Durkheim's works they will provide useful pointers for further study.

IV

The Durkheim bibliography is in three sections. The first gives the works of Durkheim in which religion is mentioned in some significant way. Here, with his kind permission, the dating-enumeration of Steven Lukes, which itself is based on that of Alpert, has been adopted. Durkheimian studies can be helped at a mundane level if there can be a common agreement on the dating and enumeration of his works. Lukes's comprehensive and, it would seem, complete bibliography is without rival. References to English translations, where applicable, also follow his enumeration.

The second section of the bibliography relates to totemism. The subject of totemism is a perplexing one to any student of Durkheim. All too well known is the fact that Durkheim in *Les Formes élémentaires* made the totemism of the Australian aboriginal tribe, the Arunta, the 'well conducted experiment' to demonstrate his conclusions about the nature of religion. Further, before the publication of the book he wrote extensively on totemism and allied matters, and reviewed many books on the subject. Today, totemism no longer assumes the critical place it did amongst anthropologists in Durkheim's time: gone is the contention supported by Durkheim and others that it was the most primitive form of social organization known to man, which, moreover, constituted a religious system. The question therefore arises, should the student of Durkheim pay as much attention to his writings on totemism as he should pay to his other and more general analyses of religion? Judged, on the one hand, by the present interest in Durkheim's religious thought, and on the other, by the relatively scant attention given today to those arguments about totemism in which Durkheim was immersed, the answer would appear to be towards the negative. However, in order to be comprehensive, and to serve those who wish to examine Durkheim's writings on totemism in detail, a bibliography on that subject has been provided.

The third section of the bibliography consists of books and articles, written by other scholars, which refer to Durkheim's analysis of religion, and, as might be expected, includes a fair number of reviews of *Les Formes élémentaires*. Also, some books

and articles have been mentioned which speak of Durkheim's life
and of his deep interest in religion; others in which he is named deal
with the religious situation in France during the Third Republic to
which he showed so much devotion. Since the list is moderately
extensive, no comments are made on individual items. The virtue of
many of these contributions, some of which are unknown to the
English-reading public, will become apparent in the projected
second book on Durkheim. This third section cannot claim to be
complete, for references to Durkheim's thought are as numerous as
the sand on the sea shore.

From these brief introductory remarks, it should be apparent that
this volume is a reference book, a source book, on Durkheim's
religious thought. As such it is hoped that it will be of some service
to students studying sociology and anthropology, as well as those of
other disciplines such as the history of religions or the philosophy
of religion—in fact to all those who want to gain some insight into
Durkheim's thought on religion. To this end they are given a
selection of texts or parts of texts, and are also encouraged to turn to
scholarly commentaries that have been written on the subject. The
deficiencies of this volume can best be overcome by reading the
complete works of the great master himself, preferably in the
original language.

W.S.F.P.

Durkheim

Unless otherwise stated the translations are
by Jacqueline Redding and W. S. F. Pickering.

1

1886a

Review 'Herbert Spencer—*Ecclesiastical Institutions: being Part VI of the Principles of Sociology*'

First published in French in *Revue philosophique de la France et de l'étranger*, XXII, pp. 61–9.

After a silence of three and a half years, partly as the result of his bad state of health, Spencer has just published a further volume of his *Sociology*. The sixth part which he now gives us is devoted to the study of ecclesiastical institutions. In accordance with his usual method, he follows the evolution of religious life from the earliest and most obscure origins to its full growth: he even attempts to outline its probable development in the future.

Religion began at that point when man found he was able to picture a supernatural being, and the first supernatural being thus imagined was a spirit. In the first part of his *Sociology*, the reader will find the history of this belief. Our earliest ancestors were unable to account for the apparently contradictory double phenomenon of dreaming and sleeping, except by discerning two men in each man, one who remained motionless, lying down, asleep, whilst the other wandered freely through space. This other self—this double, as Spencer calls it—is the spirit. Death is merely a longer separation of these two beings: what characterizes it is that its length is indefinite. Consequently, the savage imagines that all around him there is a multitude of wandering spirits which he fears just as man fears everything that is invisible and mysterious. To ward off the effect of their malevolence and ensure their protection, he seeks to propitiate them by means of offerings and sacrifices, and later by prayers. It is in this way that the cult of spirits, the initial form of every religion, was founded.

All the complicated and subtle religious systems that are to be found in history are merely the development of this first germ. Fetishism is nothing more than the cult of the spirit transferred to things which the spirit is supposed to inhabit. Naturism is simply the result of an error of language, a crude figure of speech which in their naïvety primitive men ended by taking literally. Through flattery, certain particularly feared and respected personages were given names used to describe the great forces of nature, and in time tradition no longer distinguished the men and the things described by the same word. It is this confusion which gave rise to the personification of these natural agents and to the human origins and adventures attributed to them.

Naturally, the spirits which each family held in the greatest reverence were those of its ancestors. However, when several families combined and became subject to the leadership of a single chief, each began to worship the ancestors of the common patriarch in addition to its own. In fact it seemed that the protective spirits of such a powerful man would necessarily be themselves very powerful and it was therefore prudent to gain their good will. All this gave rise to polytheism, each individual participating in two cults at the same time; one strictly domestic and the other common to the whole tribe. Yet there were no qualitative differences between these various gods. They all had the same role and the same functions and the only way to differentiate them was that they were not all equally powerful. Men did not succeed in imagining truly heterogeneous gods until different societies had reached the stage where they interacted with each other. The extent to which war contributed to this development is well known: conquerors annexed the gods of the vanquished along with the vanquished themselves. The same phenomenon occurred whenever a substantial fragment broke away from an over-large tribe, found another location, and created new gods whose cult was added to that of the ancient deities brought from the mother country. Conflicts inevitably arose between the supernatural beings born of popular imagination, since all the gods fought over the credulity and piety of their worshippers. According to the circumstances and skill of the priests, some appeared to be more powerful than others in the eyes of the faithful and so a kind of hierarchy amongst the gods was established. Step by step they even became subordinate to a supreme god who was thought to be the source of their power and who, with the help of developing thought, ended by absorbing them all and becoming the unique and true god. Polytheism had changed itself into monotheism.

This is what we might call the physiology of religion, but what of its morphology? From function we pass to structure, from the religious idea to ecclesiastical institutions. Whilst the witch doctor or exorcist is called upon only to combat evil spirits, the role of the priest is above all to propitiate benevolent spirits. For each family these spirits are those of the ancestors. Here is the explanation why, in the first instance, sacerdotal functions were private and domestic and all the members of the family exercised them indiscriminately. In the same way as every homogeneous body is unstable, so the priestly functions did not remain in this diffused state for long. As the family became constituted, the functions were concentrated in the hands of the father and eldest son. At the same time their nature changed: from being purely domestic they became simultaneously political and indeed religious. It is no longer only out of affection that we mourn the dead, it is out of duty. Just as the heir is seen only as a provisional steward of the goods left to him for which he will have to render an account to their legitimate owner, so when the wandering spirit comes back to reanimate the body, which it has momentarily left behind, the funeral offerings constitute a sort of debt or legal obligation which must be borne by the estate. On the other hand, as they are no longer destined to express the personal sentiments of the survivor but to ensure the protection of a supernatural being for the whole family, the person entrusted with the task of making these offerings takes on a truly ecclesiastical character.

In the patriarch there is vested a threefold power: at one and the same time he presides over domestic, political and religious life. Successively these three functions become dissociated and the religious function separates itself from the two others so that it is established on its own. When the family had developed to the point of becoming a village community, strangers eventually infiltrated it and settled in it. Under these conditions the patriarch controlling the composite group naturally had to abandon his domestic character. He remained the political and religious chief, however, for he acted

as intermediary between the other families and his personal
ancestors which the whole tribe worshipped together with him. From
that moment it was but a step to ecclesiastical functions becoming
quite independent. As society increased, so political preoccupations
were enough to occupy the whole of the chief's attention; he
delegated his religious powers to one of his near relatives and the
priesthood was finally established. Once formed, this special organ
continued to evolve along with the function, integrating and
differentiating itself. In other words, it developed into a hierarchical
system which was ever more complex and centralized.

As religious and political power has been intermingled for many
centuries, the process was a slow one and never quite complete.
Religious functions have been mixed up with others for a long time
and it is only with difficulty that they can be disentangled from
them. That is why the priest retained genuinely military functions at
the height of the Middle Ages—the last vestige of those times when
he was entrusted with the responsibility of making known and
respected the whims of a jealous and often cruel god. History is full
of examples of the influence exercised by the clergy even in recent
times over the civil, political and legal administration of states. By
the very fact that it held supernatural power in its hands, this caste
which was always rich and highly organized, could not fail to have a
dominant influence in primitive societies. Besides, by repressing
people's minds, the military government prepared them for all forms
of slavery and thus cleared the way for religious despotism.
Consequently, as industrialism replaced militarism, a revolution
took place in men's minds; they assumed the habit of resisting any
kind of oppression, religious along with the rest. According to the
rule of free contract, there can only be freely accepted beliefs. At the
same time as it popularized scientific knowledge, industrial progress
undermined for ever the preconceived notion of supernatural
causation. Dissidence took place and has been proliferating ever
since.

For all that, the ideal of religion will not disappear because it
contains a germ of truth already to be found in the superstitions of
savages and which time has gradually isolated and developed.
Indeed, the cult of spirits implies the belief that internal events and
external phenomena reveal two different but analogous forces, that is
to say, these two forces are themselves only two different forms of
one and the same energy, the source of all life and all change, of

which reason clearly conceives the necessity but which intelligence is for ever powerless to imagine. It is this unknowable with which science comes into collision and which it fails to explain. To be sure, it does away with absurd preconceptions and infantile explanations; nevertheless there remains an unintelligible residuum which transcends scientific knowledge. This eternal mystery is the object and *raison d'être* of religion. It follows that if religion is destined to survive, the same is true of the priesthood but it too will be purified and increasingly transformed. It will no longer consist of a highly centralized corporation, subject to more or less authoritarian rule but become a vast system of local and autonomous institutions, as is appropriate in a truly industrial society. At the same time, the functions of the priest will be more spiritual and more moral. His role will no longer consist in appeasing the gods by means of sacrifices or other propitiatory measures, but in teaching us our duty, in discussing the great and difficult problems of morality, and finally, in giving us either by word or by all the means at the disposal of art, the sentiment of the relations that we maintain with the unknown cause.

As can be seen, the germ of most of these ideas was put forward in the *First Principles*. However, we find them condensed here into a system and supported by an incalculable number of facts taken from the whole span of history. In its erudition, which is prodigious, this sixth part of the *Sociology* concedes nothing to the other parts. At the same time all these facts are grouped and organized with the great ingenuity which is the hallmark of this eminent philosopher. It is wonderful to see how there emerges from the belief in ghosts, a weak enough idea in all conscience, the refined idealism of our modern religions. What is more, it is impossible to spot the slightest gap in the long process of evolution. At first sight there seems to be nothing in common between such dissimilar dogmas, such varied ceremonies and rites. If, however, with Spencer we go below the surface and penetrate the external layer, we find everywhere the same development and the same original germ.

Naturally, this system suffers from the same shortcomings as all other systems and it has, perhaps with good reason, been accused of over-simplification. Indeed, the proposed formula seems very limited when one thinks of the prodigious complexity of religious phenomena. One cannot help but see that the explanation of the process whereby the mind moves from the cult of the dead to the cult of nature, is a singularly tenuous one. Are we to believe that naturism, the religion which for so long has been the richest source of poetic inspiration, and to which people tired and worn out by all other forms of religious speculation have an almost instinctive tendency to return, has a figure of speech and an ambiguity as its essential and almost unique cause? It is difficult to understand why once men had formulated the concept of a spirit distinct from but animating the body, they should not have made use of it to attempt to understand natural phenomena. As they visualized a sort of soul inside the human body, why should they not have visualized in a similar way a mysterious force beneath the waters of a river regulating its course, or visualized a secret energy behind the bark of a tree bringing it to life? Far from having been spawned by animism, naturism could be quite independent of it—and many facts have been quoted in support of this thesis. Furthermore, one might well ask whether, of these two religions, the latter might not necessarily have preceded the former. In fact, to be able to imagine spirits which can by intervening in the course of events disturb them in their natural course, one must already suspect the existence of an order and a sequence in the concatenation of phenomena. Now, this is too complex an idea to have been other than late in its emergence: it must therefore have been subsequent to the first religious sentiments. That is why, according to Réville, the first religious manifestations would have consisted in the worship, pure and simple, of the personification of the great forces of nature.[1]

It is with some hesitation that we open a debate in a field where we feel unqualified to speak, which brings us to the gravest objection we dare level at Spencer. Sociology has often been reproached for being a very vague and badly defined science; and it must be admitted that on more than one occasion it has merited this reproach. If, indeed, it wishes to study all the phenomena which are to be observed at the heart of societies, as it often aspires to, it is not a science but science itself. It is a complete system of all human knowledge and nothing stands outside it. For our part, we believe that its scope is more restricted and that it has a more precise object. For a fact to be sociological, it must not only concern all individuals taken in isolation, but society itself, that is to say, the collective being [être collectif]. The army, industry, the family, all have social functions, since the object of the one is to defend society, the other to feed society and the third to assure its renewal and continuity. If, however, religion is reduced to being merely a collection of beliefs and practices relating to a supernatural agent which is conjured up by the imagination, it is difficult to see in it anything more than a fairly complex aggregate of psychological phenomena. One can even readily imagine that religious sentiment might have been developed outside organized society altogether. That is how Spencer's book comes to include a great number of questions which are not relevant to our science. Sociology and the history of religions are and must remain separate disciplines.

That is not to say that religion has no place in sociology, but the sociologist must apply himself uniquely to the determination of its social role. We believe that this question, which Spencer dealt with in passing,[2] should have dominated the whole work. However, if the problem is presented in these terms, everything is transformed. The idea of God which seemed to be the sum total of religion a short while ago, is now no more than a minor accident. It is a psychological phenomenon which has got mixed up with a whole sociological process whose importance is of quite a different order. Once the idea of divinity had been formed in a certain number of *consciences* under the influence of completely personal sentiments, it served to symbolize all sorts of traditions, customs and collective needs. What must concern us then is not the symbol, but what it hides and expresses. We might perhaps be able to discover what is thus hidden beneath this quite superficial phenomenon if we compare it with others which resemble it in certain respects. In fact, what difference is there between the prescriptions of religion and the injunctions of morality? They are equally directed at the members of the same community, they are supported by sanctions which are sometimes identical and always analogous; finally, if any of them, no matter what their kind, is violated, the same sentiments of anger and disgust are aroused in people's *consciences*. If we re-read the Ten Commandments, we see that they make us rest on the Sabbath and eschew idols as insistently as we are ordered to respect the life and property of our neighbour. The history of uncivilized peoples could furnish even more conclusive examples in support of this thesis. It is consequently impossible to study these two classes of facts by separating them from each other. That is not all. The law, too, is merely a collection of commandments, of imperatives sustained by material sanctions. Here then, we have three kinds of phenomena whose origin is manifest and which can usefully shed light on each other. Now, it is the object of law and morality to maintain the equilibrium of society and to adapt it to environmental conditions. This must also be the social role of religion. It is a part of sociology to the extent that is exercises such a regulating influence on society. The problem confronting social science is to determine the content of this influence and to compare and contrast it with other influences. It is of little consequence whether the action is performed in the name of polytheism, monotheism or fetishism; it is of little consequence to know how humanity has progressed from one of these cults to the next and what took place in the obscure *consciences* of primitive men. That is for historians to decide. Moreover, when social institutions which are under the authority of religion come to change, it is not on account of the transformation of the popular conception of the deity. To the contrary, if this idea changes it is because the institutions have changed, and if they have changed, it is because external conditions are no longer the same. Each variation in the symbol presupposes a corresponding variation in the thing symbolized.

It is true that in the ordinary way one visualizes this evolution taking place in the inverse order. From time to time, Spencer himself appears to do so. Indeed, he attributes to the enquiring mind a somewhat extravagant role in the development of civilization. According to him, the main progress of religious ideas has been the result of the sentiment of independence and the taste for free enquiry, awoken and fostered by industrial society. We take the contrary view that the role of the *conscience collective*, like that of the *conscience individuelle*, can be reduced to noting facts without making them. It reflects more or less faithfully what is happening in the innermost recesses of the organism. It does no more than that. A prejudice is not dispelled because it is seen to be irrational; rather, one sees that it is irrational because it is in the process of being removed. When it no longer fulfils its function, that is to say when it no longer ensures the adaptation of individuals or the group to external circumstances, because these have changed, confusion and uneasiness result. The person with an alert conscience then intervenes, perceives that a social instinct is in the process of dissolution, records this dissolution; but at the most only accelerates it a little. It is no doubt true that if the Graeco-Roman religion was transformed it was partly because philosophers submitted it to a critical examination. That they did submit it to a critical examination was because it was no longer capable of ensuring the equilibrium of those great communities of men created by the Roman conquest.

Thus the sociologist will pay scant attention to the different ways in which men and peoples have conceived the unknown cause and mysterious depths of things. He will set aside all such metaphysical speculations and will see in religion only a social discipline. The power and authority of every discipline resides in habit: it is a totality of ways of behaving fixed by custom. Religion, therefore, is merely a form of custom, like law and morality. What, perhaps, best distinguishes this from all others is that it asserts itself not only over conduct but over the *conscience*. It not only dictates actions but ideas and sentiments. In short, religion starts with faith, that is to say, with any belief accepted or experienced without argument. Belief in God is only one kind of belief. There are many others. Do not most of us believe in progress in the same naïve way as our fathers believed in a beneficent God and in the saints? Moreover, we have no intention of maintaining that there is nothing more to religion. It is only too clear that, for a certain number of people, more than anything else it gives full scope to that need for idealism, to those aspirations towards the infinite, to that vague disquiet which stirs within all warm hearts. However incontestable and noble these sentiments may be, they are not of interest to sociology but to intimate [*intime*] and familiar [*familière*] morality. These phenomena do not arise out of the *conscience privée* and do not give rise to social consequences, at least not appreciable ones. Religion is far too complex a phenomenon for us to be able to consider all its aspects and characteristics even in a major work. Everyone has the right to his own point of view. We have simply indicated the one which is relevant in our opinion to sociology; in other words, that aspect of religion which we see when it is viewed purely as a social phenomenon.

If then we look at things from this angle, the future of religion appears to be quite different from that predicted by Spencer. How difficult it is, in fact, to admit that the confused *représentation* of the unknowable should provide such rich material for the speculations of men and exercise an effective influence over their conduct! Moreover, the very reasons given to demonstrate the existence of the unknowable are not always very conclusive. For, in the end, if reason cannot understand that everything is relative, no more can it conceive of the absolute. How is one to choose between these two absurdities and why should one prefer the second to the first? But let us leave all these logical arguments and focus attention on our own particular point of view. To turn religion into some sort of idealistic and popular metaphysic, to reduce it to a mere collection of personal and considered judgments on the relativity of human knowledge and on the necessity for an after-life, is to divest it of all social significance. It can only remain a collective discipline if it imposes itself on every mind with the overpowering authority of habit; if, on the other hand, it becomes a voluntarily accepted philosophy, it is nothing more than a simple incident in the private life and *conscience* of the individual. This theory would have as its consequence the tendency of religion to disappear as a social institution. It is far from stating, as does Spencer, that the status and importance of custom declines with civilization. How extraordinary it is that this great mind should have subscribed so completely to the common error regarding the growing omnipotence of free enquiry. In spite of the current meaning of the word, a prejudice is not a false judgment but simply an established judgment or one regarded as such. It conveys to us, in the form of a summary, the results of experiences undergone by others and which we ourselves have not experienced. In consequence, the more the field of knowledge and action is widened, the more there are things which we must believe on the authority of someone else. In other words, progress only serves to increase the number of prejudices;[3] and when we affirm that, on the contrary, its effect is to substitute clear reason for blind instinct everywhere and in everything, we are the victims of a downright illusion. A host of hereditary prejudices are in the course of crumbling and disappearing because they are no longer adapted to the new conditions of social life. In the midst of all these ruins reason alone remains standing, and it seems as if every endeavour of humanity has been channelled into preparing for its advent and for ensuring its supremacy. What we assume to be an ideal is only an unhealthy and temporary condition. A society without prejudices would be like an organism without reflexes: it would be a monster incapable of living. Sooner or later, therefore, custom and habit will claim their rights and that is what authorizes us to presume that religion will survive the attacks of which it is the object. For so long as men live together, they will hold some belief in common. What we cannot foresee and what only the future will be able to decide, is the particular form in which this faith will be symbolized.

To sum up, the law, morality, and religion are the three great regulating functions of society; these three groups of phenomena must be studied by a special branch of sociology. This is the essential conclusion to emerge from the whole discussion.

Notes

1 For an interesting discussion on this subject see Harrison and Spencer, *The Nineteenth Century*. January, March, July, September [also November— W.S.F.P.] 1884.
2 Ch. IX, pp. 763–74.
3 Quite simply, the prejudices of today are perhaps more flexible than those of the past.

2

1887b

Review   'Guyau—*L'Irréligion de l'avenir, étude de sociologie*'[1]

First published in French in *Revue philosophique de la France et de l'étranger*, XXIII, pp. 299–311.

In an article published in this journal last July,[2] we expressed the wish that someone should take up the task of studying religion as a social phenomenon. It seemed to us that most of the currently fashionable theories, which make religion a simple event in the *conscience individuelle*, were failing to recognize its essential characteristic. Unknown to us, the same feeling was at that time shared by several people. Our article was already printed but not published, when there appeared in the *Revue philosophique* two interesting articles by Lesbazeilles, in which religion was presented as a predominantly sociological fact.[3] A similar kind of thought is the leading idea of the fine book that Guyau has just given us. It is worth drawing attention to this quite spontaneous convergence of views and trends.

I. The work comprises three parts: the genesis of religions, the disintegration of religions, and the irreligion of the future.

According to Guyau the two contrasting theories which have been used to try to explain the genesis of religions are equally unsatisfactory. The *henotheism* of Müller and Hartmann—an idealistic doctrine which locates the beginnings of religion in a vague sentiment of the infinite and divine—suffers from the grave defect of imagining that modern ideas have existed since the evolutionary process began. Spencer's *spiritism* is an ingenious system but its scope is hardly in proportion to the complex phenomenon of which it claims to be the expression. What was to prevent man from deifying the phenomena of nature in the same way that he immortalized his ancestors? Spencer argues that in order to imagine spirits concealed in the heart of objects and animals, it is first necessary to have formed the idea of spirits and that as a result *naturism* cannot be accounted for unless spiritism preceded it. A fetish, however, is not necessarily seen by the worshipper to be an object inhabited by a mysterious agent; it is the object taken as a whole and conceived exactly as it presents itself to the senses, and with the good or evil virtues which experience reveals in it. The primitive believer does not in the least feel the need to explain these properties to himself by visualizing invisible forces and occult powers underlying the material mass before his eyes.

In truth, the animate and the inanimate are abstract and scholarly distinctions beyond the comprehension of minds as simple as those of the child and the savage. For them, everything is animate because everything moves and acts as they themselves act and move. They are thus quite naturally led to see living beings capable of action in things everywhere. They conceive this life to be like their own and so they imagine it to be accompanied by intelligence, *conscience*, and will. On the other hand, experience quickly teaches them that these living beings are not negligible quantities to be disregarded with impunity. At times they serve us and at other times they are harmful to us; in short they have an influence on our destiny. Here we have the second element in the idea of the deity. A god is a living being with whom man must reckon. It is more than this however. He is a living being whose power transcends ordinary experience. Men acquire this idea when they observe in certain great phenomena the manifestation of a much more powerful will than the human will and one which is, consequently, much more worthy of respect.

We now have gods and religion at one fell swoop. The gods are beings more powerful than man but who are similar to him and who live in society with him. The religious bond which has the effect of attaching man to these superior beings is accordingly a social bond. Men and gods are in close contact with each other; they are, so to speak, constantly in touch with each other; they perpetually act and react on each other. Religion is the totality of laws which regulate these social actions and reactions. Naturally such laws will be conceived in the image of those governing the relations of men among themselves. To ensure the protection and favour of these formidable powers, man employs the same methods he uses in similar circumstances relating to his fellows: prayers, offerings, marks of submission, etc. Religion is a sociology then, but one which has entirely emerged from the human imagination: it is the result of reasoning by analogy. Besides, as it was invented to explain the universe, one can define religion as 'a universal sociological explanation in mythical form' (III).

Naturally this sociology evolves along with the human society it reflects. It goes through three phases. In the beginning it is wholly physical. The society of the gods includes all the natural objects, animals, plants, minerals, with which man is in ceaseless communicaion, without anyone having yet thought of making a distinction between the soul and the body, spirit and matter. The dissociation of these two ideas which were originally intermingled, along with the advent of spiritism or animism, marks a new era in the history of religions. The conception of spirits as distinct from the bodies they animate is the beginning of a metaphysical explanation. As these spirits are at the same time powerful, far seeing, and in some cases benevolent and others hostile, it was not long before they came to be viewed as providences, continually intervening in the course of things and mingling with the life of the family or the tribe. As a result, man continually felt himself under the protection of the deity, and as he was incapable of ruling himself, he profited from this continual dependence. As it developed, the concept of a providential force naturally led to the idea of a controlling god and then creator of the world. So the second phase of religious evolution, the metaphysical phase, comes to an end. During the first, force is the divine attribute *par excellence*; during the second, intelligence, knowledge and foresight; in the third, which is taking place before our eyes, it is morality. With the passing of time, providence was seen more and more as a moral force. The deity was the prop of the social order, the recognized avenger of virtue, and so the idea of the sanction was born. At first, it was believed that sanctions would be finally imposed during this life, but gradually the time of reckoning was postponed beyond the tomb. 'Heaven and hell will open to correct this life which has become too imperfect and too evil' (p. 88).

Cult is religion become visible and tangible; like religion it is based on a sociological relationship, formed by an exchange of services. 'The man who thinks he is receiving something from the gods also feels himself under an obligation to give them something in exchange.' He believes that he can be useful or agreeable to them and in this way has a hold over them. Later, by attaching themselves to higher sentiments, the external cult and the rite assumed a symbolical character. They helped to express some great mythological or legendary drama. Finally there came the interior cult, 'the mental obeisance of the entire soul before God', and the rite has since then become no more than the symbol of this interior adoration which finds its highest form in the love of the deity. In such a way the society of gods and men grew more and more refined and spiritualized. God became the very principle of good, and the personification of the moral law.

II. That is how religions were established. What is happening to them today? (2nd Part.) We should have to close our eyes to the evidence in order not to notice that they are in the process of disintegration. Their dogmas are disappearing. In its positive and constructive part, science on certain points is already in a position to replace it. On a multitude of questions, on the genesis of the world for example, it gives us wider and more detailed explanations than the Bible. However, it gains even more importance by its destructive and disintegrating influence. Geology overthrew the traditions of most religions at a stroke; the physiology of the nervous system has explained many a miracle; and the historical sciences have attacked religions at the point of their very formation. These established scientific facts are gradually being transmitted from the scientists to the masses through the agency of primary education. At the same time, commerce and industry are developing a spirit of initiative and a feeling of responsibility. Self-confidence is substituting the direct action of man in particular events for the intervention of God. Yet even today, faith still has a last sanctuary in which it can take refuge, namely, the sphere of physical and moral accidents. There, our current helplessness and especially an ignorance which is too widespread inclines many people to seek the hope they need beyond this world. As the sciences progress and become better known, they will succeed in dislodging faith from this last outpost and religion will end 'by disappearing or at least by being centred on a small number of believers'.

To be sure, it has been said that dogma is untenable if taken literally, but why should we be confined to its literal expression? Words have no meaning in themselves; the mind has to seek the idea, and even the most sacred texts need interpretation. Unfortunately, once Luther had given the believer the authority to be an interpreter, he was instantly persuaded to put his own ideas in the place of divine thought; and soon there were everywhere nothing but symbols, even in the most essential dogmas, including that of revelation. Christ and the miracles now merely represent the deity. Why should not God himself be a symbol? As a result, we now in effect see God only as the moral ideal personified. It seems clear that such a doctrine is no more than a philosophy without consequence and does not merit the name religion. If Christ is not a god, why pray to him or why see the ultimate truth in his words? Because he is an extraordinary kind of man? But it is contrary to historical continuity and the laws of progress to see in a man, even a superior man, the expression of all the centuries.

Apart from dogmas, be they taken literally or interpreted symbolically, there is in religion something which seems likely to be much more resistant to criticism and which will uphold the faith. It is morality. Morality has developed at the heart of religion which has acted as a protective envelope for it. But will such a protection always be necessary? In responding to this question, the author analyses carefully all the elements of religious morality. He distinguishes two essential elements: respect and love. However, respect as it is taught by religion is only a form of fear: it is not the veneration of the ideal, it is the fear of divine vengeance. Now fear is a pathological sentiment which has nothing of the moral about it. As for love, religions have corrupted it by claiming it entirely for God. This mystical love detaches man from the world and from himself, it makes him indifferent to everything around him, and ends in disenchantment and disgust. Today, in place of this contemplative and passive love, we have the active and living love of the family, the motherland, humanity and the ideal. In so far as prayer is concerned, there is nothing to show that this great help to religious morality is indispensable. Out of love and charity, action will replace prayer, and the ecstasy which engulfs the spirit in sterile exaltation will be advantageously replaced by meditation and philosophical reflection.

Accordingly, there seems to be nothing in religion which looks as if it might escape the ravages of disintegration. However, in the ab-

sence of intrinsic worth, it will perhaps endure because it is necessary to a certain number of people. It has indeed been maintained
that only those of superior intelligence can do without religion and
the same is not true of the mass of people, of children, and of
women. Guyau has devoted three chapters to the refutation of this
thesis (*la religion et l'irréligion chez le peuple, chez l'enfant, chez la
femme*). They are difficult to analyse but are stimulating and are full
of interest. It is stated that without religions people will not be contained in the matter of social issues. It seems odd to make God a
means of saving the capitalist in this way! If there is a social issue,
let people study it. It is also said that religion is the safeguard of
popular morality, but the greatest religiosity may well go hand in
hand with extreme crimes. It is often the most Catholic countries
which provide most criminals. People are much less demoralized by
unbelief than they are by the wealth of some and the poverty of
others. Religion consolidates morality by means of faith but it does
not create it. If we have been defeated, it is not, as Matthew Arnold
has said, because we love the arts and sciences too much, and Jahveh
too little; it is because we have loved an art which was too facile and
a science which was too superficial. We must not try to remedy our
faults by repudiating our virtues, but perfect them and purify them.
Exclusively religious education for children produces a blunting of
the intellect. It accustoms the mind to a blind respect for tradition
and for passive obedience; and once the mind of a child has been
moulded in this way, it is not easy either to change it or even to
make it more flexible and open. We must not be afraid to speak to a
child on the subject of death as we might speak to an adult, though
avoiding the abstractions.[4] Women are no more dedicated to piety
than children. All the qualities of the feminine intelligence, credulity,
the spirit of conservation, meticulous care, may quite easily be
turned to the profit of science. Everything depends on the education
she receives from her husband. The feminine sentiments *par
excellence*—modesty and love—did not originate in religion for it is
only indirectly associated with them.

On one point only, religion has the advantage: it alone is
preoccupied with the problem of depopulation. The chapter dealing
with this question (2nd Part, VII) is among the best in the book.
Having denounced everything that is narrow and superficial about
the theory of Malthus, Guyau looks for the causes of our declining
birth rate, and shows that they are primarily moral ones. People

believe that the best way of making a child happy is to give him a
fortune. They do not seem to understand that it would be far better
to provide him with the means of earning one; that men are all the
happier for being busy; that riches which do away with action are
the enemies of happiness. So far, religion alone has fought the
doctrines and practices of Malthus. Secular morality and politics
have ignored the question although it is a vital one. This neglect
must stop and action must be taken. There are several methods at
our disposal. First of all there is legislation. We could reform the law
on filial duties, so as to offer better protection to parents against
the ingratitude of children; the law of succession in order to relieve
as much as possible taxes on any inheritance to be divided among a
large number of children; the law on military service in such a way
as to favour large families. Finally and most importantly, we should
act through the channel of education to open up new horizons to
people's minds and ambitions. 'Every time unlimited possibilities of
action are placed before any nation, it stops restricting the number
of its children' (p. 297).

III. Since the old religions are disappearing, and the accelerating
progress of science allied to the popularization of the scientific spirit
prevents the appearance of a new religion, the only religious ideal
possible is *religious anomy*, that is to say, the emancipation of the
individual, and the suppression of all dogmatic faith. The author has
shown elsewhere that the moral ideal consists in moral anomy. That
part of religions to survive will be everything in them which is worthy
of respect and which is eternal, namely, the desire to explain, the
sentiment of the unknown and the unknowable, and the need for an
ideal. 'Thanks to this double sentiment of the limits of our
knowledge and the infinity of our ideal, it is inadmissible that man
will ever turn his back on the great problems of the origin and end of
things' (p. 332). In other words, what will remain of religion is the
metaphysical and philosophical instinct which is the love of
speculation, and indeed of free speculation. What radically separates
philosophical systems and religious beliefs is that the first depends
solely on pure reason. Consequently, it is a misuse of the word to
apply the name religion to every hypothesis about the unknowable,
as does Spencer. The true religion of the future is irreligion.

However, religion is not entirely found in metaphysical
aspiration: we have indeed seen that originally it was essentially
sociological. Alongside the speculative view, there is a practical idea

found in all religions, which is the idea of association. This idea will outlive them. More and more, humanity will convince itself that the supreme ideal lies in the establishment of growing close-knit relations between people. But the associations of the future will not resemble those of the past. The individual will enter into them freely and will retain his full freedom within them. Even now, friendly societies are associations of this kind.

Every association presupposes certain common ideas. As free speculation replaces beliefs, an ever-widening gulf between opinions will become inevitable. The author hopes that, on the contrary, hypotheses will show a tendency to come closer to each other as they come closer to reality. A process of classifying metaphysical and moral doctrines is taking place which will continue into the future. At the same time, the more we are able to examine reality at close quarters and the more we are able to observe it in detail, the better and more penetrating our minds will be. Consequently, minds will diverge increasingly from a common centre on which they have converged. This will simultaneously bring about that fusion of intellects without which there is no collective life, and the growing differentiation which is the law of progress.

In the last chapters of the work, the author tries to foresee the main groups into which will fall the great metaphysical and moral hypotheses. He does not try to assess their scientific value, but only tries to determine their essential characteristics, and their speculative as well as practical role. Accordingly, he surveys theism; pantheism in its double form, optimistic (Spinoza) and pessimistic (Schopenhauer, Hartmann); and finally idealistic, materialistic, and monist naturalism. Although naturalism is restricted to the study of nature, it cannot escape the question of being. Is being matter or is it spirit? As Taine and Lange have shown, materialism taken to its logical conclusion ends up by reverting to idealism; for it leads to an abstract mechanism which loses itself in the laws of logic and thought. The idealistic evolutionism, as presented by Fouillée, is not far removed from monism. This is the doctrine which shows the greatest tendency to carry all before it. Monism reduces neither thought to matter, nor matter to thought; it unites them in the great synthesis of life. Life engenders the *conscience* by centring on itself and diffuses itself in the form of action, quite spontaneously and mechanically. There is no question of introducing the attraction of a desirable end at the beginning to set things in motion. The major

advantage of monism is to leave room for the great metaphysical
and moral hopes which humanity has so far been unable to do
without. If there is nothing to give us grounds for believing that
evolution is moving towards a precise goal, there is nothing to
prevent us from 'conceiving it as leading to beings capable of
providing a goal for themselves and striving towards this goal and
drawing nature along behind them. . . . It is unlikely that we
represent the last stage of life, thought and love. Who even knows
whether evolution will be able or has already been able to make
what the ancients called gods' (p. 439). It is not only about the
destiny of the world but also about our own destiny that
evolutionism is able to offer us fairly consoling prospects. In the first
place it ensures the immortality of our thoughts and actions. The
cerebral waves issuing from our brains will continue their way when
we are no longer there and will even travel further. And is not
atavism a guarantee of resurrection? Even if the works of the
individual survive him, is he himself doomed to annihilation?
Science says yes, but love protests, for love is attached to the
individual and wants to preserve him. So, in magnificent language,
Guyau outlines for us a hypothesis, less than that, a dream, but a
beautiful dream which, he says, is in no way anti-scientific and
which would resolve this cruel paradox. The *conscience*, the self, is
no more than a very flexible association of ideas and customs, but
there is nothing to show that instability is its ultimate and
everlasting characteristic. Perhaps it will end by forming compound
states of *conscience* strong enough to last for ever, whilst remaining
sufficiently flexible to be able to adapt to a constantly changing
environment. What is to prevent progress resulting in the formation
of psychic vortices which will become increasingly resistant? Thus
at the highest level of evolution, the struggle for life would become a
struggle for immortality and that is how the dream would become
reality. Psychology already admits that *consciences* can
interpenetrate each other. Might not the day come when we shall see
an infinitely more complete form of interpenetration taking place?
Might not *consciences* united in a common love not finish by *really*
intermingling at the heart of a *conscience supérieure*, where each
would nevertheless retain its own differences? Then, communication
would be so intimate that the *conscience individuelle*, which would
be overtaken by death, would live on in the beloved heart not as a
more or less faded memory as is the case today, but as an image so

intense that it could not be distinguished from reality. It would be like having the influence and prolongation of the extinct *conscience* in the surviving one. Then 'the only problem left would be that of being both sufficiently loving and sufficiently loved to live and survive in others.' There is only one thing for those who decline to participate in this dream to do, and that is not to be faint hearted since cowardice serves no useful purpose either.

IV. In this major work the reader will find those many fine qualities everyone attributes to the author: a great imagination allied to an exquisite sensibility; a shrewd dialectic which sometimes becomes over-refined; a rare ability to understand and experience the most diverse things; and profound ideas joined with subtle and discerning analyses. The literary merits as always are of the first order. However, what seems to us above all to be the distinguishing mark of Guyau's writings is a quite individual flavour of sincerity. His books are truly lived; it is easy to see that the ideas, which are always there, have for a long time been part and parcel of all the events of his daily life. His books, particularly this one, are sprinkled with personal memories, the impressions of travel, fortuitous observations made in the street and in society, and noted in passing. All these are nevertheless an integral part of the development of the idea. Sometimes one tends to regret that the tone does not have a little more of that impersonality which is so appropriate to science.

His doctrine marks an important step forward in the scientific study of religions. As we have said, hitherto people have only seen in religions the product of the individual imagination, and no causes have been ascribed to them other than the need to understand the world or the sentiment of the ideal. Accordingly, the marooned Robinson Crusoe could have had a religion all of his own. Religions have only been found at the heart of established societies; among sick people who have been rigorously excluded from the rest of society by a physical accident (blindness allied to deafness), religious sentiment has never been found before the day it was communicated to them (see the cases of Laura Bridgmann and Julia Brace). Finally, history teaches us that religions have evolved and changed with the very societies which gave birth to them. Do not all these facts imply that religion is wholly, or for the most part, a sociological phenomenon? That in order to study it we must first take up a sociological position and that it is only after having viewed it sociologically that we shall be able to seek its psychological roots in the *conscience individuelle*? Guyau understood this and made it his task. That is what is new about the book.

Guyau, like Spencer, ascribes an exaggerated role to pure speculation in the genesis of religions. Indeed, for him the efficient cause of religious beliefs is above all the need to understand and to explain. Social life would merely have provided the popular imagination with the blueprint for the construction of the fantastic world of religion.[5] Generally speaking, Guyau has a tendency to intellectualize which is already apparent in his previous works. It will be recalled that in his *Morale anglaise* and in his *Esquisse d'une morale*, he maintained that the spirit of enquiry would be sufficient to erode moral instincts and sentiments. In this book, he states that education alone is enough to restore them.[6] Thought, therefore, is all powerful; it can destroy everything and create anything. This theory, moreover, seems to be increasingly incompatible with the teaching of psychology. It assumes without reason that considered thought—science—is the ultimate end of mental (*psychique*) evolution, so much so that everything within us changes according to the requirements of the intellect. A scientific discovery then would be all that was needed to turn the world upside down. To the contrary, the intellect is only a means, and normally it is content to play its part as a means. The life of the psyche has as its goal action; it must adapt to the surrounding physical or social environment by means of appropriate modifications. If spontaneous and uncalculated adaptation is sufficient in practice, the intellect remains quiescent because its intervention is unnecessary. It is only required if instinctive adaptation is impeded and if pain utters a note of warning; then its co-operation becomes indispensable in re-establishing the lost equilibrium. What is true of the individual intelligence is even more true of the social intelligence. Consequently, each time anyone attempts the study of a collective *représentation*, he can rest assured that a practical and not a theoretical cause has been the determining reason for it. This is the case with that system of *représentations* we call a religion.

Perhaps Guyau would have been led to correct his intellectual excesses himself if he had not kept a very important fact so much in the background, namely, the obligatory nature of religious prescriptions. He refuses, it is true, to include morality and law among the legitimate elements of religion. In the beginning religion was merely a superstitious physics; only at the end of its evolution, when it was on the verge of disappearing and no longer quite itself, did it assume an ethical character. It might perhaps be more accurate to invert the terms of the proposition. Today morality has become independent of religion; originally, to the contrary, moral, legal and religious ideas were part of a somewhat confused synthesis, which was nevertheless primarily religious in character. Even today, side by side with secular morality, is there not a quite different confessional but no less categorical morality? Does not the believer feel impelled to go to mass and to take communion, just as he feels impelled to respect life and the property of his neighbours? The Christian who for the first time eats a normal meal on Good Friday, and the Jew who for the first time eats pork, experience a remorse which it is impossible to distinguish from moral remorse. Within each religious community, the believer who transgresses the ritual regulations becomes the object of censure which is analogous in all respects to that with which we condemn immoral acts. It is obvious that if religion had merely been a metaphysical hypothesis or a hypothesis concerned with moral philosophy—'a badly drawn scientific conclusion'—it would never have become an *obligation of social dimensions.*

Nevertheless, Guyau's theory can and must be kept as at least a partial explanation of the phenomenon of religion, on the condition that it is modified. For the author, religion originates from a double source; first, the need to understand, and secondly, sociability. To begin with, we should like to call for a reversal of the order of the factors and for sociability to be made the determining cause of religious sentiment. Men did not start by imagining the gods; that they felt bound to them by social sentiments was not because they visualized the gods in a certain way. They began by attaching themselves to the things they used or suffered from, just as they attached themselves to each other, spontaneously, without thinking, without the least degree of speculation. The theory to explain and make sense of the habits which had been formed in this way came only later to these primitive *consciences.* As these sentiments were moderately similar to those which man observed in his relations with his fellows, he visualized the powers of nature as beings like himself; and at the same time he set them apart from himself and attributed to these exceptional beings distinctive qualities which turned them into gods. Religious ideas, then, result from the interpretation of pre-existing sentiments. In order to study religion, these sentiments have to be penetrated: the *représentations*, which only symbolize them and provide them with a superficial shell, have to be discarded.

There are two kinds of social sentiments. One links each individual to his fellow citizens. This kind manifests itself within the community in the relationships of daily life—the sentiments are esteem, respect, affection and fear, all of which we can feel for one another. They could be described as inter-individual or inter-social sentiments. The second kind consist of those which link me as an individual to the social entity [*être*] taken as a whole; above all they show themselves in the relationships of one society with another and they might be called inter-social. The first kind leave me with my autonomy and personality more or less intact; it is true that they make me and others interdependent, but they do this without taking away much of my independence. On the other hand, when I act under the influence of the second kind, I am now only part of a whole whose movements I follow and whose pressure I accept. That is why the latter kind are the only ones which can give rise to an idea of obligation. Which of these two tendencies is the one which has played a part in the genesis of religions? According to Guyau it is the first. He affirms that the relationships which in the beginning united man to the deity are analogous to those which he maintains with individuals who constitute his society, that is to say, they are personal relationships. Now, the facts seem to point to the contrary. Amongst primitive peoples, and even in modern societies, the gods are not the appointed protectors or enemies of the individual but of society (the tribe, the clan, the family, the city, etc.). The individual has no claim to their help and no reason to fear their hostility unless provoked; if he has dealings with them it is not in a personal capacity but as a member of society. It is society which they persecute or favour directly. In fact, natural forces which show an exceptional degree of power are of even less interest to the isolated individual than to the group as a whole. It is the entire tribe which is menaced by thunder, enriched by rain, ruined by hail, etc. Of cosmic forces, only those which are of collective interest will be deified. In other words, it is the inter-social tendencies which give birth to religious sentiment. Religious society is not human society ideally projected beyond the stars; and the gods are not conceived as members of the tribe. They form one or rather several societies which are separate and are located in special regions, some friendly, others hostile; and men have maintained relationships with them of an international character. Not only does this hypothesis conform to the facts better, it enables us to understand why the superstitious physics of religions is obligatory, whilst that of scientists is not. Indeed, everything which affects the community quickly becomes a categorical law; society does not allow its members to do anything with impunity which is contrary to the social interest. This accounts for the analogies and differences between the commandments of morality and those of religion. Such is the second correction we should like to make to Guyau's theory.

These intellectualist tendencies are naturally to be found in the last two parts of the work, where Guyau is explaining how religions are in the process of disappearing and outlining which aspects of them will survive. In this, a leading role in the process of disintegration is attributed to science and the spirit of enquiry. If the only mistake that religions had ever made was to be in disagreement with scientific truths, they would still be in a healthy state today. But despite this conflict, societies which still needed religious faith would have circumvented the difficulty by denying science; alternatively, religions would have been modified and adapted to embrace new ideas, for there is nothing to lead us to suppose that the religious organism is at the present as fully developed as its flexibility and plasticity will allow. In fact, if we go back to the arguments, each in turn, which science musters against religion, we see that though they may be strong enough to entrench the unbeliever yet further in his opinion, there is not one of them capable of converting a believer. It is not with the aid of logic that we shall stamp out faith, logic can just as easily be used to defend as to attack it, and the theologian can reason just as well in order to prove it as the free thinker to refute it. Even if we admit that among cultivated minds beliefs have become so accommodating that they yield to a single proof, it is quite obvious that such is not the case with most people. Since faith is the result of practical causes, it must continue to exist for as long as they exist, whatever the state of science or philosophy. To show that it has no future, it has to be demonstrated that the reasons which make its existence necessary have disappeared; and since these reasons are of a sociological kind, we must look for the change which has taken place in the nature of societies and which henceforward makes religion useless and impossible.

Similarly, in order to be able to say how much of it will survive, we would need to know how much will survive of the social causes which have for so long sustained it. It can then be understood that if any essential part of religion has to remain, it is not the metaphysical sentiment or the taste for great syntheses. Besides, who can guarantee that metaphysics must be eternal? The great service which it has rendered to science has been to remind it constantly of its limits and that is why it has lasted. Some day might not this sentiment about the limits of our knowledge, confirmed as it is by long experience, permeate science itself and become an integral element of scientific thought? Might we not even say that this evolution is actually taking place before our eyes? From that moment it would become unnecessary to perpetually demonstrate a truth which is no longer in dispute. As to the reply that the mind aspires to go beyond such limits, it remains to see whether this aspiration is legitimate and reasonable, and whether indefinitely repeated failure will not discourage humanity in the end. Moreover, is it not somewhat contradictory to declare that knowledge is limited and then to immediately set out to go beyond its limits? Candolle remarked somewhere that the less people were educated, the more they had a taste for insoluble questions. If this observation is correct, it would be necessary to recognize that the development of metaphysics does not run parallel with the development of the human mind.

Notes

1 [The book was translated into English anonymously as *The Non-Religion of the Future*, and published by Heinemann in 1897. Jean-Marie Guyau (1854–88), philosopher and poet, was something of a prodigy. From the age of seventeen he published translations of the classics and at twenty-four, *La Morale d'Epicure*. Although he died when he was only thirty-four, he had written at least nine books, including *L'Art au point de vue sociologique*. *L'Irréligion de l'avenir* proved to be popular and had extended to seven editions by 1906. For the life and work of Guyau see A. Fouillée, *La Morale, l'art et la religion d'après Guyau*, Paris, 1906 (6th ed.)—W.S.F.P.]

2 'Études récentes de science sociale', July 1886. [This reference is to 1886a—W.S.F.P.]

3 'Les Bases psychologiques de la religion', April and May 1886.

4 See some excellent pages on primary education and on the way the priest can be made use of in education.

5 See the whole of ch. I. Guyau too calls religion a kind of sociomorphic physics; social life only provides the framework.

6 p. 350.

3

1897a

Suicide: a Study in Sociology

Book II, chapter 2. Translation by J. A. Spaulding and G. Simpson. Free Press, Chicago, 1951; Routledge & Kegan Paul, London, 1952. First published in French as *Le Suicide: étude de sociologie*, Alcan, Paris, pp. 149–73/t.152–70.

Egoistic suicide

First let us see how the different religious confessions affect suicide.

I

If one casts a glance at the map of European suicide, it is at once clear that in purely Catholic countries like Spain, Portugal, Italy, suicide is very little developed, while it is at its maximum in Protestant countries, in Prussia, Saxony, Denmark. The following averages compiled by Morselli confirm this first conclusion:

	Average of suicides per million inhabitants
Protestant states	190
Mixed states (Protestant and Catholic)	96
Catholic states	58
Greek Catholic states	40

The low proportion of the Greek Catholics cannot be surely attributed to religion; for as their civilization is very different from

[handwritten: Acc. to Durkheim, suicide is more profound in protestant countries or populations with many Protest. inhabiting]

that of the other European nations, this difference of culture may be the cause of their lesser aptitude. But this is not the case with most Catholic or Protestant societies. To be sure, they are not all on the same intellectual and moral level; yet the resemblances are sufficiently essential to make it possible to ascribe to confessional differences the marked contrast they offer in respect to suicide.

Nevertheless, this first comparison is still too summary. In spite of undeniable similarities, the social environments of the inhabitants of these different countries are not identical. The civilizations of Spain and Portugal are far below that of Germany and this

Bavarian Provinces (1867–75)*					
Provinces with Catholic minority (less than 50%)	Suicides per million inhabitants	Provinces with Catholic majority (50 to 90%)	Suicides per million inhabitants	Provinces with more than 90% Catholic	Suicides per million inhabitants
Rhenish Palatinate	167	Lower Franconia	157	Upper Palatinate	64
Central Franconia	207	Swabia	118	Upper Bavaria	114
Upper Franconia	204			Lower Bavaria	19
Average	192	Average	135	Average	75

* The population below 15 years has been omitted.

inferiority may conceivably be the reason for the lesser develop-ment of suicide which we have just mentioned. If one wishes to avoid this source of error and determine more definitely the in-fluence of Catholicism and Protestantism on the suicidal tendency, the two religions must be compared in the heart of a single society.

Of all the great states of Germany, Bavaria has by far the fewest suicides. There have been barely 90 per million inhabitants yearly since 1874, while Prussia has 133 (1871–75), the duchy of Baden 156, Wurttemberg 162, Saxony 300. Now, Bavaria also has most Catholics, 713·2 to 1,000 inhabitants. On the other hand, if one compares the different provinces of Bavaria, suicides are found to be in direct proportion to the number of Protestants and in inverse proportion to that of Catholics (see Table above). Not only the proportions of averages to one another confirm the law but all the numbers of the first column are higher than those of the second and those of the second higher than those of the third without exception.

It is the same with Prussia:

Prussian Provinces (1883–90)			
Provinces with more than 90% Protestant	Suicides per million inhabitants	Provinces with from 89 to 68% Protestant	Suicides per million inhabitants
Saxony	309·4	Hanover	212·3
Schleswig	312·9	Hesse	200·3
Pomerania	171·5	Brandenburg and Berlin	296·3
		E. Prussia	171·3
Average	264·6	Average	220·0
Provinces with from 40 to 50% Protestant	Suicides per million inhabitants	Provinces with from 32 to 28% Protestant	Suicides per million inhabitants
W. Prussia	123·9	Posen	96·4
Silesia	260·2	Rhineland	100·3
Westphalia	107·5	Hohenzollern	90·1
Average	163·6	Average	95·6

There are only two slight irregularities among the 14 provinces thus compared, so far as detail is concerned; Silesia, which because of its relatively high number of suicides should be in the second category, is only in the third, while on the contrary Pomerania would be more in its place in the second than in the first column.

Switzerland forms an interesting study from this same point of view. For as both French and German populations exist there, the influence of the confession is observable separately on each race. Now, its influence is the same on both. Catholic cantons show four and five times fewer suicides than Protestant, of whichever nationality.

Confessional influence is therefore so great as to dominate all others.

Besides, in a fairly large number of cases the number of suicides per million inhabitants of the population of each confession has been

French cantons		German cantons		Total of cantons of all nationalities	
Catholics	83 suicides per million inhabitants	Catholics	87 suicides	Catholics	86·7 suicides
				Mixed	212·0 suicides
Protestants	453 suicides per million	Protestants	293 suicides		
				Protestants	326·3 suicides

directly determined. The following figures were obtained by various observers:

TABLE XVIII *Suicides in different countries per million persons of each confession*

		Protestants	Catholics	Jews	Names of observers
Austria	(1852–9)	79·5	51·3	20·7	Wagner
Prussia	(1849–55)	159·9	49·6	46·4	Id.
Prussia	(1869–72)	187	69	96	Morselli
Prussia	(1890)	240	100	180	Prinzing
Baden	(1852–62)	139	117	87	Legoyt
Baden	(1870–4)	171	136·7	124	Morselli
Baden	(1878–88)	242	170	210	Prinzing
Bavaria	(1844–56)	135·4	49·1	105·9	Morselli
Bavaria	(1884–91)	224	94	193	Prinzing
Wurttemberg	(1846–60)	113·5	77·9	65·6	Wagner
Wurttemberg	(1873–6)	190	120	60	Durkheim
Wurttemberg	(1881–90)	170	119	142	Id.

Thus, everywhere without exception,[1] Protestants show far more suicides than the followers of other confessions. The difference varies between a minimum of 20 to 30 per cent and a maximum of 300 per cent. It is useless to invoke with Mayr[2] against such a unanimous agreement of facts, the isolated case of Norway and Sweden which, though Protestant, have only an average number of suicides. First, as we noted at the beginning of this chapter, these international comparisons are not significant unless bearing on a considerable number of countries, and even in this case are not conclusive. There are sufficiently great differences between the peoples of the Scandinavian peninsula and those of Central Europe for it to be reasonable that Protestantism does not produce exactly the same effects on both. But furthermore, if the suicide-rate is not in itself very high in these two countries, it seems relatively so if one considers their modest rank among the civilized peoples of Europe. There is no reason to suppose that they have reached an intellectual level above Italy, to say the least, yet self-destruction occurs from twice to three times as often (90 to 100 suicides per million inhabitants as against 40). May Protestantism not be the cause of this relatively higher figure? Thus the fact not only does not tell against the law just established on the basis of so many observations, but rather tends to confirm it.[3]

The aptitude of Jews for suicide is always less than that of Protestants; in a very general way it is also, though to a lesser degree, lower than that of Catholics. Occasionally however, the latter relation is reversed; such cases occur especially in recent times. Up to the middle of the century, Jews killed themselves less frequently than Catholics in all countries but Bavaria;[4] only towards 1870 do they begin to lose their ancient immunity. They still very rarely greatly exceed the rate for Catholics. Besides, it must be remembered that Jews live more exclusively than other confessional groups in cities and are in intellectual occupations. On this account they are more inclined to suicide than the members of other confessions, for reasons other than their religion. If therefore the rate for Judaism is so low, in spite of this aggravating circumstance, it may be assumed that other things being equal, their religion has the fewest suicides of all.

These facts established, what is their explanation?

II

If we consider that the Jews are everywhere in a very small minority and that in most societies where the foregoing observations were made, Catholics are in the minority, we are tempted to find in these facts the cause explaining the relative rarity of voluntary deaths in these two confessions.[5] Obviously, the less numerous confessions, facing the hostility of the surrounding populations, in order to maintain themselves are obliged to exercise severe control over themselves and subject themselves to an especially rigorous discipline. To justify the always precarious tolerance granted them, they have to practice greater morality. Besides these considerations, certain facts seem really to imply that this factor has some influence. In Prussia, the minority status of Catholics is very pronounced, since they are only a third of the whole population. They kill themselves only one-third as often as the Protestants. The difference decreases in Bavaria where two-thirds of the inhabitants are Catholics; the voluntary deaths of the latter are here only in the proportion of 100 to 275 of those Protestants or else of 100 to 238, according to the period. Finally, in the almost entirely Catholic Empire of Austria, only 155 Protestant to 100 Catholic suicides are found. It would seem then that where Protestantism becomes a minority its tendency to suicide decreases.

But first, suicide is too little an object of public condemnation for the slight measure of blame attaching to it to have such influence, even on minorities obliged by their situation to pay special heed to public opinion. As it is an act without offence to others, it involves no great reproach to the groups more inclined to it than others, and is not apt to increase greatly their relative ostracism as would certainly be the case with a greater frequency of crime and misdemeanor. Besides, when religious intolerance is very pronounced, it often produces an opposite effect. Instead of exciting the dissenters to respect opinion more, it accustoms them to disregard it. When one feels himself an object of inescapable hostility, one abandons the idea of conciliating it and is the more resolute in his most unpopular observances. This has frequently happened to the Jews and thus their exceptional immunity probably has another cause.

Anyway, this explanation would not account for the respective situation of Protestants and Catholics. For though the protective influence of Catholicism is less in Austria and Bavaria, where it is in the majority, it is still considerable. Catholicism does not therefore owe this solely to its minority status. More generally, whatever the proportional share of these two confessions in the total population, wherever their comparison has been possible from the point of view of suicide, Protestants are found to kill themselves much more often than Catholics. There are even countries like the Upper Palatinate and Upper Bavaria, where the population is almost wholly Catholic (92 and 96 per cent) and where there are nevertheless 300 and 423 Protestant suicides to 100 Catholic suicides. The proportion even rises to 528 per cent in Lower Bavaria where the reformed religion has not quite one follower to 100 inhabitants. Therefore, even if the prudence incumbent on minorities were a partial cause of the great difference between the two religions, the greatest share is certainly due to other causes.

We shall find these other causes in the nature of these two religious systems. Yet they both prohibit suicide with equal emphasis; not only do they penalize it morally with great severity, but both teach that a new life begins beyond the tomb where men are punished for their evil actions, and Protestantism just as well as Catholicism numbers suicide among them. Finally, in both cults these prohibitions are of divine origin; they are represented not as the logical conclusion of correct reason, but God Himself is their authority. Therefore, if Protestantism is less unfavourable to the development of suicide, it is not because of a different attitude from that of Catholicism. Thus, if both religions have the same precepts with respect to this particular matter, their dissimilar influence on suicide must proceed from one of the more general characteristics differentiating them.

The only essential difference between Catholicism and Protestantism is that the second permits free inquiry to a far greater degree than the first. Of course, Catholicism by the very fact that it is an idealistic religion concedes a far greater place to thought and reflection than Greco-Latin polytheism or Hebrew monotheism. It is not restricted to mechanical ceremonies but seeks the control of the conscience. So it appeals to conscience, and even when demanding blind submission of reason, does so by employing the language of reason. None the less, the Catholic accepts his faith ready made, without scrutiny. He may not even submit it to historical examination since the original texts that serve as its basis are proscribed. A whole hierarchical system of authority is devised, with marvellous ingenuity, to render tradition invariable. All *variation* is abhorrent to Catholic thought. The Protestant is far more the author of his faith. The Bible is put in his hands and no interpretation is imposed upon him. The very structure of the reformed cult stresses this state of religious individualism. Nowhere but in England is the Protestant clergy a hierarchy; like the worshippers, the priest has no other source but himself and his conscience. He is a more instructed guide than the run of worshippers but with no special authority for fixing dogma. But what best proves that this freedom of enquiry proclaimed by the founders of the Reformation has not remained a Platonic affirmation is the increasing multiplicity of all sorts of sects so strikingly in contrast with the indivisible unity of the Catholic Church.

We thus reach our first conclusion, that the proclivity of Protestantism for suicide must relate to the spirit of free inquiry that animates this religion. Let us understand this relationship correctly. Free inquiry itself is only the effect of another cause. When it appears, when men, after having long received their ready made faith from tradition, claim the right to shape it for themselves, this is not because of the intrinsic desirability of free enquiry, for the latter involves as much sorrow as happiness. But it is because men henceforth need this liberty. This very need can have only one cause: the overthrow of traditional beliefs. If they still asserted themselves with equal energy, it would never occur to men to criticize them. If they still had the same authority, men would not demand the right to verify the source of this authority. Reflection develops only if its development becomes imperative, that is, if certain ideas and instinctive sentiments which have hitherto adequately guided conduct are found to have lost their efficacy. Then reflection intervenes to fill the gap that has appeared, but which it has not created. Just as reflection disappears to the extent that thought and action take the form of automatic habits, it awakes only when accepted habits become disorganized. It asserts its rights against public opinion only when the latter loses strength, that is, when it is no longer prevalent to the same extent. If these assertions occur not merely occasionally and as passing crises, but become chronic; if individual consciences keep reaffirming their autonomy, it is because they are constantly subject to conflicting impulses, because a new opinion has not been formed to replace the one no longer existing. If a new system of beliefs were constituted which seemed as indisputable to everyone as the old, no one would think of discussing it any longer. Its discussion would no longer even be permitted; for ideas shared by an entire society draw from this consensus an authority that makes them sacrosanct and raises them above dispute. For them to have become more tolerant, they must first already have become the object of less general and complete assent and been weakened by preliminary controversy.

Thus, if it is correct to say that free inquiry once proclaimed, multiplies schisms, it must be added that it presupposes them and derives from them, for it is claimed and instituted as a principle only in order to permit latent or half-declared schisms to develop more freely. So if Protestantism concedes a greater freedom to individual thought than Catholicism, it is because it has fewer common beliefs and practices. Now, a religious society cannot exist without a collective *credo* and the more extensive the *credo* the more unified and strong is the society. For it does not unite men by an exchange and reciprocity of services, a temporal bond of union which permits and even presupposes differences, but which a religious society cannot form. It socializes men only by attaching them completely to an identical body of doctrine and socializes them in proportion as this body of doctrine is extensive and firm. The more numerous the manners of action and thought of a religious character are, which are accordingly removed from free inquiry, the more the idea of God presents itself in all details of existence, and makes individual wills converge to one identical goal. Inversely, the greater concessions a confessional group makes to individual judgment, the less it dominates lives, the less its cohesion and vitality. We thus reach the conclusion that the superiority of Protestantism with respect to suicide results from its being a less strongly integrated church than the Catholic church.

This also explains the situation of Judaism. Indeed, the reproach to which the Jews have for so long been exposed by Christianity has created feelings of unusual solidarity among them. Their need of resisting a general hostility, the very impossibility of free communication with the rest of the population, has forced them to strict union among themselves. Consequently, each community became a small, compact and coherent society with a strong feeling of self-consciousness and unity. Everyone thought and lived alike; individual divergences were made almost impossible by the community of existence and the close and constant surveillance of all over each. The Jewish church has thus been more strongly united than any other, from its dependence on itself because of being the object of intolerance. By analogy with what has just been observed apropos of Protestantism, the same cause must therefore be assumed for the slight tendency of the Jews to suicide in spite of all sorts of circumstances which might on the contrary incline them to it. Doubtless they owe this immunity in a sense to the hostility surrounding them. But if this is its influence, it is not because it imposes a higher morality but because it obliges them to live in greater union. They are immune to this degree because their religious society is of such solidarity. Besides, the ostracism to which they are subject is only one of the causes producing this result; the very nature of Jewish beliefs must contribute largely to it. Judaism, in fact, like all early religions, consists basically of a body of practices minutely governing all the details of life and leaving little free room to individual judgment.

III

Several facts confirm this explanation.

First, of all great Protestant countries, England is the one where suicide is least developed. In fact, only about 80 suicides per million inhabitants are found there, whereas the reformed societies of Germany have from 140 to 400; and yet the general activity of ideas and business seems no less great there than elsewhere.[6] Now, it happens at the same time that the Anglican church is far more powerfully integrated than other Protestant churches. To be sure, England has been customarily regarded as the classic land of individual freedom; but actually many facts indicate that the number of common, obligatory beliefs and practices, which are thus withdrawn from free inquiry by individuals, is greater than in Germany. First, the law still sanctions many religious requirements: such as the law of the observance of Sunday, that forbidding stage representations of any character from Holy Scripture; the one until recently requiring some profession of faith from every member of political representative bodies, etc. Next, respect for tradition is known to be general and powerful in England: it must extend to matters of religion as well as others. But a highly developed traditionalism always more or less restricts activity of the individual. Finally, the Anglican clergy is the only Protestant clergy organized in a hierarchy. This external organization clearly shows an inner unity incompatible with a pronounced religious individualism.

Besides, England has the largest number of clergymen of any Protestant country. In 1876 there averaged 908 church-goers for every minister, compared with 932 in Hungary, 1,100 in Holland, 1,300 in Denmark, 1,440 in Switzerland and 1,600 in Germany.[7] The number of priests is not an insignificant detail nor a superficial characteristic but one related to the intrinsic nature of religion. The proof of this is that the Catholic clergy is everywhere much more numerous than the Protestant. In Italy there is a priest for every 267

Catholics, in Spain for 419, in Portugal for 536, in Switzerland for 540, in France for 823, in Belgium for 1,050. This is because the priest is the natural organ of faith and tradition and because here as elsewhere the organ inevitably develops in exact proportion to its function. The more intense religious life, the more men are needed to direct it. The greater the number of dogmas and precepts the interpretation of which is not left to individual consciences, the more authorities are required to tell their meaning; moreover, the more numerous these authorities, the more closely they surround and the better they restrain the individual. Thus, far from weakening our theory, the case of England verifies it. If Protestantism there does not produce the same results as on the continent, it is because religious society there is much more strongly constituted and to this extent resembles the Catholic church.

Here, however, is a more general proof in confirmation of our thesis.

The taste for free inquiry can be aroused only if accompanied by that for learning. Knowledge is free thought's only means of achieving its purposes. When irrational beliefs or practices have lost their hold, appeal must be made, in the search for others, to the enlightened consciousness of which knowledge is only the highest form. Fundamentally, these two tendencies are one and spring from the same source. Men generally have the desire for self-instruction only in so far as they are freed from the yoke of tradition; for as long as the latter governs intelligence it is all-sufficient and jealous of any rival. On the other hand, light is sought as soon as customs whose origins are lost in obscurity no longer correspond to new necessities. This is why philosophy, the first, synthetic form of knowledge, appears as soon as religion has lost its sway, and only then; and is then followed progressively by the many single sciences with the further development of the very need which produced philosophy. Unless we are mistaken, if the progressive weakening of collective and customary prejudices produces a trend to suicide and if Protestantism derives thence its special pre-disposition to it, the two following facts should be noted: 1, the desire for learning must be stronger among Protestants than among Catholics; 2, in so far as this denotes a weakening of common beliefs it should vary with suicide, fairly generally. Do facts confirm this twofold hypothesis?

If Catholic France is compared with Protestant Germany merely at their highest levels, that is, if only the upper classes of both are compared, it seems that France may bear the comparison. In the great centers of our country, knowledge is no less honored or widespread than among our neighbours; we even decidedly outdistance several Protestant countries in this respect. But if the desire for learning is equally felt in the upper reaches of the two societies, it is not so on their lower levels; and whereas the maximal intensity is approximately the same in both, the average intensity is less among us. The same is true of the aggregate of Catholic nations compared with Protestant nations. Even assuming that the highest culture of the former is about the same as the latter's, the situation is quite otherwise as regards popular education. Whereas among the Protestant peoples of Saxony, Norway, Sweden, Baden, Denmark and Prussia, from 1877–78 among 1,000 children of school age, that is, from 6 to 12 years, an average of 957 attended school, the Catholic peoples, France, Austria-Hungary, Spain and Italy, had only 667, or 31 per cent less. Proportions are the same for the periods of 1874–75 and 1860–61.[8] Prussia, the Protestant country having the lowest figure here, is yet far above France at the head of the Catholic countries; the former has 897 pupils per 1,000 children, the latter only 766.[9] In all of Germany, Bavaria has most Catholics and also most illiterates. Of all Bavarian provinces, the Upper Palatinate is one of the most profoundly Catholic and has also the most conscripted men who do not know how to read or write (15 per cent in 1871). In Prussia the same is true for the duchy of Posen and the province of Prussia.[10] Finally, in the whole kingdom there numbered in 1871, 66 illiterates to every 1,000 Protestants and 152 to 1,000 Catholics. The relation is the same for the women of both faiths.[11]

Perhaps it will be objected that primary instruction can be no measure of general education. The degree of a people's education, it is often said, does not depend on the greater or smaller number of illiterates. Let us agree to this qualification, though the various degrees of education are perhaps more closely interrelated than seems to be the case and the development of one is difficult without the simultaneous growth of the others.[12] In any case, although the level of primary instruction may only imperfectly reflect that of scientific culture, it has a certain reference to the extent of the desire for knowledge of a people as a whole. A people must feel this need very keenly to try to spread its elements even among the lowest classes. Thus to place the means of learning within everyone's reach, and even legally to forbid ignorance, shows a national awareness of the indispensability of broadened and enlightened intelligence of the individual for the nation's own existence. Actually, Protestant nations have so stressed primary instruction because they held that each individual must be able to understand the Bible. Our present search is for the average intensity of this need, the value attached by each people to knowledge, not the standing of its scholars and their discoveries. From this special point of view, the state of advanced learning and truly scientific production would be a poor criterion; for it would show only what goes on in a limited sector of society. Popular and general education is a more accurate index.

Having thus proved our first proposition, let us attack the second. Does the craving for knowledge to the degree that it corresponds to a weakening of common faith really develop as does suicide? The very facts that Protestants are better educated and commit suicide more than Catholics is a first presumption for this. But the law can not only be verified by comparison of one faith with the other but also be observed within each religious confession.

Italy is wholly Catholic. Public instruction and suicide are identically distributed (see Table XIX).

Not only do the averages correspond exactly, but the agreement extends to details. There is a single exception: Emilia, where under the influence of local causes suicides have no relation to the extent of literacy. Similar observations may be made in France. The departments containing most illiterate couples (above 20 per cent) are Corrèze, Corsica, Côtes-du-Nord, Dordogne, Finisterre, Landes, Morbihan, Haute-Vienne; all relatively free from suicides. More generally, among departments with more than 10 per cent of couples unable either to read or write, not one belongs to the northeastern region which is classical territory for French suicides.[13]

If Protestant countries are compared with one another, the same parallelism will be found. More suicides occur in Saxony than in Prussia; Prussia has more illiterates than Saxony (5·52 per cent compared with 1·3 in 1865). Saxony is even peculiar in that the school population is above the legal requirement. For 1,000 children of school age in 1877–78, 1,031 attended school: that is, many children continued their studies after the required time. The fact is not met with in any other country.[14] Finally England, as we know, is the one Protestant country with the fewest suicides; it also most resembles Catholic countries with respect to education. In 1865

TABLE XIX* Comparison of Italian provinces with reference to suicide and education

First group of provinces	% of marriages with both husband and wife literate	Suicides per million inhabitants
Piedmont	53·09	35·6
Lombardy	44·29	40·4
Liguria	41·15	47·3
Rome	32·61	41·7
Tuscany	24·33	40·6
Averages	39·09	41·1
Second group of provinces		
Venice	19·56	32·0
Emilia	19·31	62·9
Umbria	15·46	30·7
Marches	14·46	34·6
Campania	12·45	21·6
Sardinia	10·14	13·3
Averages	15·23	32·5
Third group of provinces		
Sicily	8·98	18·5
Abruzzi	6·35	15·7
Apulia	6·81	16·3
Calabria	4·67	8·1
Basilicata	4·35	15·0
Averages	6·23	14·7

* The figures for literate couples are from Oettingen, *Moralstatistik*, supplement, Table 85; they refer to the years 1872–78, suicides to the period 1864–76.

there were still 23 per cent of naval seamen who could not read and 27 per cent unable to write.

Still other facts may be compared with the foregoing and confirm them.

The liberal professions and in a wider sense the well-to-do classes are certainly those with the liveliest taste for knowledge and the most active intellectual life. Now, although the statistics of suicide by occupations and classes cannot always be obtained with sufficient accuracy, it is undeniably exceptionally frequent in the highest classes of society. In France from 1826 to 1880 the liberal professions lead, with 550 suicides per million of the professional group, while servants, immediately following, have only 290.[15] In Italy, Morselli succeeded in computing the groups exclusively devoted to letters and found that they far surpass all others in their relative contribution. Indeed, for 1868–76, he estimates it as 482·6 per million members of this profession; the army follows with only 404·1 and the general average of the country is only 32. In Prussia (1883–90) the corps of public officials, which is most carefully recruited and forms an intellectual elite, surpasses all other professions with 832 suicides; the health services and public instruction, though much lower, still have very high figures (439 and 301). Bavaria shows the same picture. Omitting the army, the position of which is exceptional from the point of view of suicide for reasons to be given below, public officials hold second place with 454 suicides and almost achieve first place, for they are barely exceeded by business, with the rate of 465; the arts, literature and the press follow closely with 416.[16] To be sure, the educated classes in Belgium and Wurttemberg seem less gravely afflicted; but professional nomenclature in these countries is too imprecise to permit much importance being attributed to the two irregularities.

Further, we have seen that in all the countries of the world women commit suicide much less than men. They are also much less educated. Fundamentally tradionalist by nature, they govern their conduct by fixed beliefs and have no great intellectual needs. In Italy, between 1878–79, there were 4,808 married men out of 10,000 who could not sign their marriage contract; of 10,000 married women, 7,029 could not.[17] In France, the proportion in 1879 was 199 husbands and 310 wives per 1,000 couples. In Prussia the same difference is found between the sexes, among Protestants as well as among Catholics.[18] In England it is much less than in other European countries. In 1879, 138 illiterate husbands were found per thousand to 185 wives, and since 1851 the proportion has been practically the same.[19] But England is also the country where women come closer to men with respect to suicides. To 1,000 suicides of women there were 2,546 of men in 1858–60, 2,745 in 1863–67, 2,861 in 1872–76, while everywhere else[20] suicides of women are four, five or six times less frequent than those of men. Finally, circumstances are almost reversed in the United States, which makes them particularly instructive. Negro women, it seems, are equally or more highly educated than their husbands. Several observers report[21] that they are also very strongly predisposed to suicide, at times even surpassing white women. The proportion in certain places is said to be 350 per cent.

There is one case, however, in which our law might seem not to be verified.

Of all religions, Judaism counts the fewest suicides, yet in none other is education so general. Even in elementary education the Jews are at least on a level with the Protestants. In fact, in Prussia (1871), to 1,000 Jews of each sex there were 66 illiterate men and 125 women; for the Protestants the numbers were practically the same, 66 and 114. But the Jews participate proportionally more, particularly in secondary and higher learning, than the members of other religions, as the following figures taken from Prussian statistics (years 1875–76)[22] show

	Catholics	Protestants	Jews
Share of each religion in 100 inhabitants of all sorts	33·8	64·9	1·3
Share of each religion in 100 secondary school pupils	17·3	73·1	9·6

Taking into account differences of population, Jews attend Gymnasia, *Realschulen*, etc., about 14 times as often as Catholics and 7 times as often as Protestants. It is the same with higher education. Among 1,000 young Catholics attending institutions of learning of every sort, there are only 1·3 at a university; among 1,000 Protestants, 2·5; for the Jews the proportion increases to 16.[23]

But if the Jew manages to be both well instructed and very disinclined to suicide, it is because of the special origin of his desire for knowledge. It is a general law that religious minorities, in order to protect themselves better against the hate to which they are exposed or merely through a sort of emulation, try to surpass in knowledge the populations surrounding them. Thus Protestants themselves show more desire for knowledge when they are a minority of the general population.[24] The Jew, therefore, seeks to learn, not in order to replace his collective prejudices by reflective thought, but merely to be better armed for the struggle. For him it is a means of offsetting the unfavorable position imposed on him by opinion and sometimes by law. And since knowledge by itself has no influence upon a tradition in full vigor, he superimposes this intellectual life upon his habitual routine with no effect of the former upon the latter. This is the reason for the complexity he presents. Primitive in certain respects, in others he is an intellectual and man of culture. He thus combines the advantages of the severe discipline characteristic of small and ancient groups with the benefits of the intense culture enjoyed by our great societies. He has all the intelligence of modern man without sharing his despair.

Accordingly, if in this case intellectual development bears no relation to the number of voluntary deaths, it is because its origin and significance are not the usual ones. So the exception is only apparent; it even confirms the law. Indeed, it proves that if the suicidal tendency is great in educated circles, this is due, as we have said, to the weakening of traditional beliefs and to the state of moral individualism resulting from this; for it disappears when education has another cause and responds to other needs.

IV

Two important conclusions derive from this chapter.

First, we see why as a rule suicide increases with knowledge. Knowledge does not determine this progress. It is innocent; nothing is more unjust than to accuse it, and the example of the Jews proves this conclusively. But these two facts result simultaneously from a single general state which they translate into different forms. Man seeks to learn and man kills himself because of the loss of cohesion in his religious society; he does not kill himself because of his learning. It is certainly not the learning he acquires that disorganizes religion; but the desire for knowledge wakens because religion becomes disorganized. Knowledge is not sought as a means to destroy accepted opinions but because their destruction has commenced. To be sure, once knowledge exists, it may battle in its own name and in its own cause, and set up as an antagonist to traditional sentiments. But its attacks would be ineffective if these sentiments still possessed vitality; or rather, would not even take place. Faith is not uprooted by dialectic proof; it must already be deeply shaken by other causes to be unable to withstand the shock of argument.

Far from knowledge being the source of the evil, it is its remedy, the only remedy we have. Once established beliefs have been carried away by the current of affairs, they cannot be artificially re-established; only reflection can guide us in life, after this. Once the social instinct is blunted, intelligence is the only guide left to us and we have to reconstruct a conscience by its means. Dangerous as is the undertaking there can be no hesitation, for we have no choice. Let those who view anxiously and sadly the ruins of ancient beliefs, who feel all the difficulties of these critical times, not ascribe to science an evil it has not caused but rather which it tries to cure! Beware of treating it as an enemy! It has not the dissolvent effect ascribed to it, but is the only weapon for our battle against the dissolution which gives birth to science itself. It is no answer to denounce it. The authority of vanished traditions will never be restored by silencing it; we shall be only more powerless to replace them. We must, to be sure, be equally careful to avoid seeing a self-sufficient end in education, whereas it is only a means. If minds cannot be made to lose the desire for freedom by artificially enslaving them, neither can they recover their equilibrium by mere freedom. They must use this freedom fittingly.

Secondly, we see why, generally speaking, religion has a prophylactic effect upon suicide. It is not, as has sometimes been said, because it condemns it more unhesitatingly than secular morality, nor because the idea of God gives its precepts exceptional authority which subdues the will, nor because the prospect of a future life and the terrible punishments there awaiting the guilty give its proscriptions a greater sanction than that of human laws. The Protestant believes in God and the immortality of the soul no less than the Catholic. More than this, the religion with least inclination to suicide, Judaism, is the very one not formally proscribing it and also the one in which the idea of immortality plays the least role. Indeed, the Bible contains no law forbidding man to kill himself[25] and, on the other hand, its beliefs in a future life are most vague. Doubtless, in both matters, rabbinical teaching has gradually supplied the omissions of the sacred book; but they have not its authority. The beneficent influence of religion is therefore not due to the special nature of religious conceptions. If religion protects man against the desire for self-destruction, it is not that it preaches the respect for his own person to him with arguments *sui generis*; but because it is a society. What constitutes this society is the existence of a certain number of beliefs and practices common to all the faithful, traditional and thus obligatory. The more numerous and strong these collective states of mind are, the stronger the integration of the religious community, and also the greater its preservative value. The details of dogmas and rites are secondary. The essential thing is that they be capable of supporting a sufficiently intense collective life. And because the Protestant church has less consistency than the others it has less moderating effect upon suicide.

Notes

1 We have no data on confessional influence in France. Leroy, however, tells us the following in his study on Seine-et-Marne: in the communes of Quincy, Nanteuil-les-Meaux, Mareuil, Protestants show one suicide to 310 inhabitants, Catholics 1 to 678 (*Etude sur le suicide et les maladies mentales dans le département de Seine-et-Marne*, p. 203).

2 *Handwörterbuch der Staatswissenschaften*, supplement, vol. I, p. 702.

3 The case of England is exceptional, a non-Catholic country where suicide is infrequent. It will be explained below.

4 Bavaria is still the only exception: Jews there kill themselves twice as often as Catholics. Is there something exceptional about the position of Judaism in this country? We do not know.

5 Legoyt, *Le Suicide ancien et moderne*, p. 205; Oettingen, *Moralstatistik*, p. 654.

6 To be sure, the statistics of English suicides are not very exact. Because of the penalties attached to suicide, many cases are reported as accidental death. However, this inexactitude is not enough to explain the extent of the difference between this country and Germany.

7 Oettingen, op. cit., p. 626.

8 Oettingen, op. cit., p. 586.

9 Bavaria slightly exceeds Prussia in one of these periods (1877–78); but only this once.

10 Oettingen, op. cit., p. 582.

11 Morselli, *Il suicidio*, p. 223.

12 Moreover it will appear below that both secondary and higher education are more developed among Protestants than among Catholics.

13 See *Annuaire statistique de la France*, 1892–94, pp. 50 and 51.

14 Oettingen, op. cit., p. 586.

15 General report of criminal justice for 1882, p. cxv.

16 See Prinzing, *Trunksucht und Selbstmond*, pp. 28–31. It is noteworthy that in Prussia journalism and the arts show a rather ordinary figure (279 suicides).

17 Oettingen, op. cit., supplement, Table 83.

18 Morselli, op. cit., p. 223.

19 Oettingen, op. cit., p. 577.

20 Except Spain. But not only is the accuracy of Spanish statistics open to doubt, but Spain cannot compare with the great nations of Central and Northern Europe.

21 Baly and Boudin. We quote from Morselli, p. 225.

22 According to Alwin Petersilie, *Zur Statistik der höheren Lehranstalten in Preussen*. In *Zeitschr. d. preus. stat. Bureau*, 1887, p. 109 ff.

23 *Zeitschr. d. pr. stat. Bureau*, 1889, p. xx.

24 In fact, the following shows the variation of Protestant enrolment in secondary schools in the different provinces of Prussia:

Proportion of Protestant population to total		Average proportion of Protestant pupils to total no. of pupils	Difference between first and second
1st group 98·7–87·2%	Average 94·6	90·8	−3·8
2nd group 80–50%	Average 70·3	75·3	+5
3rd group 50–40%	Average 46·4	56·0	+10·4
4th group Below 40%	Average 29·2	61·0	+31·8

Thus, where Protestantism is in a great majority, its scholastic population is not in proportion to its total population. With the increase of the Catholic minority, the difference between the two populations, from being negative, becomes positive, and this positive difference becomes larger in proportion as the Protestants became fewer. The Catholic faith also shows more intellectual curiosity when in the minority. (See Oettingen, op. cit., p. 650.)

25 The only penal proscription known to us is that mentioned by Flavius Josephus in his *History of the War of the Jews against the Romans* (III, 25), which says simply that 'the bodies of those who kill themselves voluntarily remain unburied until after sunset, although those who have been killed in battle may be buried earlier.' This is not even definitely a penal measure.

4

1898c

'Individualism and the intellectuals'

Translation by S. and J. Lukes in *Political Studies*, XVII, 1969, pp. 19–30. First published in French as 'L'Individualisme et les intellectuels' in *Revue bleue*, 4th series, X, pp. 7–13.

The question which, for six months now, has so grievously divided the country is in the process of transformation; having begun as a simple question of fact, it has become more and more general in scope. The recent intervention of a well-known *littérateur*[1] has contributed greatly to this development. It seems to have been felt that the time had come to renew with a great fanfare a controversy that was dying out through repetition. That is why, instead of returning yet again to a discussion of the facts, that writer wanted, in one leap, to rise immediately to the level of principles: the state of mind of the 'intellectuals',[2] the fundamental ideas to which they adhere, and no longer the detail of their arguments, is what has been attacked. If they obstinately refuse 'to bend their logic at the word of an army general', this is, evidently, because they have arrogated to themselves the right to judge the matter; they are putting their own reason above authority, and the rights of the individual appear to them to be imprescriptible. It is, therefore, their individualism which has brought about their schism. But in that case, it has been said, if one wants to restore peace to men's minds and prevent the return of similar discords, it is this individualism which must be directly confronted. This inexhaustible source of domestic divisions must be silenced once and for all. And a veritable crusade has begun against this public scourge, 'this great sickness of the present time'.

We fully agree to conducting the debate in these terms. We too believe that the controversies of yesterday were only superficial expressions of a deeper disagreement; and that men's minds have been divided much more over a question of principle than over a question of fact. Let us therefore leave on one side the minutely detailed arguments which have been exchanged from side to side; let us forget the Affair itself and the melancholy scenes we have witnessed. The problem confronting us goes infinitely beyond the current events and must be disengaged from them.

I

There is a preliminary ambiguity which must be cleared up first of all.

In order to facilitate the condemnation of individualism, it has been confused with the narrow utilitarianism and utilitarian egoism of Spencer and the economists. This is to take the easy way out. It is not hard, in effect, to denounce as an ideal without grandeur that narrow commercialism which reduces society to nothing more than a vast apparatus of production and exchange, and it is only too clear that all social life would be impossible if there did not exist interests superior to the interests of individuals. Nothing is more just than that such doctrines should be treated as anarchical, and with this attitude we are in full agreement. But what is inadmissible is that this individualism should be presented as the only one that there is or even that there could be. Quite the contrary; it is becoming more and more rare and exceptional. The practical philosophy of Spencer is of such moral poverty that it now has scarcely any supporters. As for the economists, even if they once allowed themselves to be seduced by the simplicity of this theory, they have for a long time now felt the need to temper the rigour of their primitive orthodoxy and to open their minds to more generous sentiments. M. de Molinari is almost alone, in France, in remaining intractable and I am not aware that he has exercised a great influence on the ideas of our time. In truth, if individualism had no other representatives, it would be quite pointless to move heaven and earth in this way to combat an enemy that is in the process of quietly dying a natural death.

However, there exists another individualism over which it is less easy to triumph. It has been upheld for a century by the great majority of thinkers: it is the individualism of Kant and Rousseau, that of the *spiritualistes*, that which the Declaration of the Rights of Man sought, more or less successfully, to translate into formulae, that which is currently taught in our schools and which has become the basis of our moral catechism. It is true that it has been thought possible to attack this individualism under cover of the first type, but that differs from it fundamentally and the criticisms which apply to the one could not be appropriate to the other. So far is it from making personal interest the object of human conduct, that it sees in all personal motives the very source of evil. According to Kant, I am only certain of acting well if the motives that influence me relate, not to the particular circumstances in which I am placed, but to my quality as a man *in abstracto*. Conversely, my action is wicked when it cannot be justified logically except by reference to the situation I happen to be in and my social condition, my class or caste interests, my passions, etc. That is why immoral conduct is to be recognized by the sign that it is closely linked to the individuality of the agent and cannot be universalized without manifest absurdity. Similarly, if, according to Rousseau, the general will, which is the basis of the social contract, is infallible, if it is the authentic expression of perfect justice, this is because it is a resultant of all the particular wills; consequently it constitutes a kind of impersonal average from which all individual considerations have been eliminated, since, being divergent and even antagonistic to one another, they are neutralized and cancel each other out.[3] Thus, for both these thinkers, the only ways of acting that are moral are those which are fitting for all men equally, that is to say, which are implied in the notion of man in general.

This is far indeed from that apotheosis of comfort and private interest, that egoistic cult of the self for which utilitarian individualism has justly been reproached. Quite the contrary: according to these moralists, duty consists in averting our attention from what concerns us personally, from all that relates to our empirical individuality, so as uniquely to seek that which our human condition demands, that which we hold in common with all our fellow men. This ideal goes so far beyond the limit of utilitarian ends that it appears to those who aspire to it as marked with a religious character. The human person, whose definition serves as the touchstone according to which good must be distinguished from evil, is considered as sacred, in what one might call the ritual sense of the word. It has something of that transcendental majesty which the churches of all times have given to their Gods. It is conceived as being invested with that mysterious property which creates an empty space around holy objects, which keeps them away from profane contacts and which draws them away from ordinary life. And it is exactly this feature which induces the respect of which it is the object. Whoever makes an attempt on a man's life, on a man's liberty, on a man's honour inspires us with a feeling of horror, in every way analogous to that which the believer experiences when he sees his idol profaned. Such a morality is therefore not simply a hygienic discipline or a wise principle of economy. It is a religion of which man is, at the same time, both believer and God.

But this religion is individualistic, since it has man as its object, and since man is, by definition, an individual. Indeed there is no system whose individualism is more uncompromising. Nowhere are the rights of man affirmed more energetically, since the individual is here placed on the level of sacrosanct objects; nowhere is he more jealously protected from external encroachments, whatever their source. The doctrine of utility can easily accept all kinds of compromises, without denying its fundamental axiom; it can allow that individual liberties should be suspended whenever the interest of the greatest number demands this sacrifice. But there is no possible compromise with a principle which is thus put above and beyond all temporal interests. There is no reason of State which can excuse an outrage against the person when the rights of the person are placed above the State. If, therefore, individualism by itself is a ferment of moral dissolution, one can expect to see its anti-social essence as lying here.

One can now see how grave this question is. For the liberalism of the eighteenth century which is, after all, what is basically at issue, is not simply an armchair theory, a philosophical construction. It has entered into the facts, it has penetrated our institutions and our customs, it has become part of our whole life, and, if we really must rid ourselves of it, it is our entire moral organization that must be rebuilt at the same time.

II

Now, it is a remarkable fact that all these theorists of individualism are no less sensitive to the rights of the collectivity than they are to those of the individual. No one has insisted more emphatically than Kant on the supra-individual character of morality and law. He sees them rather as a set of imperatives that men must obey because they are obligatory, without having to discuss them; and if he has sometimes been reproached for having carried the autonomy of reason to excess, it could be equally said, with some truth, that he based his ethics on an act of unreasoning faith and submission. Besides, doctrines are judged above all by their products, that is to say by the spirit of the doctrines that they engender. Now Kantianism led to the ethics of Fichte, which was already thoroughly imbued with socialism, and to the philosophy of Hegel whose disciple was Marx. As for Rousseau, one knows how his individualism is complemented by an authoritarian conception of society. Following him, the men of the Revolution, in promulgating the famous Declaration of Rights, made France one, indivisible, centralized, and perhaps one should even see the revolutionary achievement as being above all a great movement of national concentration. Finally, the chief reason for which the *spiritualistes* have always fought against utilitarian morality is that it seemed to them to be incompatible with social necessities.

Perhaps it will be said that this eclecticism is self-contradictory? Certainly, we do not propose to defend the way in which these different thinkers have set about combining these two aspects in the construction of their systems. If, with Rousseau, one begins by seeing the individual as a sort of absolute who can and must be sufficient unto himself, it is obviously difficult then to explain how civil society could be established. But here it is a question of ascertaining, not whether such and such a moralist has succeeded in showing how these two tendencies may be reconciled, but rather whether they are in principle reconcilable or not. The reasons that have been given for establishing their complementarity may be worthless, and yet that complementarity may be real. The very fact that they are generally to be found together in the same thinkers offers at least a presumption that they are contemporaneous with one another; whence it follows that they must depend on a single social condition of which they are probably only different aspects.

And, in effect, once one has ceased to confuse individualism with its opposite, that is to say, with utilitarianism, all these apparent contradictions vanish as if by magic. This religion of humanity has all that is required to speak to its believers in a tone that is no less imperative than the religions it replaces. Far from confining itself to indulging our instincts, it offers us an ideal which infinitely surpasses nature; for we do not naturally have that wise and pure reason which, dissociated from all personal motives, would make laws in the abstract concerning its own conduct. Doubtless, if the dignity of the individual derived from his individual qualities, from those particular characteristics which distinguish him from others, one might fear that he would become enclosed in a sort of moral egoism that would render all social cohesion impossible. But in reality he receives this dignity from a higher source, one which he shares with all men. If he has the right to this religious respect, it is because he has in him something of humanity. It is humanity that is sacred and worthy of respect. And this is not his exclusive possession. It is distributed among all his fellows, and in consequence he cannot take it as a goal for his conduct without being obliged to go beyond himself and turn towards others. The cult of which he is at once both object and follower does not address itself to the particular being that constitutes himself and carries his name, but to the human person, wherever it is to be found, and in whatever form it is incarnated. Impersonal and anonymous, such an end soars far above all particular consciences and can thus serve as a rallying-point for them. The fact that it is not remote from us (for the very reason that it is human) does not prevent it from dominating us.

Now all that societies require in order to hold together is that their members fix their eyes on the same end and come together in a single faith; but it is not at all necessary that the object of this common faith be quite unconnected with individual persons. In short, individualism thus understood is the glorification not of the self, but of the individual in general. Its motive force is not egoism but sympathy for all that is human, a wider pity for all sufferings, for all human miseries, a more ardent desire to combat and alleviate them, a greater thirst for justice. Is this not the way to achieve a community of all men of good will? Doubtless it can happen that individualism is practised in quite a different spirit. Certain people use it for their own personal ends, as a means for disguising their egoism and escaping more easily from their duties towards society. But this deceptive misuse of individualism proves nothing against it, just as the utilitarian fictions of religious hypocrites prove nothing against religion.

But I now immediately come to the great objection. This cult of man has for its first dogma the autonomy of reason and for its first rite freedom of thought. Now, it will be said, if all opinions are free, by what miracle will they then be harmonious? If they are formed without knowledge of one another and without having to take account of one another, how can they fail to be incoherent? Intellectual and moral anarchy would then be the inevitable consequence of liberalism. Such is the argument, always being refuted and always reappearing, which the perennial adversaries of reason take up periodically, with a perseverance that nothing can discourage, each time a passing weariness of the human spirit puts it more at their mercy. Certainly, it is true that individualism does not go without a certain intellectualism; for liberty of thought is the first of all liberties. But why has it been seen to have as a consequence this absurd self-infatuation which would confine each within his own desires and would create a gap between men's minds? What it demands is the right for each individual to know those things that he may legitimately know. It does not sanction unlimited right to incompetence. Concerning a question on which I cannot pronounce with expert knowledge, my intellectual independence suffers no loss if I follow a more competent opinion. The collaboration of scientists is only possible thanks to this mutual deference. Each science continuously borrows from its neighbours propositions which it accepts without verifying them. The only thing is that my intellect requires reasons for bowing to the authority of others. Respect for authority is in no way incompatible with rationalism provided that authority be rationally based.

This is why, when one seeks to summon certain men to rally to a sentiment that they do not share, it is not sufficient, in order to convince them, to remind them of that commonplace of banal rhetoric, that society is not possible without mutual sacrifices and without a certain spirit of subordination. It is still necessary to justify *in this particular case* the submission one asks of them, by showing them their incompetence. When, on the other hand, it is a matter of one of those questions which pertain, by definition, to the common judgment of men, such an abdication is contrary to all reason and, in consequence, contrary to duty. For, in order to know whether a court of justice can be allowed to condemn an accused man without having heard his defence, there is no need for any special expertise. It is a problem of practical morality concerning which every man of good sense is competent and about which no one ought to be indifferent. If, therefore, in these recent times, a certain number of artists, but above all of scholars, have believed that they ought to refuse to assent to a judgment whose legality appeared to them to be suspect, it is not because, as chemists or philologists, philosophers or historians, they attribute to themselves any special privileges, or any exclusive right of exercising control over the case in question. It is rather that, being men, they seek to exercise their entire right as men and to keep before them a matter which concerns reason alone. It is true that they have shown themselves more jealous of this right than the rest of society; but that is simply because, as a result of their professional activities, they have it nearer to heart. Accustomed by the practice of scientific method to reserve judgment when they are not fully aware of the facts, it is natural that they give in less readily to the enthusiasms of the crowd and to the prestige of authority.

III

Not only is individualism distinct from anarchy; but it is henceforth the only system of beliefs which can ensure the moral unity of the country.

One often hears it said today that only a religion can bring about this harmony. This proposition, which modern prophets feel it necessary to utter in a mystical tone of voice, is really no more than a simple truism over which everyone can agree. For we know today that a religion does not necessarily imply symbols and rites in the full sense, or temples and priests. All this external apparatus is merely its superficial aspect. Essentially, it is nothing other than a system of collective beliefs and practices that have a special authority. Once a goal is pursued by a whole people, it acquires, as a result of this unanimous adherence, a sort of moral supremacy which raises it far above private goals and thereby gives it a religious character. On the other hand, it is clear that a society cannot hold together unless there exists among its members a certain intellectual and moral community. However, having recalled this sociological truism, one has not advanced very far. For if it is true that religion is, in a sense, indispensable, it is no less certain that religions change, that yesterday's religion could not be that of tomorrow. Thus, what we need to know is what the religion of today should be.

Now, all the evidence points to the conclusion that the only possible candidate is precisely this religion of humanity whose rational
expression is the individualist morality. To what, after all, should
collective sentiments be directed in future? As societies become
more voluminous and spread over vaster territories, their traditions
and practices, in order to adapt to the diversity of situations and
constantly changing circumstances, are compelled to maintain a
state of plasticity and instability which no longer offers adequate
resistance to individual variations. These latter, being less well
contained, develop more freely and multiply in number; that is,
everyone increasingly follows his own path. At the same time, as a
consequence of a more advanced division of labour, each mind finds
itself directed towards a different point of the horizon, reflects a
different aspect of the world and, as a result, the contents of men's
minds differ from one subject to another. One is thus gradually
proceeding towards a state of affairs, now almost attained, in which
the members of a single social group will no longer have anything in
common other than their humanity, that is, the characteristics which
constitute the human person in general. This idea of the human
person, given different emphases in accordance with the diversity of
national temperaments, is therefore the sole idea that survives,
immutable and impersonal, above the changing tides of particular
opinions; and the sentiments which it awakens are the only ones to
be found in almost all hearts. The communion of minds can no
longer form around particular rites and prejudices, since rites and
prejudices have been swept away in the natural course of things. In
consequence, there remains nothing that men may love and honour
in common, apart from man himself. This is why man has become a
god for man, and it is why he can no longer turn to other gods
without being untrue to himself. And just as each of us embodies
something of humanity, so each individual mind has within it
something of the divine, and thereby finds itself marked by a
characteristic which renders it sacred and inviolable to others. The
whole of individualism lies here. That is what makes it into the
doctrine that is currently necessary. For, should we wish to hold
back its progress, we would have to prevent men from becoming
increasingly differentiated from one another, reduce their
personalities to a single level, bring them back to the old
conformism of former times and arrest, in consequence, the
tendency of societies to become ever more extended and centralized,

and stem the unceasing growth of the division of labour. Such an undertaking, whether desirable or not, infinitely surpasses all human powers.

What, in any case, are we offered in place of this individualism that is so disparaged? The merits of Christian morality are extolled to us and we are subtly invited to rally to its support. But are those who take this position unaware that the originality of Christianity has consisted precisely in a remarkable development of the individualist spirit? While the religion of the Ancient City was entirely made up of material practices from which the spiritual element was absent, Christianity expressed in an inward faith, in the personal conviction of the individual, the essential condition of godliness. It was the first to teach that the moral value of actions must be measured in accordance with intention, which is essentially private, escapes all external judgments and which only the agent can competently judge. The very centre of the moral life was thus transferred from outside to within and the individual was set up as the sovereign judge of his own conduct having no other accounts to render than those to himself and to his God. Finally, in completing the definitive separation of the spiritual and the temporal, in abandoning the world to the disputes of men, Christ at the same time opened the way for science and freedom of thought. In this way one can explain the rapid progress made by scientific thought from the date that Christian societies were established. Let no one therefore denounce individualism as the enemy that must be opposed at all costs! One only opposes it so as to return to it, so impossible is it to escape. Whatever alternative is offered turns out to be a form of it. The whole question, however, is to know how much of it is appropriate, and whether some advantage is to be gained by disguising it by means of symbols. Now, if individualism is as dangerous as people say, it is hard to see how it could become inoffensive or salutary, by the mere fact of having its true nature hidden with the aid of metaphors. And, on the other hand, if that restricted individualism which constitutes Christianity was necessary eighteen centuries ago, it seems probable that a more developed individualism should be indispensable today; for things have changed in the interval. It is thus a singular error to present individualist morality as antagonistic to Christian morality; quite the contrary, it is derived from it. By adhering to the former, we do not disown our past; we merely continue it.

We are now in a better position to understand the reason why certain people believe that they must offer an unyielding resistance to all that seems to them to threaten the individualist faith. If every attack on the rights of an individual revolts them, this is not solely because of sympathy for the victim. Nor is it because they fear that they themselves will suffer similar acts of injustice. Rather it is that such outrages cannot rest unpunished without putting national existence in jeopardy. It is indeed impossible that they should be freely allowed to occur without weakening the sentiments that they violate; and as these sentiments are all that we still have in common, they cannot be weakened without disturbing the cohesion of society. A religion which tolerates acts of sacrilege abdicates any sway over men's minds. The religion of the individual can therefore allow itself to be flouted without resistance, only on penalty of ruining its credit; since it is the sole link which binds us one to another, such a weakening cannot take place without the onset of social dissolution. Thus the individualist, who defends the rights of the individual, defends at the same time the vital interests of society; for he is preventing the criminal impoverishment of that final reserve of collective ideas and sentiments that constitutes the very soul of the nation. He renders his country the same service that the ancient Roman rendered his city when he defended traditional rites against reckless innovators. And if there is one country among all others in which the individualist cause is truly national, it is our own; for there is no other whose fate has been so closely bound up with the fate of these ideas. We gave the most recent expression to it, and it is from us that other people have received it. That is why we have hitherto been held to be its most authoritative exponents. We cannot therefore renounce it today, without renouncing ourselves, without diminishing ourselves in the eyes of the world, without committing real moral suicide. Lately it has been asked whether it would not perhaps be convenient for us to agree to a temporary eclipse of these principles, so as not to disturb the functioning of a system of public administration which everyone, anyway, recognizes to be indispensable to the security of the state. We do not know if the antinomy really presents itself in this acute form; but, in any case, if a choice really must be made between these two evils, we would choose the worst of them were we to sacrifice what has hitherto been our historical *raison d'être*. A public institution, however important it may be, is only an instrument, a means that relates to an end.

What is the point of so carefully preserving the means if one abandons the end? And what a deplorable calculation to make—to renounce, in order to live, all that constitutes the worth and dignity of living,

Et propter vitam vivendi perdere causas!

IV

In truth, it is to be feared that this campaign has been mounted with a certain lack of seriousness. A verbal similarity has made it possible to believe that *individualism* necessarily resulted from *individual*, and thus egoistic, sentiments. In reality, the religion of the individual is a social institution like all known religions. It is society which assigns us this ideal as the sole common end which is today capable of providing a focus for men's wills. To remove this ideal, without putting any other in its place, is therefore to plunge us into that very moral anarchy which it is sought to avoid.[4]

All the same, we should not consider as perfect and definitive the formula with which the eighteenth century gave expression to individualism, a formula which we have made the mistake of preserving in an almost unchanged form. Although it was adequate a century ago, it is now in need of being enlarged and completed. It presented individualism only in its most negative aspect. Our fathers were concerned exclusively with freeing the individual from the political fetters which hampered his development. Freedom of thought, freedom to write, and freedom to vote were thus placed by them among the primary values that it was necessary to achieve, and this emancipation was certainly the necessary condition for all subsequent progress. However, carried away by the enthusiasm of the struggle, solely concerned with the objective they pursued, they ended by no longer seeing beyond it, and by converting into a sort of ultimate goal what was merely the next stage in their efforts. Now, political liberty is a means, not an end. It is worth no more than the manner in which it is put to use. If it does not serve something which exists beyond it, it is not merely useless: it becomes dangerous. If those who handle this weapon do not know how to use it in fruitful battles, they will not be slow in turning it against themselves.

It is precisely for this reason that it has fallen today into a certain discredit. The men of my generation recall how great was our enthusiasm when, twenty years ago, we finally succeeded in toppling the last barriers which we impatiently confronted. But alas! disenchantment came quickly; for we soon had to admit that no one knew what to do with this liberty that had been so laboriously achieved. Those to whom we owed it only made use of it in internecine strife. And it was from that moment that one felt the growth in the country of this current of gloom and despondency, which became stronger with each day that passed, the ultimate result of which must inevitably be to break the spirit of those least able to resist.

Thus, we can no longer subscribe to this negative ideal. It is necessary to go beyond what has been achieved, if only to preserve it. Indeed, if we do not learn to put to use the means of action that we have in our hands, it is inevitable that they will become less effective. Let us therefore use our liberties in order to discover what must be done and with the aim of doing it. Let us use them in order to alleviate the functioning of the social machine, still so harsh to individuals, in order to put at their disposal all possible means for developing their faculties unhindered, in order, finally, to work towards making a reality of the famous precept: to each according to his works! Let us recognize that, in general, liberty is a delicate instrument the use of which must be learnt, and let us teach this to our children; all moral education should be directed to this end. One can see that we will not be short of things to do. However, if it is certain that we will henceforth have to work out new objectives, beyond those which have been attained, it would be senseless to renounce the latter so as to pursue the former more easily; for necessary advances are only possible thanks to those already achieved. It is a matter of completing, extending, and organizing individualism, not of restricting it or struggling against it. It is a matter of using and not stifling rational faculties. They alone can help us emerge from our present difficulties; we do not see what else can do so. In any case, it is not by meditating on the *Politique tirée de l'Écriture sainte* that we will ever find the means of organizing economic life and introducing more justice into contractual relations!

In these circumstances, does not our duty appear to be clearly marked out? All those who believe in the value, or even merely in the necessity, of the moral revolution accomplished a century ago, have the same interest: they must forget the differences which divide them and combine their efforts so as to hold positions already won. Once this crisis is surmounted, it will certainly be appropriate to recall the lessons of experience, so that we may avoid falling once more into that sterile inaction for which we are now paying; but that is the task of tomorrow. As for today, the urgent task, which must be put before all else, is that of saving our moral patrimony; once that is secure, we shall see that it is made to prosper. May the common danger we confront at least help us by shaking us out of our torpor and giving us again the taste for action! And already, indeed, one sees initiatives awakening within the country, men of good will seeking one another out. Let someone appear who can combine them and lead them into the struggle: perhaps victory will then not be long in coming. For what should, to a certain extent, reassure us is that our adversaries are only strong by virtue of our weakness. They have neither that deep faith nor those generous enthusiasms which sweep people irresistibly to great reactions as well as to great revolutions. Of course, we would not dream of doubting their sincerity; yet who can fail to notice the improvised quality of all that they believe? They are neither apostles who allow themselves to be overwhelmed by their anger or their enthusiasm, nor are they scholars who bring us the product of their research and their deliberations. They are literary men seduced by an interesting theme. It seems therefore impossible that these games of dilettantes should succeed in keeping hold for long of the masses, providing that we know how to act. Moreover, what a humiliation it would be if, having no stronger opponents than these, reason were to end by being defeated, even if only for a time![5]

Notes

1 See the article by M. Brunetière: 'Après le procès', in *Revue des Deux Mondes* of 15 March 1898.
2 Let us note in passing that this word, which is most appropriate, does not properly have the pejorative meaning that has so maliciously been attributed to it. The intellectual is not a person who has a monopoly of understanding (*intelligence*); there are no social functions where understanding is unnecessary. But there are those in which it is at once both the means and the end, the instrument and the goal. Here understanding is used to extend understanding, that is to say, to enrich it with knowledge, ideas, and new sensations. It is thus the basis of these professions (art, science) and it is in order to express this peculiarity that it has come to be natural to call those who practise them intellectuals.
3 See *Contrat social*, 1. II, ch. III.
4 This is how it is possible, without contradiction, to be an individualist while asserting that the individual is a product of society, rather than its cause. The

reason is that individualism itself is a social product, like all moralities and all religions. The individual receives from society even the moral beliefs which deify him. This is what Kant and Rousseau did not understand. They wished to deduce their individualist ethics not from society, but from the notion of the isolated individual. Such an enterprise was impossible, and from it resulted the logical contradictions of their systems.

5 [For introductory comments on this article, written by Durkheim at the time of the Dreyfus Affair, see S. Lukes, 'Durkheim's "Individualism and the intellectuals" ', *Political Studies, XVIII,* 1969, pp. 14–19.—W.S.F.P.]

5

1899a (ii)

'Concerning the definition of religious phenomena'

First published in French as 'De la Définition des phénomènes religieux' in *L'Année sociologique*, II, pp. 1–28.

Since the sociology of religion deals with religious facts, it is necessary to begin by defining them. We say *religious facts*, and not *religion*, for religion is a totality of religious phenomena, and the whole can only be defined in terms of the parts. Moreover, there are innumerable religious manifestations which do not belong to any properly recognized religion. In every society, there are scattered beliefs and practices, be they individual or local, which are not integrated into a definite system.

Obviously, this initial definition cannot claim to put into words the essence of the thing defined. It can only mark the boundaries of the territory of facts to be covered by the research—only indicate how they can be recognized and distinguished from those with which they might be confused. Although this preliminary process does not directly reach the heart of the matter, it is indispensable in order to know accurately what we are talking about. For it to be of use, it is not even necessary to produce rigorously defined results at once. There can be no question of immediately discovering the exact boundaries limiting the field of the religious, always assuming they exist. We can only make a general survey of the ground, register a first impression, and separate and characterize an important group of phenomena which must attract the closest attention of the scholar. No matter how unpretentious this problem may be, it will be seen that the manner in which it is solved has some bearing on the general direction the science will take.

In other words, in order to proceed towards this definition, we must begin by completely leaving aside the more or less vague idea that each of us has about religion; it is the religious fact itself that we are trying to get to grips with, not our view of it. We must be objective and try to see things as they really are. Besides, the way to achieve this is a simple one and we have explained it so often as to feel it unnecessary to justify it once again. If we can find some social facts which have immediately apparent characteristics in common, and if these characteristics have enough affinity with those vaguely denoted by the word religion in everyday language, we shall group them under the same heading. In this way, we shall form a distinct group which will be defined quite naturally by the very characteristics which serve to form it. To be sure, it is possible that the concept thus formulated may not completely coincide with the current idea of what religion is. This does not matter; for our aim is not simply to state precisely the usual meaning of the word, but to give ourselves a subject for research which can be tackled by ordinary scientific method. To this end, it is necessary and sufficient that it should be recognized and observed from the outside, and that it should include all the facts capable of clarifying each other, but only those facts. None the less, we can easily justify our right of keeping the common expression, so long as the differences are not so marked that they entail the creation of a new word.[1]

Since this definition must apply to all facts presenting the same distinctive characteristics, we must not be selective about them, whether they refer to the more highly developed societies, or conversely, to the lowliest forms of civilization. Both must be covered by the same formula if they have the same characteristics. It is true that some minds are repelled by such lack of discrimination. They see only gross superstition in the religions of primitive peoples and refuse to compare them too closely with the idealized cults of civilized people. At least, anything properly religious about these primitive religions, they say, remains only of the most rudimentary kind. It is an unknown germ whose true nature is only revealed as it grows. If then we wish to discover the true nature of religion, we must observe it as the zenith of its evolution; it is in the most refined

forms of Christianity and not in the puerile magic of the Australian
aboriginal or the Iroquois that we must expect to find the elements of
the definition we are seeking. Only when *true religion* has been
defined in this manner will it be possible to consider the others and
to single out whatever religious content they may have. But by what
token can we recognize that one religion is superior to another?
Because it is more recent? But Islam came later than Christianity.
Because it demonstrates better the characteristics of religiosity? To
be certain of this, these characteristics must already be known; but
we are now arguing in a circle. In fact, the definitions established by
this method do no more than express in abstract form the
denominational prejudices of the scholars putting them forward;
accordingly, they are quite bereft of all scientific value. If we want to
obtain more impersonal and objective results, we must take care to
set aside all preconceptions. We must, so to speak, let things classify
themselves according to their similarities and their differences,
whatever period in history they may refer to and however they may
affect our personal feelings.

But before applying these principles ourselves, it would be of
interest to examine a few of the definitions in common use.

I

In his *Introduction to the Science of Religions* (p. 13), Max Müller
has given the following definition:

> Religion is a mental faculty or disposition which . . . enables man
> to apprehend the Infinite under different names and under
> varying disguises. Without that faculty, no religion, not even the
> lowest worship of idols and fetishes, would be possible; and if we
> will but listen attentively, we can hear in all religions a groaning
> of the spirit, a struggle to conceive the inconceivable, to utter the
> unutterable, a longing after the Infinite.

In a subsequent work,[3] he upholds this definition in its essentials.
Religion thus consists of a system of beliefs and practices relative to
a *nescio quid*, as unfathomable to the senses as to reason. It would
be defined in terms of its object, which would always be the same
and this object would be the mysterious, the unknowable, the
incomprehensible. This is the very conclusion arrived at by Spencer,
and along with him, all the members of the agnostic school.

'Religions diametrically opposed in their overt dogmas, are perfectly at one', he writes, 'in the tacit conviction that the existence of the world with all it contains and all which surrounds it, is a mystery calling for interpretation.'[4]

Quite apart from the fact that these formulae are very vague, they make the mistake of ascribing to primitive peoples, and even to the lower strata of population in the most advanced societies, an idea which is completely foreign to them. Undoubtedly, when we see them attributing extraordinary properties to unimportant objects, populating the universe with strange forces, endowed with some unintelligible ubiquity or other, and made up of such incompatible elements that as a result they cannot be described, it is easy to find that these conceptions are cloaked in mystery. It seems to us that men can only have resigned themselves to such disconcertingly irrational ideas because they were unable to discover other more rational ones. As a matter of fact, these explanations, which to us seem so surprising, are to the primitive mind the simplest explanations in the world. Primitive man does not see in them a sort of *ultima ratio* to which the intellect only turns when all else fails, but the most direct method of understanding and visualizing what he sees about him. For him it is no miracle that with an utterance or gesture, one should be able to command the elements, stop or hasten the movements of the stars, or conjure up rain by imitating the sound of rainfall, etc. Consequently, in certain cases, anybody can exercise this power over things, however remarkable it may seem in our eyes; it is just a question of knowing an effective formula.[5] If, in other circumstances, one can only succeed with the help of the intervention of certain special beings, priests, sorcerers, diviners, etc., it is because these privileged people are in direct communication with exceptionally intense sources of energy. But this energy has nothing particularly mysterious about it. It is a force of the kind understood by the present-day scientist which he relates to the phenomena he is studying. It is no doubt true that such forces behave in a different manner and that they cannot be managed and disciplined by the same processes. But both kinds are to be found in nature and are at the disposal of mankind, though not all men are in a position to make use of them.

Far from seeing the supernatural everywhere, primitive man sees it nowhere. Indeed for him to have any sort of conception of it, he would also have to have a conception of the opposite, the first being merely the negative aspect of the second. He would have to have a feeling for a *natural order* and there can hardly be anything less primitive than that. It is an idea which implies that we have reached the stage where we can see things interconnected according to necessary relationships called laws; thus, we say of an event that it is natural when it conforms to the appropriate known laws, or at least is not at variance with them. When an event is at variance with them, we say that it is supernatural. This idea of necessary laws is a relatively recent one; there are branches of knowledge from which the idea is still almost completely absent, and moreover only a few minds are imbued with it. Consequently, for any stranger to scientific culture, nothing is outside nature, because for him there is no such thing as nature. He multiplies miracles unconsciously, not because he feels surrounded by mysteries, but on the contrary, because nothing has any secrets for him.

Therefore, what seems a miracle to us is no such thing for primitive man. As his understanding is not yet formed (because the understanding is only formed with and by knowledge), it is with his imagination that he views the world. Now the imagination, when given a free rein, orders things quite haphazardly, never encountering any sort of resistance. The inner states which it is fashioning, that is to say the images, are made up of such insubstantial, plastic material, their contours are so blurred and wavering, that they are easily modified according to the whim of the subject. The subject, then, has no difficulty in arranging them in the order most closely conforming to his desires, to his habits and to the demands of his method; in other words, he has no trouble in explaining things. If human intelligence really has limits, primitive man knows nothing about them because he has not yet reached them. What gives us this impression of a limit, of a milestone which cannot be passed, is the effort that we are obliged to make when we step outside ourselves and into the shoes of the unscientifically cultured in order to understand things. Despite our endeavours to grasp things and to bring them into our purview, we feel them partially escaping us. Man only knows all this effort, all this suffering, all these laborious and complete explanations, when he has reached a certain degree of mental development. Let us assume for a moment the existence of the most perfect science that the most uncompromising idealist might dream of; imagine the whole world expressed in clear and distinct ideas. For anyone who had this complete knowledge, there would obviously no longer be any mystery in the universe: the whole of reality would be fully visible to him, since it would be totally reduced to a system of manageable ideas which he would hold, as it were, in the hollow of his hand. A completely uncultivated mind finds itself in a similar position but for the opposite reasons. For this mind, too, everything is readily explicable. For it, too, the universe, or at least the part of the universe in which it is interested, is fully expressed in a system of inner states which it arranges with the same facility. Undoubtedly, the substance of these two minds is quite different. One is exclusively made up of vague and confused images; the other, of clear ideas. In one case man is conscious that nature yields to mind because mind has subjected nature; in the other case, man is not aware of nature's resistance because mind has not yet got to grips with nature. But in a sense, the result is the same: for the one as for the other, mystery does not exist.

Thus, the idea of mystery is in no sense primordial. It is not innate in man, but man himself has invented it. He has progressively built it up along with its opposite, for each entails the other and neither can evolve separately. Consequently, the idea only plays an important part in a small number of very advanced religions, and even there, it does not constitute the whole. One cannot, therefore, make it the characteristic of religious phenomena without arbitrarily excluding from the definition the greater part of the facts to be defined. It is narrowing the field of religion to a great extent if one only includes a few Christian dogmas.

Another definition, an even more popular one, expresses religion as a function of the idea of God. 'Religion', says Réville, 'is the determination of human life by the sentiment of a bond uniting the human mind to that mysterious Mind whose domination of the world and of itself it recognizes, and to whom it delights in feeling itself united.'[6] It is true that the word mystery is to be found in this formula as in the preceding one; but here, it only plays a secondary part and could be left out. The really essential thing is that it makes religion a kind of superior ethic, whose object is to regulate the relationships of man to certain beings of a superhuman nature, on whom he is supposed to depend. These beings are gods.

At first glance, the proposition seems a truism and as such incontestable. The idea of God and the idea of religion are indeed so closely linked in our minds that they seem inseparable and, again, we are accustomed to imagining every god as a force which dominates man and lays down the laws he must observe. There are, nevertheless, whole religions which do not satisfy this definition.

In the first place, it is not true to say that the gods have always been thought of in this way; man very often treats them as absolute equals to himself. No doubt he depends on them, but they depend just as much on him. He needs their assistance but they need his sacrifices. So when he is not content with the service they provide, he stops his offerings to them; he cuts off their supplies. The relationship between them is of a contractual kind and is based on the principle of *do ut des*.[7]

> Once the savage has made offerings according to his means to his fetish, he firmly expects benefits in return. The fact is that however great may be his fear of the fetish, we cannot, for all that, represent the relationship existing between them as if the savage were necessarily and in every instance the subject of his fetish, as if the fetish were superior to the savage. He is not a being of superior nature to the one who worships him; he too is a savage and, should the occasion arise, must be treated as such.

Supposing he freely refuses to do what is asked of him, despite the prayers addressed to him and the offerings donated? The fetish must be compelled to respond by ill-treatment; for example, if the hunt has been unsuccessful, he is whipped. It is not that his power is held in any doubt; once the punishment has been inflicted there is a reconciliation, he is newly clothed and fresh offerings are made. Only his good will is suspect and it is hoped that a timely chastisement will restore him to a better frame of mind. In China, when the countryside is suffering from a prolonged drought, the people construct an enormous paper dragon which represents the rain god and carry it in solemn procession; but if no rain comes, abuse is hurled at it and it is torn to pieces.[8] In a similar situation, the Comanches whip a slave who is supposed to represent the god. Another way of forcing the rain god out of his inactivity is to go and disturb him in his lair: to do this, stones are thrown into the sacred lake where he is thought to live.[9]

One could quote a multitude of examples showing that man does not always have a very high opinion of the gods he worships. This is also proved by the ease with which he attributes divine characteristics to himself or confers them on one of his fellow men.

Indeed, human deities [*Hommes-Dieux*] crop up frequently in inferior societies; this dignity is lavishly distributed because so little is needed to be eligible for it. In India, if anyone is above average in the matter of courage or strength or some other personal quality, he readily obtains the honour of divinization. The Todas consider the dairy to be a sanctuary; so the dairyman in charge is treated like a god. In Tonkin, it is frequently the case that some vagabond or beggar succeeds in persuading the inhabitants of the village that he is their divine protector. It has been said of the ancient religion of the Fijians that it establishes no clear line of demarcation between gods and men.[10] The way in which primitive man visualizes the world explains, moreover, this conception of divinity. Nowadays, as we have a better idea of what nature is and what we are, we are conscious of our insignificance and our weakness in the face of cosmic forces. In consequence, we cannot conceive that a being should have the power over them which we attribute to the deity, without endowing him with a power superior to our own, without setting him infinitely above ourselves, without being under his domination. But, so long as we are not fully aware of the intransigence of things, so long as we do not know that their manifestations are necessarily predetermined by their nature, extraordinary powers do not seem necessary to control them.

Thus, even if the idea of God is really the point where all religious phenomena converge, it would still need a different definition of God for the idea of God to serve as a definition of religion. Again, it is not true to say that in all the manifestations of religious life, this idea has played the superior role attributed to it.

In fact, there are religions in which there is no idea of God at all. One example is Buddhism, whose teaching is contained in the following four propositions, called by the faithful the four noble truths:

1. *The existence of suffering.* To exist is to suffer. Everything within us and around us is in a perpetual state of flux. Now only unhappiness can exist where there is continual insecurity. Bliss can only consist in the calm and assured possession of something permanent. Life, therefore, can only be suffering because it is nothing but instability.

2. *The cause of suffering.* This lies in the desire which grows by its very satisfaction. Since life is suffering, the cause of suffering is the desire to live, which is the love of life.

3. *The cessation of suffering.* This is achieved by the suppression of desire.

4. *The path leading to this suppression.* There are three stages. In the first place there is uprightness which is essentially contained in the following five precepts: there must be no killing of any living creature, no stealing the property of others, no unchastity with another man's wife, no telling of untruths, no drinking of intoxicating liquor. The second stage is self-concentration by means of which the Buddhist turns away from the outside world to retire within himself 'and savour in advance in the calm of the self, the cessation of the perishable'. Finally, over and above meditation, there is wisdom, that is to say, the possession of the four truths. Having travelled along these three stages one reaches the end of the road; here is deliverance, salvation by achieving Nirvana.[11]

These are the essential dogmas of Buddhism. It is evident that the question of a deity does not arise. Alone and without outside help the holy man delivers himself from suffering. Instead of praying and instead of turning to a being superior to himself, whose assistance he implores, he retires within himself and meditates; and the object of his meditation is not goodness, not glory, not the greatness of a god, but the self into which he is absorbed by the very fact of his meditation. That is not to say that he bluntly denies the existence of beings called Indra, Agni, and Varuna, but he believes that in any case, even if they exist, he owes them nothing; for their power only extends over worldly things which to him are valueless. He is an atheist then in the sense that he has no interest in the question of knowing whether or not there are gods. Besides, even if there were any gods and no matter what their power the holy man who has found salvation considers himself to be superior to them, for human dignity does not lie in the extent of the power which human beings exercise over things, nor does it lie in the intensity of the life they lead; but exclusively in the degree of progress they have made along the road to salvation.

Another great Indian religion, Jainism, presents the same characteristics. Moreover, the two doctrines have the same conception of the world and the same philosophy of life. Both offer to mankind a purely human ideal: the attainment of a state of wisdom and beatitude, in one instance brought about by Buddha, in the other, by Jaina.[12] 'Like the Buddhists, the Jainists are atheists. They admit of no creator; the world is eternal; and they explicitly deny the possibility of a perfect being from all eternity.'[13] It is true that along with the northern Buddhists, certain Jains have come to embrace a sort of deism, since the Jina has been deified as it were, but in so doing they have gone against the opinion of their most authoritative scholars.

If indifference to the divine is complete in Buddhism and in Jainism, it is because the seeds of it were already present in Brahmanism from which both religions derived. Indeed, according to Barth, Brahmanic metaphysics often consists 'in an explanation of the universe which is frankly materialistic and atheistic'.[14] It is true that in general it takes the form of pantheism; but this pantheism is such that it is almost completely identifiable with atheism. It states the fundamental identity of things, the unity of being; but this unique being is not a primary cause greater than man in every respect, enveloping him and transcending him in all his immensity, which as a result, naturally attracts love and demands worship. It is quite simply the substance of which each one of us is made and which is to be found everywhere, identical to itself; it is that part of us which is lasting and constant. Consequently, to attain wisdom, which consists in leaving behind the ephemeral multiplicity of things in order to rediscover this immutable, basic substance, it is sufficient to concentrate our attention on ourselves and to meditate. The aspiration towards the deity is replaced by the turning in of the individual upon himself. The idea of God, therefore, is absent from behaviour and morality. 'When the Buddhist', says Oldenberg,[15]

> sets out on that great venture of imagining a world of salvation where man saves himself and creates a religion without God, Brahmanic speculation has already prepared the ground for this attempt. The idea of divinity has retreated step by step, the faces of the ancient gods have grown paler and are gradually fading away; Brahma sits enthroned in his eternal quietude, high above the terrestial world, and, apart from him, there remains but a single person to play an active part in the great work of deliverance: it is man.

Consequently the Brahmin who has attained this state considers himself to be the equal of the gods: even, Tiele says, 'the solitary penitents consider themselves to be their superiors in power and in dignity'.[16]

These examples are particularly striking; but there are many

others which would not have passed unnoticed if a little more care
had been taken to state precisely the meaning of the word god. If,
indeed, one wishes to get it clear in one's own mind and not to
confuse the most disparate things under the same heading, one must
not extend this expression to include everything which inspires in a
rather pointed manner the special feeling conventionally called
religious awe. A god is not simply an eminently sacred object:
temples, ritual objects, presiding priests, etc., are not gods. One
notable trait distinguishes gods from other religious beings: it is that
each one of them is an individuality *sui generis*. It is not a general
kind of thing, an animal, vegetable or mineral species; it is a specific
animal, star, stone, spirit, a specific mythical personality. It is
because he is that particular tree, that particular plant, that
legendary hero, that he is a god and that he is that god. The
characteristic or characteristics which make a deity of him and to
which religious practices are directed, are not common to other
beings as well as to him; he possesses them in his own right. At least,
if they are found elsewhere, it is always to a lesser degree and in a
different way; he only imparts reflections and small fragments of
those characteristics. It is these same attributes which make up his
essential constitution, which is the basis of divine substance. The
power to hurl down thunderbolts from the sky was the epitome of
Zeus,[17] just as the power to preside over the life of the fields was the
epitome of Ceres. A god, then, is a force which gives rise to certain
more or less clearly defined manifestations. These are always related
to a particular, determined subject. When, conversely, this same
property remains diffused throughout an indeterminate class of
things instead of being thus incarnated in an individual, we simply
have sacred objects, as opposed to profane objects, but no god. For
a god to be constituted in such a way, it is necessary for the obscure
property which confers on the former objects their religious nature,
to be separated, conceived apart and given substance. It is of little
importance, moreover, whether it be imagined in the guise of a pure
spirit, or whether it be attached to a material substratum; the
essential thing is that it should be individualized.

Of course we are not thinking of presenting these few remarks as
a true definition. They suffice, however, to show that the idea of
divinity, far from being the most fundamental aspect of religious life,
is only in fact a secondary aspect of it. It is the product of a special
process by virtue of which one or more religious characteristics are

concentrated and made concrete in the shape of a more or less definite individuality. It may well happen that this process of becoming concrete does not take place. This is the case with all the practices which make up the cult of totemism. Indeed, the totem is not a given member of the animal or vegetable species which acts as a symbol for the group; it is the species as a whole. In a clan which has the wolf as its totem, all wolves are equally venerated, those existing today, along with those which existed yesterday, along with those which will exist tomorrow. The same honours are rendered to them without distinction. In this example there is neither god nor gods, but a vast category of sacred things. In order to be able to apply the word god, it would be necessary for the principle common to all these particular beings to be separated from them, and, personified in some form or other, to become the focal point of the cult itself. It is true that certain tribes have progressed to the idea of an incredible being from which descended, simultaneously, the clan and the species adopted as its totem. This eponymous ancestor, however, is the object of no special rites; and he plays no active or personal role in the religious life of the group; he is not the one to be invoked; nor is his presence that which is sought out or feared. It is simply a way for the mind to visualize the unity of the totem species and the relationships of kin that the clan is supposed to maintain with it. Far from such a *représentation* being the very basis of totemism, it is obvious that it has only been invented after the event, to allow man to explain to himself a system of practices already in existence.

The same could be said of agrarian cults. Their aim is to ensure the regular renewal of vegetation in all its forms, fruit trees and other trees, and plantations of every kind. It is by no means always the case that the diversity of operations which make up these cults are invariably addressed to gods. Very often it is that religious action exercises itself directly on the vegetation itself, on the soil which bears it and which nourishes it, with no divine intermediary being invoked by the faithful. The principle from which the life of the forest or that of the field is supposed to derive, does not reside in a specific wheatsheaf, or in a specific tree, or in a specific ideal personality, distinct from all particular trees and fields; it is diffused throughout the whole expanse of fields and woods.[18] It is not a god, it is simply a characteristic common to a whole class of things, from which it has only progressively emerged to become a divine entity.[19]

Besides, there is no religion where one cannot discover rites whose effectiveness is independent of all divine power. The rite acts by itself, by virtue of sympathetic action; it brings about the phenomenon that it is intended to produce almost mechanically. It is neither an invocation, nor a prayer addressed to a being on whose good graces the outcome depends. The result is obtained by the automatic bringing into play of the ritual operation. This is notably the case with sacrifices in the Vedic religion. 'Sacrifice', writes Bergaigne, 'exercises a direct influence on celestial phenomena';[20] it is all-powerful by itself and *without any form of divine intervention.* For example, it broke down the doors of the cave where the Dawn was imprisoned and caused the light of day to shine forth (p. 133); *despite the gods,* appropriate hymns caused the waters of heaven to spread upon the earth (p. 135).

No text bears better witness to the consciousness of a magical action performed by man on the waters of heaven than line [Rig-Vedal] X, 32, 7 where this belief is expressed in general terms, applicable to contemporary man as much as to his ancestors, whether real or mythological: *ignorant man has enquired of the knowing man and, instructed by the knowing man, he acts and we see how he has profited from the instruction, he has made the mighty torrents flow.*

The practice of certain austerities has the same power as the ceremonies of sacrifice. Again,[21]

sacrifice is so much the pre-eminent principle that not only the origin of man, but the origin of the gods is ascribed to it. . . . Such an idea might well seem strange. It is explained, however, as one of the final consequences of the idea of the omnipotence of sacrifice.

The whole of the first part of Bergaigne's book is given up to the discussion of sacrifices in which the gods have played no part. If, moreover, we borrow an example from the Vedic religion, it is not because the occurrence is peculiar to it; on the contrary, it is generally widespread. In every cult there are practices which act by themselves, by virtue of some power of their own, and no god interposes himself between the individual performing the rite and the goal which he pursues. This explains the primordial importance attached by almost all cults to the material part of the ceremonies.

Such religious formalism, which is probably a preliminary form of judicial formalism, results from the fact that the formula pronounced, the movements made which contain within themselves the source of their effectiveness, would necessarily lose it if they did not conform exactly to the model made sacred by success.

In short, the distinction made between sacred and profane things is very often independent of the idea of god. The idea cannot then have been the original point of departure from which this distinction was made; it was formulated later on to introduce the beginnings of organization into the confused mass of sacred things. In fact, each god became a sort of centre around which gravitated a certain section of the religious world. The different spheres of divine influence have progressively co-ordinated themselves and grown subordinate to each other. In this way the notion of divinity has played a role in the religious life of people, somewhat analogous to that of the idea of the ego in the psychic life of the individual: it is a principle of grouping and unification. But just as there exist psychological phenomena which cannot be attributed to an ego, there are religious phenomena which cannot be linked to a god. It is now easier to understand how one can have atheistic religions like Buddhism and Jainism. For a diversity of reasons, this organization has not been necessary. One can find holy things in them (the deliverance from suffering is a holy thing as is the whole of life which is a preparation for it), but they do not look back to a divine being for their source.

II

The mistake common to all these definitions is the desire to state from the beginning the content of religious life. Quite apart from the fact that this content is infinitely varied in relation to different periods of time and different societies, it can only be determined slowly and progressively in the light of growing scientific knowledge; it is the main object of the sociology of religion to succeed in discovering it, and consequently it cannot provide the material for an initial definition. Only the exterior and apparent form of religious phenomena is immediately accessible to observation; it is to this therefore that we must apply ourselves.

There is a category of religious facts which is commonly accepted as being especially characteristic of religion and which as a result ought to give us what we are looking for, namely ritual. When one tries to define ritual, however, one notices that left on its own and unrelated to anything else, it has nothing specific about it. In fact, it consists in practices, that is to say, in clearly defined ways of behaviour. There are no social practices, however, which do not have the same characteristic: it is therefore necessary to indicate how one can distinguish the former kind of practices. Perhaps we should say that they are, certainly for the most part, obligatory. But then, are law and ethics any different? How can we distinguish between ritual prescription and moral and legal maxims? Some people have thought it possible to differentiate between them by saying that, in one case, they regulate the relations between men, and in the other, they regulate the relations between men and gods. But we have just seen that some cults do not concern themselves with gods. The distinction is even less easy to draw for, until recent times, religious morality and secular morality, secular law and divine law, were one and the same. In many societies, offences against one's fellow men have been considered as offences against the deity. Even today, for the well-informed believer, the fulfilment of one's duty towards one's neighbour is a part of ritual: it is the best way of honouring God. It is true one can avoid all these difficulties if one says in a general way that ritual is the totality of practices concerned with *sacred things*; even if there are rites without gods, the objects to which they refer are always by definition of a religious nature. But we are merely replacing one word by another and this substitution in itself brings about no clarification. We should also need to know what constitutes these sacred things and how we are to recognize them. This is precisely the problem we are considering. Stating it in a different way is not the same as solving it.

Here we have a group of phenomena which are irreducible to any other group of phenomena. Certain communities which at times correspond to a political society, but at others are distinct from it, all present the same characteristics; not merely do their members adhere to a common faith, but are required to adhere to it. Not only does the Israelite believe that Jahveh is God, that he is the sole God, the creator of the universe, the revealer of the Law; he must believe it. He must also believe that Jahveh saved his ancestors from the slavery of Egypt, in the same way as the Athenian must believe that Athens was founded by Athene and not cast any doubts on the fundamental myths of the city, and as the Iroquois must admit that

his clan is descended from a certain animal, and as the Christian
must accept the basic dogmas of his Church. These beliefs vary in
nature and in importance. Sometimes the object of the faith of the
believer is a purely ideal being created by the imagination;
sometimes it is a directly observable concrete reality, and the
obligation to believe relates only to certain properties attributed to
it. At times they form an erudite and systematized creed; at others
they are reduced to a few simple articles. Here, they are of a moral
order, constituting a doctrine for living (Buddhism, Christianity);
there, they are purely cosmogonic or historical. In the first case, they
are specifically known as dogmas, in the second, as myths or
religious legends. In all these forms, however, they present the same
distinctive peculiarity: the society which professes them does not
allow its members to deny them.

This prohibition is not always upheld by punishments as such. In
any religion common to a specific society,[22] the denial of certain
beliefs does not constitute a crime which must be explicitly
punished. But even when this is the case, society always brings
pressure to bear on its members to prevent them from deviating from
the common faith. Whoever shows signs of moving away from it,
even on minor points, is to some extent found fault with, held at
arm's length, shunned. Dissidents never enjoy more than a very
relative level of tolerance. The fact which best serves to demonstrate
the extent to which this imperative characteristic is inherent in all
religious opinion is that everywhere basic dogmas are protected
from outspoken criticisms by the direst of punishments. Where a
religious society corresponds to a political society, it is in the name
of the state, and very often by the state, that these sanctions are
applied. Where these two communities are dissociated, there are
purely religious sanctions which are in the hands of the spiritual
authority and which range from excommunication to penitence.
There is always an exact parallel between the religious character of
the beliefs and the intensity of the repression which imposes respect
for them, that is to say, the more religious they are, the more they
are obligatory. This obligation results from their nature and can
consequently serve as a definition for them.

Thus, *représentations* of a religious kind are in opposition to
others in the same way that obligatory opinions are in opposition to
freely held opinions. To this difference in *représentations*
corresponds another between their objects. Some myths, some

dogmas, are mental states *sui generis* that we can easily recognize, it is not necessary to give a scientific definition of them, and they cannot be confused with the products of our personal ideas. Since they do not have the same origins, they do not share the same characteristics. The former are traditions which the individual finds ready-made and to which he respectfully conforms his thought; the latter are our own work and, for this reason, do not curtail our liberty. Things which reach our minds by such very different routes cannot appear to us in the same light. All tradition inspires a very special respect and this respect necessarily communicates itself to its object, whatever it may be, real or ideal. That is why we feel that there is about these beings, whose myths and dogmas teach us about existence or describe nature to us, something majestic which sets them apart. The special way by which we begin to know them cuts them off from those we know by the normal processes of empirical *représentation*. This explains why there is this division of things into sacred and profane, which is fundamental to all religious organization. It has been said, it is true, that the distinctive trait of the sacred is to be found in the exceptional intensity of the energy which it is supposed to unleash. The inadequacy of the characteristic is proved by the fact that there are extraordinarily intense natural forces to which we do not ascribe a religious character, and conversely, that there are religious objects whose active properties are fairly weak: an amulet, a rite of secondary importance, are religious things without being very awesome. The sacred therefore distinguishes itself from the profane by a difference, not only of degree but of quality. It is not only a temporal force of frightening aspect because of the effects it can produce, it is something else. The line of demarcation which separates these two worlds results from the fact that their nature is different, and this duality is only the objective expression of that which exists in our *représentations*.

We now face a sufficiently definite group of phenomena. No confusion is possible between law and morality; obligatory beliefs are quite a different matter from obligatory practices. It is true that both are imperative by definition, but the first force us to think in certain ways, the second to behave in certain ways. One kind compels us to accept certain *représentations*; the other to perform certain actions. There is then all the difference between them as that which exists between thinking and acting, between representative functions and motivating or practical functions. Seen from another angle, if science is also made up of *représentations*, and collective *représentations* at that, the *représentations* which constitute it can be distinguished from the preceding ones in that they are not strictly obligatory. It is sensible to believe in them but we are not obliged to do so morally or legally. Indeed, very few of them can be considered completely beyond question. It is a fact that there are beliefs intermediate between science and religious faith; these are general beliefs of all kinds which appear to be relevant to secular objects, things like the flag, one's country, some form of political organization, some hero, or some historical event or other, etc. They are obligatory in a certain sense, because of the very fact of their being held in common; the community will not tolerate open denial of them without resistance. It would seem then that they can be included in the preceding definition. As a matter of fact, however, they are to some extent indistinguishable from religious beliefs proper. The mother country, the French Revolution, Joan of Arc, etc., are sacred to us all, and we refuse to allow anyone to interfere with them. Public opinion will not willingly tolerate the challenging of the moral superiority of democracy, the reality of progress, and the idea of equality, just as the Christian will not allow his fundamental dogmas to be questioned. At least, if there are differences between these two kinds of collective beliefs, they are only noticeable in the light of a third set of facts which we are about to discuss.

Beliefs are not the only phenomena which must be called religious; there are practices as well. Ritual is an element of all religion, which is no less essential than faith. If we have been unable to make it the prime element of our definition, it is because, considered by itself and in its intrinsic characteristics, it is indistinct from morality and law. Religious practice is a way of behaving which is clearly defined and obligatory, like moral and legal practices; such ways of behaving are differentiated only by their object. At the beginning of our research, we had no means of saying what was specific about this object. That is the question we have just answered. We now know what religious things are. What distinguishes them from all others is the way in which they are pictured in people's minds. We are not free to believe them or disbelieve them; the mental states conveying them to us thrust themselves upon us obligatorily. The specific character of the corresponding practices is determined by that very fact. What prevents them

from being confused with other obligatory practices is that the beings
on whom they act, or are supposed to act, are known to us only
through those very particular collective *représentations* known as
myths and dogmas, and whose characteristics we have stated above.
The same is not true of morality. *In so far as it has no religious
characteristics*, it has as its basis neither mythology nor cosmogony
of any kind.[23] Here, the system of rules which predetermine conduct
is not bound up with a system of rules which predetermine thought.
Since religious practices and beliefs are so interdependent, they
cannot be separated by science and must belong to a single study.
The one and the other are only two different aspects of the same
reality. The practices translate the beliefs into action and the beliefs
are often only an interpretation of the practices. That is why,
combining them in one single definition, we state: religious
phenomena is the name given to obligatory beliefs as well as the
practices relating to given objects in such beliefs.[24]

There is, however, a feature of religious phenomena to which this
formula does not give enough prominence. It demonstrates that
practices are bound up with beliefs; it does not sufficiently
emphasize the inverse relationship which is no less real. Indeed, one
may ask oneself if beliefs which do not lead to practices are really
religious. Religion is not exclusively either an obligatory
philosophy, or a practical discipline: it is both one and the other at
the same time. Thought and action are closely linked to the point of
being inseparable. Religion corresponds to a stage of social
development where these two functions are not yet dissociated and
established apart from each other, but are still so interrelated that it
is impossible to draw a clear line of demarcation between them.
Dogmas are not purely speculative states or simple phenomena
of conceptualization. They are always directly connected with
definite practices: the dogma of transubstantiation in the Christian
mass, that of the Trinity in the feasts and prayers addressed to
the triune God, etc. This is the way they distinguish themselves
from commonly held secular beliefs like the belief in progress,
democracy, etc. Although they exercise a general influence
on conduct, these beliefs are not connected with definite ways of
behaving which are the expression of them. Doubtless, one cannot
believe firmly in progress without it having some effect on one's way
of life; however, there are no precise practices attached to such an
idea. It is a faith without a corresponding ritual. We have here the

inverse phenomenon of the one we had been discussing earlier in relation to morality. The precepts of law and morality are identical with those of religion, except that they do not rest on a system of obligatory beliefs. Those collective beliefs which are not religious are similar in all respects to properly recognized dogmas, except that they are not necessarily translated into a system of definite practices. Finally, we propose the following definition: *phenomena held to be religious consist in obligatory beliefs, connected with clearly defined practices which are related to given objects of those beliefs.*[25] As for religion, it is a more or less organized and systematized whole, composed of phenomena of the kind mentioned.

III

However precise may be the criterion by which religion has just been defined, such a criterion stands at the heart of our study. Consequently, by the very fact that this definition has been accepted, the science of religions becomes orientated in a definite direction which makes it a truly sociological science.

Indeed, what characterizes religious beliefs and practices alike is that they are obligatory. Now everything that is obligatory has a social origin. An obligation implies a command and consequently an authority which commands. For the individual to be forced to behave in conformity with certain rules, the rules must proceed from a moral authority which imposes them; and in order to be able to impose them, the authority must dominate the individual. Otherwise, where would the influence necessary to bend people's will come from? We comply with orders spontaneously only if they come from someone more exalted than ourselves. If, however, we refuse to move outside the realm of experience, there is no moral authority superior to the individual, except that of the group to which he belongs. From empirical knowledge, the only thinking being which is greater than man is society. It is infinitely superior to each individual, since it is a synthesis of individuals. The state of perpetual dependence in which we find ourselves in the face of society inspires in us a feeling of religious awe. Thus, society dictates to the believer the dogmas he must uphold and the rites he must observe; if this is so, it is an indication that the rites and dogmas are its own handiwork.

We have as a corollary to our definition the fact that religion originates not in individual feelings but in collective states of mind, and that it varies according to these states. If it sprang from the nature of the individual, it would not present itself to him in this coercive way: ways of behaving and thinking, which are in direct accord with the tendencies of our dispositions, cannot appear to us invested with an authority superior to that which we attribute to ourselves. Therefore it is not in human nature in general that we must seek the determining cause of religious phenomena; it is in the nature of the societies to which they relate, and if they have evolved in the course of history, it is because their social organization has been transformed. From now on, the traditional theories which pointed to the source of religiosity as being in the feelings of individuals, like the awe inspired in each one of us by such things as great cosmic forces at work, or the spectacle of certain natural phenomena like death, must be viewed with more than suspicion. Henceforth we can predict with some assurance that research will have to be conducted in quite a different manner. The problem presents itself in sociological terms. The powers before which the believer prostrates himself are not simply physical forces, such as are given to the senses and the imagination: they are social forces. They are the direct product of collective sentiments which have clothed themselves in a material covering. What are these sentiments? What social causes have aroused them and led them to express themselves in this form or that? What social ends are satisfied by the organization arising in this way? These are the questions that the science of religions must consider; and to deal with them we have to observe the conditions of collective existence.

From this point of view, religion becomes something natural and explicable to the human intelligence, while at the same time retaining in relation to the reason of the individual, its characteristic transcendence. If it emanates from the individual, it constitutes an incomprehensible mystery. Since by definition it expresses things as being other than they are, it seems like some great hallucination and phantasmagoria which has duped humanity and whose existence has no apparent justification. It is understandable that in these circumstances, certain thinkers have seen fit to look for the origins in sleep and dreams; the whole thing has something of the substance of a dream, now genial and now sombre, that humanity has lived through. Only this does not explain why experience did not rapidly teach men that they were victims of error. If, however, we accept that religion is essentially a social thing, these difficulties disappear. There is no further need to enquire why the things in whose existence religion asks us to believe appear so disconcerting to individual reason. It is quite simply that the *représentation* of them it offers us is not the handiwork of the individual reason but that of the collective mind [*l'esprit collectif*].[26] Now, it is quite natural for this collective mind to see reality in a different way from us, because its nature is of a different order. Society has its own mode of existence which is peculiar to it; correspondingly, its own mode of thought. It has its passions, its habits, and its needs, which are not those of the individual, and which leave their mark on everything it conceives. It is not surprising, therefore, that as mere individuals, we do not feel at home with these conceptions which are not ours and which do not express our nature. That is why they are shrouded in an air of mystery which disturbs us. This mystery, however, is not inherent in the object itself which they represent, it is entirely the result of our ignorance. It is a provisional mystery like those which science invariably clears up step by step as it advances. It stems uniquely from the fact that religion belongs to a world which human science has only just begun to explore and which to us is still unknown. If we can succeed in finding the laws of collective conceptualization, these strange *représentations* will lose their strangeness.

This is how the distinction between sacred and profane things to be found in all religions takes on its full meaning. Sacred things are those whose *représentation* society itself has fashioned; it includes all sorts of collective states, common traditions and emotions, feelings which have a relationship to objects of general interest, etc.; and all those elements are combined according to the appropriate laws of social mentality. Profane things, conversely, are those which each of us constructs from our own sense data and experience; the ideas we have about them have as their subject matter unadulterated, individual impressions, and that is why they do not have the same prestige in our eyes as the preceding ones. We only put into them and see in them what empirical observation reveals to us. Now, these two sorts of mental states constitute two kinds of intellectual phenomena, since one type is produced by a single brain and a single mind, the other by a plurality of brains and minds acting and reacting on each other. This duality of the temporal and the spiritual is not an invention without reason and without foundation in reality;

it expresses in symbolic language the duality of the individual and the social, of psychology proper[27] and sociology. That is why for a long time the initiation into sacred things was also the operation by which the socialization of the individual was completed. At the same time, as man entered into the religious life, he assumed another nature and became a new man.

It will be objected that there are beliefs and practices which indeed seem to be religious and which are however partly the result of individual spontaneity. In fact, there are no religious societies where, as well as the gods whom everybody is compelled to worship, there are not also others which anyone can freely create for his own personal use. From the very beginning, in addition to the collective totem venerated by the whole clan, there have been the private totems that everyone chooses as he wishes and which nevertheless are the objects of a true cult. Similarly today there is hardly a believer who does not view more or less in his own way the God commonly worshipped, and who does not modify traditional concepts on some point or other. There are even some people who refuse to recognize any other deity than the one which free meditation has led them to believe exists; and in this case they are the real legislators of the cult to which they adhere. Finally, even when the believer addresses himself to the God worshipped by the community, he does not always confine himself to the practices rigorously prescribed. He takes others upon himself and he forces himself to make sacrifices or to undergo disciplines which religious law does not positively demand. But if all these facts are undeniable, and no matter what the relationship they may have to those we have discussed so far, they require none the less to be distinguished from them. If one does not want to be open to grave misunderstanding, it is necessary to be aware of confusing a free, private, optional religion, fashioned according to one's own needs and understanding, with a religion handed down by tradition, formulated for a whole group and which it is obligatory to practise. The two disciplines which are so different cannot meet the same needs: one is completely orientated towards the individual, the other towards society.

Yet, it remains true that they belong to the same family. Indeed, in both cases gods and sacred things are found equally, and the relations we establish in one case or the other are palpably the same: it is still a matter of sacrifices, offerings, prayers, lustrations, etc. If, however, for this reason, it is convenient to integrate these facts into the general definition of religious phenomena, it can only be as a secondary consideration. In the first place, it is certain that at all times and in all countries, the bulk of religious facts has been formed by those we defined in the first instance. Individual beliefs and practices[28] have always been of little significance in comparison with collective beliefs and practices. Moreover, if there is a relation between these two sorts of religion, which would seem to be *a priori* probable, it is obviously private belief which is derived from public belief. Indeed, by the definition as it were, obligatory religion cannot have individual origins. The obligation which characterizes it would be inexplicable if it did not emanate from some authority superior to the individual. On the other hand, it is easy to believe in the reverse. The individual is not present as a passive witness in the religious life which he shares with his group. He visualizes it, thinks about it, seeks to understand it and, by that very fact, changes its nature.

When he meditates about it, he pictures it in his own way and partially personalizes it. Thus, owing to the force of circumstances, there are in every church almost as many heterodox as orthodox, and unorthodox opinions multiply and become more obvious in proportion to the growth of individual thought. It is even inevitable that by imitation the believer comes to construct for himself and his own use a system analogous to that which he sees functioning with his own eyes in the interests of society. That is why he imagines totems, gods, and guardian spirits are there exclusively for him. This intimate and personal religion is then only the subjective aspect of the external, impersonal and public religion. And in order to be able to accept this idea, it is not at all necessary to imagine that these two religions correspond to two distinct and successive historic phases. In all probability, they are contemporaneous. Indeed, the individual is affected by the social states which he helps to fashion at the very moment he is fashioning them. They influence him as they are being formed and he changes their nature as he is influenced by them. It is not a question of two distinct time-scales. To whatever extent he may be absorbed into society, he always retains some personality of his own; the social life to which he contributes becomes in him, at the very moment of its coming into being, the germ of an interior and personal life which grows parallel to the first one. Moreover, there are no forms of collective activity which do not become personalized in this way. Each one of us has his personal moral code, his personal approach, which differs from the common morality and general approach of society although they spring from them.

Thus, to give these facts a rightful place within the whole of religious phenomena, we should add to the definition suggested above, the following words: *In addition, the optional beliefs and practices which concern similar objects or objects assimilated into the previous ones, will also be called religious phenomena.* This correction leaves intact the methodological conclusions we have drawn. It continues to be the case that the idea of the sacred is of social origin and can be explained only in sociological terms. If it influences individual minds and is developed in them in an original manner, it is by way of secondary effect. The forms it takes cannot be understood if they are not related to the public institutions of which they are only the extension.

Notes

1 See a more complete exposition in our *Règles de la méthode sociologique*, pp. 43 ff. [English translation, *The Rules of the Sociological Method*, by S. A. Solovay and J. H. Mueller, London, 1938, pp. 34 ff.—W.S.F.P.]

2 See E. Caird, *The Evolution of Religion*, I, p. 46. This theological and denominational preoccupation is fairly general among British anthropologists. See also the book by Jevons. [Probably F. B. Jevons, *An Introduction to the History of Religion*, London, 1897—W.S.F.P.]

3 *Origin and Growth of Religion*, 1882, p. 23. It will be observed that in this definition and in the following ones, religion is defined, not religious facts. It is assumed that all religion is a reality with clearly drawn contours and that it does not exclude any religious facts outside itself. This idea is far from being a true representation of the facts.

4 *First Principles*, p. 37. See Caird, I, pp. 60 ff.

5 See Frazer, *Golden Bough*, pp. 13 ff.

6 Prolégomènes à l'histoire des religions, p. 34. [English translation, *Prolegomena of the History of Religions*, by A. S. Squire, London, 1884, p. 25—W.S.F.P.]

7 Schultze, *Fetichismus*, p. 129.

8 Huc, *L'Empire chinois*, I, p. 266.

9 *Golden Bough*, I, p. 19.

10 Ibid., I, pp. 30–56.

11 See Oldenberg, *Le Bouddha*, pp. 214 ff. [English translation from the German, *Buddha: his Life, his Doctrine, his Order*, by W. Hoey, London, 1882—W.S.F.P.]

12 [Mahavira is traditionally regarded as the founder of Jainism in the sixth century BC. He is looked upon as the twenty-fourth Jina by Jains. Jina means conqueror or victor. A Jaina or Jain means a follower of the Jina.—W.S.F.P.]

13 Barth, *The Religions of India*, p. 146.

14 *Encyclopédie des sciences religieuses*, VI, p. 548.

15 Ibid., VI, p. 51.

16 *Histoire des religions*, p. 175.

17 Of course, we are not trying to say that each god, Jupiter or any other, can be defined by one attribute and one only: on the contrary, it is known that the most different attributes can merge and unite in the same deity. We are merely thinking of an elementary example to simplify the argument.

18 See the facts in Mannhardt. Also Philpot, *The Sacred Tree*, London, 1897, analysed in *L'Année sociologique*, vol. I, p. 218.

19 See further on, in the article on sacrifice, the developments concerning agrarian sacrifice. [The reference is to 'Essai sur la nature et la fonction de sacrifice' by H. Hubert and M. Mauss, which followed this article in the same issue of *L'Année sociologique*. English translation, *Sacrifice: its Nature and Function*, by W. D. Halls, London, 1964—W.S.F.P.]

20 *La Religion Védique*, p. 122.

21 Ibid., pp. 137, 138, 139.

22 Note that for the moment we are only discussing religions common to a group. We deal with individual religions further on.

23 In so far as morality still rests on some dogma, for example on the idea that the human personality is a sacred thing because it is created by God, it ceases to be secular, ceases to be morality proper and becomes part of the cult.

24 This definition enables one to distinguish between religious rites proper and magical rites. A radical distinction is not possible in this sense in that there are religious rites in great number which are magical too. It very often happens that a god is asked to bring about a certain desired event by means of a ceremony which imitates that event. Symbolic feasts may well have originated in this way. There are, however, rites which are solely magical: they are not directed towards the gods or sacred things, they are in no way dependent on any obligatory belief. Sympathetic magic is a case in point. There is nothing sacred about either the statue or the poor unfortunate who is to be bewitched and, generally, the sorcerer calls for the intervention of either deity nor demon. Like is automatically supposed to cause like by itself.

25 This definition lies mid-way between the two opposite theories which are at the moment dividing the science of religions. According to one, the essence of religious phenomena is myth; according to the other, it is ritual. It seems clear, however, that there can be no ritual without myth, for a rite necessarily assumes that things are represented as being sacred and this *représentation* can only be mythical. On the other hand, one must recognize that in less advanced religions, rites are already developed and definite when myths are still very rudimentary. Besides, it seems equally unlikely that there should be myths which are not dependent on some rite or other. Between these two sorts of fact there is a very close connection. Perhaps the debate partly arises out of the fact that the word myth is reserved for more highly developed and more or less systematized religious *représentations*. This restriction may be legitimate; but another word is needed to designate simpler religious *représentations*, distinguishable from myths proper by reason of their greater simplicity.

26 There is no need to repeat that we are only referring to the way *sui generis* in which men think when they think collectively.

27 It is to be remembered that by psychology we mean the science of the individual mentality; we reserve the name sociology for anything concerning the collective mentality.

28 We speak of strictly individual beliefs and not those common to small groups within the body of the Church. The religion of a group, even a small one, is still collective, for example, domestic religion.

6

1910a (ii) (2)

Note   'Religious systems of primitive societies' (I)

First published in French as 'Systèmes religieux des sociétés inférieures' in *L'Année sociologique*, XI, pp. 75–6 (unsigned: probably by Durkheim).

Until now, we have confusedly grouped under this title all those religions which are not clearly national or universal. This, however, has meant cataloguing some very dissimilar systems under the same heading. As far as political structure and judicial organization are concerned, the societies of Australia, of North America and kingdoms like that of Dahomey, cannot be grouped together. Parallel distinctions must be introduced into the classification of religious systems. That is why in the future, among the religions of primitive societies, a distinction will have to be made between those which are properly and essentially totemic and those which we shall call totemic religions, on the one hand, and on the other, those where totemism, although still existing, is none the less in the process of giving birth to new forms of religion. Totems are still to be found among them, attached to family groups, phratries or clans; but the cult of totems is either being modified or effaced, and is being replaced by the cult of spirits and even true deities. The clans themselves, whilst sometimes remaining recognizable, include religious subgroups which are changing and which are differently organized. These are the brotherhoods so often and wrongly called secret societies. We shall call those religions which are to be found particularly among the Indians of North America, *primitive religions evolved from totemism*. They bring us closer to a higher form of religious system but at the same time cannot be classified under the same heading as the great national religions. A notable example is the religion of the Ewhe which is considered later. In it there is no longer any question of clans or phratries; religion has become tribal and will be described as such. A tribe, in so far as it can sometimes attain to quite considerable dimensions, is still not sufficiently organized as a society to merit being called a nation. There is a gulf between a state like ancient Egypt and the great kingdoms of western Africa; naturally, the gap is also to be found between the corresponding religions.

This innovation in our classification has the advantage that it distinguishes more clearly the intermediate stages connecting totemism with the most highly evolved types of religion. The very object of the several analyses that we shall read is the marking out of some of the stages in this evolution.

7

The Elementary Forms of the Religious Life: the Totemic System in Australia

Introduction, I, II (part); Book I, chapter I, sections III and IV; Book II, chapter VII, sections I, II, IV, and VI; Conclusion, sections I and II. First published in French as *Les Formes élémentaires de la vie religieuse. Le système totémique en Australie*, Alcan, Paris, pp. 1–15; 49–66; 293–307, 320–8, 336–42; 593–616.

Introduction
The Subject of the Research

Sociology of religion and theory of knowledge

I
1–15

In this book we intend to study, analyse and attempt to explain the most primitive and simple religion currently known to man. Among the religious systems we have had the opportunity of observing, we consider the most primitive to be one that fulfils the two following conditions: to begin with, it must be found in societies whose organization is so simple that no other could be simpler;[1] in addition, it should be possible to explain it without recourse to any element borrowed from an earlier religion.

We shall endeavour to describe the economy of this system with the exactness and accuracy which an ethnographer or historian might bring to the task. Our task, however, will not stop there. Sociology deals with problems different from those of history or ethnography. It does not attempt to study earlier forms of civilization with the sole aim of understanding and reconstructing them. Like all positive science its object is above all to explain present reality: a reality which touches us closely and which, as a result, is capable of affecting our ideas and actions. This reality is man, and particularly present-day man, assuming that we are hardly concerned with understanding any other kind of man. We shall not, then, be studying the very archaic religion in question for the sole pleasure of recounting its oddities and peculiarities. If we have made it the subject of our research, it is because we considered it to be more suited than any other religion to the task of clarifying the religious nature of man, that is to say, of revealing an essential and permanent aspect of humanity.

Still, this proposition inevitably gives rise to strong objections. It might seem strange that in order to succeed in understanding humanity today, we should have to begin by turning our back on it and returning to the beginnings of history. This method of procedure appears to be particularly paradoxical when applied to the question which concerns us. Indeed, religions are not thought to be equal in terms of value and importance, for it is generally accepted that some have a greater share of the truth than others. Accordingly, it would seem that we cannot compare the highest forms of religious thought with the lowest, without reducing the first to the level of the second. In granting that the crude forms of worship of the Australian tribes can help us to understand Christianity for example, are we not implying that the latter religion issues from the same mentality, that is to say, it is made up of the same superstitions and is based on the same errors? For this reason the theoretical importance sometimes attributed to primitive religions has been taken as the sign of a systematic hostility to religion which, by prejudging the results of research, invalidate them in advance.

This is not the place to enquire into whether or not some scientists must be reproached for turning religious history and ethnography into an engine of war to combat religion. In any case, this cannot be true of the sociologist. It is an essential postulate of sociology that a human institution cannot be based on error and falsehood, otherwise it could not have lasted. If it did not have its roots in the very nature of things, it would have encountered opposition to things which it could not overcome. Consequently, we approach the study of primitive religions secure in the knowledge that they are the products of reality of which they are the expression. This principle will recur time and again in the course of the analyses and arguments which follow, and we blame the schools from which we dissociate ourselves precisely with having failed to appreciate it. It is true that if we take things quite literally, these religious beliefs and practices sometimes seem disconcerting and we might be tempted to attribute them to a sort of fundamental aberration. Underlying the symbol there is a reality which it represents which we must grasp, and which gives it its true meaning. The most barbarous or bizarre rites and the strangest myths all express some human need, some aspect of life, be it individual or social. The reasons employed by the believer to justify them may be, indeed often are, erroneous; nevertheless, real reasons exist and it is the job of science to discover them.

Fundamentally then there are no false religions. They are all true in their own way: they all answer, albeit in different ways, the given conditions of human existence. Naturally, it is not impossible to arrange them in hierarchical order. Some may be said to be superior to others in the sense that they bring into play a higher order of mental functions, that they are richer in ideas and sentiments, that they include more concepts and fewer sensations and images, and that their systematization is better. Yet, however real their greater complexity and higher conceptualization may be, they are not enough to place the corresponding religions into separate genera. They are all severally religions, just as all living beings are equally living, from the lowest plastid to man himself. So, when we set ourselves to study primitive religions, it is not with the ulterior motive of disparaging religion in general; for primitive religions are no less worthy of respect than any other. They answer the same necessities, they play the same role, they are subject to the same causes. Just as much as any other religions, they are able to demonstrate the nature of religious life and consequently help to resolve the problem that we intend to study.

Why should they be granted some kind of prerogative? Why choose them in preference to all others as the subject of our research? It is simply for reasons of method.

In the first place, we cannot hope to succeed in understanding the most recent religions unless we follow the way in which they have been progressively built up in the course of history. History is indeed the only method of analysis which can possibly be applied to them.

It alone enables us to break down an institution into its constituent elements since history reveals them to us, one after the other as they are born in time. Then again, by situating each one of them within the pattern of circumstances in which it developed, it offers the only tool we have of determining the causes which gave rise to it. Every time we proceed to explain some human fact, related to a specific moment in time—whether it be a question of a religious belief, a moral law, a legal precept, an aesthetic technique, or an economic system—it is necessary to go back to its most primitive and simplest form. We must seek to account for the characteristics which help to define it at that period of its existence and then try to see how it has gradually developed and grown more complex, and how it has become what it is now. It is easy to imagine the importance of determining the starting point of this series of progressive explanations. It is a Cartesian principle that in a chain of scientific truths, the first link is of prime importance. To be sure, there can be no question of having an idea formulated in the Cartesian manner as the foundation of the science of religions, that is to say a logical concept, a pure construct, erected by the unaided power of thought. What we must find is a concrete reality which historical and ethnographical observation can alone reveal. If, however, this cardinal idea has to be derived by different methods, it remains true that it is destined to have a considerable amount of influence on the whole sequence of propositions established by the science. Biological evolution was viewed in a totally different light from the moment it became known that there existed unicellular beings. Likewise, the pattern of religious facts is explained differently if one places naturism, animism or some other such religious form at the base of evolution. Even the most specialized scientists are obliged to choose one or other of these hypotheses. If they do not intend to limit themselves to the task of erudition pure and simple, and if they want to understand the facts they are analysing, they must work from the chosen hypothesis. Whether they like it or not, the questions they ask necessarily take the following form: how has naturism or animism been led to take this particular form, and in some way or the other become developed or despoiled? Since a decision has to be reached on this initial point and since that decision is bound to affect the whole of the science, it must be met face to face and that is what we propose to do.

Moreover, quite apart from these consequential effects, the study of primitive religions is in itself of direct interest and prime importance.

If it is useful to know the contents of a given religion, it is even more important to try to discover what religion is in general. This problem has always whetted the curiosity of philosophers and with good reason, for it concerns the whole of humanity. Unfortunately, the method which they normally employ in solving it is purely dialectical: they limit themselves to analysing the idea they have of religion, and illustrating the results of this mental analysis with examples borrowed from the religions which come closest to their ideal. Although the method must be abandoned, the problem itself has not been forgotten, thanks to the philosophers who grappled with it when other scholars ignored it. It can now be approached again from a different angle. Since all religions are comparable and since they are all species of one and the same genus, they necessarily have certain essential elements in common. By that we do not simply mean the external and visible characteristics which they all have in equal measure, and which enable us to define them provisionally at the outset. To discover these obvious signs is relatively easy as the observation required need not penetrate below the surface of things. These external resemblances, however, imply the existence of others which are more deep rooted. At the heart of all systems of beliefs and of all cults, there must necessarily be a certain number of fundamental *représentations* and ritual attitudes which, despite the diversity of forms they have each been able to assume, have everywhere the same object meaning and universally fulfil the same functions. It is these permanent elements which constitute the eternal and human aspect of religion; they make up the whole of the objective content of the idea we are expressing when we speak of *religion* in general. How then are we to reach them?

Certainly not by observing the complex religions which have appeared in the course of history. They are all compounded of such a variety of elements that it is very difficult to distinguish between what is secondary and what is primary, and between the essential and the non-essential. Consider religions like those of Egypt, India or classical antiquity. In them we have an involved tangle of multifarious cults varying according to their locality, temples, generations, dynasties, invasions, etc. In them, too, popular superstition is mingled with the most subtle dogmas. Neither religious thought nor religious activity is equally distributed among the masses of the faithful; depending on individuals, the environment or circumstances, beliefs and rites alike are experienced in different ways. Here we have priests, there monks, elsewhere laymen; there are mystics and rationalists, theologians and prophets, etc. Under these conditions, it is difficult to see what they have in common. Use can be made of one or other of these systems to provide a fruitful field of study for some particular fact which is manifested in them and in an especially well-developed form, like sacrifice or prophecy, monasticism or cultic mysteries; but how do we set about discovering the common foundation of the religious life beneath the luxuriance of vegetation covering it? How can the fundamental states which are characteristic of the religious mentality in general be found behind the clash of theologies, the variations in ritual, the multiplicity of groupings and the diversity of individuals?

The situation is quite different in lower societies. The limited development of individuality, the restriction of the group, the homogeneity of external circumstances all contribute to reduce the differences and variations to a minimum. The group consistently realizes an intellectual and moral conformity such as we rarely find in more advanced societies. Everything is common to everybody. Movements are stereotyped; everybody does similar things in similar circumstances and this conformity of behaviour only reflects the conformity of thought. As all *consciences* are carried along by the same current, the individual type is almost submerged in the generic type. Just as everything is uniform, everything is simple. Nothing is more crude than those myths made up of a single theme which is endlessly reiterated, than those rites which are composed of a small number of gestures repeated to the point of oblivion. The popular or priestly imagination has not yet had either the time or the means to refine and transform the raw material of religious ideas and practices; this starkly presents itself to the eyes of the observer who has only to make the merest effort to see what he wants to see. The accessory, the non-essential, indeed, superfluous developments of any kind have not yet emerged to obscure the primary.[2] Everything is reduced to the indispensable, to that without which there can be no religion. But the indispensable is also the essential, that is to say, what above all else we must know.

Primitive civilizations, then, are privileged cases because they are simple cases. That is why the observations of ethnographers have often been veritable revelations which have invigorated the study of human institutions. For example, before the middle of the nineteenth century, people were convinced that the father was the essential element in the family; it seemed inconceivable that there might be a family organization in which paternal authority was not the keystone. Bachofen's discovery overthrew this old idea. Until quite recent times, it was thought obvious that the moral and legal relations which constitute kinship were merely another aspect of the physiological relations resulting from common descent: Bachofen and his successors, MacLennan, Morgan and many others, were still subject to the influence of this preconception. Since we have known about the nature of the primitive clan, we have also known that, on the contrary, kinship cannot be defined in terms of consanguinity. To revert to religions. The exclusive consideration of those religious forms which are most familiar to us, has created a long-standing belief that the idea of God is characteristic of everything religious. But the religion which we shall be studying later is, for the most part, quite alien to any idea of divinity; in it, the forces to which the rites are offered are very different from those which have the prominent place in our modern religions, and yet they will help us to understand them better. There is nothing more unjust than the contempt with which too many historians still view the work of ethnographers. On the contrary, it is a fact that, within different branches of sociology, ethnography has very often been at the heart of the most fruitful revolutions. For the same reason, the discovery of unicellular beings, which was discussed earlier, transformed current ideas about life. As life is reduced to its essential features among these very simple beings, it is more difficult to fail to recognize what these features are.

Primitive religions, however, do not only enable us to isolate the constituent elements of religion, they also have the great advantage of facilitating the explanation of religion. Because the facts are simple, the relations between them are also more apparent. The reasons which men give to explain their own actions have not yet been elaborated and dissected by studied reflections; they are nearer, more akin to the motives which really determine these actions. In order to understand a delirium properly and to be able to carry out the best course of treatment, a doctor needs to know how it started. But this is much more easily ascertained if one can observe the delirium soon after it began. On the other hand, the longer the illness is allowed to develop, the more it eludes observation. The reason is that, as it develops, all sorts of interpretations intervene which tend to drive the original condition into the unconscious, and to replace it with others which sometimes conceal the way leading to the first. There is often a considerable gap between the completed study of a delirium and the first impressions which gave rise to the study. The same is true of religious thought. In its progress through history, the causes which called it into existence, though still active, can now only be seen through a vast system of interpretations which distort them. Popular mythologies and subtle theologies have done their work: they have superimposed on primitive sentiments very different sentiments which, despite being an elaboration of the former from which they have evolved, only give us a very imperfect view of the true nature of the primitive form. The psychological distance between cause and effect, between apparent cause and effective cause, has become greater and more difficult for the mind to grasp. The remainder of this work will be an illustration and verification of this methodological point. It will be seen how, in primitive religions, the religious fact still bears the visible mark of its origins: it would have been much more difficult for us to infer them from an exclusive consideration of the more highly developed religions.

The study that we are undertaking is, then, a kind of reconstruction, *in different terms*, of the old problem of the origin of religions. To be sure, if by origin we mean an absolute first beginning, the question is not a scientific one and must be dismissed out of hand. There is no such thing as a radical moment when religion came into existence and there is no question of trying to find an expedient which would enable us to travel mentally to that moment. In common with every human institution, religion had no beginning. Consequently, all speculations of this kind are rightly discredited; they can only consist in subjective and arbitrary constructions without any form of control. The problem we intend to consider is quite a different one. What we should like to do is to find a way of detecting the ever-present causes behind the most essential forms of religious thought and practice. For the reasons we have just stated, these causes are most easily observed when the society under consideration is of the least complicated kind. That is why we are trying to revert to origins.[3] It is not that we intend to ascribe particular virtues to the lower forms of religion. On the contrary, they are rudimentary and uncivilized. There can therefore be no question of using them as some form of model for the development of subsequent religions. However, their very lack of refinement makes them instructive for they can be viewed as convenient experiments where facts and relationships are easier to determine. When the physicist is trying to discover the laws governing the phenomena which he is studying he seeks to simplify the latter and to rid them of their secondary characteristics. As far as institutions are concerned, nature made spontaneous simplifications of the same kind at the beginning of history. We only want to profit from them. It is no doubt true that we shall only be able to find very elementary facts by this method. When we have perceived them, in so far as it is possible for us to do so, innovations of every kind which have been produced in the wake of evolution will still remain unexplained. Although we would not think of denying the importance of the problems which they present, we feel that they will gain from being dealt with at the right time, and that there is an advantage to be gained in not tackling them until after we have examined those whose study we are about to undertake.

II

None the less our research is not solely concerned with the science of religions. It is a fact that in some respect every religion goes beyond the bounds of religious ideas proper and, because of that, the study of religious phenomena provides a means of reviving the problems which, until now, have only been discussed amongst philosophers.

It has been known for a long time that the earliest systems of *représentations* constructed by man of the world and of himself were religious in origin. Every religion proclaims a cosmology, as well as speculating about the divine. If philosophy and the sciences were born of religion, it was because in the beginning religion assumed the role of the sciences and philosophy. Less notice has been taken of the fact that it did not restrict itself to enriching the human mind formed beforehand by a certain number of ideas, but that it contributed to its formation. Men are not only indebted to it for the greater part of the substance of their knowledge, but also the form in which this knowledge was formulated.

At the root of our judgments, there exists a certain number of essential ideas which dominate the whole of our intellectual life; they are those which philosophers since Aristotle have called the categories of understanding: notions of time, space,[4] genus, number, cause, matter, personality, etc. They correspond to the most universal properties of things. They are like solid frames enclosing thought and thought does not appear to be able to break out of them without destroying itself, as we do not seem to find it possible to think of objects which are not found in time or space, which are not numerable, etc. Other notions are contingent and changeable; a man, a society, or an era might be aware of the lack of them but the former appear to be almost inseparable from the normal func- *signific* tioning of the mind. They might be described as the skeleton of *Aristotle* the intellect. Now when we analyse primitive religious beliefs methodically, we naturally come across the main categories. They are born in religion and of religion; they are a product of religious thought. This statement is one that we shall reiterate several times in the course of this work.

The point is already of interest in itself but is given its full significance by what follows.

The general conclusion of the book before the reader is that religion is something pre-eminently social. Religious *représentations* are collective *représentations* which are the expression of collective realities. Rites are ways of behaving which only come into being at the heart of assembled groups and whose function is to create, maintain and to re-establish certain mental states within these groups. Yet if categories are religious in origin, they must have some of the characteristics of the nature common to all religious facts: they too must be social things, products of collective thought. Given the current state of our knowledge of these matters, we must beware of all radical and exclusive propositions. At the very least, it is legitimate to assume that categories are rich in social elements.

This is, moreover, what we can already forsee for some of them. Let us try for example to imagine what our notion of time would be if we disregarded the processes by which we divide it up, measure it, express it by means of objective signs: time would not consist in a succession of years, months, weeks, days, hours! It would be literally unthinkable. We cannot visualize time other than in terms of separate moments. What was the origin of this differentiation? It is true that the states of consciousness which we have already experienced can be revived in us in the very order in which they originally took place; in this way parts of our past become present to us again while at the same time spontaneously remaining distinct

from the present. But however important this distinction may be for
our private experience, it falls far short of constituting the notion or
category of time. This does not simply consist in the memory,
partial or complete, of our past life. It is an abstract and impersonal
frame which encloses not only our individual existence, but that of
humanity. It is like an unframed picture in which the whole of
duration is spread out beneath the gaze of the mind and in which all
possible events can be situated in relation to fixed and well-defined
landmarks. It is not *my time* which is organized in this way; it is
time as it is objectively imagined by all men in the same civilization.
That alone is a sufficient indication that such organizations must be
collective. Indeed, observation establishes that these indispensable
landmarks, in relation to which all things are temporarily classified,
are borrowed from social life. The divisions into days, weeks,
months, years, etc., correspond to the periodicity of rites, festivals
and public ceremonies.[5] A calendar is the expression of the rhythm
of collective activity, at the same time as it serves to ensure its
regularity.[6]

[The rest of the Introduction is devoted to the development of further
epistemological issues.—W.S.F.P.]

Book I

Chapter I

Definition of the Phenomenon of Religion and of Religion

[In the first two sections of this opening chapter, Durkheim deals with problems of defining religion and rejects the possibilities which make the notions
of mystery and spiritual beings key terms. He discusses the case of Buddhism. These sections approximate to 1899a(ii): 1–16/t.74–87 in this
volume.—W.S.F.P.]

III

49–56

Having set aside these definitions, let us face up to the problem
ourselves.

First of all, let it be noted that in all these formulae, the attempt is
made to deal specifically with the nature of religion as a whole. An
approach is made to the subject as if religion constituted a kind of
indivisible entity when in fact it is a whole made up of parts. It is a
more or less complex system of myths, dogmas, rites, and

ceremonies. Now a whole can only be defined in terms of its parts. Accordingly, it is more methodical to seek to characterize the elementary phenomena which constitute every religion, before dealing with the system produced by their combination. This method seems all the more obvious in that there are some religious phenomena which belong to no specific religion. Those which make up folk-lore are of such a kind. For the most part they are the remains or disorganized survivals of religions which have now disappeared. Some came into being spontaneously as the result of local influences. In Europe, Christianity endeavoured to absorb and assimilate them; it tinged them with its own colours. Nevertheless, many persisted till quite recently and still persist with a relative degree of autonomy: festivals associated with May Day, the summer solstice, Shrove Tuesday, various beliefs about spirits, local demons, etc. Although the religious character of these facts is gradually disappearing, their religious importance is still such that they enabled Mannhardt and his school to revive the science of religions. A definition which did not take these facts into account would in consequence not include everything which is religious.

Religious phenomena arrange themselves quite naturally into two fundamental categories: beliefs and rites. The first are states of opinion and consist of *représentations*; the second are determined modes of action. Between these two classes of facts, there is all the difference which separates thought from action.

Rites cannot be defined and distinguised from other human practices, notably moral practices, except by the special nature of their object. Indeed a moral rule, like a rite, prescribes ways of behaving but these apply to objects of a different kind. Thus we need to characterize the object of the rite in order to characterize the rite itself. Now the special nature of this object is expressed in belief. One cannot therefore define a rite until belief has been defined.

All known religious beliefs, be they simple or complex, have one characteristic in common: they imply a classification realized by man of things, real or ideal, into two classes—two contrasting genera usually designated by two distinct terms, which are well expressed by the words *profane* and *sacred*. The division of the world into two domains which include everything that is sacred in the one and everything that is profane in the other, is the characteristic feature of religious thought. Beliefs, myths, dogmas and legends are either *représentations* or systems of *représentations* which express the nature of sacred things, the virtues and powers attributed to them, their history, their relations to each other and to profane things. By sacred things, however, we must not just understand those personal beings called gods or spirits: a rock, a tree, a spring, a pebble, a piece of wood, a house, in short any miscellaneous thing can be sacred. A rite may have this characteristic; indeed, there is no rite which does not possess it to some degree. There are words, utterances, and formulae which can only come from the mouths of sacred persons; there are gestures and movements which cannot be carried out by everyone. If Vedic sacrifice was particularly efficacious, if even, according to mythology, it generated gods as opposed to being merely a means of winning their favour, it was because it had a virtue comparable to that of the most sacred beings. Thus the circle of sacred objects cannot be determined once and for all; its extent is infinitely variable according to different religions. For this reason Buddhism is a religion: it is so because, in the absence of gods, it admits the existence of sacred things, namely the four noble truths and the practices based on them.[7]

So far, we have restricted ourselves to listing as examples a certain number of sacred things. We must now indicate by what general characteristics they may be distinguished from profane things.

First of all there might be the temptation to define them in terms of the place which is normally assigned to them in the hierarchy of beings. They are readily considered superior in dignity and in power to profane things and particularly to man, when he is just a man, and there is nothing sacred about him. He is seen as occupying an inferior and dependent position in relation to them; and this *représentation* is certainly not without some truth. However, there is nothing in that which is really characteristic of the sacred. It is not enough for a thing to be subordinate to another for the second to be sacred in relation to the first. Slaves depend on their masters, subjects on their king, soldiers on their officers, the lower classes on the ruling classes, the miser on his gold and the ambitious person on power and the hands in which it is vested. If we say of some man that he makes a religion out of those beings or things which he acknowledges to be of particular value and possessing some form of superiority in relation to himself, it is clear that in all these cases the word religion is used in a metaphorical sense and that there is nothing in the relations which is truly religious.[8]

Then again, we must not lose sight of the fact that there are many degrees of sacred things and that there are some with which man feels relatively at ease. An amulet is sacred in character and yet there is nothing exceptional about the awe which it inspires. Even when confronting his gods, man is not always in an unduly marked state of inferiority, for it very often happens that he is able to impose a real physical constraint on them in order to obtain the object of his desire. He beats the fetish who displeases him and becomes reconciled with him, if in the end the fetish shows himself more amenable to the hopes of the worshipper.[9] To make it rain, man throws stones into the spring or sacred lake where the god of rain is supposed to dwell; he believes that in this way he will make him emerge and show himself.[10] Moreover, although man depends on his gods, the dependence is mutual. The gods, too, need man; without offerings and sacrifices they would die. We shall have the opportunity of showing that this dependence of the gods on the faithful is continued even in the most developed religions.

If, however, a purely hierarchical distinction is at one and the same time too general and too imprecise a criterion, the only way that remains of defining the sacred in relation to the profane is by their heterogeneity. This heterogeneity is enough to characterize the classification of things and to distinguish it from all others because it is very special: *it is absolute*. In the history of human thought there exists no other example of two categories of things so fundamentally differentiated and so radically contrasted to each other. The traditional dichotomy between good and evil is insignificant in comparison: good and evil are two sides of the same coin, namely morality, just as good health and illness are only two different aspects of the same order of facts, that is to say, life. The sacred and the profane have always and everywhere been imagined by the human mind as separate genera, two worlds which have nothing in common. The forces operating in the one are not simply those found in the other raised a few degrees; they are of a different order. In different religions, this dichotomy has been visualized in different ways. In order to separate these two kinds of things, it seemed sufficient in one case to locate them in regions distinct from the physical universe; in another, some have been cast into an ideal and transcendental environment, whilst the material world has been quite properly given over to the others. Though the forms of the contrast may vary,[11] the very fact of the contrast is universal.

We are not saying that a being can never pass from one of these worlds to the other, but that the way in which this takes place, when it does take place, demonstrates the essential duality of the two kingdoms. It involves a genuine metamorphosis. This is notably demonstrated by initiation rites as they are practised by a multitude of peoples. Initiation consists of a long series of ceremonies whose object is to introduce the young man to religious life: for the first time he leaves behind the purely profane world where he has lived his early childhood, to enter into the circle of sacred things. Now this change of state is visualized, not as the simple and regular growth of already existing germs, but as a transformation *totius substantiae*. It is said that at that moment the young man dies, that the particular person he was has ceased to exist and that instantaneously another has taken the place of the preceding one. He is reborn in a new form. Appropriate ceremonies are supposed to have brought about this death and rebirth which are not understood in a purely symbolic sense but are taken literally.[12] Does this not show that there is a gap between the profane being he once was and the religious being he has become?

This heterogeneity can even be of such a kind that it often degenerates into a veritable antagonism. The two worlds are not only thought of as being separate, but as hostile and the jealous rivals of each other. Since one cannot fully belong to the one without having completely left behind the other, man is urged to withdraw totally from the profane in order to live an exclusively religious life. For example, alongside and outside the natural environment where the majority of men live the life of their time, monasticism artificially organizes another life, shut off from the first and almost tending to run counter to it. A further example is mystical asceticism, the object of which is to eradicate from man even the last vestiges of an attachment to the profane world. And finally, there are all forms of religious suicide which is the logical consummation of this asceticism, for the only ultimate escape from the profane life is, in short, to run away from life altogether.

The dichotomy between these two genera, moreover, expresses itself outwardly by a visible sign which enables us to recognize without any difficulty this very special classification wherever it occurs. Because the notion of the sacred is always and everywhere separate from the notion of the profane in men's thoughts, because we imagine a sort of logical void between them, the mind shrinks automatically from allowing the corresponding things to intermingle or even to come into contact with each other. Such promiscuity or even close contiguity is strongly inconsistent with the state of dissociation surrounding these ideas in people's *consciences*. The sacred thing is pre-eminently that which the profane must not and cannot touch with impunity. It is true that this prohibition cannot go so far as to make all communication between the two worlds impossible; if the profane were prevented from entering into relations with the sacred, the sacred would serve no useful purpose. In addition to the fact that this creation of contact is always in itself a delicate operation necessitating precautions and a more or less complicated initiation,[13] it is not even possible unless the profane loses its specific characteristics, unless it becomes to some extent and to some degree sacred itself. The two genera cannot be brought together and retain their own nature at the same time.

We have now a preliminary criterion for religious beliefs. Doubtless, included in these two basic genera there are secondary species which are, in themselves, more or less incompatible with each other.[14] The truly characteristic thing about the religious phenomenon is that it always presupposes a bipartite division of the known and knowable universe into two genera which encompass everything that exists, but which radically exclude each other. Sacred things are those which are protected and isolated by prohibitions: profane things are those to which the prohibitions apply, and they must keep their distance from sacred things. Religious beliefs are *représentations* which express the nature of sacred things and the relations they maintain with each other, or with profane things. In fact, rites are rules of conduct which prescribe how man must behave in relation to sacred things.

When a certain number of sacred things maintain relations of co-ordination and subordination with each other in such a way as to form a system with a certain unity but which does not itself fit into any other system of the same genus, the totality of the beliefs and the corresponding rites makes up a religion. It can be seen by this definition that a religion is not necessarily contained in one single idea, that it cannot be reduced to a unique principle which, whilst varying according to the circumstances to which it applies, would be basically identical to itself everywhere. It is a whole made up of distinct and relatively individualized parts. Each homogeneous group of sacred things, or even each sacred thing of some importance, constitutes the centre of an organization towards which gravitates a group of beliefs and rites, a particular cult. There is no religion, however integrated it might be, which does not recognize a plurality of sacred things. Even Christianity, at least in its Catholic form, allows in addition to the divine personality—which is itself three in one—the Virgin, the angels, the saints, the souls of the dead, etc. Consequently, a religion cannot normally be reduced to a single cult, but consists of a system of cults endowed with a certain autonomy. This autonomy is, furthermore, variable. Sometimes the cults are arranged in a hierarchy and subordinated to some dominant cult into which they may finally be absorbed. It also happens, however, that they are simply juxtaposed and grouped together. The religion that we are about to study will provide us with an example of just this kind of organization.

At the same time, one can see that there might be groups of religious phenomena which belong to no constituted religion: this is because they are not or are no longer integrated into a religious system. If, for special reasons, one of the cults we have just been discussing succeeds in maintaining its identity although the whole which included it disappears, it will survive only in a state of disintegration. That is what has happened to so many agrarian cults which have survived in folk-lore. In certain cases, it is not even a cult but a simple ceremony, a particular rite which persists in such a form.[15]

Although this is only a preliminary definition, we can already forsee the terms governing the problem which necessarily dominates the science of religions. When it is held that sacred beings can only be distinguished from other beings by the greater intensity of the powers attributed to them, the question of knowing how men first acquired the idea of them is a fairly simple one. It is enough to look for those forces which, because of their exceptional energy, were able to impress themselves on the human mind so forcibly as to inspire religious sentiments. If, however, as we have tried to establish, sacred things differ from profane things in their very nature, and if their essence is different, the problem is far more complex. We must then ask ourselves what caused man to see in the world two heterogeneous and incompatible worlds, when there was nothing in tangible experience which might suggest the idea of such a radical dualism.

IV

Nevertheless, this definition is not yet complete for it fits equally two orders of facts which, whilst being related to each other, still require to be distinguished from each other—they are magic and religion.

Magic is also made up of beliefs and rites. Like religion it has its myths and its dogmas, only they are more rudimentary: doubtless because it pursues technical and utilitarian ends, magic does not waste time on pure speculation. Similarly, it has its ceremonies, sacrifices, lustrations, prayers, chants and dances. The beings invoked by the magician, the forces he brings into play, are not only of the same nature as the forces and beings appealed to by religion, they are frequently identical with them. Thus, from the most inferior societies onwards, the souls of the dead have been essentially sacred things and the object of religious rites. At the same time, they have played a considerable role in magic. In Australia[16] as well as in Melanesia,[17] in Greece as well as among Christians,[18] the souls of the dead, their bones, their hair, have been included among the intermediaries most often employed by the magician. Demons also are a common instrument of magical action. They too are beings surrounded by prohibitions; they are separate, live in a world apart, and, in fact, it is often difficult to distinguish them from true gods.[19] Besides, even in Christianity, is not the devil a fallen god, and quite apart from his origins, does he not acquire a religious character from the very fact that the hell he was given to rule is an indispensable cog in the Christian religion? There are even regular and official deities who are invoked by the magician. Sometimes they are the gods of a foreign people, for example, Greek magicians appealed to Egyptian, Assyrian or Jewish gods. Sometimes they are even national gods: Hecate and Diana were the objects of a magical cult; the Virgin, Christ, the saints, have all been utilized in the same way by Christian magicians.[20]

Must it be admitted then that magic cannot be rigorously distinguished from religion, that magic is full of religion as religion is of magic, and that it is, consequently, impossible to separate them and to define the one without the other? However, this thesis is difficult to uphold because of the marked aversion of religion to magic, and conversely, the hostility of the second towards the first. Magic takes a sort of professional pleasure in desecrating sacred things;[21] in its rites it inverts the actions of religious ceremonies.[22]

Religion, if it has not always condemned and prohibited magical rites, generally views them with disfavour. As Hubert and Mauss have pointed out, there is something fundamentally anti-religious in the methods of the magician.[23] Whatever connections there may be between these two kinds of institutions, it would be difficult for them not to be opposed at some point and it is all the more necessary to find out how they can be distinguished from each other, given that we intend to limit our researches to religion and to stop short at the point where magic begins.

This is how a line of demarcation can be drawn between these two domains.

True religious beliefs are always common to a particular collectivity which professes to support them and to practise the rites which are an integral part of them. Not only are they agreed to individually and by all the members of the collectivity, but they are something belonging to the group and bringing about its unity. The individuals who constitute it feel bound to each other by the very fact that they have a common faith. A society, whose members are united because they visualize the sacred world and its relations to the profane world in the same way, and because they express this common *représentation* in identical practices, is called a church. In the course of history, a religion without a church is never encountered. Sometimes the church is rigidly nationalistic, sometimes it extends beyond frontiers, sometimes it embraces a whole people (Rome, Athens, the Hebrews), sometimes it includes only a fraction of a people (Christian societies since the advent of Protestantism), sometimes it is led by a body of priests, sometimes it is almost completely free from any properly appointed leader.[24] Wherever religious life is observed, a substratum of a clearly defined group is also found. Even so-called private cults, like the domestic cult or the public cult, satisfy this condition for they are always observed by a collectivity, the family or the corporation. Besides, just as these particular religions are simply and for the most part special forms of a more general religion which embraces the whole of life,[25] such limited churches are in reality merely chapels in a far vaster church, which by reasons of its size is even more worthy of being called by that name.[26]

With magic the story is altogether different. It is true that magical beliefs are always fairly widespread. More often than not they are diffused throughout the broad layers of the population and there are even peoples among whom there are as many believers in magic as believers in orthodox religion. These beliefs do not, however, have the effect of binding together the men who hold them, or of uniting them in the same group in which they share a common life. *In magic there is no church.* Between the magician and the individuals who consult him, as between these individuals themselves, there are no durable links which would make them members of the same moral body, a body comparable to that formed by the followers of the same god, or the observers of the same cult. The magician has a clientele, not a church, and his clients may well not come into contact with each other, to the extent of not knowing who each other is: even the contacts they have with each other are usually accidental and transitory. They are perfectly comparable with those of a sick person and his doctor. The fact that the magician is sometimes invested with an official and public character does not alter the situation; he may operate in public but this does not unite him in a more regular and lasting way to those having recourse to his services.

It is true that in some cases magicians form societies among themselves: they may meet periodically to celebrate in common certain rites, and the place held in European folk-lore by assemblies of witches is well known. But first of all, it will be noted that these associations are in no way indispensable to the execution of magic: they are fairly exceptional and indeed rare. In order to practise his art, the magician has no need to link himself with his colleagues. He is something of an isolated person, and usually, far from seeking society, he shuns it. 'Even with regard to his colleagues, he always stands on his dignity.'[27] On the other hand, religion is inseparable from the idea of a church. From this point of view, there is already an essential difference between magic and religion. But what is significant is that when a society for magic is formed, it never includes all the believers in magic, but only the magicians. The laymen, if they may be called that, who gain benefit from the rites that are celebrated and who in fact correspond to the faithful attending regular cults, are excluded from the rites. Now the magician is to magic what the priest is to religion, and a college of priests is not a church, any more than is a religious congregation living in the shadow of a cloister and dedicated to a particular cult of some saint. A church is not simply a brotherhood of priests, it is the moral community formed by all the believers in one and the same faith, believers and priests alike. Normally, magic is absent from communities of this kind.[28]

If the idea of a church is introduced into the definition of religion, does it not exclude at the same time the individual religions which each person establishes for himself and celebrates for himself? There is scarcely a society in which these are not found. Each Ojibway, as will be seen later, has his personal *manitou* which he chooses for himself and to which he owes particular religious duties; the Melanesian of the Banks Islands has his *tamaniu*;[29] the Roman has his *genius*;[30] the Christian has his patron saint and guardian angel, etc. All these cults seem by definition independent of any idea of the group. Not only do such individual religions occur frequently in the course of history, but certain people today are asking themselves whether or not they are destined to become the prominent form of religious life, and whether the day is far off when the only form of worship will be that which each of us will freely perform in his own heart.[31]

If, leaving aside these speculations on the future for a moment, we limit ourselves to a consideration of religions as they are at the present time and have been in the past, the evidence appears to show that these individual cults constitute, not distinct and autonomous religious systems, but elemental aspects of the religion common to the church as a whole, of which individuals are a part. The patron saint of the Christian is chosen from the official list of saints recognized by the Catholic church, and canon law prescribes how each believer must behave with regard to the particular cult. Similarly, the idea that each man of necessity has a protecting genius is, in varying forms, behind a great number of American religions as it is behind Roman religion (to quote only two examples); for as we shall see later on, it is closely bound up with the idea of the soul which is not an idea which can be left entirely to the discretion of the individual. In short, the church of which he is a member teaches the individual what these personal gods are, what their role is, how he must enter into relations with them and how he must honour them. When we analyse methodically the doctrines of this church, no matter what its kind, sooner or later we come across those relating to special cults. We are not, then, confronted with two different types of religion pulling in opposite directions; we have the same ideas and the same principles, applied in the first case to circumstances affecting the whole of the collectivity, and in the second to the life of the individual. Indeed, among certain peoples[32] the solidarity is so marked that the believer enters into relations with his protecting genius for the first time in the course of ceremonies combined with rites whose public character is incontestable, namely, initiation rites.[33]

We are left with contemporary aspirations towards a religion which would consist entirely of interior subjective states and which would be freely fashioned by each of us. However real these aspirations, they cannot affect our definition, for this can only be applied to established and recorded facts, not to uncertain potentialities. One can define religions as they are or have been, not as they show signs of developing. It may be that religious individualism is destined to become a fact; but in order to be able to say to what extent, we ought to know what religion is, of what elements it is compounded, what brings it about, what function it fulfils. We must not give premature answers to all these questions since we are still standing at the threshold of our research. Only when we reach the end of the study shall we be able to attempt to anticipate the future.

Thus we reach the following definition: *A religion is a unified system of beliefs and practices relative to sacred things, that is to say, things set apart and forbidden, beliefs and practices which unite into one single moral community called a church all those who adhere to them.* The second element which thus finds a place in our definition is no less essential than the first; for in showing that the idea of religion is inseparable from the idea of a church, it foreshadows the fact that religion must be a pre-eminently collective thing.[34]

Book II

Chapter VII

The Origins of these Beliefs (End)

Origin of the notion of the totemic principle or mana

293–307

The proposition established in the previous chapter defines the terms in which the problem of the origins of totemism must be expressed. Since totemism is entirely dominated by the notion of a quasi-divine principle, immanent in certain categories of men and things and visualized in animal or vegetable form, an examination of the religion is essentially an explanation of this belief—it is necessary to seek how men have been impelled to construct this idea and the materials they have used in its construction.

I

Obviously, the idea did not emerge from the feelings aroused in *consciences* by the things serving as totems and we have already shown that they are often insignificant. The lizard, the caterpillar, the rat, the ant, the frog, the turkey, the bream, the plum tree, the cockatoo, etc., to quote only names which occur frequently in the lists of Australian totems, are not of such a nature as to produce great and strong impressions on man so that they can in some respects resemble religious emotions, and thus impress a sacred character on the objects which give rise to them. The same cannot be said of the stars, of the great celestial phenomena which, on the contrary, are fully equipped to make a vivid impact on people's imaginations. However, it so happens that they but very rarely serve as totems and it is even probable that they were only called upon to fulfil that function at a late stage.[35] It is not, therefore, the intrinsic nature of the thing whose name the clan bears which marks it out to become the cult object. Besides, if the sentiments which the intrinsic nature inspires were really the determining cause of the totemic rites and beliefs, it would also be the sacred being *par excellence*: the animals or plants used as totems would play the dominant role in religious life. In fact, we know that the focal point of the cult is to be found elsewhere. It is the figurative *représentations* of these plants or animals, the totemic emblems and symbols of all kinds which are the most holy. Accordingly we find in them the source of the religious nature which the real object which these emblems represent merely reflects.

Thus, the totem is above all a symbol, a material expression of some other thing.[36] But of what?

From the very analysis which we have made, it is evident that it expresses and symbolizes two different kinds of things. On the one hand, it is the external and tangible form of what we call the totemic principle or god. On the other hand, it is also the symbol of that particular society which we call the clan. It is its flag. It is the sign by which each clan distinguishes itself from the other clans, the visible mark of its personality, the sign which is borne by everything that is in some way a part of the clan, men, beasts and things. If, then, it is at once the symbol of god and of society, is this not because god and society are one and the same thing? How could the emblem of the group have become the form of this quasi-deity, if the group and the deity were two distinct realities? The god of the clan, the totemic principle, cannot therefore be anything other than the clan itself hypostasized and represented to the imagination in the form of the tangible species of vegetable or animal which serves as the totem.

But how was this deification possible, and how did it come about in such a fashion?

II

In a general way, there is no doubt that a society contains all that is necessary to arouse in people's minds the feeling of the divine by the very influence it exercises over them; for society is to its members what a god is to the faithful. A god, indeed, is above all a being whom man imagines to be superior to himself in some way and on whom he believes himself to be dependent. Whether it be a question of a conscious personality, like Zeus or Jahveh, or abstract forces like those which are called into play in totemism, in each case the believer thinks himself bound to behave in a certain way, which is imposed on him by the very nature of the sacred principle with which he feels himself to be in communication. Society, too, fosters in us a feeling of perpetual dependence. Because of its own nature which differs from our nature as individuals, it pursues ends which are equally peculiar to it. As, however, it can only attain them through us, it imperiously demands our co-operation. Forgetful of our interests, it demands that we should become its servants and it subjects us to all kinds of constraints, privations, and sacrifices without which social life would be impossible. We are thus continually obliged to submit to rules of conduct and thought that we have neither drawn up nor desired, and which are sometimes the very opposite of our most basic tendencies and instincts.

Yet, if society only obtains these concessions and sacrifices from us by material constraint, it can arouse in us only the idea of a physical force to which we yield out of necessity, rather than a moral force of the kind worshipped in religion. In reality, the dominion it exercises over our *consciences* depends much less on the physical supremacy which is its prerogative than on the moral authority with which it is vested. If we accede to its orders, it is not simply because its weapons would vanquish our resistance, it is above all because it is the object of genuine respect.

We say of an individual or collective object that it inspires respect when the *représentation* which expresses it in people's *consciences* is endowed with such force that automatically it compels or inhibits actions, *regardless of every consideration relating to the useful or harmful effects of any of them*. When we obey a person by reason of the moral authority which we acknowledge in him, we follow his advice, not because it seems judicious, but because a particular kind of psychic energy is immanent in the idea we have of this person, and it influences our will and predisposes it in the right direction. Respect is the emotion we experience when we feel this internal and quite spiritual pressure working within us. We are not, then, impelled by the advantages or disadvantages of the attitude prohibited or recommended; it is the way in which we visualize the being who recommends or prohibits it. That is why a command generally takes a short, precise form which leaves no room for hesitation; it is because the command itself works by reason of its own power and excludes all notion of reflection and calculation. It owes its effectiveness to the intensity of the mental state in which it is given. This intensity constitutes what we call moral ascendancy.

Society is so strongly attached to certain ways of behaving that it imposes them on its members, and in so doing stamps them with a distinctive sign which provokes respect. Because they are worked out in common, the intensity with which they are accepted by each individual mind echoes reciprocally in all other minds. The *représentations* which express them in each one of us have, then, an intensity which purely private states of *conscience* can never attain; for they have the strength of the innumerable individual *représentations* which have helped to form each one of them. It is society which speaks through the mouth of those who assert them in our presence; it is society we hear when we hear them and their voice has a power which one single voice could not have.[37] The very violence of society's reaction towards attempts at dissent—censure or material suppression—is at one and the same time a patently obvious manifestation of the fervour of the common conviction and an aid to the enforcement of its authority.[38] In short, when a thing is the object of a state of opinion, the *représentation* each individual has of it derives from its origins and from the conditions which gave birth to it—a power of influence felt even by those who do not submit to it. It tends to suppress the *représentations* which are at variance with it; it remains aloof from them. On the other hand, it compels actions which bring it into being, and, what is more, this is achieved, not by means of material coercion or by the possibility of it, but by the simple effulgence of mental energy within it. Its effectiveness comes uniquely from its psychic properties and it is precisely by this sign that moral authority can be recognized. Opinion, then, essentially a social thing, is a source of authority and we might even ask ourselves whether all authority is not the offspring of opinion.[39] The objection will be raised that science is often the antagonist of opinion, whose errors it combats and rectifies. It can, however, only succeed in this task if it has sufficient authority and it can only derive this authority from opinion itself. If people have no faith in science, no scientific demonstration will have any influence over their minds. Even today, if science happens to run counter to a strong current of public opinion, it risks losing its credibility.[40]

Since it is through the mind that social pressure is exerted, man could not fail to see that there exists outside him one or more moral, as well as effective forces on which he depends. In part he has had to visualize these forces as being outside himself, since they speak to him in commanding tones, and sometimes even call upon him to act against his most natural inclinations. It is true that if he could at once see that the influences to which he submits himself emanate from society, the system of mythological interpretations would never have seen the light of day. Nevertheless, social action follows paths which are too circuitous and too indistinct, and it makes use of psychic techniques which are so complex that the common observer finds it impossible to see where it came from. Until scientific analysis was able to make things clear to him, he felt that he was being manipulated, but did not know by whom. Accordingly, he had to construct the notion of these forces, with which he felt he was in contact, out of nothing. Hence, we can already see how he was led to visualize them in forms alien to them and to transfigure them by thought.

A god, however, is not only an authority on whom we depend, it is also a force on which we rely for strength. The man who has obeyed his god and who, for that reason, believes him to be on his side, faces the world with confidence and a feeling of increased energy. Similarly, social action is not limited to demanding sacrifices, privations and effort from us. The collective force is not entirely external to us; it does not wholly drive us from outside, but, since society can only exist in and by individual *consciences*,[41] it is necessary for it to enter into us and begin to work within us. In this way it becomes an integral part of our being and by that very fact it is ennobled and enriched.

There are circumstances in which this stimulating and invigorating influence of society is especially manifest. When we find ourselves at the heart of an assembly animated by a common passion, we become capable of sentiments and actions of which we are not capable when we are reduced to our own efforts; and when the assembly breaks up, when we are once more on our own and return to our normal level, we can measure the extent to which we were lifted above ourselves. History abounds in examples of this kind. We only have to think back to the night of the fourth of August, when a meeting was suddenly swept into an act of sacrifice and self-denial which each of its members had recoiled from on the previous day and at which all were surprised on the following day.[42] It is for this reason that all parties, political, economic and confessional, periodically take the trouble to instigate meetings at which their followers can refurbish their common faith by manifesting it in common. To confirm sentiments which if left to themselves would atrophy, it is enough to bring those who experience them nearer together and to put them into closer and more active relations. This also explains the attitude peculiar to the man addressing a crowd, when he has succeeded in getting through to it. His language has a form of grandiloquence which would be ridiculous in ordinary circumstances; there is something dictatorial about his gestures; even his ideas lose all sense of proportion and easily fall into every kind of excess. It is because he feels in himself a sort of abnormal plethora of forces bubbling up and spilling out around him. Sometimes he even has the impression that he is dominated by a moral power which transcends him and of which he is merely the mouthpiece. By this trait we recognize what has often been called the demon of oratorical inspiration. But this exceptional increase of forces is quite real for it derives from the very group the man addresses. The feelings stirred up by his words rebound towards him, magnified and amplified, and so intensify his own feeling. The passionate energy he arouses reverberates within him and increases his vitality. It is no longer a single individual speaking, rather it is a group incarnate and personified.

Apart from these transitory or intermittent states, there are more lasting ones in which society's strengthening influence makes itself felt more effectively and often even more ostentatiously. There are periods in history when, under the influence of some great collective upheaval, social interaction becomes much more frequent and more active. Individuals seek each other out and assemble more often. As a result there is a general effervescence characteristic of revolutionary or creative periods. Now, this abnormal activity has the effect of being a general stimulus on individual forces. Men's lives are more intense and different than they are normally. The changes are not merely those of nuance or degree; men become quite different. The passions which excite them are so strong that they can only be satisfied by violent, immoderate acts, acts of superhuman heroism or bloodthirsty barbarism. That is what explains, for example, the Crusades[43] and so many of the events, sublime or brutal, of the French Revolution.[44] Under the influence of the general over-excitement, we saw the most moderate and inoffensive of the bourgeois transformed into either hero or executioner.[45] All these mental processes so obviously belong to those which are at the root of religion, which the individuals concerned have often visualized in an explicitly religious form, the pressure to which they yielded in this way. The Crusaders believed that they felt the presence of God in their midst enjoining them to go and conquer the Holy Land. Joan of Arc believed that she was obeying celestial voices.[46]

However, it is not only in such exceptional circumstances that this stimulating influence of society makes itself felt, there is, so to speak, not a moment of our lives when we are unaffected by some rush of energy reaching us from outside. Any man who does his duty finds in the many manifestations of the sympathy, esteem and affection of his fellows for him, an impression of comfort of which he may not be fully aware but which none the less supports him. The feeling that society has for him enhances that feeling he has about himself. Like the believer who is conscious of the gaze of his god turned benevolently towards him, he has more confidence, courage, boldness in action, because he is in moral harmony with his contemporaries. In this way, our moral being is given a kind of perpetual support. We cannot but feel that this *moral quality* [*tonus*] is dependent on an external cause, since it varies according to a multiple of external factors and according to the nature of the social groups around us, and whether our relations with them are more or less active. But we are not aware of the location of this cause or what it is. Consequently, we usually imagine it to be in the form of a moral force which, whilst being immanent in us, is at the same time representative in us of something other than ourselves. This moral conscience is, moreover, something which the majority of men have never been able to visualize at all clearly without the help of religious symbols.

In addition to these unattached forces which are ceaselessly renewing our own, there are those which we employ but which are embedded in all kinds of techniques and traditions. We speak a language which we did not invent, we make use of instruments which we did not make, we invoke laws that we did not establish, a treasure house of knowledge is passed on to each generation which it did not amass, etc. It is to society that we owe these varied benefits of civilization and although we are not usually aware of the source from which they came, we know at least that they are not of our doing. It is these which mark out the specific character of man amongst all other beings; for man is a man only because he is civilized. He cannot, therefore, escape the feeling that outside him there are active causes which are the source of the characteristic attributes of his nature, and benevolent forces which are there to help him, protect him, and ensure him an advantageous destiny. He necessarily has to confer on these forces a dignity commensurate with the great value of the benefits which he attributes to them.[47]

Thus, the environment in which we live seems to be peopled with forces with which we are in contact and which are also imperious and helpful, majestic and benevolent. Since they exert a pressure on us of which we are conscious, we must locate them outside ourselves, as we do with the objective causes of our sensations. On the other hand, however, the sentiments which they inspire in us differ in nature from those we feel for simple, tangible things. So long as these are reduced to the empirical characteristics observable in common experience, so long as the religious imagination has not changed their nature, we can feel nothing approaching respect for them and they are in no way able to raise us above ourselves. The *représentations* expressing them thus appear to be very different from those aroused in us by collective influences. Each form in our *conscience* two circles of mental states, which are distinct and separate: like the two forms of life to which they correspond. In consequence, we have the impression of being in communication with two sorts of reality, which are distinct in themselves and are clearly separated from each other by a line of demarcation. On the one hand there is the world of profane things, and on the other that of sacred things.

Besides, as much today as in the past, we see society ceaselessly creating sacred things out of nothing. If society happens to take to some man, and if it believes that it has found in him the main aspirations which preoccupy it, together with the means of satisfying them, we may be sure that such a man will be set above his fellows and virtually deified. Opinion will bestow on him a majesty completely analogous to that which protects the gods. This is what happened to so many kings in whom their contemporaries had faith: even if they were not turned into gods, people saw in them at least the direct representatives of the deity. If proof were needed that society alone is the originator of such apotheoses, it can be found in the fact that often it has sanctified in this way men whose merits did not entitle them to it. Besides, men invested with important social functions inspire a simple deference which is no different in nature from religious respect. It expresses itself in the same actions: men keep their distance from a great personage; they only approach him with caution; when they talk to him, they use a different language and different gestures from those which are adequate for ordinary mortals. The sentiment felt in these circumstances is so closely related to religious sentiment that many people have confused them. To explain the special consideration enjoyed by princes, nobles, heads of state, a sacred character has been attributed to them. In Melanesia and in Polynesia, for example, an influential man is said to have mana and this mana is alleged to be responsible for his influence.[48] Yet it is evident that his special position rests uniquely on the importance attributed to him by general opinion. The fact is that the moral force conferred by opinion and that vested in sacred beings have basically the same origin and are made up of the same elements. This explains why the one word can be used for both.

As well as men, society sanctifies things, notably ideas. The moment a belief is unanimously shared by a group of people, it is forbidden for reasons stated above to interfere with it, that is to say, to deny or dispute it. The prohibition of criticism is a prohibition like any other and proves that we are face to face with a sacred thing. Even today, when we allow each other a great measure of freedom, a man who totally denies progress, who scoffs at the human ideal to which modern societies attach so much importance, would in effect be committing an act of sacrilege. There is, at the very least, one principle which the devoted disciples of free enquiry tend to put above argument and to look upon as sacrosanct, that is to say sacred—it is the very principle of free enquiry itself.

This tendency of society to set itself up as a god or to create gods was never more in evidence than during the early years of the Revolution. At that particular time, under the influence of general enthusiasm, things that were purely secular in nature were transformed into sacred things by public opinion, for example, the Motherland, Liberty, Reason.[49] A religion was established which had its dogmas, [50] its symbols,[51] its altars,[52] and its holy days.[53] It was to these spontaneous aspirations that the cult of Reason and the Supreme Being attempted to give some form of official recognition. It is true that this religious revival lasted only a very short time because the patriotic enthusiasm which at first caught the imagination of the masses, gradually waned.[54] As the cause disappeared, the effect could not be prolonged. Even though the experiment was short-lived, it retains sociological interest. The fact is that in one specific case, we saw society and its essential ideas become the object of a genuine cult, directly and without any kind of transfiguration.

All these facts give some indication of how the clan can arouse in its members the idea that forces exist outside them which dominate them and at the same time support them: in short, they are religious forces. There is no society in which primitive men are more directly and more closely dependent on other men. The bonds which tie them to the tribe are looser and less consciously felt. Even though the tribe is certainly not strange to them, it is with the people of their own clan that they have most in common. They are immediately conscious of the influence of this group and accordingly it is the same influence which, in preference to all others, has to be expressed in religious symbols.

This initial explanation is too general, however, as it can be applied indiscriminately to every species of society, and consequently to every religion. Thus we must try to state precisely what particular form this collective action takes in the clan and how it gives rise to the sensation of the sacred. Certainly, nowhere else can it be more easily observed, and nowhere else are its results more apparent.

[Section III considers the two phases of aboriginal life—one when the tribes are broken up and the other when they are gathered together. Totemism is discussed in relation to clan life. The totemic emblem is seen to be akin to the embodiment of the god: the sacred spreads to everything associated with the totemic being.—W.S.F.P.]

IV

320–8

The first religious conceptions have often been attributed to the feelings of weakness and dependence, fear and anguish, which seized man when he came into contact with the world. As the victim of a sort of nightmare of his own making, he is supposed to have felt himself surrounded by hostile and deadly forces which his rites sought to appease. We have just shown that the origin of the earliest religions was quite different. The celebrated saying *Primus in orbe deos fecit timor* is by no means justified by the facts. Primitive man does not see his gods as being strangers or enemies, or fundamentally and necessarily evil beings whose good will he is obliged to gain at all costs. To the contrary, they are rather his friends, relatives, and natural protectors. Is this not implied in the names he gives to the beings of the totemic species? The power to which the cult is addressed is not visualized as one looking down from on high and overwhelming him with its superiority. In fact man sees it as being close to him and bestowing on him useful powers which he does not naturally possess. Never perhaps has the deity been closer to man than at that moment in history when it was present in the things filling his immediate environment, and it is to some extent immanent in man himself. In short, at the root of totemism are to be found sentiments of joyous confidence rather than of terror and repression. Apart from burial rites—the black side of every religion—the totemic cult is celebrated amidst songs, dances and dramatic performances. As we shall see, cruel expiations are relatively rare, and even the obligatory and painful mutilations of initiation do not have this characteristic. Jealous and terrible gods only make their appearance at a later stage of religious evolution. The fact is that primitive societies are not kinds of Leviathan overwhelming man with the enormity of their power and subjecting him to a hard discipline.[55] To them he gives himself spontaneously and without resistance. Since at that stage the social soul [*âme sociale*] is only made up of a small number of ideas and sentiments, it easily becomes wholly embodied in each *conscience individuelle*. The individual carries it entirely within him; it is a part of him and consequently, when he yields to the impulses that it imprints on him, he does not consider that he is yielding to a constraint but that he is following the dictates of his own nature.[56]

This way of understanding the origin of religious thought avoids the objections raised by the most widely accepted classical theories.

We have seen how naturists and animists claim to construct the notion of sacred beings out of the sensations induced in us by various phenomena of a physical or biological order, and we have shown how this was an impossible and even contradictory undertaking. Nothing arises out of nothing. The impressions made on us by the physical world cannot, by definition, embody anything which transcends this world. The tangible can only be made into the tangible; the vast cannot be made into the minute. Moreover, in order to be able to explain how the idea of the sacred took shape under such conditions, most of these theorists have been compelled to admit that man had superimposed an unreal world on the reality of observation. This unreal world was one entirely constructed with either the fantastic images which disturbed his mind during dreams, or the often monstrous aberrations to which the mythological imagination gave birth under the wondrous but misleading influence of language. But then it became incomprehensible how for the course of centuries man should have persisted in errors which experience ought to have demonstrated very quickly to him.

From our standpoint these difficulties disappear. Religion ceases to be some sort of inexplicable hallucination: it takes root in reality. We can indeed say that the believer is not deluding himself when he believes in the existence of a moral force on which he depends and to which he is indebted for the best of himself: this force indeed exists—it is society. When the Australian is carried away, when he feels flowing in him a life whose intensity surprises him, he is not the victim of an illusion. This exaltation is real and it is actually the product of forces external and superior to those of the individual. To be sure, he is mistaken in believing that this heightening of vitality is the work of a force in the form of an animal or plant. The error, however, relates exclusively to the literal symbol by which the mind visualizes this being, to the external aspect with which the imagination has clothed it, and not to the very fact of its existence. Behind these forms and metaphors, be they crude or sophisticated, there is a concrete, living reality. Religion thus becomes meaningful and is open to reason in a way that even the most intransigent rationalist cannot fail to recognize. Its chief aim is not to give man a *représentation* of the physical universe, for if that were its essential task we cannot understand how it could have survived, since in this matter it is scarcely more than a tissue of lies. Above all, it is a system of ideas by means of which individuals represent to themselves the society of which they are members, and the obscure but intimate relations that they maintain with it. It is its primordial role; and although metaphorical and symbolic, this *représentation* is by no means inaccurate. Quite to the contrary, it conveys everything essential about the relations that must be expressed: for it is an eternal truth which is outside us that there exists something greater than ourselves with which we are able to enter into communion.

That is why we are assured in advance that the practices of the cult, whatever they may be, are more than meaningless motions and ineffectual gestures. By the very fact that their apparent function is to strengthen the bond attaching the believer to his god, they actually strengthen at the same time the bonds uniting the individual to the society to which he belongs, assuming that the god is only the figurative expression of the society. It is even conceivable that the fundamental truth thus contained within religion has been sufficient to offset the secondary errors which it almost necessarily implies, and that consequently the faithful have been prevented from breaking away from it, despite the mistakes which come as the inevitable result of these errors. More often than not the prescriptions which it urged man to employ in order to bring about certain reactions in things were doubtless ineffective, but these failures could not have had a profound influence because they did not attack religion at its centre.[57]

However, the objection will be made that even in this hypothesis, religion remains the product of a certain form of delirium. But what other name can be given to the state in which men find themselves, when as a result of collective effervescence, they believe themselves

[handwritten margin note: religious life is related to delirium as that's what causes intensity]

to be transported into an entirely different world from the one before their eyes?

It is quite true that religious life cannot attain a given degree of intensity without implying a certain psychic exaltation, not unrelated to delirium. It is for this reason that prophets, founders of religions, great saints, in short, the men whose religious *conscience* is exceptionally sensitive, very often show signs of an excessive nervous instability, which is even pathological. These physiological defects preordain them to play great religious roles. The ritual use of intoxicating liquors can be explained in the same way.[58] It is certainly not the case that ardent faith is necessarily a product of drunkenness and the mental disorder which accompanies it; but as experience quickly awakens people to the analogies between the mentality of the person who is delirious and that of the seer, it is natural to seek a way of reaching the second by artificially provoking the first. If for this reason it can be said that religion has its share of delirium, it must be remembered that this delirium is *well founded* if it results from the causes we have attributed to it. The images of which it is made up are not pure illusions like those the naturists and animists see as the base of religion: they correspond to some aspect of reality. To be sure, it is in the nature of the moral forces which they express that they are unable to have a vigorous effect on the human mind without taking it outside itself, without plunging it into a state that might be described as *ecstatic*, provided that the word is taken in its etymological sense (ἔκστασις); but it does not follow that they are imaginary. Quite the contrary, the mental excitement that they arouse bears witness to their reality. It is simply a further proof of the fact that a very intense social life always imposes a kind of strain on the organism, as it does on the *conscience* of the individual, which upsets its normal functioning. Therefore, it can only last for a very limited time.[59]

Moreover, if we are going to call delirium every state in which the minds adds to data immediately perceived by the senses, and projects its sentiments and impressions on to things, there is perhaps no *représentation collective* which is not delirious in some sense or the other. Religious beliefs are only a specific instance of a very general law. The whole social environment appears to us to be populated with forces, which, in reality, only exist in our minds. We know what the flag is for the soldier: in itself it is but a piece of cloth. Human blood is only an organic liquid; yet even today we cannot see it spilt

[handwritten margin note: Social environment exercises great influence over our minds.]

[handwritten: it is society which makes us conform to seeing these things with respect]

without being profoundly moved in a way which its physico-chemical properties cannot explain. From the physical point of view man is nothing more than a system of cells, and from the mental standpoint, a system of *représentations*: in both respects he only differs from the animal in degree. Yet, society sees him and compels us to see him as a being endowed with a character *sui generis* which isolates him, preserves him from rash encroachments, and in short inspires respect. This unrivalled dignity seems to us to be one of his distinguishing attributes, although it is impossible to find anything in the empirical nature of man to justify it. A used postage stamp may be worth a fortune but it is obvious that its value is in no way implicit in its natural properties. In a sense it is true that our *représentation* of the external world is also only a fabric of hallucinations; for the odours, tastes, and colours that we ascribe to bodies are not there, or at least they are not what we perceive them to be. Nevertheless, our olfactory, gustatory and visual sensations correspond to certain objective states of the things represented. In their way they express the properties of either the material particles or the movements of the ether which have their origin in the bodies that we perceive as odorous, savoury or coloured. But *représentations collectives* very often attribute to the things to which they refer properties which do not exist in any form or to any degree. Out of the commonest object they make a sacred and very powerful being.

Yet, for all that they are purely ideal, the powers thus bestowed on it operate as if they were real. They determine the conduct of man with the same necessity as physical forces. The Arunta who has rubbed himself in the correct fashion with his churinga feels stronger; he is stronger. If he has eaten the flesh of an animal, which although perfectly wholesome is none the less forbidden, he will feel ill and may die. The soldier who falls defending his flag certainly does not believe that he has sacrificed himself for a piece of cloth. Because of the imperative authority vested in it, social thought is effective in a way which individual thought cannot be. Because of the influence it has over our minds, it can make us see things in the light which suits it, and it adds to reality or subtracts from it according to circumstances. There is thus a part of nature where the formula of idealism applies almost literally: it is the social kingdom. There, much more than elsewhere, ideas constitute reality. Doubtless even in this case, idealism is only true if [*représentations* can be] modified. We can never escape from the duality of our nature and free ourselves completely from physical necessity. To express our own ideas to ourselves, we need, as we shall see later, to attach them to material things which symbolize them. Here, however, the part played by matter is reduced to a minimum. The object which acts as a support to the idea is of very small account in comparison with the ideal superstructure beneath which it disappears and to which, moreover, it contributes nothing. The pseudo-delirium to be found at the base of so many *représentations collectives* is nothing more than a form of this essential idealism.[60] It is not a delirium proper, for the ideas which objectify themselves in this way are founded, not in the nature of the material things onto which they graft themselves, but in the nature of society.

One can now understand how the totemic principle and, more generally, how every religious force is external to the things in which it resides.[61] It is because the idea of it is not constructed out of the impressions that this thing produces directly on our senses and on our minds. Religious force is merely the sentiment which the collectivity inspires in its members, but it is projected outside the *consciences* which experience it and is objectified. To be objectified, it attaches itself to an object which as a result becomes sacred: any object, however, can play this role. In principle, none are by nature predestined to it in preference to others; similarly there are none which are necessarily excluded.[62] Everything depends on circumstances which allow the sentiment which generates religious ideas to fall here or there, at this point rather than at another. The sacred character which a thing assumes is not implied in the intrinsic properties of that thing: *it is superadded to it.* The religious world is not one particular aspect of empirical nature: *it is superimposed on it.*

Finally, this conception of the religious enables us to explain an important principle which we find at the root of a multitude of myths and rites and which can be stated as follows: when a sacred being subdivides itself, it remains whole and equal to itself in each of its parts. In other words, as far as religious thought is concerned, the part is equal to the whole; it has the same powers, it is equally effective. The fragment of a relic has the same virtues as the entire relic. The merest drop of blood contains the same active principle as blood as a whole. As we shall see, the soul can be fragmented into almost as many parts as there are organs and tissues in the organism, and each of these partial souls is the equivalent to the entire soul. This conception would be inexplicable if the sacred character were dependent on the constituent properties of the thing serving it as a substratum; for then it would have to vary according to that thing, and to grow and shrink with it. If, however, the virtues it is considered to possess are not intrinsic to it, if they are the result of certain sentiments which it evokes and symbolizes, although their origins are to be found outside—given that it has no need of determined dimensions to fill this evocative role—it will have the same value whether it be whole or not. Since the part recalls the whole, it also evokes the sentiments recalled by the whole. A mere fragment of the flag represents the Motherland just as well as the flag itself. Therefore, it is sacred in the same way and to the same degree.[63]

[Section V returns to specific issues associated with totemism, notions of group consciousness, tattooing, and animal emblems.—W.S.F.P.]

VI

336–42

This theory of totemism will provide us with the key to a curious feature of human mentality which, although more marked formerly than now, has nevertheless not disappeared, and which in any case has played a considerable part in the history of thought. It will be a further opportunity for establishing that logical evolution is closely bound up with religious evolution and depends like the latter on social conditions.[64]

If there is a truth that seems obvious today, it is that objects [êtres], such as minerals, plants, animals and men, which differ not only in their external appearance, but in their most essential properties, cannot be considered as equivalent to each other nor as direct substitutes for each other. Long-established custom, which scientific culture has rooted even more firmly in our minds, has taught us to erect between the kingdoms of nature barriers of which even transformism does not deny the existence. Although it admits that life can be born from non-living matter and man from animal, it does not fail to recognize that once living things have been formed, they are different from minerals, and that man is different from animals. Within each kingdom, the same barriers separate the different classes. We cannot imagine how a mineral could have the distinctive characteristics of another mineral, or an animal species those of another species. These distinctions, which seem so natural to us, are in no way primitive. Originally, all the kingdoms were intermingled with each other. Rocks had a sex and were able to breed. The sun, moon, stars were men or women who felt and expressed human sentiments; whilst men on the other hand were imagined as animals or plants. This state of confusion is to be found at the root of all mythologies. Hence, there is the ambiguous character of the beings which the myths portray. They cannot be classified in any definite genus, for at one and the same time they have some of the characteristics of the most contrasting genera. There is no difficulty about them being transmuted into each other; indeed, it is by transmutations of this kind that men for a long time thought that they could explain the origin of things.

That the anthropomorphic instinct with which the animists have endowed primitive man cannot account for this mentality, is shown by the nature of the confusion which characterizes it. They arise, in fact, not because man has inordinately extended the human kingdom to the point of including all others, but because he has mingled the most disparate kingdoms. He has no more conceived the world in his own image than he has conceived himself in the image of the world: he has done both at one and the same time. In his idea of things, he has undoubtedly included human elements; but in his idea of himself, he has included elements derived from things.

However, there is nothing in experience to suggest to him these comparisons or combinations. As perceived by the senses, everything is different and discontinuous. Nowhere in the world of reality do we find beings intermingling their natures and becoming metamorphosed into each other. It is therefore obvious that some exceptionally powerful cause must have intervened and transfigured reality in such a way as to give it an appearance which is not really its own.

Religion was the agent which brought about this transfiguration. Religious beliefs were responsible for substituting a different world for the world perceived by the senses. This is exemplified in the case of totemism. The fundamental thing about this religion is that the people of the clan and the various beings whose form is reproduced in the totemic emblem are considered to have the same essence. Now, once this belief was accepted, a bridge was thrown between the different kingdoms. Man was represented as a sort of animal or plant; plants and animals were related to man, or rather all these beings, so different to the senses, were imagined as sharing some of the characteristics of one and the same nature. Thus, this remarkable aptitude for confusing things which seem to us to be so manifestly distinct, results from the fact that the first forces by which the human intelligence populated the universe were formulated by religion. Because they were made up of elements borrowed from the different kingdoms, men created the principle common to most heterogeneous things, which in this way became endowed with one and the same essence.

On the other hand, we know that these religious conceptions are the product of determined social causes. Because the clan cannot exist without a name and without an emblem, and because this emblem is constantly before the eyes of every individual, it is towards this and towards the objects of which it is the image that the sentiments which society awakens in its members are directed. As a result, men are forced to imagine the collective force whose influence they experience in the form of the thing which serves as the flag of the group. The idea of this force therefore allows the intermingling of the most widely different kingdoms: in a sense, it is essentially human since it is made up of human ideas and sentiments; but at the same time it cannot fail to appear narrowly akin to the animate or inanimate being which gave it its external form. Besides, the cause whose influence we recognized here is not in any case peculiar to totemism alone; there is no society in which it is not active. Generally speaking, a collective sentiment cannot become conscious of itself unless it attaches itself to some material object;[65] by virtue of that very fact, however, it takes on some of the characteristics of the nature of that object, and vice versa. It was social necessity then which coalesced ideas which at first sight seemed distinct, and social life has facilitated this amalgamation by the great mental effervescence which it determines.[66] It is further proof that logical understanding is a function of society, since it assumes the forms and attitudes which society stamps on it.

It is true that we find this logic disconcerting. We must, however, be careful not to undervalue it: no matter how crude it may seem, it constituted for the intellectual evolution of humanity a contribution of the highest importance. Indeed, it was the means by which an early explanation of the world was possible. To be sure, the mental habits implicit in this logic prevented man from seeing reality as shown to him by his senses, but the reality they showed him had the major disadvantage of being proof against all explanation. To explain is to connect things with each other, it is to establish relations between them which make them appear to be functions of each other, vibrating sympathetically, as it were, according to an interior law grounded in their nature. But sensation, which only sees things from the outside, cannot make us see these relationships and internal links: the mind alone can create the notion of them. When I learn that A regularly comes before B, my consciousness is enriched by a new knowledge; my intelligence is not at all satisfied by a statement which does not in itself give a reason for itself. I only begin to *understand* if I am able to imagine B in such a way that I can see that it is connected with A, as if it were linked to A by some tie of kinship. The great service which religions have rendered to thought is to have constructed a first *représentation* of what these relations of kinship between things might be. Given the conditions in which it was attempted, the undertaking obviously could only attain uncertain results. In the first place, however, does it ever produce any more final ones and is it not necessary to reconsider them again and again? Besides, what mattered was not so much to succeed as to dare to try. The main thing was to liberate the mind from its enslavement to tangible appearances, indeed, to teach it to dominate them and to connect what is separated by the senses. For from the moment that man had the sentiment that there existed internal connections between things, science and philosophy became possible. Religion opened up the way. If, however, it was able to play this role, it was because it was a social thing. To be able to make a law about the impressions of the senses and to substitute for them a new way of representing reality, it was necessary for a new kind of thought to be established, namely, collective thought. If by itself it was able to be effective, it was because in order to create a whole world of ideals through which the world of experienced realities seemed transfigured, a great excitement of intellectual forces was needed which is only possible in and through society.

This mentality then is far from being unrelated to ours. Our logic was born of that logic. The explanations of contemporary science are more certain of being objective because they are more methodical and because they are based on observations which are more vigorously controlled, but they do not differ in nature from those which satisfy primitive thought. Today, just as much as in the past, to explain is to show how a thing participates in one or more other things. It has been said of the participations where existence is postulated by mythologies, that they violate the principle of contradiction, and that as a result they are opposed to those involved in scientific explanations.[67] In saying that a man is a kangaroo, that the sun is a bird, is it not implied that they are considered to be identical to each other? But are we thinking any differently when we say of heat that it is motion, of light that it is a vibration of the ether, etc.? Each time we unite heterogeneous terms by an internal link, we are inevitably considering them as being identical. Assuredly, the terms which we unite in this way are not those which the Australian brings together: we choose them according to other criteria and for other reasons, but the actual approach by which the mind connects them is not essentially different.

It is true that if primitive thought had not the kind of general and systematic indifference to contradiction attributed to it,[68] it would be in sharp contrast at this point to modern thought which is always careful to remain consistent. We do not believe, however, that it is possible to characterize the mentality of less-developed societies by a sort of unilateral and exclusive tendency towards vagueness. If primitive man merges things which we separate, inversely he separates others which we group together, and he even sees these distinctions in the form of violent and clear-cut contrasts. Between two beings who are classified into two different phratries, there is not merely separation but antagonism.[69] For this reason, the same Australian who merges the sun and the white cockatoo, contrasts the latter with the black cockatoo which is viewed as its opposite. They each appear to him to belong to two separate genera which have nothing at all in common. A contrast which is even more marked is the one between sacred and profane things. They repel and contradict each other so forcibly that the mind refuses to think of them at the same time. They mutually exclude each other from the *conscience*.

Thus, there is not an abyss between the logic of religious thought and the logic of scientific thought. Both are made up of the same essential elements but are unequally and differently developed. The thing that seems most of all to characterize the first is a natural taste for immoderate confusions as well as jarring contrasts. It freely tends to excesses in both directions. When it relates things together, it confounds them; when it distinguishes between things, it opposes them. It knows nothing of restraint or gradations, it seeks extremes; as a result, it uses logical mechanisms in a clumsy way, but it does not overlook any of them.

Conclusion

593–616

At the beginning of this work, we declared that the religion whose study we were undertaking contained within it the most characteristic elements of the religious life. The accuracy of this proposition can now be verified. However simple the system that we have studied may be, we have discovered in it all the major ideas and all the principal ritual attitudes which are at the base of even the most advanced religions: the distinction between sacred and profane things; the idea of the soul, of spirit, of mythical personality, of a national and even international deity; the negative cult accompanied by ascetic practices which are its exaggerated form, oblatory and communion rites, imitative rites, commemorative rites, expiatory rites—nothing essential is lacking. We are thus justified in hoping that the results we have reached are not peculiar to totemism alone but can help us to understand what religion is in general.

The objection will be raised that a single religion, whatever its area of influence may be, constitutes a limited basis on which to make such an inference. We do not fail to appreciate that extended examination can add authority to a theory. But it is no less true that when a law has been proved by one well-conducted experiment, such a proof is universally valid. Even in one single case, if a scientist succeeded in discovering the secret of life, be the instance that of the simplest protoplasmic being imaginable, the facts so obtained would apply to all living beings, even the most developed. If then in the very lowly societies which we have just studied, we have really succeeded in perceiving some of the elements which make up the most fundamental religious ideas, there is no reason for not extending the more general results of our research to other religions. It is indeed inconceivable that according to circumstances the same effect could be the result of one cause now and of another at some other time, unless basically the two causes are really one and the same. A single idea cannot express one reality here and a different reality there, unless this duality is only apparent. If the ideas of the sacred, the soul, and the gods can be explained sociologically among certain peoples, we must assume scientifically that in principle the same explanation is valid for all these peoples, among whom the same ideas are to be found, along with the same essential characteristics. Therefore, supposing we are not mistaken, we can legitimately generalize at least certain of our conclusions. The time has now come to put these forward. An inference of this kind, which has as its basis a clearly defined experiment, is less hazardous than many a summary generalization, which, whilst trying to reach the essence of religion at the first attempt without undertaking the analysis of any religion in particular, runs the risk of missing the mark altogether.

I

More often than not, the theorists who have proceeded to explain religion in rational terms have seen it to be above all a system of ideas corresponding to a definite object. This object has been visualized in many ways: nature, the infinite, the unknowable, the ideal, etc., but the differences are not important. In all these cases it is the *représentations*, the beliefs, which are considered to be the essential element of religion. From this point of view, the rites appear as merely an external, contingent and material expression of those internal states which alone are considered to have an intrinsic value. This idea is so widespread that the arguments on the subject of religion mostly turn on the question of knowing whether or not religion can be reconciled with science, in other words, whether alongside scientific knowledge there is room for another form of thought which is specifically religious.

But the believers, those who live the religious life and who have the direct sensation of what it really is, object to this way of looking at it on the grounds that it does not bear out their day to day experiences. In fact they feel that the true function of religion is not to make us think, to enrich our own knowledge, to add to the *représentations* that we owe to science others of a different origin and character, but to urge us to action, to help us to live. The believer who has entered into communion with his god is not only a man who sees new truths which the unbeliever does not know, he is a man who is *capable* of doing more. He is given greater strength whether it be in enduring the difficulties of existence or in conquering them. It is as if he were raised above human misery because he is set above his condition as a man. He believes that he is delivered from evil in whatever form he visualizes it. The first article of every creed is the belief in salvation by faith. Now, it is difficult to see how a simple idea could be so effective. An idea is only a part of ourselves; how can it confer on us powers superior to those which are ours by nature? However rich it may be in affective virtues it cannot add to our natural vitality; it can only release the emotive forces which are within us, and neither create nor augment them. From the fact that we imagine an object worthy of being loved and sought after, it does not follow that we feel stronger. But it is necessary that the superior energies to those which we have at our command should emanate from this object and that, moreover, there should be some means of allowing these energies to penetrate within us and combine with our interior life. For that to be possible it is not enough to think about them. It is essential that we put ourselves within their sphere of influence and that we should turn to embrace their influence: in short, we must act and repeat the necessary action each time we need to renew their effects. It can be seen how from this point of view the regular repetition of the set of actions which make up the cult assumes its full importance. In fact, anyone who has really practised a religion well knows that it is the cult which gives rise to those impressions of joy, internal peace, serenity and enthusiasm which are for the believer a kind of experimental proof of his faith. The cult is not merely a system of symbols by which faith is expressed externally, it is the collection of the means by which it periodically creates and recreates itself. Whether it consists in material manoeuvres or mental operations, the cult is always that which is effective.

The whole of our study rests on the assumption that this unanimous sentiment of believers all through history cannot be purely illusory. Along with a recent apologist for the faith,[70] we admit that religious beliefs are based on a specific experience whose demonstrative value is in a sense no way inferior to that of scientific experiments, whilst, at the same time being different. We also believe that 'by their fruits ye shall know them',[71] and that its fruitfulness is the best proof of the health of its roots. From the fact that there exists, if you like, a 'religious experience' which can to some extent be justified—is there any case of an experience which cannot?—it does not follow that the reality justifying it conforms objectively to the believers' conception of it. The very fact that the way in which it has been conceived has varied infinitely according to time, is sufficient proof that none of these conceptions expresses it adequately. If the scientist takes it as axiomatic that the sensations of heat and light experienced by men correspond to some objective cause, he does not conclude that this is what it appears to be to the senses. Similarly, the impressions experienced by the faithful, although they are not imaginary, do not however constitute privileged intuitions. There is no reason to believe that they tell us more about the nature of their object than do ordinary sensations about the nature of bodies and their properties. In order to discover what constitutes this object, we must accordingly subject the impression to an examination analogous to that which substitutes for the tangible *représentation* of the world one that is scientific and conceptual.

Now this is precisely what we have attempted to do. We have seen that the reality is society, which mythologies have visualized in so many different forms and which is the objective, universal and eternal cause of those *sui generis* sensations which make up religious experience. We have shown what moral forces society develops and how it awakens the feeling of support, protection and tutelary dependence which links the believer to his cult. It is society which raises him above himself: we might even say that he is made by society, for the thing that makes man is that totality of intellectual assets which constitutes civilization, and civilization is the work of society. This explains the leading role of the cult in every kind of religion. It is because society can only make its influence felt if it is active, and it is only active if the individuals of which it is composed are assembled together and act in common. In common action it becomes aware of itself and establishes itself: it is above all an active co-operation. As we have shown, collective ideas and sentiments are only possible because of the external movements which symbolize them.[72] Thus action dominates religious life simply because it is society which is its source.

To all the reasons which have been given to justify this conception, a final one may be added which emerges from our work seen as a whole. As we have proceeded, we have established that the fundamental categories of thought, and consequently of science, have religious origins. We have seen that the same is true of magic and as a result of the various techniques derived from it. On the other hand, it has been known for a long time that, until a relatively recent stage of evolution, the rules of morality and law were indistinguishable from ritual prescriptions. In short, we can say that almost all the great social institutions were born of religion.[73] If the main aspects of collective life began as mere aspects of the religious life, it is obvious that the religious life must have been the eminent form of collective life and a shorthand expression of it viewed in its entirety. If religion has given birth to everything that is essential in society, the reason is that the idea of society is the soul of religion.

Religious forces are therefore human and moral forces. No doubt because collective sentiments cannot become conscious of themselves without being attached to external objects, these moral forces have assumed some of the characteristics of things in order to become established. In this way they have acquired a kind of physical nature which has enabled them to intermingle with the life of the material world and through them an explanation of what is happening in it has been thought possible. When, however, they are considered strictly from this angle and in this role, only the most superficial aspects of them are seen. In fact, it is from the *conscience* that the essential elements of which they are composed are borrowed. Normally it seems that they only have a human character when they are imagined in human form:[74] but even the most impersonal and anonymous of them are nothing more than objectified sentiments.

In so far as religions are seen from this point of view, it is possible to perceive their true significance. If we judge by appearances, rites often give the impression of being purely manual operations: for example, unctions, lustrations, meals. In order to consecrate some thing it is put into contact with a source of religious energy, just as today, to heat a body or to electrify it, it is put into contact with a source of heat or electricity. The processes used in each case are not essentially different. Looked at in this way, religious technique seems to be a sort of mystical mechanics. These physical manoeuvres however are only an outer envelope which conceals mental operations. Finally, it is not a question of exercising a kind of physical constraint on blind and, moreover, imaginary forces, but of reaching peoples' *consciences*, of invigorating and disciplining them. Primitive religions have sometimes been described as materialistic. Such an expression is inaccurate. All religions, even the crudest, are in a sense spiritual; the forces that they bring into play are above all spiritual, and besides, their main function is to act on moral life. Thus, it can be readily understood that whatever has been done in the name of religion cannot have been done in vain: for it is necessarily society that did it, it is humanity which has reaped the harvest.

But one asks, what exactly is this society which has been made into the substratum of religious life? Is it real society as it exists and functions before our eyes, with the moral and legal organization that it has laboriously fashioned for itself in the course of history? But this society is riddled with defects and imperfections. In it, evil is found alongside the good and injustice often reigns supreme, while truth is continually obscured by error. How can any being so crudely constituted inspire the sentiments of love, ardent enthusiasm and the spirit of self-denial which all religions expect from their faithful? Those perfect beings which are the gods cannot have assumed their characteristics from such a mediocre, sometimes even base reality.

On the other hand, what about the perfect society, where justice and truth reign unchallenged and from which evil, in all its forms, has been rooted out? No one would deny its close relationship with the religious sentiment, for the tendency of religions is to realize such a society. However, as such it is not an empirical, definite and observable fact; it is a chimera, a dream to beguile men's sorrows, and it has never existed in reality. It is a simple idea which through the *conscience* expresses our vague, indistinct aspirations towards the good, the beautiful, and the ideal. Now these aspirations have their roots in us; they come from the very depths of our being so that there is nothing outside us which can account for them. Besides, in themselves they are already religious, and far from being able to explain religion, the ideal society presupposes it.[75]

But in the first instance, to visualize religion only in its idealistic aspect is to arbitrarily simplify things: in its own way religion is realistic. There is no physical or moral ugliness, there are no vices or evils, which have not been deified. There have been gods of robbery and trickery, of lechery and war, of sickness and death. No matter how noble its ideas of the deity may have been, Christianity itself has found it necessary to make a place in its mythology for the spirit of evil. Satan is an essential part of the Christian system; he may be an impure being but he is not a profane being. The anti-god is a god, inferior and subordinate it is true, yet he is endowed with extensive powers. He is even the object of rites, of negative ones at least. Far, then, from ignoring real society and turning it into an abstraction, religion is the image of it; it is its reflection in every aspect, even the most common and repulsive. It includes everything and, if as is more often the case, good is seen to prevail over evil, life over death, the forces of light over the forces of darkness, it is because this is what happens in reality. If the relation between these opposing forces were reversed, life would be impossible: in actual fact, it maintains itself and even tends to develop.

Although we see reality clearly discernible in mythologies and theologies, it is nevertheless true that we only see it magnified, transformed, and idealized. In this respect, the most primitive religions do not differ from the most recent and sophisticated. For example, we have seen that the Arunta believe that at the beginning of time there was a mythical society, whose organization exactly reproduced the one which still exists today. It included the same clans and phratries. It was subject to the same matrimonial rules. It practised the same rites. But the people who made it up were ideal beings endowed with powers and virtues to which the common mortal could lay no claim. Not only was their nature superior, it was different because it combined at the same time some of the characteristics of both animal and human nature. Evil forces underwent a similar metamorphosis: evil itself seemed to become sublime and idealized. The question is to know whence this idealization comes.

In reply it might be said that man has a natural faculty for idealization, that is to say, for substituting for the world of reality a different world to which he is transported by thought. But this is changing the terms of the problem; it neither resolves it nor advances it. This systematic idealization is an essential characteristic of religions. To explain them by an innate power of idealization is to substitute quite simply one word for another which is its equivalent; it is akin to saying that man created religion because he has a religious nature. Nevertheless, the animal only knows one world, namely that which it perceives through internal as well as external experience. Man alone has the faculty to imagine the ideal and to add to the real. Whence comes this singular privilege? Before making it a key fact or a mysterious virtue which eludes scientific explanation, it is essential to make sure that it does not depend on conditions which are empirically determinable.

The explanation of religion which we have proposed has precisely this advantage in giving an answer to the question. What defines the sacred is its being superadded to the real. Now the ideal satisfies the same definition and we cannot therefore explain the one without explaining the other. Indeed, we have seen that when it attains a certain degree of intensity, the collective life excites religious thought because it gives rise to a state of effervescence, which changes the conditions of psychic activity. Vital energies are overstimulated, passions become more animated, sensations are stronger; there are even some which are only produced at that moment. Man no longer recognizes himself; he feels transformed and as a result he transforms his immediate environment. In order to understand the extraordinary impressions that he experiences, he attributes to the things with which he is in most direct contact properties they do not have, exceptional powers, and virtues which the objects of common experience do not possess. In short, he superimposes onto the real world in which he lives his profane life, another world which in a sense only exists in his thoughts, but upon which, compared with the first, he bestows some kind of higher dignity. Thus, it is an ideal world on both counts.

In this way the formation of an ideal does not constitute an irreducible fact which is outside science; it depends on conditions amenable to observation; it is a natural product of social life. For a society to become aware of itself and to sustain at the necessary level of intensity the sentiment it has about itself, it is obliged to assemble and to focus on itself. This inner concentration gives rise to an exaltation of mental life which is expressed in a set of ideal conceptions in which is depicted the new life awakened in such a way. They correspond to the upsurge of psychic forces which are then superadded to those which are available for the everyday tasks of existence. A society can neither create nor re-create itself without at the same time creating the ideal. This process of creation is not some kind of act of supererogation by which it completes itself once it is formed; it is the act by which it makes and remakes itself periodically. So when we contrast the ideal society with the real society, as if they were two antagonists pulling in opposite directions, we realize and contrast abstractions. The ideal society does not stand outside the real society: it is a part of it. Far from being torn between two opposite poles, we cannot be part of the one without being part of the other. A society is not simply constituted by a mass of individuals who compose it, by the territory they occupy, by the things they use and the actions they perform, but above all by the idea it has about itself. To be sure, it hesitates about the way it ought to see itself: it feels pulled in different directions. When these conflicts do break out, however, they do not take place between the ideal and the real but between different ideals, between the ideal of yesterday and the ideal of today, between that backed by the authority of tradition and that which is only beginning to gain favour. There is certainly every reason to investigate how these ideals evolve, but no matter what the solution to the problem may be, the fact nevertheless remains that everything that happens happens in the world of the ideal.

The collective ideal which religion expresses is not the result of some innate power or other of the individual, rather it is in the school of collective life which the individual has learnt to idealize. It is by assimilating the ideals elaborated by society that he has become capable of imagining the ideal. It is society which, by drawing him into its sphere of influence, has made him feel the need to rise above the world of experience and has provided him at the same time with the means of conceiving another. For society has constructed this new world in constructing itself, since it is society which it expresses. Thus, for the individual just as much as for the group, there is nothing mysterious in the ability to idealize. It is not a sort of luxury which man could do without but a condition of his existence. He would not be a social being, that is to say he would not be a man, if he had not acquired this ability. By incarnating themselves in individuals, collective ideals have a tendency to assume individual characteristics. Everyone understands them in his own way, puts his own stamp upon them, subtracts some elements from them and adds others. The personal ideal thus emerges from the social ideal as the individual personality develops and becomes an autonomous source of action. If we want to understand this disposition for living outside reality which is apparently so odd, we should see it against the social conditions on which it depends.

Care must be taken not to see our theory of religion as a simple revival of historical materialism: this would show a complete misunderstanding of our ideas. By holding that religion is essentially something social, we are by no means trying to imply that it is limited to translating the material forms of society and its immediate and vital necessities into another language. Certainly, we regard it as obvious that social life depends on its substratum and bears its marks, just as the mental life of the individual depends on the brain and in fact on the whole organism. The *conscience collective* is something more than a simple epiphenomenon of its morphological base, just as the *conscience individuelle* is something more than a simple efflorescence of the nervous system. In order to obtain the first, a synthesis *sui generis* of particular *consciences* is necessary. The effect of this synthesis is to produce a whole world of sentiments, ideas, images which once created obey the laws appropriate to them. They attract each other, repel one another, amalgamate, divide themselves, and proliferate; but none of these combinations is directly commanded or necessitated by the state of the underlying reality. The life thus aroused even enjoys enough independence to indulge occasionally in aimless manifestations serving no useful purpose but for the sole pleasure of asserting itself. We have shown precisely that this is often the case with ritual activity and mythological thought.[76]

But if religion is the product of social causes, how can we explain the individual cult and the universal character of religions? If it was born *in foro externo*, how was it able to enter the innermost heart of the individual and penetrate it even more deeply? If it is the work of definite and individual societies, how was it able to dissociate itself from them to the extent of being thought common to humanity?

In the course of our research we have encountered the germs of individual religions and of universal religion, and we have seen how they were formed. The general elements of an answer to this double question are here available.

In fact, we have shown how the religious force which animates the clan has become particularized by incarnating itself in particular *consciences*. This accounts for the formation of secondary sacred beings. Each individual has his own made in his image, associated with his interior life, and bound up with his destiny—the soul, the individual totem, the protective ancestor, etc. These beings are the object of rites which the believer can celebrate by himself and outside any group. Here is the first and genuine form of the individual cult. Assuredly, it is but a very rudimentary cult. The fact is that since the individual personality at that stage was not very pronounced, and little value was attributed to it, the cult which expressed it could not as yet be very developed. However, as individuals became increasingly differentiated and the value of the person increased, the corresponding cult took a greater part in the totality of religious life, and at the same time became more hermetically closed against the outside.

The existence of individual cults does not imply anything which might contradict or obstruct a sociological explanation of religion, for religious forces to which they apply are merely individualized forms of collective forces. Even though religion seems to be entirely contained within the innermost recesses of the individual, the living spring which feeds it is still to be found in society. We are now in a position to assess the value of that radical individualism which seeks to make religion purely individualistic. It misunderstands the fundamental conditions of religious life. If it has so far remained at the level of unrealized theoretical aspirations, it is because it is unrealizable. A philosophy can easily be formulated in solitary meditation, but not a faith. A faith is above all, warmth, life, enthusiasm, the exaltation of the whole of mental activity, and the raising of the individual to a higher plane. How can a man supplement the energies he has without going outside himself? How can he surpass himself if he only has his own unaided strength? The only source of moral warmth that man has is that provided by the society of his fellow men; the only moral forces which he can sustain and augment are those obtained from other people. Let it be admitted that there really do exist beings more or less analogous to those represented to us by mythologies. In order that they may have a useful influence over souls—the very reason for their existence—it is essential to believe in them. Beliefs are only active when they are shared. They may well be maintained for some time by a purely personal effort but this is not the way they are born or acquired, and it is even doubtful whether they can be retained under these conditions. Indeed, the man who has a true faith feels an inconquerable need to spread it. To do this he comes out of his isolation, draws closer to others, seeks to convince them; and it is the ardour of the convictions aroused which help to strengthen his own faith, which would otherwise atrophy.

The same is true of religious universality as of individualism. Far from being an exclusive attribute of certain great religions, we have found it not at the base, it is true, but at the summit of the Australian system. Bunjil, Daramulun, Baiame are not simple tribal gods, for each of them is recognized by many different tribes. In a sense their cult is international. This conception then is very near to that which is found in the most recent theologies. Consequently, for this reason, some writers have seen fit to deny its authenticity, however incontestable it may be.

We ourselves have been able to show how it was formed.

Neighbouring tribes belonging to the same civilization cannot fail to be in constant contact with each other. All sorts of circumstances create opportunities for this: besides trade—at that stage rudimentary—there are weddings, since intertribal weddings are very frequent in Australia. In the course of these meetings men naturally grow aware of the moral kinship which unites them. They have the same social organization, the same division into phratries, clans, matrimonial classes; they practise the same initiation rites, or rites which are very similar. Mutual cultural borrowings or conventions help to reinforce these spontaneous resemblances. The gods which are linked to institutions so manifestly identical, can only with great difficulty remain distinct in people's minds. Everything conspires to bring them together and consequently, even if each tribe formulates the idea independently, they would necessarily have a tendency to merge with one another. It is in any case probable that they were originally conceived in intertribal assemblies. Of primary importance are the gods of initiation, and in initiation ceremonies different tribes are generally represented. If then, sacred beings were formed which are not connected with any geographically determined society, it is not because they have an extra-social origin. Over and above these geographical groupings, there already exist others whose outlines are more blurred. They do not have fixed frontiers but include all kinds of tribes which are more or less adjoining and are akin to each other. The particular social life which is created by them is liable to spread over an area unbounded by any precise limits. Quite naturally the mythical personages corresponding to them share the same characteristic; their sphere of influence is undefined; they exist above individual tribes and even beyond space. They are the great intertribal gods.

There is nothing in this situation which is peculiar to Australian societies. There is no people, no state, which is not linked to some other more or less unlimited society, which includes all the peoples and states with which the former is directly or indirectly related. There is no national life which is not dominated by some collective life of an international nature. As we proceed into history, these international groups assume a greater importance and become more widespread. Thus we are able to see how in certain cases the tendency to universality has developed to the point of affecting not only the highest ideas of the religious system but the very principles on which it rests.

II

There is then something eternal in religion which is destined to survive all the particular symbols which have successively veiled religious thought. There can be no society which does not feel the need at regular intervals to maintain and strengthen collective sentiments and ideas which constitute its unity and personality. This moral tonic can only be obtained by means of reunions, assemblies, and meetings, where individuals who are brought into contact with one another, mutually reaffirm their common sentiments. The result is ceremonies which by their object, by the effects they produce, by the methods they employ, are not inherently different from religious ceremonies as such. What essential difference is there between an assembly of Christians celebrating the main events of the life of Christ, or Jews keeping either the Exodus from Egypt or the promulgation of the Decalogue, or a gathering of citizens commemorating the institution of a new moral charter or some great event in the life of the nation?

Today we may have difficulty in imagining what form feasts and ceremonies of the future might take. This is because we are passing through a period of transition and moral mediocrity. The great things of the past, those which fired our fathers with enthusiasm, do not arouse in us the same fervour, either because they have passed into common usage to such a degree that we are no longer conscious of them, or because they do not meet our current aspirations; but nothing has yet come to replace them. We no longer become impassioned by the principles which prompted Christianity to exhort masters to treat their slaves humanely. Again, the Christian concept of equality and human brotherhood seems to us today to leave too much room for unjust inequalities. Its pity for the outcast seems too platonic; we should prefer something more practical but we cannot see clearly yet what this would be, or how in actual fact it would be realized. In brief, the old gods are growing old or are dying and other gods have not been born. This is what reduced to nothing Comte's attempt to organize a religion out of old historic memories which were artificially reawakened. It is from life itself and not from a dead past that a living cult emerges. But such a state of uncertainty and confused agitation cannot last for ever. The day will come when our societies will know once again hours of creative effervescence, in the course of which new ideals will be born and new formulae emerge which will for a time serve as a guide to humanity. Once these hours have been experienced, men will spontaneously feel the necessity from time to time to relive them in their thoughts, that is to say, to keep them alive in the memory by means of festivals which would regularly revive their creations. We have already seen how the Revolution instituted a whole cycle of festivals to maintain the principles which were its inspiration in a state of perpetual vigour. The reason why the institution quickly disintegrated was because revolutionary faith lasted but a short time, and disappointments and discouragement quickly followed the first flush of enthusiasm. Although the effort was abortive, it enabled us to visualize what might have happened under different conditions; and everything leads us to suppose that sooner or later the effort will be made again. There are no gospels which are immortal but neither is there reason to believe that humanity will be incapable of inventing new ones in the future. How the new faith will be symbolized, whether or not the symbols will resemble those of the past, whether they will be more appropriate to the reality they are trying to express—these are questions which the human mind is not equipped to answer and which in any case do not constitute the basic issue.

Festivals and rites, in a word the cult, are not, however, the whole of religion. Religion is not only a system of practices, it is also a system of ideas whose object is to express the world. We have seen that even the most primitive people have their cosmology. Whatever connection there may be between these two elements of religious life, they are none the less quite different. The one is oriented towards action which it demands and regulates; the other towards thought which it enriches and organizes. They do not depend on the same conditions and, in consequence, there are grounds for asking whether the second answers to such universal and permanent necessities as the first.

When specific characteristics are attributed to religious thought, when it is believed that its function is to express in its own way a whole aspect of reality, which is as much outside common knowledge as it is outside science, there is naturally reluctance to admit that religion could ever abandon its speculative role. However, the analysis of the facts does not seem to have demonstrated this particular point. The religion we have just studied is one example of religions whose symbols the mind finds particularly disconcerting. Everything in its appears mysterious. Those beings who belong at the same time to the most heterogeneous kingdoms, who multiply without losing their unity, who divide without growing smaller, seem at first sight to belong to a world which is completely different from the one we inhabit, of which it has even been said that the thought which constructed it was totally ignorant of the laws of logic. Never perhaps has the contrast between reason and faith been so pronounced. If there was ever a moment in history when their heterogeneity had to stand out clearly it was in this one. Contrary to appearances, we have established that the realities to which religious speculation was then applied are the very ones which later serve as objects of reflection by scientists: namely, nature, man and society. The mystery which seems to surround them is quite superficial and disappears in the face of more careful observation. It is only necessary to draw aside the veil with which the mythological imagination has covered them and they appear as they really are. Religion attempts to express these realities in an intelligible language which does not differ in nature from that used by science. In both cases it is a question of linking things to each other, of establishing internal relations between them, of classifying them, and of systematizing them. We have even seen that the essential ideas of scientific logic are religious in origin. To be sure, science thinks them out afresh in order to make use of them, it frees them from all sorts of accidental elements, it generally brings to all its proceedings a critical mind unknown to religion, it surrounds itself with safeguards to 'avoid haste and bias', and to eliminate passions, prejudices and all subjective influences. However, these methodological improvements are insufficient to differentiate it from religion. In this respect, they are both pursuing the same end; scientific thought is merely a more perfect form of religious thought. It seems natural then that the second should progressively give way to the first as it becomes better fitted to perform the task.

There is no doubting the fact that this regression has indeed taken place in the course of history. Born of religion, science is tending to substitute itself for religion in everything that concerns the cognitive and intellectual functions. Already Christianity has definitely accepted this substitution with regard to material phenomena.

Seeing in matter the profane *par excellence*, it has readily abandoned knowledge of it to an alien discipline, *tradidit mundum hominum disputationi*. In this way the natural sciences have been able to establish themselves and have their authority acknowledged without very great difficulty. But it could not let go of the world of souls so easily, for the God of the Christians aspires above all else to reign over souls. This is why for a long time the idea that the life of the psyche should be submitted to science seemed a form of profanation and even today it is still distasteful to many people. Nevertheless, experimental and comparative psychology was established and now it has to be reckoned with. But the world of religious and moral life still remains a forbidden subject. The great majority of men continue to believe that it constitutes an order of things into which the mind can only enter by very special paths; hence the lively resistance encountered every time men try to deal with religious and moral phenomena in a scientific way. Despite opposition, however, these attempts are persistently being repeated and this enables us to predict that the last barrier will in the end give way and that science will dominate even this preserve.

This is what is at stake in the conflict between science and religion. People often receive the wrong impression of it. Science is said to deny religion in principle but religion exists; it is a system of given facts; in short, it is a reality. How can science deny a reality? Moreover, in so far as religion is action, in so far as it is a way of life, science cannot take its place, for though it expresses life, it does not create it; it may well explain faith but by that very fact it presupposes it. There is no conflict except on a limited front. Of the two functions that religion originally fulfilled, there is one and only one which is showing an increasing tendency to fall outside the scope of religion, that is, its speculative function. There is but one point at issue between science and religion: it is not the right of religion to exist, it is its right to dogmatize about the nature of things, and the special competence religion claims for itself to know about man and the world. As a matter of fact, it does not know itself. It knows neither what it is made of, nor what needs it satisfies. Far from being able to dictate to science, it is itself the subject of scientific investigation! Again, apart from that reality which is the subject of scientific thought, there exists no proper object for religious speculation to be concerned with, and it is obvious that it will be unable to play the same role in the future as it did in the past.

Yet it seems destined to be transformed rather than to disappear. We have said that there is something eternal about religion: it is cult and faith. But men cannot take part in ceremonies which seem to have no point, nor accept a faith which is totally incomprehensible to them. In order to extend religion or simply to keep it alive, its justification is necessary, that is to say, there has to be a theory about it. Such a theory is without doubt bound to depend on the different sciences as soon as they come into existence; the social sciences first, because religious faith has its origins in society; psychology, because society is a synthesis of human *consciences*; finally, the natural sciences because man and society are functions of the universe and can only be artificially separated from it. However important the borrowings made from organized sciences may be, they are inadequate. Faith is above all an impulse to action, while science, however far one extends it, always remains removed from action. Science is fragmentary, incomplete; it only advances slowly and its work is never complete. Life cannot wait. Theories which are aimed at helping people live and act are by that very reason compelled to be ahead of science and to force it to a premature conclusion. They are only possible if practical requirements and vital necessities, as we experience them without clearly visualizing them, propel thought beyond the limits science lays down. Thus, even the most rational and laicized religions cannot and never will be able to do without some special form of speculation which, although it has the same object as science itself, nevertheless is not really scientific. In these religions the obscure intuitions of sensation and sentiment often take the place of logical reasoning. On the one hand, this speculation resembles that encountered in the religions of the past; but on the other, it differs from it. Although it gives itself the right to go beyond science, it must begin by knowing it and drawing inspiration from it. Once the authority of science is established, it must be taken into consideration. We can go beyond science because of the pressures of necessity; however, it must be our starting point. We can affirm nothing it denies, deny nothing it affirms, and establish nothing which directly or indirectly contradicts the principles on which it depends. From now on, faith no longer exercises over the system of *représentations*, which we can continue to call religious, the same hegemony as before. Confronting it stands a rival power, its offspring which will subject it to its own criticism and control. All the signs indicate that this control will continually increase and be ever more effective, while no limit can possibly be fixed on its future influence.

[Sections III and IV, which complete the Conclusion, deal with epistemological issues raised in the Introduction.—W.S.F.P.]

Notes

1 Similarly, we shall call these societies primitive societies and the men constituting them primitive. It is true that the term is not a precise one but it is difficult to avoid and once trouble has been taken to define its meaning, it is a convenient expression.

2 That is not to say, naturally, that all primitive cults are lacking in the superfluous. We shall see, on the contrary, that one can find in every religion beliefs and practices which do not aim at narrowly defined utilitarian ends (Bk III, ch. IV, section II). This superfluity, however, is indispensable to religious life. It is part of its very essence. It must be added that it is much more rudimentary in lower religions than in others and that very fact will enable us to define more satisfactorily the reason for its existence.

3 It can be seen that we are attributing to this word 'origins' as to the word 'primitive' a purely relative meaning. By that, we do not imply beginning in an absolute sense but the simplest social state which is currently known, the state beyond which we can go no further at the present time. When we refer to origins, the beginning of religious history or thought, it is in that sense that these expressions must be understood.

4 We say of time and space that they are categories because there is no difference between the role played by these notions in intellectual life and that which is ascribed to the notions of genus or cause. (On this point see Hamelin, *Essai sur les éléments principaux de la représentation*, pp. 63, 76, F. Alcan, Paris).

5 In support of this assertion see Hubert and Mauss, *Mélanges d'histoire religieuse (Travaux de l'Année sociologique)*, the chapter on *La représentation du temps dans la religion* (F. Alcan, Paris).

6 This points to the differences that exist between the group of sensations and images which locate us in time, and the category of time. The former are a summary of individual experiences which are only valid for the individual who understands them. On the other hand, what the category of time expresses is a time common to the group, it is social time so to speak. It is a genuine social institution in itself. Consequently it is peculiar to man; animals have no *représentation* of this kind. This distinction between the category of time and the corresponding sentiments could equally be made with regard to space and causality. Perhaps it will help to clear up a certain amount of confusion which feeds the controversies surrounding these questions. We shall return to this point in the conclusions of the book (section IV).

7 Not to mention the wise man and the saint who practise these truths and who are themselves sacred for that reason.

8 That is not to say that these relations cannot assume a religious character, but they do not necessarily possess it.

9 Schultze, *Fetichismus*, p. 129.

10 Examples of these customs are to be found in Frazer, *Golden Bough*, 2nd ed., I, pp. 81 ff.

11 The idea according to which the profane is contrasted to the sacred, as the irrational to the rational, and the intelligible to the mysterious, is only one of the forms in which this dichotomy is expressed. Once science came into being, it assumed a profane character, especially in the eyes of the Christian religion; consequently as it emerged it could not be applied to sacred things.

12 See Frazer, 'On Some Ceremonies of the Central Australian Tribes' in *Australasian Association for the Advancement of Science*, 1901, pp. 313 ff. Furthermore, the idea is extremely widespread. In India, simple participation in the sacrificial act has the same effects; by virtue of the fact that he enters into the circle of sacred things, the sacrificer changes his personality. See Hubert and Mauss, 'Essai sur le sacrifice' in *L'Année sociologique*, II, p. 101.) [English translation, *Sacrifice: its Nature and Function*, by W. D. Halls, London, 1964, p. 63—W.S.F.P.]

13 See above what we have to say about initiation, p. 54[t.116 above—W.S.F.P.]

14 We ourselves shall demonstrate later on how, for example, certain incompatible species of sacred things are mutually exclusive in the same way that the sacred excludes the profane (Bk II, ch. I, section II).

15 This is the case with certain nuptial or funeral rites, for example.

16 See Spencer and Gillen, *Native Tribes of Central Australia*, pp. 534 ff., *Northern Tribes of Central Australia*, p. 463; Howitt, *Native Tribes of S.E. Australia*, pp. 359–61.

17 See Codrington, *The Melanesians*, ch. XII.

18 See Hubert, art. 'Magia' in *Dictionnaire des antiquités*.

19 For example, in Melanesia, the *tindalo* is sometimes a religious and sometimes a magical spirit (Codrington, pp. 125 ff., pp. 194 ff.).

20 See Hubert and Mauss, *Théorie générale de la magie*, in *L'Année sociologique*, VII, pp. 83–4. [English translation, *A General Theory of Magic*, by R. Brain, London, 1972, pp. 84–5—W.S.F.P.]

21 For example, the host is desecrated in the black mass.

22 One turns one's back on the altar or goes round it from the left instead of setting off from the right.

23 Hubert and Mauss, loc. cit., p. 19.

24 It is true that it is rare for a ceremony not to have a leader at the time it is taking place; even in the most crudely organized societies, one generally finds men whose important social role marks them out for playing a leading role in religious life (for example, the chiefs of local groups in certain Australian societies). This allocation of functions, however, still remains vague.

25 In Athens, the gods appealed to by the domestic cult were only specialized forms of the gods of the city (Ζεύς κτήσιος, Ζεύς έρκεῖος). Similarly, in the Middle Ages, the patrons of the guilds were saints mentioned in the calendar.

26 As a rule the name of the church is only applied to a group whose common beliefs relate to a circle of less special things.

27 Hubert and Mauss, loc. cit., p. 18.

28 Robertson Smith has already shown that magic is the antithesis of religion as the individual is the antithesis of the social (*The Religion of the Semites*, 2nd ed., pp. 264–5). It must be added that by distinguishing magic from religion in this way, we do not intend to create a gap between them. The frontiers between the two domains are often doubtful.

29 Codrington, in *Trans. and Proc. Roy. Soc. of Victoria*, XVI, p. 136.

30 Negrioli, *Dei Genii presso i Romani*.

31 This is the conclusion reached by Spencer in his *Ecclesiastical Institutions* (ch. XVI). It is also that of Sabatier, in his *Esquisse d'une philosophie de la religion d'après la psychologie et l'histoire* [translated by T. A. Seed, *Outlines*

of a Philosophy of Religion Based on Psychology and History, London, 1897—
W.S.F.P.], and of all the school to which he belongs.

32 Especially among many Indian peoples of North America.

33 This statement of fact does not, it must be added, solve the question of knowing whether external and public religion is merely the development of an internal and personal religion which would be the primitive fact, or whether, on the other hand, the second might merely be an extension of the first within individual *consciences.* The problem will be dealt with later on (Bk II, ch. V, section II. Cf. chs. VI and VII, section I). For the time being we confine ourselves to noting that the individual cult is seen by the observer as an element dependent on the collective cult.

34 In this way our present definition supersedes the one we formerly put forward in *L'Année sociologique.* In that work, we defined religious beliefs exclusively in terms of their obligatory character; but this obligation evidently arises, as was demonstrated, from the fact that these beliefs belong to a group which imposes them on its members. The two definitions, thus, partly overlap. We felt it necessary to put forward a new one because the first was too formal and completely neglected the content of religious *représentations.* The advantage in immediately revealing what is characteristic about it will be obvious in the ensuing discussion. Furthermore, if this imperative characteristic is really a distinctive trait of religious beliefs, it permits an infinite number of degrees; consequently, there are cases where it is not easily perceptible. Hence, we are avoiding certain difficulties and obstacles by substituting for this criterion the one we have employed above.

35 See *Les Formes élémentaires,* p. 145. [t.1915d:103. To Durkheim's references to *Les Formes élémentaires* have been added the corresponding pages in the English translation by J. W. Swain with the notation t.1915d.—W.S.F.P.]

36 Pikler, in the short article referred to above, has already expressed in a rather dialectical manner the sentiment that here lies the essential nature of the totem. [G. Pikler and F. Somló, *Ursprung des Totemismus Ein Beitrag zur Materialistischen Geschichtstheorie,* Berlin, 1900—W.S.F.P.]

37 See our *Division du travail social,* 3rd ed., pp. 64 ff. [English translation, *The Division of Labor,* by G. Simpson, New York, 1933, pp. 96 ff.—W.S.F.P.]

38 Ibid., p. 76 [English translation, p. 108—W.S.F.P.]

39 At least this is true of all moral authority recognized as such by a collectivity.

40 We hope that this analysis and those which follow will put an end to the incorrect interpretation of our ideas which has caused more than one misunderstanding. Because we made coercion the *external characteristic* by which social facts can be most easily recognized and distinguished from the facts of individual psychology, it has been thought that we saw physical constraint as the prime essential of social life. In actual fact, we have only ever considered it to be the material and outward expression of a profound internal fact which is totally ideal, namely, *moral authority.* The sociological problem—if one can say there is *a* sociological problem—consists in seeking among the different forms of external constraint, the different kinds of moral authority corresponding to them and discovering the causes which have determined them. In particular, the question we are dealing with in the present work has the main object of finding out what form this specific kind of moral authority, which is inherent in everything religious, first took and its composition. Furthermore, it will be seen later that although we make social pressure one of the distinctive characteristics of sociological phenomena, we do not intend to imply that it is the only one. We will show another aspect of collective life which is almost the antithesis of the first one, but no less real. [See

Les Formes élémentaires, p. 303 (t.1915d:212)—W.S.F.P.]

41 That it not to say, of course, that the *conscience collective* has no specific characteristics (see on this point 'Représentations individuelles et représentations collectives' in *Revue de métaphysique et de morale*, 1898, pp. 273 ff.). [Reproduced in *Sociologie et philosophie*, Paris, 1924, pp. 1 ff. English translation, *Sociology and Philosophy*, by D. F. Pocock, London, 1953, pp. 1 ff.— W.S.F.P.]

42 This is substantiated by the lengthy and impassioned character of the debate in which a legal form was given to the resolutions of principle made in a moment of collective enthusiasm. More than one person, drawn from the clergy and nobility alike, referred to this famous night as the 'night of the Dupes', or along with Rivarol, as the St Bartholomew's Night Massacre of the Estates (see Stoll, *Suggestion und Hypnotismus in der Voelkerpsychologie*, 2nd ed., 618, n. 2). [The date referred to in the text was 4 August 1789. A report of the committee on the state of the nation to the National Assembly created such great enthusiasm that noblemen denounced their feudal rights and privileges.— W.S.F.P.]

43 See Stoll, op. cit., pp. 353 ff.

44 Ibid., pp. 619, 635.

45 Ibid., pp. 622 ff.

46 The sentiments of fear and sadness can just as easily develop and be intensified by the same influences. As we shall see, they correspond to a whole aspect of religious life (see Bk II, ch. V).

47 This is the other aspect of society which, as well as being imperious, is also good and benevolent. It dominates us and it assists us. If we have defined the social fact in terms of the first of these characteristics rather than the second, it is because it is more easily observable and because it expresses itself in external and visible signs; far be it from us to have ever thought of denying the reality of the second (see *Règles de la méthode sociologique*, preface to the second edition, p. xx, n. 1). [English translation, *The Rules of Sociological Method*, by S. A. Solovay and J. H. Mueller, Chicago, 1938, p. liv—W.S.F.P.]

48 Codrington, *The Melanesians*, pp. 50, 103, 120. Besides, it is generally considered that, in the Polynesian languages, the word 'mana' originally had the meaning of authority. (See Tregear, *Maori Comparative Dictionary*.)

49 See Albert Mathiez, *Les Origines des cultes révolutionnaires* (1789–92).

50 Ibid., p. 24.

51 Ibid., pp. 29, 32.

52 Ibid., p. 30.

53 Ibid., p. 46.

54 See Mathiez, *La Théophilanthropie et le culte décadaire*, p. 36.

55 At least, when he has reached adulthood and is fully initiated, for the initiation rites which introduce the young man into social life in themselves constitute a severe discipline.

56 On this particular nature of primitive societies, see *De la Division du travail social*, 3rd ed., pp. 123, 149, 173 ff. [English translation, op. cit., pp. 151, 174, 196 ff.—W.S.F.P.]

57 Provisionally we shall limit ourselves to this general information. We shall return to the idea and provide a more explicit proof of it when we deal with rites (see Bk III).

58 On this point see Achelis, *Die Ekstase*, Berlin, 1902, notably ch. I.

59 Cf. Mauss, 'Essai sur les variations saisonnières des sociétés eskimos', in *L'Année sociologique*, IX, p. 127.

60 One can see everything that is wrong with the theories which, like Ratzel's

geographical materialism (see especially his *Politische Geographie*), attempt to derive the whole of social life from its material substratum (be it economic or territorial). They perpetuate an error quite comparable with that made by Maudsley in individual psychology. Just as the latter reduced the psychic life of the individual to being merely an epiphenomenon of his physiological basis, they want to reduce the whole of the psychic life of the collectivity to its physical basis. This ignores the fact that ideas are realities and forces, and that *représentations collectives* are forces which are even more active and effective than *représentations individuelles*. On this point see our article 'Représentations individuelles et représentations collectives', in *Revue de métaphysique et de morale*, May 1898. [See note 41 in this section—W.S.F.P.]

61 See *Les Formes élémentaires*, pp. 269, 277. [t.1915d:188, 194—W.S.F.P.]

62 Even the *excreta* have a religious character. See Preuss, 'Der Ursprung der Religion und Kunst', particularly ch. II entitled 'Der Zauber der Defäkation' (*Globus*, LXXXVI, pp. 325 ff.).

63 The principle has passed from religion into magic: it is the *totem ex parte* of the alchemists.

64 The mental state which is studied in this paragraph is identical to that which Lévy-Bruhl calls the law of participation (*Les Fonctions mentales dans les sociétés inférieures*, pp. 76 ff.) [English translation, *How Natives Think*, by L. A. Clare, London, 1926, pp. 76 ff.—W.S.F.P.] The pages which follow were already written when this work made its appearance; we are publishing them in their original form without changing anything and we limit ourselves to adding a few explanations where we indicate how we dissociate ourselves from Lévy-Bruhl in our interpretations of the facts.

65 See *Les Formes élémentaires*, p. 307 [t.1915d:230—W.S.F.P.].

66 Another cause has contributed to a great extent to this amalgamation; it is the extreme contagiousness of religious forces. They invade every object within reach, whatever it may be. It is thus that a single religious force is able to animate the most disparate things which by virtue of that fact, are brought closely together and classified in the same genus. We shall return to this contagiousness later at the same time that we shall show that it derives from the social origins of the idea of the sacred (see Bk III, ch. I, in fine).

67 Lévy-Bruhl, op. cit., pp. 77 ff. [English translation, op. cit., pp. 77 ff.—W.S.F.P.]

68 Ibid., p. 79. [English translation, op. cit., p. 78—W.S.F.P.]

69 See *Les Formes élémentaires*, p. 207 [t.1915d:146—W.S.F.P.].

70 William James, *The Varieties of Religious Experience* (1902).

71 Ibid., p. 19 (French translation). [The words in the original English text are given in our translation; in the same text there is the added phrase, 'not by their roots'. Durkheim writes: 'qu'un arbre se connaît à ses fruits' (pp. 596–7—W.S.F.P.].

72 See *Les Formes élémentaires*, pp. 329 ff. [t.1915d:230 ff.—W.S.F.P.].

73 One single form of social activity has not yet been explicitly linked with religion, namely economic activity. However, the techniques derived from magic are found by that very fact to have origins which are indirectly religious. Moreover, economic value is a kind of power, an efficiency, and we are aware of the religious origins of the idea of power. Wealth can confer mana; it follows that it possesses it. Consequently we can see that the idea of economic value and religious value are not unconnected. The question of knowing what is the nature of this connection however has not yet been studied.

74 It is for this reason that Frazer and even Preuss place impersonal religious forces outside, or at least on the threshold of religion, to link them with magic.

75 Boutroux, *Science et religion*, pp. 206–7. [English translation, *Science and Religion*, by J. Nield, London, 1909, pp. 212–13—W.S.F.P.]
76 See *Les Formes élémentaires*, pp. 542 ff. [t.1915d:379 ff.—W.S.F.P.] Cf. on this same question our article 'Représentations individuelles et représentations collectives', in *Revue de métaphysique et de morale*, May 1898. [See note 41 above—W.S.F.P.]

8

Note 'Religious systems of primitive societies' (II)

First published in French as 'Systèmes religieux des sociétés inférieures' in
L'Année sociologique, XII, pp. 90–1 (unsigned: probably by Durkheim).

In volume XI of *L'Année sociologique* (p. 75) we recognized the
necessity of introducing into the somewhat confused category of so-
called primitive religions, subdivisions which indicate their real
diversity. We distinguished between three different phases of
religious evolution corresponding to three types of society; purely
totemic systems of the kind to be found in Australia; systems where
totemism, although extant, is evolving and being transformed, for
example into naturism, where the clans are being transformed into
brotherhoods; finally, tribal religions. At the same time, readers
were warned that this classification was and could only be a
provisional one and that it would be gradually improved as
opportunities arose. On one point, we shall now introduce a
modification.

We included among tribal systems, certain degenerate religions
like those of the Koryak and the Chuckchee along with those of the
Ewhe or the Bantu. Doubtless, for the most part one can still find
within degenerate societies the most characteristic traits of the
normal organization which once vigorously flourished there and, for
this reason, classify them under one or other of the adopted headings. In the first place, however, this work of reconstruction is not al-

ways possible; it very often remains purely conjectural. Moreover, it is useful to study the states of degeneration in themselves and for their own sake. The religious facts found there show valuable peculiarities; it is a significant process and we must make use of it, while at the same time retaining all its specific characteristics. In observing how religions decay, we can better understand how they originally evolved: it is desirable to know which are the more persistent phenomena and which on the other hand disintegrate the quickest. The creation of a special heading is all the more necessary in that we have sometimes considered as primitive and simple those religious systems which were in the process of decay: this is notably the case with the Vedda. It has generally been thought that the more the cult of spirits—especially minor spirits—and that of the souls of the dead predominate the more a religion is near to its origins, when in fact on the contrary, this preponderance is generally characteristic of religious regression.

The time has come when it seems desirable to improve our classification further. There are many possible degrees of tribal religion: they vary from a fairly diffuse and vague naturism to some form of monotheism. Unfortunately, by making too clear a distinction between these different forms of tribal religion, it is easy to classify in different categories religions which are in fact a part of the same civilization. For example, the Bantu religions are sometimes the aggregate of associated cults, and sometimes religions unified around a god and a central cult. Inversely, from this point of view, we should have to put into the same group religions belonging to quite distinct families of peoples and civilizations, like those of the Baganda and certain Nilotic peoples. It seemed obviously desirable that the reader should be able to follow at a glance how the same religion in the same culture can move by degrees from diffusion to unity; that is why we have avoided introducing new distinctions within tribal systems.

9

1913a (ii) (6) and (7)

Review 'Lévy-Bruhl—*Les Fonctions mentales dans les sociétés inférieures*'[1] and 'Émile Durkheim—*Les Formes élémentaires de la vie religieuse Le système totémique en Australie*'

First published in French in *L'Année sociologique*, XII, pp. 33–7.

Our task here is not to make a complete and critical analysis of the works which have appeared in a collected form in the *Travaux de l'Année sociologique*. However, it is necessary to set out briefly the main findings, so that our survey of sociological activity during the last three years is a complete one.

The aim of Lévy-Bruhl's book is to establish the fact that human mentality is not as unchanging as certain philosophers, as well as the representatives of the anthropological school, would have us believe. Working on the assumption that types of mentality must vary according to types of society, he undertakes the construction of the mental type found in the ill-defined group of societies which are normally classified as primitive. He is well aware that as vastly different societies are grouped together under this heading, the corresponding logical mentality will necessarily have to be a party to the same relative want of definition; so we shall only be able to obtain a very comprehensive genus which will include a great number of distinct species. Given the present conditions of research, the only thing to do is to make a start on some rough preliminary work: the future alone will be able to evaluate the results accurately.

What characterizes the primitive mentality, according to Lévy-

Bruhl, is that it is essentially religious or, as the author says, mystical. Beings and things are represented to the mind as having very different properties from those revealed by the observation of the senses. Primitive man sees occult powers everywhere, mysterious forces whose existence experience neither establishes nor can establish. They are the objects of faith and, what is more, experience is as powerless to invalidate this faith as it is to prove it. It is also a characteristic of this mentality to be unwilling to accept any kind of experimental proof.

It is already obvious that the mind of primitive man is clearly differentiated from ours. The way in which he connects his ideas is no less specific: his logic is not our logic. The factor dominating the first of these is what Lévy-Bruhl calls the law of participation which he states as follows (p. 77):

> In the collective *représentations* of the primitive mentality, objects, beings and phenomena may all be in some way incomprehensible to us, at the same time themselves and yet something other than themselves. In a way which is no less incomprehensible, they emit and receive various forces, virtues, qualities and mystical actions which can make themselves felt outside them and yet never escape from being within them.

In short, primitive thought is not subject to the law of contradiction and that is why Lévy-Bruhl calls it prelogical.

Having thus defined this mentality, Lévy-Bruhl shows how it accounts for certain peculiarities of language (pp. 151–204), of numeration (pp. 204–57) and of institutions appropriate to societies of this kind (pp. 261–421).

The work which we have published on *Les Formes élémentaires de la vie religieuse* inevitably led us to ask questions closely related to or connected with those already referred to; it is obviously not possible to understand the lower forms of religion without studying the mentality of the peoples practising them. Without actually dealing with the problem directly, we could not but fail to find it crossing our path and we have not neglected the opportunities to consider it which have been given to us.

It goes without saying that we hold fundamental principles in common with Lévy-Bruhl. Like him, we believe that various types of mentality have succeeded each other in the course of history. Similarly we claim—and we have tried to establish this by analysing the facts—that the primitive mentality is essentially religious, that is to say, that the ideas which at that time controlled the movement of the *représentations* originated at the very heart of religion. On the other hand, as the main object of this book is to demonstrate that the origins of religion are social, it follows that these ideas and the corresponding logic have the same origins. That is what is shown in detail in considering the most important of these *représentations*. Yet, our point of view is somewhat different from that of Lévy-Bruhl. Preoccupied above all with differentiating this mentality from ours, he has sometimes gone so far as to present these differences in the form of a positive antithesis. Religious and primitive thought on the one hand, scientific and modern thought on the other, are set up as opposites. With the one there reigns an almost complete indifference to experimental demonstration and to contradiction, and with the other, the principle of identity and the sovereignty of experience are undisputed. On the contrary we consider that these two forms of human mentality, however different they may seem, are mistakenly thought to have originated from different sources: they grew out of each other and represent two stages in the same process of evolution. Indeed we have shown that the most essential of human ideas, ideas of time, space, genus and species, force and causality, personality, in short those to which philosophers have given the name of categories and which dominate the whole of logical activity, were developed at the very heart of religion. Science borrowed them from religion. There is no gap between these two stages of the intellectual life of mankind (pp. 12 ff., 205 ff., 290, 386, 518).

At the same time as we were establishing the religious origins of categories, we showed that they were pregnant with social elements, that they were even made in the image of social things. Physical space was originally constructed on the model of social space, that is to say of the territory occupied by society and such as society visualized it; time was the expression of the rhythm of collective life; the idea of genus was in the first instance merely another aspect of the idea of the human group; the collective force and its power over its *consciences* served as prototypes for the notion of force and causality, etc. One might think, it is true, that by the very reason of these origins, the fundamental *représentations* would necessarily lack all objective value and consist only in artificial constructions without foundation in reality; for society is generally seen as something alogical or illogical which is not at all formed to satisfy speculative needs. It is therefore difficult to see at first sight how ideas, which are the work of society and which express it, could have come to play such a leading role in the history of thought and of science. We have, however, applied ourselves to the task of showing that, contrary to appearances, the primary source of logical activity is society. The thing that characterizes the concept in relation to sensation and the image is its impersonality: it is a *représentation* which, in so far as it maintains its identity, is common and communicable; it can pass from one mind to another; it is by means of the concept that intelligent beings communicate with one another. Thus a *représentation* can only be common to all men in the same group if it has been formulated by them in common, if it is the work of the community. If conceptual thought has a special value for us, it is precisely because being collective it has been enriched by all the experience and all the knowledge accumulated by the collectivity throughout the course of time. The intellectual power of society is infinitely greater than that of the individual, simply because it results from the co-operation, the collaboration of a multitude of minds and even of generations (pp. 616–27). As for these *sui generis* concepts which we call categories, if they are social not only in their origins but in their content, it is because they are superior concepts; they dominate and encompass all other concepts. 'Now, in order to be able to include a given object, they must necessarily be based on a common order of reality' (p. 628). A time which includes all the individual intervals of time, a space which encompasses all the individual regions of space, a total genus which takes in all known beings can only be the time, space, and totality of things imagined by a subject formed by the totality of individual subjects and which transcends them. It is society which taught men there was a point of view other than that of the individual and which made him see things under the form of a totality.

If then human mentality has varied over the centuries and with societies—if it has evolved—the different types of mentality it has successively produced have each given rise to the other. The higher and most recent forms are not the antithesis of the more primitive and lower forms, but were born of them. Even some of the contrasts that have been pointed out ought to be qualified. We have given examples to show that although the primitive mind is disposed to confusion, it is just as inclined to striking contrasts, and often applies the principle of contradiction to an exaggerated degree.

Inversely, the law of participation is not peculiar to it: our ideas, now as formerly, participate in each other. It is the very condition of all logical activity. The difference lies above all in the way in which this participation becomes established (pp. 329 ff).

Note

1 [English translation, *How Natives Think*, by L. A. Clare, London, 1926—W.S.F.P.]

10

Review with M. Mauss   'Frazer—*Totemism and Exogamy*, vol. IV' and 'Durkheim—*Les Formes élémentaires de la vie religieuse. Le système totémique en Australie*'

First published in French in *L'Année sociologique*, XII, pp.91–8.

Frazer's work is essentially a *corpus* of the best ethnographical documents on totemism and exogamy. It is not a book of doctrine. It is true that Frazer ultimately proposes a new theory regarding the two institutions he is studying. However, this theory takes up little space in relationship to the whole work (vol. IV, pp. 40–169), whose principal aim is to present students with all the arguments of the debate. Consequently, the author finds it necessary not only to remind us of the opinions of his predecessors on these questions, but also to reproduce those of his earlier writings which refer to them. Thus volume I begins with a re-issue of *Totemism* and some articles which Frazer once published in the *Fortnightly Review* after the first discoveries of Spencer and Gillen: yet he rejects now the conclusions he formerly upheld.

Here we shall only discuss the part of the book devoted to totemism: the subject of exogamy is dealt with later on. This separation is all the more natural in that, according to our author, the two problems are independent of each other.

The method employed is a geographical one. One after another Frazer surveys the different continents and, within each of them, the main regions; according to their ethnic affinities, he groups the peoples among whom are found either proper totemic institutions or at least traces of totemism. Thus the book has the merit of tabulating for us the range of facts studied: a series of maps, found at the end of volume IV, provides material expression of the results of the work. Of course we must not attach more importance than Frazer does himself to this graphic representation of the current state of our knowledge on totemism. In the first place, there are a certain number of peoples who have kept it hidden from the European observer; as a result, it is in some respects an unknown quantity. One cannot conclude from this that it is not to be found amongst them. Many of the gaps appearing on Frazer's maps can have no more significance than this. On the other hand, Frazer does not seem to have exhausted the subject, nor has he made a thorough survey of all the ethnographical data that is at present available to us. In South America, for example, there is reason to believe that the great civilized nations of the high plateaux and of the Andean Belt, the Chibchas being the foremost amongst them, have not been unfamiliar with totemism. According to Grubb's book, which we consider later on, it would appear that if the Indians of the Chaco no longer recognize totemism, it is because they have forgotten it. In Africa, we know of no Bantu people among whom traces of it have not been found by experienced observers. We show at length later on that among the Nilotic, Guinean and Sudanese peoples there exist more than simple survivals of it.

Even where the peoples studied by the author are concerned, there are serious gaps in the recorded facts. If, on the way, Frazer's fertile genius wanders off into all sorts of questions (theories of the ritual of initiation, vol. IV, pp. 227 ff., prohibition of salt equivalent to sexual taboos, vol. IV, p. 223), he leaves aside some fundamental problems to make up for it. This is notably the case with the totemic *blason* which is not mentioned even where it plays a conspicuous role. Thus, when discussing the Cherokee (vol. II, pp. 192–3), Frazer provides us with all sorts of details and even suggests some ingenious views on the Corn Mother, but this has nothing to do with totemism. Yet he omits to tell us that they have a system of totemic emblems, which is one of the most highly developed known to man. When we think of the influence the emblem has exercised over the Sioux, in Melanesia, on the shores of the American Pacific, not only on decorative art and writing but also on class structure which is determined by the way in which emblems and masks are used, we are inclined to regret that Frazer left everything related to this question in the background, especially as he had once been more aware of its importance.

Another aspect of totemism which is just as neglected is mythology. One could almost conclude as a result of reading Frazer that nothing is known about Australian or Red Indian cosmology. Nowhere is there reference to the myth of the great god, the repository of totems, of the divisions of the world, of the migrations of totemic ancestors, of the legendary history of the clans, of the battles between the totems of the phratries, etc. Neither does he mention the intricate systems of totemic ideas developed by the Sioux, the Pueblo Indians, systems in which all mythical and natural beings take their place. The potlatches, the legends of the clans of the Americans of the North-West, their masks, the vast mythology they possess, all have equally been passed over in silence. It is true that this complexity of beliefs, which conspicuously elevates the dignity of totemism above magic and a purely animistic interpretation, is not in keeping with Frazer's present theories; this is no reason for not taking them into account. Perhaps these serious omissions might have been avoided if Frazer, in the steps of Spencer, had not treated the work of Strehlow (vol. I, p. 186, n. 2) in such a cavalier fashion. This observer's documents may well be in need of criticism but they are nevertheless a mine of information and the same is true of the books of Mrs Parker. It is to be feared that a certain amount of *a priori* reasoning, perhaps necessary in great works, bears some responsibility for these oversights.

The geographical order adopted by the author did, however, lead him to modify on one essential point, the method which he normally followed, and thus to take an important step forward. When he examined a belief or an institution, in his book on *Totemism* as well as in *The Golden Bough*, he too often allowed himself to leave it in the air, so to speak, quite unconnected with the social system of which it formed a part. He was compelled to do this by the fact that as he was making a rapid survey of all the peoples whom he thought might provide related evidence of some sort for the fact under examination, he could not stop to analyse the constitution of each one of them. Now in his present book, as he examines successively different societies—or at least the different groups within the societies related by race and civilization—he is quite naturally led to define their general organization in order to locate the totemic practices in which he is particularly interested. This change in his normal manner of doing things is deliberate on his part. In this book he says (vol. I, p. x),

> The facts are arranged in ethnographical order, tribe by tribe, and an attempt has been made to take account of the physical environment as well as of the general social conditions of the principal tribes which are passed in review. In this way I have sought to mitigate the disadvantages incidental to the study of any institution viewed abstractedly and apart from the rest of the social organism with which it is vitally connected.

In short, Frazer's method becomes intentionally sociological in character.

As for the content of the book, it is **impossible to make a proper** analysis. It includes a multitude of **ingenious views and interesting** comparisons which are especially valuable for their detail. Certain complex questions, like that of the secret societies in the American North-west (vol. II, pp. 457 ff.), are less satisfactorily dealt with; they appear to be not so well suited to Frazer's intuitive genius. The thing we find totally impossible to accept is the new theory of totemism he offers us. It makes the contrived character of the hypotheses that he had put forward previously seem even more pronounced: he would have us believe that totemism is nothing more than a particular example of the belief in miraculous births. The belief is that women are impregnated by the spirits of the animals or plants surrounding them; that the children born in this way are regarded as the products of this impregnation and for that reason are to be classified within the animal or vegetable kingdom. Finally, this belief itself would be explained by the phenomenon described in English as the 'cravings' of pregnant women. These exceedingly suggestible women imagine that the thing they crave for and the being that they give birth to are one and the same thing. Because it frequently happens that the body of the new-born baby bears marks reminiscent of the appearance of the thing concerned, these birthmarks may be considered the empirical confirmation of the totemic prejudice.

It is not our intention to discuss this hypothesis. We do not know if these 'craving' marks are to be found among the women of Australia or America; even if we suppose them to be widespread there, we are completely ignorant of whether or not the infant ever receives the totem corresponding to the mark observed on his body. This entire theory is the fruit of a sort of Voltairianism whose development in our science and in Frazer himself is cause for raised eyebrows. Have not Robertson Smith and Frazer himself contributed more than anyone to conveying an awareness of the extreme complexity of religious facts, of the profound causes on which they depend, and on the partly unconscious evolution from which they result?

Durkheim's book differs from the preceding one in its method as much as in its general approach and conclusions. In a comprehensive survey Frazer tried to cover all the peoples among whom totemism in a more or less developed form is to be found. Durkheim, on the other hand, has concentrated all his efforts on a well-defined and limited group of societies; a group, however, among whom the features displayed by totemism are sufficiently pronounced as to enable the study of them to meet with most chances of success. Australia was chosen as the area for observation and everything pointed to its fitness to play this role. Nevertheless, references have sometimes been made to American totemism on those occasions when a comparison could serve to illuminate or to define more accurately the Australian facts.

Secondly, whilst for Frazer totemism is merely a disorganized accumulation of magical superstitions, for Durkheim it is a religion in the true sense of the word. What characterizes religion, in fact, is the distinction between the sacred and the profane. Thus the totem is sacred; it cannot be approached, it is held in respect, it is surrounded by prohibitions and at the same time positive virtues are attributed to it. However, what proves the religious character of totemism better than anything else is the actual analysis of the beliefs and practices of which it is composed. All the essential elements of a religion are to be found among them.

Finally, if Frazer refused to see a proper religious system in totemism, it is because he failed to recognize its social character. Durkheim has set himself the task of throwing this character into relief. The object at the centre of totemic religion, the object which is pre-eminently sacred, is not the totemic animal but the pictorial representation of it. It is because this symbol is the emblem or flag of the clan. If the symbol of the group is sacred, is this not because the sentiments inspired by the group relate to the sign which is an expression and a reminder of it? Indeed, Durkheim shows how each collectivity inspires in its members sentiments which are identical in nature with religious sentiments. In a similar way to the deity, it acts on individuals categorically, it demands sacrifices and privations from them and it gives them comfort. It requires that they should act contrary to their nature and it sustains them. These propositions have been established not only by analyses of general psychology, but also by studies of conditions of groups peculiar to Australian societies. The individual within a group is taken out of himself, goes into a genuine state of ecstasy, lives a life *sui generis* which is contrasted in its intensity and impersonality with the one the individual leads in the course of his ordinary existence. Besides, it is a fact that society produces sacred things at will and then stamps on them the characteristics of religion.

If the moral force which is the soul of religion is divested of its material symbols, what remains is collective power. This explains why, in so many lower religions, the power worshipped by the members of the cult is known in an anonymous and impersonal form: it is the Melanesian and Polynesian mana, the *wakan* of the Sioux, etc. The same idea is also to be found in Australia where the object worshipped in totemism is a vague force which is diffused throughout the animal (or vegetable) species, throughout the whole clan, at the same time as it is inherent in the totemic emblem.

Because this anonymous force is entirely moral, that is to say made up of ideas and sentiments, it can only live and act in and through particular *consciences*. Accordingly, it permeates them, and in so doing assumes individual characteristics. The fragment which each of us carries within him takes on a particular aspect by the very fact of being intermingled with our individual life, of bearing the imprint of our organism and of our temperament. Each of these fragments is a soul. That is how the idea of a soul came into being. It gives expression to the higher part of ourselves, it is the sum of the ideals which interpret collectivity in us, and which each of us incarnates in his own fashion. The author shows, by analysing Australian and American facts, how indeed the soul is merely a particularized form of the totemic force among these peoples.

Along with the idea of the soul, the idea of the personality was introduced into the domain of religion and, as a result, mythological formations of a new kind became possible. From souls to spirits, there is but a single step. Once the idea of spirits was accepted, it was to spirits that the great social or religious institutions were attributed. Thus were born, in the popular imagination, the civilizing heroes. Finally, there is a group of rites which play a leading role in the social life of these peoples, namely, initiation rites. Initiation is not peculiar to any clan; it is a tribal and even an intertribal cult, for representatives of different tribes are summoned to them. The mythical personality connected with these rites, then, occupied a separate place in religion; it was revered not by one clan but by the tribe and even several tribes. As the purpose of the initiation was to 'make men', this personality was also considered to be the creator of humanity. Thence came the idea of a great god, acknowledged by vast groups of human beings and visualized as the father of mankind. With this conception, we are already within reach of a religion which goes beyond totemism.

Such conclusions, drawn from the analysis of the beliefs, are subsequently confirmed by a study of the cult, which also determines the meaning and functions of the different rites. On this occasion, the author attempts a classification of the principal forms of the cult. First of all, he distinguishes between the negative cult and the positive cult. The first, which is made up of abstentions, consists in the observance of prohibitions. To the negative cult are naturally linked the ascetic rites which are nothing more than the exaggerated practice of the prohibitions. As for the positive cult, it includes all active ritual performances. Those studied in this book are sacrifice, all the essential elements being included in the *intichiuma*, mimetical rites, representative or dramatic rites, and expiatory rites. The last are in contrast to all the others, as doleful rites are contrasted to joyful ones: they express a special aspect of the cult. In relation to each of these kinds of rite, the author attempts to discover which collective states of the soul they express, maintain, or restore, and in this way to demonstrate the extent to which the details of ritual action are bound up in the most essential aspects of social life.

In the end, this interpretation of religion appears, above all, to be consistent with a system of actions aimed at making and perpetually remaking the soul of the collectivity and of the individual. Although it has a speculative part to play, its principal function is dynamogenic. It gives the individual the strength which enables him to surpass himself, to rise above his nature and to keep it under control. The only moral forces superior to those which the individual *qua* individual has at his command are those issuing from individuals in association. That is why religious forces are and can only be collective forces.

11

1919b

Contribution to discussion   'Religious sentiment at
the present time'

First published in French in F. Abauzit *et al.*, *Le Sentiment religieux à
l'heure actuelle*, Vrin, Paris, pp. 97–105, 142–3.[1]

Ladies and gentlemen, I am overwhelmed by the honour you are
paying me in inviting me to speak to you. It was only in the course
of the afternoon that Monsieur Abauzit, who had been told that I
could stay only for the beginning of this session, came to ask me to
say a few words to you. Accordingly, I am going to present the
completely extemporaneous expression of an idea which is not itself
extemporaneous but which I should have preferred to set before you
in a different way. Besides, I must take care not to anticipate the
subject that Monsieur Belot will be dealing with this evening. It is
extremely kind of him to allow me to speak before he does and I am
most grateful to him. As he proposes to examine with you a book I
have recently published on certain forms of religious life, I should
like to try to indicate very briefly the spirit in which I hope it will be
studied and then discussed. Because this assembly includes two sorts
of elements, free thinkers on the one hand and free believers on the
other, I ask your permission to address each of them separately.

   First, I shall address the free thinkers, that is to say, those who
keep a completely open mind in the face of all dogmas, even the ones
which have sometimes been embellished with the great name of free
thought. In order to make them understand what it is that is rather

special about the ideas that I have developed, I would particularly draw their attention to a peculiarity of religious life. This peculiarity is one probably well known to the believer but one which the free thinker is not always sufficiently aware of and which, nevertheless, embodies the true characteristic of religious life.

As often as not, thinkers who have attempted to interpret religion in rational terms have seen in it only, or little more than a system of ideas, a system of *représentations* destined to express some part of reality like sleep, dreams, illness, death or the great dramas of nature. Now, when one sees in religion only ideas or mainly ideas, it really seems as if the individual could have brought it into being by his own efforts. No doubt these *représentations* have something disconcerting about them, they have a sort of mysterious character which disturbs us but, on the other hand, we know from experience that the workings of the mind are so varied, so diverse, so rich, and so creative that *a priori* we give the mind the credit. We willingly accept in advance that thought has been able to invent all these marvels out of nothing. However, although religious ideals may themselves have special characteristics, it is to those that we must look for what is characteristic of religion.

Indeed, religion is not only a system of ideas, it is above all a system of forces. The man who lives according to religion is not only one who visualizes the world in a certain way, who knows what others do not know, he is above all a man who feels within himself a power of which he is not normally conscious, a power which is absent when he is not in the religious state. The religious life implies the existence of very special forces. I cannot contemplate describing them here; in the words of a well-known phrase, let it suffice to say that these are the forces which move mountains. By that I mean when a man lives a religious life he believes he is participating in a force which dominates him, but which at the same time upholds him and raises him above himself. Thus strengthened it seems to him that he is better equipped to face the trials and difficulties of existence and he can even bend nature to his own designs.

This sentiment has been too widespread throughout humanity and is too established to be illusory. An illusion does not last in this way for centuries. So it is essential that this force which man feels to be there should really exist. Consequently the free thinker—that is to say, the man who methodically sets himself the task of expressing religion in terms of natural causes, without introducing any kind of notion not borrowed from our ordinary discursive faculties—this man must consider the question of religion in the following terms: which part of the world of experience can these forces come from which dominate and at the same time sustain him?

One can readily understand that it is not by trying to interpret some natural phenomenon or other that it has been possible for us to conjure up in ourselves such an upsurge of life; forces of that kind can never have arisen from an erroneous *représentation* of sleep or death. The spectacle of great cosmic forces is not likely to have produced this effect either.

As you may well know, here lies the highest rational explanation of religion which has been put forward. Physical forces, however, are only physical forces; consequently they remain outside me. I can see them from the outside, they do not influence me, they do not come and mingle with my interior life. I do not feel stronger, better equipped to face destiny, less a slave to nature, because I can see rivers flowing and crops springing up and the stars in their courses. I can only feel moral forces inside me and only these can command and comfort me. Once again, these forces must be real, they must really be there inside me, for this sentiment of comfort and dependence is not illusory.

Defined in this way the problem presents itself in fairly simple terms. To explain religion, to make it rationally intelligible—and this is what the free thinker sets out to do—we must find in the world which we can apprehend by observation, by our human faculties, a source of energy superior to that which is at the disposal of the individual and which, nevertheless, can be communicated to him. I ask myself if this source can be found anywhere other than in the very special life which emanates from an assembly of men. We indeed know from experience that when men are all gathered together, when they live a communal life, the very fact of their coming together causes exceptionally intense forces to arise which dominate them, exalt them, give them a quality of life to a degree unknown to them as individuals. Under the influence of collective enthusiasm they are sometimes seized by a positive delirium which compels them to actions in which even they do not recognize themselves.

There is no question of setting out here, even briefly, the analyses and the facts on which I have based this fundamental thesis. I will limit myself to warning those members of my audience who have not read my work that this method of understanding and explaining religion, although it does not present itself as a proven truth, does not, however, rest on purely dialectic views. It is not an abstract and purely philosophical hypothesis. Seen independently of the facts and historical observation, it has already inspired more than one particular piece of research which it has guided most usefully; it has already served to interpret various phenomena in different religions; it has then been subjected to the test of experience and so proved its validity.

I will refrain from stressing the reasons which are in favour of the idea which will be later set before you quite impartially, I am sure, and discussed with equal freedom. My sole object is to prepare you for this exposition and examination which you will be hearing; it is not my place to anticipate it. In brief, what I ask of the free thinker is that he should confront religion in the same mental state as the believer. It is only by doing this that he can hope to understand it. Let him feel it as the believer feels it; what it is to the believer is what it really is. Consequently, he who does not bring to the study of religion a sort of religious sentiment cannot speak about it! He is like a blind man trying to talk about colour. For the believer what essentially constitutes religion is not a plausible or seductive hypothesis about man and his destiny; what attaches him to his faith is that it is a part of his being; it seems to him that he cannot renounce it without losing something of himself, without a resultant dejection, a diminution of his vitality, a sort of lowering of his moral temperature.

In a word, the characteristic of religion is the dynamogenic influence it exercises on the *conscience*. In fact, to explain religion is above all to explain this influence.

Now I shall address the free believer, the man who while having a religion, who while even adhering to a denominational formula, nevertheless brings to the examination of this formula an openness of mind which he strives to keep as complete as possible. To him I will speak in a different language.

I shall ask him to bear with me. I believe that the idea which I am trying to establish merits such forbearance. To be sure, if he values a denominational formula in an exclusive and uncompromising way, if he believes that he holds the truth about religion in its definitive form, then agreement is impossible and my presence here has no meaning. If, however, he considers that formulae are only provisional expressions which last and can only last a certain time, if he thinks that they are all imperfect, that the essential thing is not the letter of these formulae but the reality they hide and which they all express inexactly to a greater or lesser degree, if he thinks that it is necessary as a consequence to look beneath the surface to grasp the underlying principle of things, I believe that up to a certain point there is an enterprise we can embark upon by common consent.

We must bring to it this openness of mind: for a time we must practise a sort of Cartesian doubt. Without going so far as to disbelieve the formula we believe in, we must forget it provisionally, reserving the right to return to it later. Having once escaped from this tyranny, we are no longer in danger of perpetrating the error and injustice into which certain believers have fallen who have called my way of interpreting religion basically irreligious.

There cannot be a rational interpretation of religion which is fundamentally irreligious; an irreligious interpretation of religion would be an interpretation which denied the phenomenon it was trying to explain. [Applause.] Nothing could be more contrary to scientific method. We may understand this phenomenon differently, we may even succeed in not understanding it, but we cannot deny it.

Indeed, when we refuse to equate religion with any given particular dogma, what we see in it above all else is a totality of ideals which has the effect of elevating man above himself, of leading him to free himself from his temporal and mundane interests, in favour of an existence which surpasses in worth and dignity the one he leads when he is only occupied with ensuring his survival. Now, the doctrine you are going to hear about and whose essential points I reminded you of a short time ago, implies that above and beyond all the dogmas and all the denominations, there exists a source of religious life as old as humanity and which can never run dry; it is the one which results from the fusion of *consciences*, of their communion in a common set of ideas, of their co-operation in one work, of the morally invigorating and stimulating influence that every community of men imposes on its members. Is not this a proposition on which we can agree? You may think, no doubt, that this religious life is not enough, that there is another one, which is higher, which springs from an altogether different origin. Is it not something to be able to recognize that there exists in us, outside us, religious forces which depend on us for their release, need us to call them into being: forces that we cannot but engender by the mere fact of coming together, thinking together, feeling together, acting together?

A short time ago, an orator, gesticulating prophetically towards the heavens, told us they were emptying and urged us to turn our eyes towards the earth, that is to say, to occupy ourselves above all with pursuing our economic interests to the best of our ability. This formula has been called impious. From my position one can say that it is false. No, there is no need to fear that the heavens will ever become finally depopulated, for we ourselves populate them. What we project there are enlarged images of ourselves. So long as human societies exist, they will draw from themselves great ideals of which men will become the servants.

In these conditions, is it nor fair to say that a social conception of religion is necessarily animated by a religious spirit which it would be unjust not to acknowledge?

To state these ideas precisely, one would like to try to imagine the composition of a future religion, that is to say, a religion more conscious of its social origins. Of course, one must be very cautious in doing this. It is quite pointless to try to guess in what precise form such a religion would be able to express itself. What one can foresee are the social forces which will give birth to it.

If today our religious life is languishing, if the passing revivals that are observed always appear as superficial and short-lived movements, it is not because we have turned away from some denominational formula or other, it is because our power for creating ideals has weakened, it is because our societies are undergoing a phase of profound agitation. In a sense they can be proud of this change they are experiencing; it stems from the fact that having passed through the period of equilibrium in which they could live peacefully in the past, they are obliged to renew themselves and so try laboriously and painfully to discover themselves. The old ideals and the divinities which incarnated them are dying because they do not meet the requirements of the new aspirations which have come to the fore, and the new ideals which we need to guide our lives are not yet born. Thus we find ourselves in a transitional period, a period of moral coldness which explains the various manifestations of which we are continually the anxious and saddened witnesses.

Who does not feel—and it is this which must reassure us—who does not feel that in the depths of society an intense life is developing which is seeking outlets and which will ultimately find them? We aspire to a higher justice than any of the existing formulae can express in a way that will satisfy us. These latent aspirations which disturb us will some day succeed in becoming more clearly conscious of themselves, in translating themselves into definite formulae which men can rally round and which will become a nucleus for the crystallization of the new beliefs. It is pointless to try to discern the content of these beliefs. Will they remain general and abstract, will they be linked with personal beings who will incarnate them and represent them? These are historical contingencies that one cannot foresee.

The only thing that matters is to sense above the moral coldness which prevails on the surface of our collective life, the sources of warmth which our societies carry in themselves. One can go further and say with some precision that it is among the working classes in particular that these new forces are in the course of formation.

Ladies and gentlemen, here is an idea that we absolutely have to get used to; it is that humanity is left on this earth to its own devices and can only count on itself to direct its destiny. As one advances through the course of history, this idea has continued to gain ground; I doubt therefore if it will lose ground in the future. At first sight it can disturb the man who is used to imagining as superhuman the forces he leans on. If, however, he succeeds in convincing himself that humanity alone can furnish the support he needs, is there not something highly comforting in this prospect, since the resources he is clamouring for are so readily available, so close to hand, as it were? Well, the theory that Monsieur Belot is going to present to you leads to that conclusion.

Some Answers to Questions[2]

As Monsieur Durkheim was prevented from being present at the end of the session, he has been kind enough to reply in writing to the questions put by Monsieur Boegner. We should like to publish in full the questions and answers.

1

Boegner: Is it legitimate to seek the essential elements of religious life in its most rudimentary forms? Would it not be advisable in determining these elements to attach the greatest importance to the most perfect forms, the most complete forms, of the religious life?

Durkheim: I explained in my *Formes élémentaires de la vie religieuse* (pp. 3–12), the reasons why the study of a very simple religion seemed to me to be particularly instructive. A science which is just beginning must pose problems in their simplest form and allow them to become progressively more complicated later. When we have understood very elementary religions we shall be able to proceed to others. These, by reason of their simplicity, have the advantage that the essential elements are more apparent and are easier to discern.

In any case, it is quite clear that the study of the more advanced forms of religious life has in itself great advantages. I will go so far as to add that a certain knowledge of more advanced forms helps in understanding the simpler forms. It is, however, with these latter that research must first concern itself.

2

Boegner: Can primitive peoples of present-day Australia be considered truly primitive? Must not primitive forms of religious life possess a spontaneity in places where this life has evolved and by this very fact contain certain essential characteristics no longer found in the religious life of contemporary Australians? Surely such religious life must inevitably have atrophied at least to some extent by remaining unchanged for so many long centuries?

Durkheim: There are no 'true primitive peoples': I said so on the first page of my book. There is no doubt that the Australians have a long history behind them like all known peoples. I chose them merely because their religion was by far the simplest of all those known to me and seemed capable of explanation without the necessity of referring back to a previous religion. If anyone discovers an even more simple religion, we shall study it, but for the moment it seems pointless to talk about it.

Similarly, it seems to be pointless to talk about the changes which might have taken place in Australian religions during the course of history, if we are ignorant of them. Besides, there are some that we do know and have an inkling of. The cults of the high gods would appear to be relatively late, the cults of phratry to have disappeared, etc.

3

Boegner: Is it possible to find in the *conscience collective* of a given time all the elements included in the religious *conscience* of the great initiators of that time, for example, Jeremiah, Jesus, in opposition to the tendencies of the collective, religious *conscience* of the period?

Durkheim: The question of great religious personalities and of their role is certainly an important one. It was not involved in the study that I undertook. I did not wish to put forward a hypothesis relative to such a complex problem: a problem which has never been methodically studied.

4

Boegner: Would it not be desirable for sociology to study the social phenomena caused by the action, of an allegedly superior religion like Christianity on the *conscience collective* of a pagan tribe or people (fetishist or animist) through the individual *consciences* it influences?

Examples: Basutoland, Uganda.

Durkheim: The study alluded to is of the greatest interest. We have there a whole range of experiences the importance of which cannot be denied.

Notes

1 [This is a report of an unprepared speech made by Durkheim on 18 January 1914 at a conference held in Paris which was organised by the Union of Free Thinkers and Free Believers.—W.S.F.P.]
2 [In this translation, instead of presenting all the questions put by Boegner and then all the answers given by Durkheim, each question is followed by the appropriate answer.—W.S.F.P.]

12

1925a

Moral Education

Chapter I, 'Introduction'. Translation by E. K. Wilson and H. Schnurer. Free Press, New York, 1961. First published in French as *L'Éducation morale*,[1] Alcan, Paris, pp. 1–16/t.1–14.

Secular Morality

I propose to talk about moral education as an educator; therefore, I ought to give you my conception of education at the very outset. I have previously suggested that we are not dealing with a science.[2] A science of education is not impossible; but education itself is not that science. This distinction is necessary lest we judge education by standards applicable only to strictly scientific research. Scientific inquiry must proceed most deliberately; it does not have to meet deadlines. Education is not justified in being patient to the same extent; it must supply the answers to vital needs that brook no delay. When a change in the environment demands appropriate action of us, our hand is forced. All that the educator can and should do is to combine as conscientiously as possible all the data that science puts at his disposal, at a given moment, as a guide to action. No one can ask more of him.

However, if education is not a science, neither is it an art. Art, indeed, is made up of habit, practice, and organized skills. Pedagogy is not the art of teaching; it is the *savoir faire* of the educator, the practical experience of the teacher.

What we have here are two clearly differentiated things: one may be a good teacher, yet not very clever at educational theory. Conversely, the educational theorist may be completely lacking in practical skill. It would have been unwise to entrust a class to Montaigne or to Rousseau; and the repeated failures of Pestalozzi prove that he was not a very good teacher. Education is therefore intermediate between art and science. It is not art, for it is not a system of organized practices but of ideas bearing on these practices. It is a body of theories. By that token it is close to science. However, scientific theory has only one goal—the expression of reality; whereas educational theories have the immediate aim of guiding conduct. While these theories do not constitute action in themselves, they are a preparation for it, and they are very close to it. Their *raison d'être* is in action. It is this dual nature that I have been trying to express in referring to education as a practical theory. The uses that may be expected of it are determined by this ambivalent nature. It is not action itself and thus cannot replace action. But it can provide *insight* into action. It is therefore useful to the extent that thought is useful to professional experience.

If educational theory goes beyond its proper limits, if it pretends to supplant experience, to promulgate ready-made formulae that are then applied mechanically, it degenerates into dead matter. If, on the other hand, experience disregards pedagogical thinking, it in turn degenerates into blind routine or else is at the mercy of ill-informed or unsystematic thinking. Educational theory essentially is the most methodical and best-documented thinking available, put at the service of teaching.

These preliminaries over, I can now go on to the problem of moral education. To treat this question methodically, we must look at the conditions under which it is posed today. It is within the framework of our traditional, national educational system that the crisis to which I have alluded before[3] has reached particularly serious proportions. Let us examine it a little more closely.

The question is not only intrinsically interesting to all teachers. It is especially urgent today. Anything that reduces the effectiveness of moral education, whatever disrupts patterns of relationships, threatens public morality at its very roots. The last twenty years in France have seen a great educational revolution, which was latent and half-realized before then. We decided to give our children in our state-supported schools a purely secular moral education. It is essential to understand that this means an education that is not derived from revealed religion, but that rests exclusively on ideas, sentiments, and practices accountable to reason only—in short, a purely rationalistic education.

Such a change could not take place without disturbing traditional ideas, disrupting old habits, entailing sweeping organizational changes, and without posing, in turn, new problems with which we must come to grips.

I know that I am now touching on questions that have the unfortunate effect of arousing passionate argument. But we must broach these questions resolutely. We cannot speak of moral education without being very clear as to the conditions under which we are educating. Otherwise we will bog down in vague and meaningless generalities. In this book, our aim is not to formulate moral education for man in general; but for men of our time in this country.

It is in our public schools that the majority of our children are being formed.[4] These schools must be the guardians par excellence of our national character. They are the heart of our general education system. We must, therefore, focus our attention on them, and consequently on moral education as it is understood and practiced in them and as it should be understood and practiced. As a matter of fact, I am quite sure that if we bring to our discussion of these questions just a modicum of the scientific attitude, it will not be hard to treat them without arousing passions and without giving offence to legitimate feelings.

In the first place, a rational moral education is entirely possible; this is implied in the postulate that is at the basis of science. I refer to the rationalist postulate, which may be stated thus: there is nothing in reality that one is justified in considering as fundamentally beyond the scope of human reason. When I call this principle a postulate, I am in fact using a very improper expression. That principle had the character of a postulate when mind first undertook to master reality—if indeed one can say that this intellectual quest ever had a beginning. When science began to organize itself, it necessarily had to postulate that it, itself, was possible and that things could be expressed in scientific language—or, in other words, rational language, for the two terms are synonymous. However, something that, at the time, was only an anticipation of the mind, a tentative conjecture, found itself progressively demonstrated by all the results of science. It proved that facts should be connected with each other in accordance with rational relationships, by discovering the existence of such relationships.

There are of course many things—in fact, an infinity of things—of which we are still ignorant. Nothing guarantees that all of them will ever be discovered, that a moment will come when science will have finished its task and will have expressed adequately the totality of things. Rather, everything leads us to think that scientific progress will never end. But the rationalist principle does not imply that science can in fact exhaust the real. It only denies that one has the right to look at any part of reality or any category of facts as invincibly irreducible to scientific thought—in other words, as irrational in its essence.

Rationalism does not at all suppose that science can ever reach the limits of knowledge. If it is understood in this fashion, we might say that this principle is demonstrated by the history of science itself. The manner in which it has progressed shows that it is impossible to mark a point beyond which scientific explanation will become impossible. All the limits within which people have tried to contain it have only served as challenges for science to surpass them. Whenever people thought that science had reached its ultimate limit, it resumed, after varying periods of time, its forward march and penetrated regions thought to be forbidden to it. Once physics and chemistry were established, it was thought that science had to stop there. The biological world seemed to depend upon mysterious principles, which escaped the grasp of scientific thought. Yet biological sciences presently came into their own. Next, the founding of psychology demonstrated the applicability of reason to mental phenomena. Nothing, then, authorizes us to suppose that it is different with moral phenomena. Such an exception, which would be unique, is contrary to all reasonable inferences. There is no ineluctable reason for supposing that this last barrier, which people still try to oppose to the progress of reason, is more insurmountable than the others. The fact is, we are witnessing the establishing of a science that is still in its beginnings, but that undertakes to treat the phenomena of moral life as natural phenomena—in other words, as rational phenomena. Now, if morality is rational, if it sets in motion only ideas and sentiments deriving from reason, why should it be necessary to implant it in minds and characters by recourse to methods beyond the scope of reason?

Not only does a purely rational education seem logically possible; it seems to be determined by our entire historical development. If our education had suddenly taken on this character several years ago, one might well doubt whether so sudden a transformation were really implied in the nature of things. In reality, however, this transformation is the result of a gradual development, whose origins go back, so to speak, to the very beginnings of history. The secularizing of education has been in progress for centuries.

It has been said that primitive peoples had no morality. That was an historical error. There is no people without its morality. However, the morality of undeveloped societies is not ours. What characterizes them is that they are essentially religious. By that, I mean that the most numerous and important duties are not the duties of man toward other men, but of man toward his gods. The principal obligations are not to respect one's neighbor, to help him, to assist him; but to accomplish meticulously prescribed rites, to give to the Gods what is their due, and even, if need be, to sacrifice one's self to their glory. Human morality in those circumstances is reduced to a small number of principles, whose violation is repressed less severely. These peoples are only on the threshold of morality. Even in Greece, murder occupied a much lower place in the scale of crimes than serious acts of impiety. Under these conditions, moral education could only be essentially religious, as was morality itself. Only religious notions could serve as the basis for an education that, before everything, had as its chief aim to teach man the manner in which he ought to behave toward religious beings.

But gradually things change. Gradually, human duties are multiplied, become more precise, and pass to the first rank of importance; while others, on the contrary, tend to become attenuated. One might say that Christianity itself has contributed most to the acceleration of this result. An essentially human religion since its God dies for the salvation of humanity, Christianity teaches that the principal duty of man toward God is to love his neighbor. Although there are religious duties—rites addressed only to divinity—the place they occupy and the importance attributed to them continue to diminish.

Essential sin is no longer detached from its human context. True sin now tends to merge with moral transgression. No doubt God continues to play an important part in morality. It is He who assures respect for it and represses its violation. Offenses against it are offenses against Him. But He is now reduced to the role of guardian. Moral discipline wasn't instituted *for his benefit*, but *for the benefit of men*. He only intervenes to make it effective. Thenceforth our duties become independent, in large measure, of the religious notions that guarantee them but do not form their foundation.

With Protestantism, the autonomy of morality is still more accentuated by the fact that ritual itself diminishes. The moral functions of divinity become its sole *raison d'être*. It is the only argument brought forward to demonstrate its existence. Spiritualistic philosophy continues the work of Protestantism. But among the philosophers who believe today in the necessity of supernatural sanctions, there are none who do admit that morality could be constructed quite independent of any theological conception. Thus, the bond that originally united and even merged the two systems has become looser and looser. It is, therefore, certain that when we broke that bond definitively we were following in the mainstream of history. If ever a revolution has been a long time in the making, this is it.

If the enterprise is possible and necessary, if sooner or later it had to be undertaken, and even if there were no reason to believe that it was long in the making, it still remains a difficult process. It is well to realize it, for only if we do not delude ourselves concerning these difficulties will it be possible to triumph over them. Gratified as we may be with what has been achieved, we ought to realize that advances would have been more pronounced and coherent had people not begun by believing that everything was going to be all too simple and easy. Above all, the task was conceived as a purely negative operation. It seemed that to secularize education all that was needed was to take out of it every supernatural element. A simple stripping operation was supposed to have the effect of disengaging rational morality from adventitious and parasitical elements that cloaked it and prevented it from realizing itself. It was enough, so they said, to teach the old morality of our fathers, while avoiding recourse to any religious notion. In reality, the task was much more complex. It was not enough to proceed by simple elimination to reach the proposed goal. On the contrary, a profound transformation was necessary.

Of course, if religious symbols were simply overlaid upon moral reality, there would indeed be nothing to do but lift them off, thus finding in a state of purity and isolation a self-sufficient rational morality. But the fact is that these two systems of beliefs and practices have been too inextricably bound together in history; for centuries they have been too interlaced for their connections possibly to be so external and superficial and for the separation to be so easily consummated. We must not forget that only yesterday they were supported on the same keystone: God, the center of religious life, was also the supreme guarantor of moral order. There is nothing surprising in this partial coalescence; the duties of religion and those of morality are both duties, in other words, morally obligatory practices. It is altogether natural that men were induced to see in one and the same being the source of all obligation. One can easily foresee, by reason of this relationship and partial fusion, that some elements of both systems approached each other to the point of merging and forming only one system. Certain moral ideas became united with certain religious ideas to such an extent as to become indistinct from them. The first ended by no longer having or seeming to have any existence or any reality independent of the second. Consequently, if, in rationalizing morality in moral education, one confines himself to withdraw from moral discipline everything that is religious without replacing it, one almost inevitably runs the danger of withdrawing at the same time all elements that are properly moral. Under the name of rational morality, we would be left only with an impoverished and colorless morality. To ward off this danger, therefore, it is imperative not to be satisfied with a superficial separation. We must seek, in the very heart of religious conceptions, those moral realities that are, as it were, lost and dissimulated in it. We must disengage them, find out what they consist of, determine their proper nature, and express them in rational language. In a word, we must discover the rational substitutes for those religious notions that for a long time have served as the vehicle for the most essential moral ideas.

An example will illustrate precisely what I mean: Even without pushing the analysis, everybody readily perceives that in one sense, a very relative sense as a matter of fact, the moral order constitutes a sort of autonomous order in the world. There is something about prescriptions of morality that imposes particular respect for them. While all opinions relating to the material world—to the physical or mental organization of either animals or men—are today entitled to free discussion, people do not admit that moral beliefs should be as freely subjected to criticism. Anybody who questions in our presence that the child has duties toward his parents or that human life should be respected provokes us to immediate protest. The response is quite different from that which a scientific heresy might arouse. It resembles at every point the reprobation that the blasphemer arouses in the soul of the believer. There is even stronger reason for the feelings incited by infractions of moral rules being altogether different from those provoked by ordinary infractions of the precepts of practical wisdom or of professional technique. The domain of morality is as if surrounded by a mysterious barrier which keeps violators at arm's length, just as the religious domain is protected from the reach of the profane. It is a sacred domain. All the things it comprises are as if invested with a particular dignity that raises them above our empirical individuality, and that confers upon them a sort of transcendent reality. Don't we say, casually, that the human person is sacred, that we must hold it in reverence? As long as religion and morals are intimately united, this sacred character can be explained without difficulty since, in that case, morality as well as religion is conceived as an attribute and emanation of divinity, the source of all that is sacred. Everything coming from it participates in its transcendence and finds itself by that very fact implicated in other things. But if we methodically reject the notion of the sacred without systematically replacing it by another, the quasi-religious character of morality is without foundation, (since we are rejecting the traditional conception that provided that foundation without providing another). One is, then, almost inevitably inclined to deny morality. It is even impossible to feel the reality of it, when, as a matter of fact, it could very well be that it is founded in the nature of things.

It may very well be that there is in moral rules something that deserves to be called by this name and that nevertheless could be justified and explained logically without implying the existence of a transcendent being or specifically religious notions. If the eminent dignity attributed to moral rules has, up to the present time, only been expressed in the form of religious conceptions, it does not follow that it cannot be otherwise expressed; consequently, one must be careful that this dignity does not sink with the ideas conventionally associated with it. From the fact that nations, to explain it to themselves, have made of it a radiation and a reflection of divinity, it does not follow that it cannot be attached to another reality, to a purely empirical reality through which it is explained, and of which the idea of God is indeed perhaps only the symbolic expression. If, then, in rationalizing education, we do not retain this character and make it clear to the child in a rational manner, we will only transmit to him a morality fallen from its natural dignity. At the same time, we will risk drying up the source from which the schoolmaster himself drew a part of his authority and also a part of the warmth necessary to stir the heart and stimulate the mind. The schoolmaster, feeling that he was speaking in the name of a superior reality, elevated himself, invested himself with an extra energy. If we do not succeed in preserving this sense of self and mission for him—while providing, meanwhile, a different foundation for it—we risk having nothing more than a moral education without prestige and without life.

Here is a first body of eminently complex and positive problems that compel our attention when we undertake to secularize moral education. It is not enough to cut out; we must replace. We must discover those moral forces that men, down to the present time, have conceived of only under the form of religious allegories. We must disengage them from their symbols, present them in their rational nakedness, so to speak, and find a way to make the child feel their reality without recourse to any mythological intermediary. This is the first order of business: we want moral education to become rational and at the same time to produce all the results that should be expected from it.

These questions are not the only ones we face here. Not only must we see to it that morality, as it becomes rationalized, loses none of its basic elements; but it must, through the very fact of secularization, become enriched with new elements. The first transformation of which I have just spoken bore only on the form of our moral ideas. The foundation itself cannot stand without profound modifications. The causes requiring the institution of a secular morality in education are too closely related to the foundation of our social organization for the content of morality itself—indeed, for the content of our duties—to remain unaffected. Indeed, if we have felt with greater force than our fathers the need for an entirely rational moral education, it is evidently because we are becoming more rationalistic.

Rationalism is only one of the aspects of individualism: it is the intellectual aspect of it. We are not dealing here with two different states of mind; each is the converse of the other. When one feels the need of liberating individual thought, it is because in a general way one feels the need of liberating the individual. Intellectual servitude is only one of the servitudes that individualism combats. All development of individualism has the effect of opening moral consciousness to new ideas and rendering it more demanding. Since every advance that it makes results in a higher conception, a more delicate sense of the dignity of man, individualism cannot be developed without making apparent to us as contrary to human dignity, as unjust, social relations that at one time did not seem unjust at all. Conversely, as a matter of fact, rationalistic faith reacts on individualistic sentiment and stimulates it. For injustice is unreasonable and absurd, and, consequently, we are the more sensitive to it as we are more sensitive to the rights of reason. Consequently, a given advance in moral education in the direction of greater rationality cannot occur without also bringing to light new moral tendencies, without inducing a greater thirst for justice, without stirring the public conscience by latent aspirations.

The educator who would undertake to rationalize education without foreseeing the development of new sentiments, without preparing that development, and directing it, would fail in one aspect of his task. That is why he cannot confine himself to commenting upon the old morality of our fathers. He must, in addition, help the younger generations to become conscious of the new ideal toward which they tend confusedly. To orient them in that direction it is not enough for him to conserve the past; he must prepare the future.

Furthermore, it is on that condition alone that moral education fulfils its entire function. If we are satisfied with inculcating in children the body of mediocre moral ideas upon which humanity has been living for centuries, we could, to a certain extent, assure the private morality of individuals. But this is only the minimum condition of morality, and a nation cannot remain satisfied with it. For a great nation like ours to be truly in a state of moral health it is not enough for most of its members to be sufficiently removed from the grossest transgressions—murder, theft, fraud of all kinds.

A society in which there is pacific commerce between its members, in which there is no conflict of any sort, but which has nothing more than that would have a rather mediocre quality. Society must, in addition, have before it an ideal toward which it reaches. It must have some good to achieve, an original contribution to bring to the moral patrimony of mankind. Idleness is a bad counsellor for collectivities as well as individuals. When individual activity does not know where to take hold, it turns against itself. When the moral forces of a society remain unemployed, when they are not engaged in some work to accomplish, they deviate from their moral sense and are used up in a morbid and harmful manner. Just as work is the more necessary to man as he is more civilized, similarly, the more the intellectual and moral organization of societies becomes elevated and complex, the more it is necessary that they furnish new nourishment for their increased activity.

A society like ours cannot, therefore, content itself with a complacent possession of moral results that have been handed down to it. It must go on to new conquests; it is necessary that the teacher prepare the children who are in his trust for those necessary advances. He must be on his guard against transmitting the moral gospel of our elders as a sort of closed book. On the contrary, he must excite in them a desire to add a few lines of their own, and give them the tools to satisfy this legitimate ambition.

You can understand better now why I have said that the educational problem poses itself for us in a particularly pressing fashion. In thus expressing myself, I was thinking especially of our system of moral education which is, as you can see, to be rebuilt very largely from top to bottom. We can no longer use the traditional system which, as a matter of fact, endured only because of a miracle of equilibrium and the force of habit. For a long time it had been resting on an insecure foundation. It was no longer resting on beliefs strong enough to enable it to take care of its functions effectively. But to replace it usefully, it is not enough to cancel out the old. It is not enough to trifle with certain external features of the system at the risk of jeopardizing what lies beneath. A complete recasting of our educational technique must now engage our efforts. For the inspiration of yesteryear—which, as a matter of fact, would awaken in the hearts of men only feebler and feebler echoes—we must substitute a new inspiration. We must discover, in the old system, moral forces hidden in it, hidden under forms that concealed their intrinsic nature. We must make their true reality appear; and we must find what comes of them under present conditions, where even they themselves could not remain immutable. We must, furthermore, take into account the changes that the existence of rational moral education both presupposes and time generates. The task is much more complex than it could possibly appear at first glance. But this should neither surprise nor discourage us. On the contrary, the relative imperfection of certain results is thus explained by reasons that authorize better hopes. The idea of the progress, remaining to be made, far from depressing us, can only urge us to more strenuous endeavor. We must resolve to face these difficulties. They become dangerous only when we try to hide them from ourselves and to sidestep them arbitrarily.

Notes

1 [See Abstracts in this volume.—W.S.F.P.]
2 [As Paul Fauconnet points out in his preface, this refers to the first two lectures in this series. The first of these was published in 1903 in the *Revue de métaphysique et de morale*. In 1922, it was reproduced in *Education et sociologie*, recently translated and published by the Free Press.—E. K. Wilson]
3 [Again, this refers to the preceding lecture, which was omitted from the 1925 volume.—E. K. Wilson]
4 [The reference here is to the elementary school system.—E. K. Wilson]

Other authors

Translations are by Jacqueline Redding
and W. S. F. Pickering

13

A. van Gennep   1913

Review   'É. Durkheim—*Les Formes élémentaires de la vie religieuse. Le système totémique en Australie*'

First published in French in *Mercure de France*, 101, pp. 389–91.[1]

In systematically attempting to make *Les Formes élémentaires de la vie religieuse* perfectly clear, Durkheim spares us none of the links in his formidable chains of reasoning, nor any of the discussions of detail in the development of his proofs. His volume is made up of two involved parts; one deals with general theory, the other is monographic. Although it goes into great detail, the latter seems to me to be the weak part. As, during the course of the years, I have examined the same documents as Durkheim, I am in a position to state positively that their theoretical value is less than the author thinks. He deals with them in the same way as commentators deal with sacred texts, namely, analysing them with a great display of erudition, and without even asking themselves whether the bulk of the original material is reliable. I hope that a perusal of the volume will attract some new initiates to ethnography; but I fear that, like Lévy-Bruhl's book, it is more likely to repel many. Take my word for it, this is bookish ethnography, the sort of thing one gets when the wrongly named German method is applied to Greek and Latin texts. There is a profusion of references to documents coming from indeterminate informants: a policeman, some colonial or other, an obtuse missionary, etc. None of this is of much use, for there are pages in Durkheim's book where the impartial ethnographer is obliged to put question-marks beside every line. 'Is this certain?' 'What is this informant worth?' 'What is this document worth or what exactly does it say?' Andrew Lang and Father Schmidt had already lost their way in the Australian labyrinth, and in turn Durkheim has gone headlong into it. In ten years the whole of his analysis of the Australian material will be completely rejected, as will the generalizations based on the most unsound group of ethnographical facts that I have come across. The idea it gave him of primitive man (relatively speaking; cf. his note on p. 11) and of 'simple' societies is entirely erroneous. As we get to know the Australians better and as we are less concerned with identifying the stage of material civilization and that of social organization, we find that Australian societies are highly complex, very far from being simple and primitive, and indeed they may be very advanced in particular directions. At this very moment, B. Spencer (who has never revealed all his documents to us, but only abstracts and notes) is exploring northern Australia; will he find something more simple and primitive there?

Every reader who is not a specialist, not merely in Australian ethnography but even in general ethnography, can see how Durkheim makes good the gaps in the documentation with innumerable hypotheses, which are always ingenious and are asserted with a disconcerting sincerity. As soon as we refuse to accept one or other of these hypotheses, the entire edifice begins to crumble. The whole of this part, alas, brings to mind the systematizations of Lombroso: their strength lies precisely in the unbelievable accumulation of linking hypotheses and it would have been almost necessary to devote a special book to each of them in order to demonstrate that it was empty of facts and deficient in logic.

Let us take leave of these unfortunate Australians who have already played many a good trick on the theorists. There is the other part of Durkheim's book which is full of solid facts. This part is taken up with two major theories: a general theory of totemism and a general theory of religion. In both cases, the documentation is not confined to Australia; it is comparative within the required limits.

In chapter V, one may read a criticism of the various theories of totemism; it is straightforward, to the point, accurate. Chapter VI, however (the origins of these beliefs), does not contain a proper theory. It is hardly putting forward a theory to say: '*totemism is the religion, not of certain animals, or man, or images, but of a sort of anonymous and impersonal force to be found in each of these beings, though not however to be confounded with any of them'*, that is to say, of the mana. This definition only applies to the substratum of totemism; in short, it gives to the word totemism the meaning of the word fetishism and removes all the difficulties of interpreting the details; it also suppresses the question: Why so many forms of totemism? Which is the true totemism?, etc. Briefly, it opens the door to all sorts of new arguments but does not provide a definition which would immediately shed light on all the obscurities which are making things difficult for us. A totem is already a force which has taken on individual characteristics: we are a long way from the so-called 'fetishist' or 'impersonalist' stage.

What Durkheim has to say about this impersonal force and these primitive dynamist ideas will perhaps startle many readers. I feel that I have drawn sufficient attention to the shortcomings of the book for people to be inclined to believe me when I say that, in this instance, Durkheim is quite right. Primitive ideas are clearly energy-giving. Furthermore, all religions do the same: the thing that differs is the name given to the sources and forms of energy, and the form in which they are visualized.

The way in which Durkheim depicts religion and its constituent elements (notions of the soul, spirits, gods; the system of prohibitions or taboos constituting the negative cult; sacrifice, mimetic rites, commemorative rites and piacular rites constituting the positive cult) depends directly on the results to which the study of the Australians led him. He continually refers to these tribes in order to demonstrate the 'genesis' of a certain religious tendency or institution. It is this very thing which makes his complete construction so unstable, since its foundations are unsound. Moreover, as a result of his well-known personal tendency to emphasize the collective element (social) above all else and to put it in the foreground, Durkheim has neglected action, the creator of institutions and beliefs, of various individuals, to which I drew attention in a volume (*Mythes et légendes d'Australie*, 1906), which Durkheim conscientiously held to be worthless. It is with great care that he points out the leading role of society in the various religious phenomena he surveys. I refuse to follow him in saying that 'society is not an alogical being', or even in saying that it is a being pure and simple. It is obvious that in the most primitive societies, social action is more pressing than individual action; but the latter can always take its revenge. Durkheim's dream is to recognize in society a natural—one might almost say cosmic—reality which would consequently be subject to laws as necessary as physico-chemical laws. If in places he alludes to biology, undoubtedly it is only to that of the lower animals. Is man one? I begin to wonder. Durkheim has discovered unicellular beings. Is an Australian society, since it exists, a unicellular organism? I suspect that Durkheim, despite his apparent concern for the ethnographical facts, is only in possession of the metaphysical meaning and even more the scholastic meaning; he ascribes true reality to concepts and words. Mistaken as he is about the meaning of life, that is to say the biological and ethnographical meaning, he turns phenomena and living beings into those scientifically dried plants to be found in a herbarium.

From there to the denial of the reality of the individual, and the dynamic part of the individual in the evolution of civilizations, there is only a small hurdle which Durkheim gleefully clears. It is indeed true that in semi-civilized societies, religion, in so far as it is a totality of beliefs and acts of a certain kind, is the most 'social' phenomenon that we know, since at that stage it embraces law, science, everything. It is for this reason, however, and because the individual has gradually grown conscious of himself—has become individualized—that the progress of humanity has consisted in the growing secularization of all mental and practical activities, and in the proportional disintegration and destruction of religion. As for replacing religion with another sociological imperative, I do not see the point of it, nor do I consider even its possibility.

Note

1 [For a short biography of van Gennep, see R. Needham's introduction to his English translation of van Gennep's *The Semi-Scholars*, Routledge & Kegan Paul, London, 1967, pp. ix–xii.—W.S.F.P.]

14

A. A. Goldenweiser 1915

Review 'Émile Durkheim—*Les Formes élémentaires de la vie religieuse. Le système totémique en Australie.* 1912'

American Anthropologist, 17, pp. 719–35. Reproduced by permission of the American Anthropological Association from the *American Anthropologist*, vol. 17, 1915.

A contribution by Émile Durkheim always commands attention. His *Les Règles de la méthode sociologique, De la division du travail social*, and *Le Suicide* have exercised an appreciable influence on sociological theory and are still remembered and read. As editor of *L'Année sociologique*, Durkheim deserves credit for a methodical and extensive survey of anthropological and sociological literature. In this task he was ably assisted by his disciples and sympathizers, Hubert, Mauss and others. It is to be regretted that this excellent annual has now gone out of existence, its place having been taken by a triennial publication supplemented by occasional monographs constituting a series of *Travaux de L'Année sociologique*, of which *La Vie religieuse* is the fourth volume.

As the title indicates, the work deals with Australian totemism, but is also meant as a general theoretical inquiry into the principles of religious experience. Durkheim is a veteran in Australian ethnology. It will be remembered that the first volume of *L'Année sociologique* (1896–1897) contained a study from his pen devoted to 'La prohibition de l'inceste et ses origines.' Volume V (1900–1901) of the Annual contains another study, 'Sur le totémisme;' and volume VIII (1903–4) one on 'L'organisation matrimoniale autralienne.' One need not therefore be surprised to find Durkheim's latest work replete with abundant and carefully analyzed data. In this respect the volume compares most favorably with much of the hazy theorizing called forth in such profusion by Spencer and Gillen's descriptive monographs. But Durkheim's work contains, of course, much more than a merely descriptive study. He had a vision and he brings a message. To these we must now turn.

While a comprehensive analysis of all of Durkheim's propositions is entirely beyond the scope of a review, his cardinal doctrines may be discussed under the headings of five theories: a theory of religion, a theory of totemism, a theory of social control, a theory of ritual, and a theory of thought.

Theory of Religion

Durkheim vigorously objects to the theories of religion which identify it with belief in God or in the supernatural. A belief in the supernatural presupposes the conception of a natural order. The savage has no such conception nor does he know of the supernatural. He does not wonder nor inquire, but accepts the events of life as a matter of course. The attempts to derive religion from dreams, reflections, echoes, shadows, etc., find as little favor with Durkheim. Is it conceivable, he exclaims, that religion, so powerful in its appeal, so weighty in its social consequences, should in the last analysis prove to be nothing but an illusion, a naïve aberration of the primitive mind? Surely, that cannot be. At the root of religion there must lie some fact of nature or of experience, as powerful in its human appeal and as universal as religion itself. Durkheim sets out in search of that fact. Presently, the field of inquiry is limited by the reflection that the beings, objects, and events in nature cannot, by virtue of their intrinsic qualities, give rise to religion, for there is nothing in their make-up which could, in itself, explain the religious thrill. This, indeed, is quite obvious, for do not the least significant beings and things in nature often become the objects of profound religious regard? Thus the source of religion may not be sought in natural experience but must in some significant way be interwoven with the conditions of human existence. Now the most fundamental and patent fact in all religion is the classification of all things, beings, events in experience into sacred and profane. This dichotomy of the universe is coextensive with religion; what will explain the one will explain the other. The next important fact to be noted is that the content of religion is not exhausted by its emotional side. Emotional experience is but one aspect of religion, the other aspects being constituted by a system of concepts and a set of activities. There is no religion without a church.

The fundamental propositions thus advanced by Durkheim do not impress one as convincing. In claiming that primitive man knows no supernatural, the author fundamentally misunderstands savage *not highly developed* mentality. Without in the least suspecting the savage of harboring the conception of a natural order, we nevertheless find him discriminating between that which falls within the circle of everyday occurrence and that which is strange, extraordinary, requiring explanation, full of power, mystery. To be sure, the line of demarcation between the two sets of phenomena is not drawn by the savage where we should draw it, but surely we should not thereby be prevented from becoming aware of the existence of the line and of the conceptual differentiation of phenomena which it denotes. If that is so, Durkheim commits his initial error, fatal in its consequences, in refusing to grant the savage the discriminating attitude towards nature and his own experience which he actually possesses. The error is fatal indeed, for the realm of the supernatural, of which Durkheim would deprive the savage, is precisely that domain of his experience which harbors infinite potentialities of emotional thrill and religious ecstasy.

Durkheim's objection to the derivation *origin* of the first religious impulses from what he calls illusions, strikes one as peculiar. For what, after all, is truth and what is illusion? Are not the highest religions, of undisputed significance and worldwide appeal, also based on illusions? Are not ideals, in more than one sense, illusions? Should one therefore be shocked if religion were shown to have its primal roots in an illusion? Thus Durkheim's search for a *reality* underlying religion does not seem to rest on a firm logical basis. The author's definition of religion, finally, represents a conceptual hybrid, the application of which could not but have the gravest consequences for his study. A religion, says Durkheim, is an integral *essential part of truth* system of beliefs and practices referring to sacred things, things that *def.* are separated, prohibited; of beliefs and practices which unite into a moral community called the church all those who participate in them. This apparently innocent definition involves a series of hypotheses. While all will concede that religion has a subjective as well as an objective side, that belief is wedded to ritual, the equating of the two factors in one definition arouses the suspicion of an attempt to derive one from the other, a suspicion justified by a further perusal of the work. Closely related, moreover, as are belief and ritual, they belong to different domains of culture, their relations to tradition, for instance, and to individual experience, are quite different, and the methodology of research in the two domains must be radically different. Unless this standpoint is taken at the outset, inextricable situations are bound to arise. That the body of believers constitutes a moral community is another proposition which one may set out to prove but which should not be taken for granted in an initial definition. The proposition further prejudices the investigator in favor of the social elements in religion and at the expense of the individual elements. The introduction of the term 'church,' finally, as well as the designation of the religious complex as an 'integral system,' brings in an element of standardization and of unification, which should be a matter to be proved not assumed.

Theory of Totemism

Durkheim takes pains to set forth his reasons for discarding the comparative method of inquiry. The pitfalls of this mode of approaching cultural problems being familiar to ethnologists, we may pass over the author's careful argumentation. As a substitute for the antiquated method Durkheim proposes the intensive study of a single area; for, he urges, the superficial comparison of half-authenticated facts separated from their cultural setting is pregnant with potentialities of error, while the thoroughgoing analysis of one instance may reveal a law. Australia is the author's choice; for from that continent come detailed and comprehensive descriptive monographs; moreover, there, if anywhere, are we likely to discover the prime sources of religion: the social organization of the Australians being based on the clan, the most primitive form of social grouping, their religions must needs be of the lowest type. The author thus takes as his starting-point the Australian clan, which he conceives as an undifferentiated primitive horde. Each horde takes its name from the animal or plant most common in the locality where the group habitually congregates. The assumption of the name is a natural process, a spontaneous expression of group solidarity which craves for an objective symbol. To the totemic design or carving an- a group of ppl who are connected coz of particular thing.

A. A. Goldenweiser 213

must be ascribed an analogous origin. Of this type of symbolism tattooing is the earliest form; not finding much evidence on that point in Australia, the author borrows some American examples. The paintings and carvings of the Australian being very crude and almost entirely unrealistic, the author is again tempted to refer to the American Indian, while ascribing the character of Australian totemic art to the low degree of their technical advancement. The theory of social control will show us how the concept of power, *mana*, the totemic principle, originates in the clan. Here we take it for granted. Thus, on ceremonial occasions the individual is aware of the presence of a mysterious power; through the vertigo of his emotional ecstasy he sees himself surrounded by totemic symbols, churingas, nurtunjas, and to them he transfers his intuition of power; henceforth, they become for him the source from which that power flows. Thus it comes that the totemic representations stand in the very center of the sacred totemic cycle of participation; the totemic animal or plant, and the human members of the totemic clan become sacred by reflection. When so much is granted, the other peculiarities of totemism follow as a matter of course. Totemism is not restricted to the clans, their members, animals, carvings, but spreads over the entire mental universe of the Australian. The whole of nature is divided and apportioned between the clans, and all the beings, objects, phenomena of nature partake, to a greater or less degree, of the sacredness of the totemic animal or plant or thing with which they are classified. This is the cosmogony of the totemic religion. Individual totemism, the worship of the guardian spirit, is a later derivative of clan totemism, for whereas clan totemism often appears alone, individual totemism occurs only in conjunction with clan totemism. Every religion has its individual as well as its social aspect. The guardian-spirit cult is the individual aspect of totemism. The subjective embodiment, finally, of the totemic principle is the individual soul. But whence the totemic principle? Before passing to the theory of social control which brings an answer to the query, we must pause to examine the theory of totemism as here outlined.

While the author's rejection of the comparative method deserves hearty endorsement, the motivation of his resolve to present an intensive study of one culture arouses misgivings. For thus, he says, he might discover a law. Applicable as this concept may be in the physical sciences, the hope of itself discovering a law in the study no matter how intensive of *one* historical complex, must be regarded as hazardous. And presently one finds that there is more to the story, for Australia is selected for the primitiveness of its social organization (it is based on the clan!) with which a primitive form of religion may be expected to occur. That at this stage of ethnological knowledge one as competent as Émile Durkheim should regard the mere presence of a clan organization as a sign of primitiveness is strange indeed. For, quite apart from the fact that no form of clan system may be regarded as primitive, in the true sense of the word, clan systems may represent relatively high and low stages of social development. Moreover, even were the social organization of the Australian to be regarded as primitive, that would not guarantee the primitiveness of his religion; just as his in reality complex and highly developed form of social organization appears side by side with a markedly low type of industrial achievement. Also from the point of view of the available data must the selection of Australia be regarded as unfortunate, for, in point of ethnography, Australia shares with South America the distinction of being our dark continent. A most instructive study in ethnographic method could be written based on the errors committed by Howitt, and Spencer and Gillen, as well as Strehlow, our only modern authorities on the tribes from which Durkheim derives all his data. The fact itself that the author felt justified in selecting the Australian area for his intensive analysis, shows plainly enough how far from realization still is the goal which his own life-work has at least made feasible, the *rapprochement* of ethnology and of sociology.

But let us pass to the concrete points. The conception of a clan name being assumed as an expression of clan solidarity is suggestive enough. On the other hand, one must not be forgetful of the fact that a name serves to differentiate group from group, and that at all times names must have been given by group to group rather than assumed by each group for itself. Not that names were never assumed by groups—such names as, 'we, the people' or 'men,' etc., bespeak the contrary—but this process must be regarded as the exception rather than the rule. Moreover, groups of distinct solidarity such as phratries or the Iroquois maternal families, often appear without names (in the instance of the maternal family this is indeed always the case), so that the consciousness of solidarity in a group may not be regarded as inevitably leading to expression in the form of a name. As to the objective totemic symbol, the totemic carvings or drawings, it is discussed most loosely by our author. Not finding the totemic tattoo in Australia, he appeals to American examples, but this device, of course, does not strengthen his case except by showing that totemic tattoo occurs in America. Also, he completely neglects the cardinal differences between the totemic art of the Northwest Coast and that of the Aranda—to both of which he refers—in failing to note that whereas among the Tlingit or Haida the carved crests are positively associated with the totemic ideas, among the Aranda the churinga or ground and rock designs are at best but passive carriers of momentary (although recurrent) totemic associations. It is, in fact, quite obvious that the geometrical art of the area has neither originated in nor been differentiated through totemic ideas, but being of an extra-totemic origin, has been subsequently drawn into the totemic cycle of associations without, however, ever becoming actively representative of them. Similarly, with the so-called totemic cosmogony, the fact that social organization tends to be reflected in mythology cannot indeed be disputed; this fact, however, altogether transcends, in its bearing, the problem of totemism. Hence, when we find a sociological classification of the universe coexisting with a totemic complex, we are fully justified in regarding the two phenomena as genetically distinct and secondarily associated. The burden of proof, at any rate, falls upon those who would assert the contrary. Durkheim's treatment of these as of other aspects of the Australian totemic complex reflects his failure to consider that view of totemism which was designed to show, at the hand of relevant data, that totemic complexes must be regarded as aggregates of various cultural features of heterogeneous psychological and historical derivation. Needless to add, the adoption of that view would strike at the very core of Durkheim's argument necessitating a complete recasting of the fundamental principles of *La Vie religieuse*. Nor does Durkheim's discussion of the relative priority of clan totemism carry conviction. Here his facts are strangely inaccurate, for far from it being the case that 'individual totemism' never occurs unaccompanied by clan totemism, the facts in North America, the happy hunting-ground of the guardian spirit, bespeak the contrary. Whereas that belief must be regarded as an all but universal aspect of the religion of the American Indian, it has nowhere developed more prolifically than among the tribes of the Plateau area who worship not at the totemic shrine. To regard the belief in guardian spirits, 'individual totemism,' as an outgrowth of clan totemism is, therefore, an altogether *unnecessary*

gratuitous hypothesis! Having satisfied himself that all the elements which, according to his conception of religion, constitute a true religion, are present in totemism, Durkheim declares totemism to represent the earliest form of a religion which, while primitive, lacks none of those aspects which a true religion must have. Thus is reached the culminating point of a series of *not based in connecting* misconceptions of which the first is Durkheim's initial view and definition of religion. For had he given proper weight to the emotional and individual aspects in religion, the aspect which unites religious experiences of all times and places into one psychological continuum, he could never have committed the patent blunder of 'discovering' the root of religion is an institution which is relatively limited in its distribution and is, moreover, distinguished by the relatively slight intensity of the religious values comprised in it. In this latter respect totemism cannot compare with either animal worship, or ancestor worship, or idolatry, or fetichism, or any of the multifarious forms of worship of nature, spirit, ghost and god. Several of these forms of religious belief are also more widely diffused than totemism and must be regarded as more primitive, differing from totemism in their independence from any definite form of social organization. Resuming the author's argument, we now return to the 'totemic principle,' the origin of which must be accounted for.

The Theory of Social Control

Analysis shows that society has the qualities necessary to arouse the sense of the divine. *Connectivit God* Social standards, ideals, moods, impose themselves upon the individual with such categorical force as to arouse the consciousness of external pressure emanating from a force transcending the powers of the individual. Through the action of this social force the individual on certain occasions behaves, feels, and thinks in a way which differs from the psychic activities of his daily experience. The psychic situation of the orator and his audience, on the one hand, and, on the other, the actions and psychic experiences of individuals in the crusades or during revolutions, may serve as examples. Now the social unit with which the Australian is most intimately allied is the clan. The life of the clan mates consists of periods of non-eventful daily activities alternating with periods of violent emotional disturbances accompanying ceremonial occasions. While 'the secrets' hold sway, to speak with the Kwakiutl, the individual lives on an exalted plane, manifesting qualities which altogether transcend those he possesses under ordinary conditions. The periodic recurrence of these two sets of ideas, emotions, acts, cannot but evoke in the individual the tendency to classify the totality of his experience into profane and sacred. The former embraces all that is strictly individual, the latter all that is social. The sense of external power which acts through the individual on social occasions will tend to crystallize into a concept of an undifferentiated, powerful, mysterious force, which pervades nature and absorbs the individual who feels himself external to that power and yet part of it. This power, as it appears to the Australian clansman, may be called the *totemic principle*. It is not the clan emblem, the totemic design, which is worshipped, nor the totemic animal, nor the various beings and things which form part of the totemic cycle of participation; but the totemic principle, the mysterious substance which pervades them all and constitutes their holiness. It was shown in the preceding section how this sense of power, craving for objective expression, attaches itself to the totemic symbols which surround the individual on ceremonial occasions and thus gives the initial stimulus to the formation of a sacred totemic world. Comparison with American data shows that the totemic principle is a forerunner of the *wakan*, the *orenda* as well as of the Melanesian *mana*. The concept is the same, the only difference being that the totemic principle, originating as it does within the clan, reflects the clan differentiation of the tribe, whereas, the *wakan*, the *orenda*, etc., belonging to a higher stage of development, have freed themselves from the constraint of the clan limit, and transcending it, have acquired that character of generality and homogeneity which distinguishes these concepts.

Thus a solution is reached not alone of the totemic problem, but of the problem of religion. The reality which underlies religion is society itself. In the Australian situation society appears in its most primitive form—the clan. The totemic principle, the nucleus of the most primitive religion, is the clan itself reflected in the psyche of the individual. Not aware of the real source of his subjective sense of power, the Australian objectifies the latter in the form of religious symbolism, thus giving rise to the infinitely varied world of the concrete carriers of religious values. Thus, while here also there is illusion, it extends only to the content not to the existence of the ultimate reality, which is eternal.

We may first consider the minor issue raised in this section, namely the identification of the totemic principle with *mana*. On reading the pages devoted to this discussion the unprejudiced student soon perceives that the facts supporting Durkheim's contention are altogether wanting. There is no indication that the beliefs underlying totemic religion are generically the same as those designated by the terms *mana* or *orenda*; and that the *wakan* and *orenda* concepts should represent later stages of religious evolution, having superseded a stage in which the totemic principle reigned, is an imaginary construction which cannot be described otherwise than *aus der Luft gegriffen*. The main issue of the section, however, is the derivation of the totemic principle. This, in fact, is Durkheim's theory of religion, which is represented as a symbol of social control. Durkheim's theory has the charm of originality, for no one else before him has, to my knowledge, held such a view, nor has the author himself, in his former writings, ever gone so far in his social interpretations of psychic phenomena. Our first objection to the derivation of the sacred from an inner sense of social pressure is a psychological one. That a crowd-psychological situation should have aroused the religious thrill in the constituent individuals, who—*nota bene*—were hitherto unacquainted with religious emotion, does not seem in the least plausible. Neither in primitive nor in modern times do such experiences, *per se*, arouse religious emotions, even though the participating individuals are no longer novices in religion. And, if on occasion such sentiments do arise, they lack the intensity and permanence required to justify Durkheim's hypothesis. If a corroborree differs from an intichiuma, or the social dances of the North American Indians from their religious dances, the difference is not in the social composition but in the presence or absence or pre-existing religious associations. A series of corroborrees does not make an intichiuma; at least, we have no evidence to that effect, and human psychology, as we know it, speaks against it. Durkheim's main error, however, seems to our mind to lie in a misconception of the relation of the individual to the social, as implied in his theory of social control. The theory errs in making the scope of the social on the one hand, too wide, on the other, too narrow. Too wide in so far as the theory permits individual factors to become altogether obscured, too narrow in so far as the society which figures in the theory is identified with a crowd, and not with a cultural, historic group. The experience of all times and places teaches that the rapport of the individual, as such, with the religious object is of prime importance in religious situaations. While, on the one hand, religious emotions are stimulated (not created) by the social setting, the leaders of religious thought, prophets, reformers, individuals whose lives must be conceived as protracted communions with the divine, do not require the social stimulant, they shun the crowd, the church, the world, their god is within them, and their emotional constitution is a guarantee of an interminable succession of religious thrills. The lives of saints are one great argument against Durkheim's theory. The psychic cast of many a savage medicineman, magician, shaman, is another. If the social pressure, the ceremonial whirl is so indispensable a factor in the religious thrill, how is it that the world over the novice, in anticipation of the most significant, if not initial religious experience of his life, withdraws from human companionship, spends days, nay months in isolation, fasts and purifies himself, dreams dreams and sees visions? If phenomena of this type are so important in religion at all times, can one with impunity brush them aside in his search for a plausible origin of religion? Or would Durkheim claim that the religious thrill, socially produced, did then in some way become part of the psychic constitution of man in the form of a hereditary predisposition? But our author has not advanced this theory, and it would perhaps be unfair to attribute it to him.

On the other hand, the scope of the social in the author's theory is too narrow. For, significant as are the functions ascribed to it, the content of the social setting, in Durkheim's religious laboratory, is curiously restricted. Religion, he says, is society, but society, we find, is but a sublimated crowd. The only aspect of the relation of the individual to the social drawn upon in Durkheim's theory is the crowd-psychological situation, the effect on the individual of the presence of other individuals who, for the time being, think, and above all, feel and act as he does. We hear nothing of the effect on the individual of the cultural type of the group of the tribal or national or class patterns of thought and action, and even emotion, patterns developed by history and fixed by tradition. Of all this we hear nothing. The only factor called upon to do such far-reaching service is that whimsical psycho-sociological phenomenon which equates a crowd of sages to a flock of sheep. Strange fact, indeed, that one who expects so much from the social should see in it so little!

Theory of Ritual

It will be impossible to fully discuss in these pages Durkheim's suggestive analysis of rituals, negative and positive, mimetic, representative, and piacular. We shall restrict our remarks to the types of ritual which bear directly on the theories here discussed. Ritual is essential for belief. Nature goes through certain periodic changes; evidently, thinks the Australian, the divinities controlling nature must go through similar transformations. To this spectacle man may not remain indifferent; he must assist the divinities with all the powers at his command. The divinities, totems, etc., derive their sacred character from man, hence, the sacredness will decline unless revived. The group gathers intent on relieving the situation. But presently they feel comforted: 'They find the remedy because they look for it together.' On such occasions society becomes rejuvenated, and with it the soul of the individual, for is it not derived from society?

In the mimetic dances of the intichiuma the performers believe that they *are* the animals whose multiplication they crave, hence they imitate them in cries and actions. This identification of man and animal exists only to the extent to which it is believed, and the rite feeds the belief. The ceremony is beneficent for it constitutes a moral re-making of the participants. Hence the feeling that the ceremony has been successful. But it was intended to further the multiplication of the totemic animal, and now the belief that such multiplication has actually been achieved arises as a correlate of the feeling that the ceremony was sucessful. Such is ritualistic mentality.

In this case as in others the real justification of a religious rite is in the rite itself, that is, in the effect it produces on the social consciousness. The economic or other uses to which a rite is put are secondary, they vary and the same rite often does service for different purposes.

Another aspect of the ritualistic situation is what one might call an overproduction of thought, emotion, and activity. The elaboration of these processes is accompanied by pleasurable emotion, it becomes an end in itself. This is the threshold of Art.

A striking example of Durkheim's conception of ritual and of its effect on belief, is presented in his interpretation of mourning. When an individual dies, the social solidarity of his family is shaken. Driven by the shock of their loss, they unite. At first this leads to an intensification of sorrowful emotion: a 'panic of grief' sets in, in the course of which the individuals sob, howl and lacerate themselves. But presently the effect of this exhibition of solidarity in sorrow begins to be felt. The individuals feel comforted, reassured. The mourning is brought to an end through the agency of the mourning itself.

But the individual remains perplexed. He must account for the strange exhibitions of mourning. Of social forces he knows nothing. All he is aware of is his suffering, and he seeks the cause for it in an external will. Now, the body of the deceased can surely not be held accountable, but his soul is there and it must be vitally concerned in the processes of the mourning rite; but these processes are highly disagreeable, hence the soul must be evil. When the mourning frenzy subsides, and a pleasurable calm ensures, the soul is again held responsible for the change, but now it appears as a benevolent agency. Not only the properties, but the survival itself of the soul, may, according to Durkheim, be an afterthought, introduced to account for the mourning rites.

Thus the ritual in this and similar cases appears as a spontaneous response of the group to an emotional situation. The beliefs, on the other hand, arise out of speculative attempts designed to interpret the phenomena of the ritualistic performance.

Durkheim's psychological interpretation of ritual, must, on the whole, be regarded as the most satisfactory part of his analysis. Nevertheless here, as elsewhere, he permits himself to lapse into a rationalistic and behavioristic attitude. While it is, of course, true that divinities exist only to the extent to which they are believed in and that belief is stimulated by ritual, this dependence of the gods on belief is certainly a fact which never enters the mind of the native. He, for one, is profoundly convinced of the externality and objectivity of his spiritual enemies or protectors, nor does he believe in the waning and waxing of their powers, to keep pace with the periodic changes in nature. Moreover, while the rite may properly be regarded as a battery by means of which the participants are periodically recharged with belief, this function of ritual may easily be exaggerated, nor should other sources be disregarded which tend to preserve accepted belief, such as the forces of tradition, teaching and more strictly individual, as contrasted with social, experience. It must be remembered that ritualism on an extensive scale is, while a common, by no means a constant nor even a predominant characteristic of primitive society. An analysis, from this point of view, of the North American area, for instance, reveals the suggestive fact that ritual *en masse* occurs mainly in the Southwest, Southeast, Northwest, Plains area, and part of the Woodland area, whereas among the Eskimo, in the Mackenzie and Plateau areas and in California, ritual is, speaking generally, an individual or family function. In other words, ritual *en masse* is associated with tribes of a complex social type, where the group is differentiated into many definite social units some of which appear as the carriers of ceremonial functions; while the tribes with a relatively simple social structure, based on the individual family and the local community, are on the whole foreign to ritualism of the above type. This generalization cannot be accepted without certain reservations. The situation is really more complex, and other factors, such, for instance, as diffusion of rituals, would have to be taken into account; such tribes, moreover, as those of the Western Plains or the Nootka combine with a relatively simple type of social organization a relatively complex type of ritualism. Within certain limits, however, the generalization holds. Now, it becomes at once obvious that the intensity of religious belief is not correlated with complex ceremonialism. Among tribes devoid of complex ritualism, other factors must be operative to strengthen and perpetuate the existing belief; and, if that is so, we are also cautioned against the exclusive emphasis on ritual as a generator of belief even where it does occur on a large scale. The gods live not by ritual alone.

As a most glaring instance of an extreme behaviorist position we must regard Durkheim's attempt to account for the qualities nay, in part, even for the survival of the soil, by means of the 'ritualistic mentality.' Elaborate criticisms of hypotheses such as this are futile, for it obviously represents a deliberate effort to disregard the many emotional and conceptual factors which go to the making of the soul-belief in all its aspects, in favor of a simplicist behaviorist explanation. When Durkheim interprets the belief in the efficacy of the intichiuma as a reflection of the rise in social consciousness brought on by the ceremony, he commits a similar error. It seems unjustifiable, for instance, to disregard as a contributing factor in furthering the belief, the observation often made by the natives that the totemic animals and plants actually do multiply soon after the performance of the ceremonies. Durkheim does, indeed, note the fact, but he fails to utilize it in his theory.

Theory of Thought

Whereas the prime object of the author's work is to trace the origin of religious beliefs and notions, he turns repeatedly to the more general problem of thought, of intellectual categories. While the author's remarks on that subject are not extensive nor systematic, enough is said before the volume draws to a close, to make his position stand out in bold relief. No less than the categories of religion the categories of thought are of social origin. The importance of individual experience and of tentative generalizations derived therefrom should not be underestimated, but isolated individual experience lacks the elements necessary to give the notions which thus arise that character of generality and imperativeness which distinguishes the mental categories. *Mana*, the totemic principle, that objectified intuition of society, is the first religious force, but also the prototype of the notion of force in general; just as the concept of soul, the active element in man, is, as shown, of social derivation. Similarly with the category of causality. The 'will to believe' aspect of ritualistic mentality, as manifested, for instance, in the intichiuma ceremonies, has been dwelt on at length. But the belief alone is not sufficient; it would, at best, result in a state of expectancy. The rites must be repeated whenever need is felt of them, and the emotional attitude must be supplemented by a concept, if the intichiuma as a method of constraining or assisting nature is to be counted on. The concept that like produces like becomes a fixed mental category, and behind it is a social mandate. 'The imperatives of thought seem to constitute but another aspect of the imperatives of Will.'

The notion that the qualities of objects can be communicated to their surroundings by a process of propagation, cannot be derived from daily experience, for the phenomenon in question does not occur within the domain of such experience, but constitutes a peculiarity of the religious world. Religious forces, qualities, being themselves but sublimated and transformed aspects of society, are not derived from objects but superadded upon them. The intrinsic virtues of the carriers of religious forces are thus indifferent, and the most insignificant things may become objects of greatest religious import. It is not strange that sacredness can be communicated by contagion from object to object for it is by contagion that sacredness becomes primarily fixed upon objects. Nor is this contagiousness of the religious irrational, for it creates bonds and relations between objects, beings, actions, otherwise disparate, and thus paves the way for future scientific explanations. What was heretofore called the cosmogony of totemism, the classificatory aspect of the most primitive religion, thus becomes the prototype of classification in general, the first source of the notions of genus, subordination, co-ordination.

The mental categories, concludes Durkheim, are not merely instituted by society, but they are, in their origin, but different aspects of society. The category of genus finds its beginning in the concept of the human group; the rhythm of social life is at the basis of the category of time; the space occupied by society is the source of the category of space; the first efficient force is the collective force of society, bringing in its wake the category of causality. The category of totality, finally, can only be of social origin. Society alone completely transcends the individual, rises above all particulars. 'The concept of Totality is but the abstract form of the concept of society: Society is the whole which compromises all things, the ultimate class which embraces all other classes.'

The author's attempt to derive all mental categories from specific phases of social life which have become conceptualized, is so obviously artificial and one-sided that one finds it hard to take his view seriously, but the self-consistency of the argument and, in part, its brilliancy compel one to do so. In criticism we must repeat the argument advanced in another connection in the preceding section: in so far as Durkheim's socially determined categories presuppose a complex and definite social system, his explanatory attempts will fail, wherever such a system is not available. The Eskimo, for example, have no clans nor phratries nor a totemic cosmogony (for they have no totems); how then did their mental categories originate, or is the concept of classification foreign to the Eskimo mind? Obviously, there must be other sources in experience or the psychological constitution of man which may engender mental categories; and, if that is so, we may no longer derive such categories from the social setting, even when the necessary complexity and definiteness are at hand.

In this connection it is well to remember that the origin of mental categories is an eternally recurring event; categories come into being within the mental world of every single individual. We may thus observe that the categories of space, time, force, causality, arise in the mind of the child far ahead of any possible influence from their adult surroundings by way of conscious or even deliberate suggestion. To be sure, these categories are, in the mind of the child, not strictly conceptualized nor even fully within the light of consciousness, but their presence is only too apparent: the individual experience of the child rapidly supplements the congenital predisposition of the mind. Instructive conclusions, bearing on these and other questions of epistemology, could be drawn from a systematic analysis of the grammars of primitive languages. Grammar is but a conceptual shorthand for experience and the means by which a relatively unlimited experience is squeezed into the frame of a strictly limited grammar is classification. Now, while the psychic processes underlying grammatical categories fall notoriously below the level of consciousness, they do nevertheless represent the deepest and most fundamental tendencies of the mind which, without doubt, provide the foundation for later, more conscious mental efforts, in similar directions. While no intensive study of primitive grammars, from the above point of view, has as yet been made, enough is known to foresee that but a fraction of the categories thus revealed will prove of specifically social derivation.

There remains another equally fundamental criticism to be made of Durkheim's doctrine. As we have seen, the author maintains that infectiousness is a specifically religious phenomenon. It does not seem that even the infectiousness of the sacred has been satisfactorily accounted for by the author. For, granting that sacredness is not inherent in objects but projected into them, that fact would not, *per se*, explain why sacredness should be so readily communicable from object to object. The Australian is not aware of the extraneous character of the sanctity of things, and surely it would be impossible for him to believe that his consciousness is if not the ultimate, yet the proximate source of that sanctity. Hence, the infectiousness of the sacred remains, from that standpoint, inexplicable. Another instance of the psychologist's fallacy! This, however, is but a minor point. But can we follow the author in his assertion that infectiousness is peculiar to the sacred and that the quality is foreign to experience outside of the religious realm? Assuredly not. Daily observations brings before the mind of the savage numerous instances of the communicability of qualities. Wet comes from wet, and cold from cold; red ochre makes things red and so does blood, while dirt makes them dirty; touching rough surfaces brings roughness of skin and soreness; intimate contact with strongly smelling substances communicates the smell; heat, finally, produces heat—and pain. If the sacred is infectious, so is profane nature, and the mind which learns from the one its first lesson in categorizing can learn it from the other as well. It will be seen that the above criticism is based on a special instance. It must now be generalized. The exclusive emphasis on the religious and ultimately on the social as the source of the fundamental categories of thought is unjustifiable in view of the rich variety of profane experience which is amenable to like conceptualization. While the point, when made in this general form, is fairly obvious, much interesting research work in this neglected field of primitive mentality remains to be done. The magico-religious aspect of primitive life and thought has for years monopolized our attention to such an extent that the less picturesque but no less real concrete experience of the savage has remained almost completely in the background. What does the savage know? should be the question. A vast store of data is available, on which to base our answer, and more can be procured.

The principal criticisms here passed on Durkheim's work may now be summarized as follows:

The selection of Australia as the practically exclusive source of information must be regarded as unfortunate, in view of the imperfection of the data. The charge is aggravated through the circumstance that the author regards the case of Australia as typical and tends to generalize from it.

The Theory of Religion is deficient in so far as it involves the commingling in one definition of disparate aspects of the religious complex. Many of the special points made in the course of the work are thus prejudged; the individual and subjective aspect of religion, in particular, thus fails to receive proper attention.

The Theory of Totemism suffers from the disregard of the ethnological point of view which forces upon us the conviction that the institution must be regarded as highly complex historically and psychologically. The resulting interpretation of the totemic complex, while giving evidence of Durkheim's superior psychological insight and often brilliant argumentation, recalls by its one-sidedness and artificiality the contributions to the subject on the part of the classical anthropologists.

The Theory of Social Control must be rejected on account of its underestimation as well as overestimation of the social, involving a fundamental misconception of the relation of the individual to society. For, on the one hand, the individual becomes, in Durkheim's presentation, completely absorbed in the social; society itself, on the other hand, is not conceived as a historical complex but as a sublimated crowd.

The Theory of Ritual, while involving much true insight, is narrowly behavioristic and rationalistic and fails to do justice to the direct effect of experience upon the mind. The conception of the subjective side of religion as an after-thought, consequent upon and explanatory of action, must be vigorously rejected.

The Theory of Thought, finally, suffers from an exclusive emphasis on socio-religious experiences as the sources of mental categories, to the all but complete exclusion of the profane experience of the savage and the resulting knowledge of the concrete facts and processes in Nature.

Thus the central thesis of the book that the fundamental reality underlying religion is society, must be regarded as unproved.

15

G. Richard   1923

'Dogmatic atheism in the sociology of religion'

First published in French as 'L'Athéisme dogmatique en sociologie religieuse' in *Revue d'histoire et de philosophie religieuse*, 1923, pp. 125–37, 229–61.

I (i)

From now on sociology will form a part of the official teaching syllabus in France. Recent regulations for higher education make it the main subject of one of the four certificates that candidates for the Licentiate in Philosophy must produce and regulations relating to elementary education have introduced a great deal of sociology into the curriculum of teachers' training colleges.[1] In future even an elementary study of this science can and must exercise a profound influence on the teaching profession at all levels. This influence will be a very fortunate one if it brings together historical and philosophical disciplines which have been rivals for far too long—if it puts an end to the conflict between scientific methods and ethical ideals—if finally it gives a common social discipline to teachers in secondary and elementary education. Before these desirable results can be obtained, however, it is undoubtedly necessary for teachers of sociology to refrain from discussing certain contentious topics and to abstain from presenting to the young in training colleges, even more than elsewhere, hypotheses or even conjectures as if they were established scientific conclusions. The specific study of social facts must never be allowed to degenerate into speculation.

Above all it is in matters of religion that this prudence is desirable. The teaching of sociology, like all other teaching, is subject to the fundamental rule of impartiality and neutrality. Properly interpreted, this rule does not prevent the teacher from examining religious thought impartially; it does not require that he should avoid or set aside questions where the expression of religious thought presents itself as part of experience. What it does exclude is the possibility of a dogmatism prescribed by the state about the origin and nature of religion, especially if this dogmatism is radically incompatible with beliefs very frequently expressed by parents and often by the teachers themselves.

On this score, the attitude apparently underlying the teaching of sociology demands examination. It cannot be denied that one school, that of Durkheim, is trying to monopolize the teaching of sociology in France, and is attempting to use the new curricula as a means of ensuring the widest possible spread of its doctrines even in teacher training colleges. Nor can it be denied that this school tends to identify sociology with a certain conception of the origins of religion, its nature, its social role, and ultimately its history. In the end, it is incontrovertible that this sociology of religion (*sociologie religieuse*),[2] as it is called, is incompatible not only with Christian faith, but even with philosophical theism, and indeed with any belief that recognizes, hypothetically at least, a divine personality.

Many first-rate minds especially among members of the teaching profession consider this to be a regrettable situation, not only because it runs counter to the hope of religious peace which is so ardently desired, particularly in Alsace, but also because it casts doubts on the very future of the teaching of sociology, which might one day give rise to a conflict between state education on the one hand and the church or the family on the other.

Consequently there is no cause for surprise if in this estimable journal, a professor of social science tries to examine the claims of the sociology of religion to be a science forming part of the education prescribed by the state.

What we are trying to discover is whether this sociology called religious (perhaps ironically) has the right to set itself up as an impartial science, neutral in the matter of belief, a science really based on observation, history and induction, or whether it conceals a metaphysics run riot, backed up by an artificial interpretation of the history of beliefs and practices.

I (ii)

The term, sociology of religion, was coined by *L'Année sociologique* which was edited by Émile Durkheim. The term first appeared in 1898, when it referred to one of the six sections of the journal which dealt with the direction taken by sociological research, and especially the objective study of the sources of the new science.[3] It was soon clear, however, that the sociology of religion was the main concern of *L'Année sociologique*, that it was inspired by a definite doctrine of nature, the origin and evolution of religion, and that this doctrine went well beyond the bounds of a special science of societies. A series of monographs, some of them from the pen of Durkheim, others from those of Mauss and Hubert, prepared and heralded the book which was to epitomize the doctrine. This book, *Les Formes élémentaires de la vie religieuse*, finally appeared in 1912.[4] Its author presented it as a study of Australian totemism but the ambition of its conclusions contrasted strangely with the modesty, even timidity, of the title. It was a theory of religion without God, of religion reduced to the level of a simple social phenomenon, of religion as a characteristic of primitive societies. It was also a theory of the origin of knowledge, a solution to the old scholastic problem of the innateness of ideas and of principles determining experience. This is in fact metaphysics, if the subject of metaphysics is above all the study not only of the nature of knowledge but its value, along with the discovery of whether or not subject and object are fundamentally identical. Durkheim accepted such a monist doctrine. Sociology of religion was used to show that society is at one and the same time subject and object, a unique rational subject and a total object, since it is equivalent to the universe.[5]

In rashly moving from an analysis of the ritual practices of the small tribes of central Australia to a complete system regarding the nature and value of knowledge, rather like Berkeley in *Siris* who led his reader from the properties of tar-water to an exposition of absolute idealism, Durkheim seemed to reject all the rules which he had laid down for sociological research in a well-known book published by him seventeen years earlier. At that time he insisted on the independence of sociology from all philosophy. This was the necessary condition for the existence of sociology.[6]

It is independent of all philosophy. Because sociology is born of great philosophical doctrines, it has retained the habit of leaning on some system on which it is then dependent. This explains why it has been successively positivist, evolutionary and *spiritualiste*, when it ought to have been satisfied with just being sociology.... It is not for sociology to take sides between the great hypotheses which divide metaphysicians. Nor must sociology come down on the side of free will against determinism. All it asks is that the principle of causality should apply to social phenomena.... Philosophy can only gain by its emancipation from sociology. *Until the sociologist has adequately rid himself of the philosopher, he will only consider social things in their most general aspect, the aspect in which they most resemble the other things of the universe.*

Less than two decades have passed and sociology has become the basis for speculation reminiscent of, but distinct from the speculation of Schelling, Hegel and Lamennais. This speculation has led to a pantheistic formula which was not very original in itself and from which the very possibility of a specific science of societies has evaporated.

From that time until the very moment of its inclusion in the official teaching syllabus, sociology has risked losing the characteristics which make it a science. It is now no more than a hypothesis about reason and its immediate objects. Teachers of philosophy are currently speaking of a *school of sociology* whose debates have become exercises in schools. Is this really what Durkheim wanted? *Ut pueris placeas et declamatio fias!*

If, however, there were no sociology, if societies and social phenomena could not be scientifically studied, there would be no need of a sociology of religion or even a school of sociology. The question then is to know why religion in France has become the principal object of sociological research and has come to be viewed as a social phenomenon. We are thus led to seek the position occupied by the study of religion in the works of Durkheim prior to the founding of *L'Année sociologique*. There we shall have the opportunity of discovering the origin of the error which led Durkheim astray and along with him a good number of teachers who studied sociology under him.

It is our opinion that, despite himself, Durkheim has been led by the inexorable demands of logic to leave the field of sociological induction which he had attempted to define in his youth and to transform the outline of a science into a noncritical metaphysical system. He has done this because from the beginning he expected too much of the science of social phenomena which, nevertheless, he intended to extricate from the hold of the positivism of Comte and the evolutionism of Spencer. His presumption consisted in creating a theory of the social milieu in order to explain moral obligation. Morality, imprisoned by him in social phenomenology, took its revenge by steering him towards metaphysics, and an initial error about the nature of morality led him into graver metaphysical errors about the nature of religion.

I (iii)

What we must do is to try to discover that conception of the relations between morality and religion which is revealed by reading the early works of Durkheim, the works which preceded the monographs which he wrote in *L'Année sociologique* and the paper he presented at the Bologna Conference on 'Jugements de valeur', and finally *Les Formes élémentaires de la vie religieuse*. There are four works to be considered. Two are doctoral theses, *De la Division du travail social*,[7] and a Latin thesis *La Contribution de Montesquieu à la sociologie*,[8] two years later came *Les Règles de la méthode sociologique*, and after a further interval of two years, *Le Suicide*.[9]

These four books can be reduced to three, for the thesis on Montesquieu is clearly a preliminary version of *Les Règles de la méthode sociologique*.[10] The *Division du travail* and *Les Règles* were conceived and elaborated at the same time. The methodology set out in the second of these publications is a justification (a very imperfect one) of the theory of the forms of social solidarity stated in the first. Is *Suicide* any different? No one can doubt it if he gives to this work (Durkheim's least known but best argued and most significant work because of its practical conclusions) all the attention it merits. If *Les Règles* constitutes the logical introduction to the *Division de travail*, *Suicide* is intended to develop its conclusions. The statistics for suicide, that is to say the indirect measure of the value which social man accords life, ratifies the law obeyed in the inevitable changes in types of solidarity. It must convince us that henceforward a morality which is totally adequate to the division of labour and to the ensuing organic solidarity, that is to say a strictly professional morality, can alone cure us of the *taedium vitae*, whose origin is the inevitable weakness of religious solidarity.

Thus it is necessary to seek (1) the definition of religion revealed by this series of books, and (2) its relation to the hypothesis of primitive totemism.

Ostensibly a reading of *Les Règles* does not enlighten us very much. Yet we cannot entirely neglect it. Indeed, we see there the method prescribed by the author for himself and for us with regard to the study of religion. *Nobody ought to study religion while taking into the slightest account his own experience of religious life.* What William James was to call 'religious experience' is totally excluded. It would be 'giving to the inferior faculties of intelligence supremacy over the highest'.[11] Until then we had believed that if the precondition for speaking with some discernment about art and poetry was to have feelings for art and poetry oneself, so the precondition for the man wishing to understand the believer and societies of believers is to have believed himself at some moment of his life, or at least been linked to a belief by affection and feeling. Obviously a grave mistake! James Darmesteter wrote[12]

> unhappy is the scholar who approaches the things of God without having in the depths of his *conscience*, in the furthermost recesses of his being, where the souls of his ancestors lie, an unknown sanctuary whence rises intermittently a perfume of incense, the line of a psalm, a cry of pain or of triumph, to which as a child he had given utterance to heaven (etc.).

Durkheim considers that there are no limits in combating 'such a mystical doctrine which is disguised as empiricism, the negation of all that is scientific'. Hence from the beginning, the sociology of religion prohibits the observation of religious feeling, of religion as an interior life of the soul. The sociologist has no intention of concerning himself with what leads a man to religion. He will take it as an external fact, which is historically given. The believer is not a man who feels and lives his belief personally, he is an automaton who receives a ready-made, pre-existing religion from outside. 'The believer has found the beliefs and practices of religious life ready made when he is born; if they existed before him, it is because they exist outside him.'[13]

What is the creative force of religion which pre-exists its adherents and which functions outside each of them? It would seem that here there is a mystery which the weakness of our understanding must find more disconcerting than any of the most subtle propositions of theology. The first two works of Durkheim are an attempt to explain this mystery.

De la Division du travail social is, one knows, a theory of the origins and changes in the nature of moral obligation. Obligation is a form of constraint which every society imposes on its members. Accordingly, it is in keeping with the nature of social solidarity. Now there are two major forms of solidarity, one of resemblance and one of conjunction, that is, co-operation among dissimilar elements. Today we only really experience the second, which is more indirect, less narrow, and less coercive than the first. Solidarity in the form of resemblance, however, which Durkheim called mechanical, is the historical antecedent of co-operative or organic solidarity and was the pre-condition of its appearance. Men were unable to achieve this division of all kinds of functions straight away, which makes each dependent on the others. History and comparative ethnography prove that men have tried many forms of social order, the horde, the tribe, and then the city prior to feudalism, from which gradually and partially sprang the modern world.

It is at this point that religion and the schematic unfolding of its history is encountered (Bk I, ch. V, section V).[14] Durkheim recognizes that he does not yet possess a 'scientific concept of religion'. He should have in fact treated the problem 'by the comparative method applicable to the phenomenon of crime' (p. 182). Let us accept the analogy although it is not necessary to push it further and to realize that [ibid.]

> religion is not at each moment of history the totality of beliefs
> and feelings of all kinds, relative to the relationships between
> man and a being or beings whose nature he regards as superior to
> his own. Such a definition is manifestly inadequate.

Many religious rules apply to relationships of quite a different kind. What are these rules? They are rules governing ritual (p. 182).

Religion forbids the Jew to eat certain kinds of meat, orders him to dress in a specific way; imposes a given doctrine regarding the nature of man and of things, as well as the origins of the world; very often regulates legal, moral and economic relationships. Accordingly, its sphere of action extends far beyond the dealings between the man and the divine. Besides we are assured that there exists at least one religion without a god. It would be sufficient for this single fact to be well established for us to no longer have the right to define religion as a function of the idea of God.

It can be seen that from the beginning and for a long time before studying totemism, Durkheim was ready (1) to identify religion with ritual, (2) to attribute social or rather collective functions to it, (3) to judge it independent of the idea of God. He takes care to inform us in a note that this religion 'without a god' on which he would base his induction is Buddhism.

We can immediately draw the conclusion that the history of religion is not an evolution but a dissolution. 'If there is one truth that history has proved without doubt it is that religion now encompasses a smaller part of social life.' It is even by virtue of this claim that its history interests sociology: it takes the place of an experiment on the transformation of solidarity in the form of resemblance.[15]

Originally it encompassed everything; everything social and religious; *the two words were synonymous.* Gradually the political, economic and scientific functions broke away from the religious function, they were separately constituted and took on an ever more obvious secular character. God, who, if we may put it in this way, was once present in all human activities, has progressively withdrawn from them; he has abandoned the world to men and their quarrels.

It is a mistake to attribute this secularization to modern free thought.[16]

Individualism or free thought can be dated not to our own time, nor to 1789, nor to the Reformation, nor to scholasticism, nor to the fall of the Graeco-Roman polytheism, nor yet to the oriental theocracies. It is a phenomenon which has no beginning but which has developed ceaselessly throughout history.

Perhaps, if the truth were told, this progress was not a rectilinear
one.[17]

We must consider only societies at the same point in their
development. For example, we must compare Christian societies
of the Middle Ages with primitive Rome, and primitive Rome
with early Greek cities. It can consequently be stated that this
progress, regression if you like, has taken place without a gap as
it were. We have here an inescapable law which it would be folly
to rebel against.

This progress or this regression! Here, it must be believed, we
have the decisive formula revealing the idea behind the beginning of
the sociology of religion. *Even before it was scientifically
constituted, the history of religions had its inescapable law. The law
was that the evolution of religion is regression or rather dissolution.*
The proof is that religion absorbs and persecutes society less and
less. It never occurred to Durkheim that religion could be a principle
of inner life for the individual and that this function of individual
morality corresponds to the growing relationship between the
conscience religieuse and the idea of God. In his eyes, religion can
only be revealed by constraint, that is to say by persecution. A
religion uniting the affirmation of the divine ideal with that of the
value of the human personality seems to be for him an impossibility.

I (iv)

A second proof was needed. It is in *Suicide* that we find it sketched
out. To anyone who wants to have an account of the formation of
the sociology of religion, the importance of this work is even greater
than that of the *Division du travail*.

This book has put off a great many readers by reason of the
numerous statistical tables that need to be studied. Such laziness is
blameworthy. In fact, anyone who has not studied *Suicide* knows
nothing and understands nothing of the work of Durkheim. It is
there that he formulates his conclusions about the reorganization of
contemporary society by corporations;[18] it is there that he states his
pathology of society.[19] Finally, it is there also that one must seek his
theory of advanced religions and the societies associated with them.
In it he satisfies one of the *desiderata* that he acknowledged in the
Division du travail; in it, too, he uses comparative statistics to study

religion in the same way as criminality. Durkheim employs three sets of comparisons: (1) Judaism and Christianity, (2) Catholicism and Protestantism, also contrasting different kinds of Protestantism, (3) monotheistic religions and the pantheism of India. Moreover, these religions are compared from one point of view only, namely, the immunity from suicide they confer on their adherents and the consequent value they accord to human life.

We must not be in too much of a hurry to judge the sets of comparisons as being superficial, or to say that they are based on pure coincidence. The major question in fact is to know whether in the process of evolution towards an abstract ideal, religion is capable of teaching man respect for his essential nature and above all respect for his own life. The frequency of suicide can be in this respect a fairly useful criterion. Suicide is indeed a form of homicide which, according to statisticians, replaces other forms of homicide. Its frequency is often in inverse ratio to that of murder. The law controls murder much more easily and effectively than suicide. Immunity against suicide can only be of a moral nature.

The plan adopted by Durkheim facilitates the comparison he makes of advanced religions—religions which have aspired to universality. He classes them according to the relations they maintain with the types of suicide that he distinguishes. In his view, suicide is not an individual act but a social act (*chose*). He applies to his study the strange method of wanting to impose on sociologists the study of social facts and the elimination of feelings and individual will. Suicide is merely the symbol of social currents of which some are altruistic, some egoistic, others anomic. (We are given to understand that anomic suicide is the result of discord in economic affairs.)[20]

If some daylight is to be shed on these subtle distinctions, we might say that man can kill himself as a result of altruism, or as a result of egoism, or finally as a result of being influenced by despair born of inadequate social support. If we disregard the unintelligible anomic form of suicide (which Durkheim could easily have classified with egoistic suicide, as it corresponds to the absence of a form of solidarity, that is, corporate solidarity) we conclude that in his system, life in the eyes of the individual loses its value just as much as being inextricably caught up in the toils of social constraint, as in ceasing to feel its importance. In both cases, religion as the expression of social solidarity will intervene and it will thus be possible to measure the progress of its decline.

Altruistic suicide is a form of sacrifice.[21] In our civilization it is to be observed among soldiers.[22] In simple societies, however, it assumes or used to assume a religious form. The religions of India can serve as an example.[23]

> The religions and metaphysical systems which serve as a logical
> framework to these moral practices,[24] succeed in proving
> that this is definitely the origin and significance of it. It has been
> known for a long time that they generally exist along with
> pantheistic beliefs. It is true that Jainism, like Buddhism, is
> atheistic, but *pantheism is not necessarily theistic.* What
> essentially characterizes it is the idea that the real part of the
> individual is foreign to his nature, that the soul which animates
> him is not his soul and that in consequence he has no personal
> existence.

We must not believe that it is the depressing influence of this pantheistic religion which, in India and among a large number of oriental peoples, has sanctioned the abasement of the individual.[25]

> We must not admit that pantheism produces suicide. . . .
> *Religious ideas are the products of the social environment rather*
> *than the reverse and if they react on the causes which engendered*
> *them, once they have been formed, this reaction cannot be very*
> *far-reaching.* If then, what constitutes pantheism is a more or less
> radical negation of all individuality, such a religion can only be
> formed at the heart of a society where in fact the individual
> counts for nothing, that is to say, is almost completely lost in
> the group. *For men can only visualize the world in the image of*
> *the small social world in which they live.*

It was necessary to reproduce this text literally despite its length. It proves to us the extent to which the sociology of religion was deductively constituted before an examination of the facts and at a date when Durkheim had not yet embarked on the study of totemism.

Indian pantheism is therefore very much at the point of the development of religion where religion, as the faithful expression of the *conscience collective*, still includes the whole of human life. Monotheistic religions, on the other hand, correspond to the stage of its dissolution (i.e. of the *conscience collective*). They enable us to follow the process, for they express this disintegration very irregularly. Here Durkheim indeed adds little to the views expressed by Auguste Comte in the *Cours de philosophie positive* and in the *Système de politique positive*. Comte sees in monotheism only an abstraction of polytheism, which itself is an abstraction of fetishism. For Durkheim the tendency towards monotheism at the successive points of its progress, expresses the slackening of this solidarity which took away from the individual the *conscience* of his personality. Durkheim only changes Comte's method by substituting the analysis of moral statistics for that of history.

The problem now is to define the relation between monotheistic religions and the egoistic form of suicide. The three religions considered are Judaism, Catholicism and Protestantism from which Anglicanism is distinguished. Durkheim recognizes that they are unanimous in condemning suicide and in threatening with eternal damnation those who commit it. Yet the immunity they confer on their faithful from the *taedium vitae* is very unequal. By dint of grouping the statistics carefully, of retaining the facts favourable to the thesis, and of leaving the embarrassing ones in the dark, Durkheim succeeds in showing (1) that the Jew is better protected from suicide than the Catholic; (2) that he in his turn is better off in this respect than the Protestant; (3) that among Protestants the Anglican is better off than the Lutheran, the Calvinist, or a member of any other denomination. *The power of immunity is in inverse ratio to the liberty of thought that these religions allow to individuals.*[26] Let us note the judgment on Protestantism.[27]

> The leaning of Protestantism towards suicide must be relative to the spirit of free enquiry which animates this religion. We must endeavour to understand this relationship properly. Liberty of thought is in itself only the effect of another cause. When, after a long time of accepting their faith ready-made by tradition, men claim the right to make it for themselves, it is not because of the intrinsic attractions of the freedom of enquiry, for this brings as much pain with it as joy; it is because from now on they have need of this liberty. Now this need can only have one cause: the undermining of traditional beliefs. If they asserted themselves with the same force as formerly, we would not ever consider questioning them. If they still retained the same authority we would not wish to verify the source of their authority.

It is still, as we can see, the same identification of religion with external constraint, akin to persecution. Tolerance is the sign of disintegration.[28]

Ideas which are shared by a whole society draw from this common assent an authority which makes them sacrosanct and sets them beyond dispute. For them to be more tolerant they must already have become the object of less general and less complete adherence, they must have been weakened by previous controversies.

I have known ministers who were moved by this appreciation of Protestantism. They were too ingenuous. Durkheim, merely in interpreting certain statistical data relating to suicide in Germany, appropriated a polemical procedure much favoured by the German Catholic clergy.[29] Protestantism here becomes a supernumerary. It represents, irrespective of its actions or aims, the last degree of disintegration of religion, in the sense that positivist sociology gives to the term—religion as the pressure of the *conscience collective* on the *conscience individuelle*. This characteristic is one it has in common with all monotheistic religions. It is an essential manifestation of the inevitable law which decrees that the development of religion is identified with its disintegration.

The sociology of religion of Durkheim was fixed in its main outlines at a date when, the author admits, religion had not been the subject of methodical study. *Suicide* and the *Division du travail* are like two volumes of the same book dealing with the nature of social solidarity. *A priori*, to some extent, Durkheim deduced from his idea of solidarity that 'religious ideas are the products of the social environment' and the environment whence they originally issued is that which leaves to the *conscience individuelle* no opportunity of forming or manifesting itself. These conclusions were not drawn from a laborious study of Indian religion or Australian totemism as is readily believed today. They preceded this study; they prejudiced later interpretations.

In setting about the task of developing the sociology of religion, Durkheim was motivated solely by the necessity of justifying his essential and basically contradictory thesis—the identity of evolution and dissolution, of development and regression, within the framework of the history of religions. Did he succeed? That is what we hope to discover in a later article.

II (i)

In 1907 the *Revue néo-scolastique* published a signed article by Simon Deploige, a professor at the University of Louvain, on the genesis of Durkheim's system. This promoted an exchange of correspondence of the greatest possible interest to us. The Belgian critic saw a reflection of German thought in Durkheim's theories. Durkheim himself was particularly concerned with re-establishing the evolution of his ideas and proclaimed himself to be, we believe with justification, a disciple of Auguste Comte who developed his ideas. In this correspondence there is one letter that we should note because it gives information about the origins of the sociology of religion and even more about its transformation. The letter in question is that dated 20 November 1907. In it we read:[30]

On page 343 note 1, it is affirmed that I found in Wundt the idea that religion is the matrix of moral and judicial ideas, etc. I read Wundt in 1887 and yet it was only in 1895 that I had a clear understanding of the important role played by religion in social life. It was in that year that I found the method of approaching the study of religion sociologically for the first time. It was a revelation to me. During 1895 a line of demarcation was drawn in the development of my thought, so much so that all my earlier research had to be looked at afresh and made to harmonize with these new views. Wundt's *Ethik* which I had read eight years previously had nothing to do with this change in direction. It was entirely the result of the studies of religious history which I had just undertaken, notably the reading of the work of Robertson Smith and his school.

Therefore, when in 1893, Durkheim published his doctoral thesis, the *Division du travail social*, he had not yet 'found the method of approaching the study of religion sociologically'. We know, however, that from that moment he thought he knew the laws of history and the identity of the development of religion along with its regression. Would he uphold this law? Would he modify it? Would he repudiate it?

A retraction was possible although it would have entailed as a consequence a fairly far-reaching modification of the theory of solidarity. Systematization had not yet been pushed so far however—the theory of collective understanding had not been sufficiently formulated—for it to be impossible to turn back in the light of more complete and certain information. Is this what happened?

In 1897, two years after the events of 1895 when 'a line of demarcation was drawn' in the development of his thought, Durkheim published *Suicide*. We have established that, far from abandoning the law of the continuous and inevitable regression of religion in his work, he affirmed it even more clearly than in the *Division du travail*.

Suicide may have only appeared in 1897 but it was in fact prepared and written long before. It was thus dependent on a scientific elaboration as yet uninfluenced by the effect of religious studies. It must be noted that in it Durkheim accepts on these terms the authorship of a plan of social and moral reorganization where religion no longer has a role to play. Can religion, will religion ever be able to remedy this collective melancholy which leads increasing numbers of men to deprive themselves of life? Not at all.[31]

> Religion moderates the leaning towards suicide only to the extent that it prevents man from thinking freely. This taking over of the individual intelligence is a difficult thing to do now and it will continue to become increasingly so. It offends our dearest sentiments. More and more we refuse to admit that we can define the limits of reason and say to it: you must go no further. This is not a movement which started only yesterday; the history of mankind is the very history of the progress of free thought. It is puerile, therefore, to wish to delete a current which so far proved irresistible. *Unless the great societies of today disintegrate irrevocably and we return to the small social groups of former times, unless humanity returns to its point of departure, religions will no longer be able to exercise great and widespread power over* consciences.

The very fact, however, that in 1898 Durkheim assumed the editorship of *L'Année sociologique* to which he became the most prolific contributor, that in 1902 he was installed in the Chair of the Science of Education at the Sorbone, that he published in his *Revue* a considerable number of monographs on the most diverse topics,[32] that in 1911 he presented at the International Congress of Philosophy held at Bologna a very important study on 'Jugements de valeur et de réalité',[33] that in the meanwhile he was actively engaged with the affairs of the *Revue philosophique* on the one hand and the *Revue de métaphysique et de morale* on the other, in which from 1909 onwards he was publishing the introduction to the great work that was to appear in 1912, *Les Formes élémentaires de la vie religieuse*—all these facts might lead us to expect a revision of the hasty and badly substantiated conclusions that he had put forward in his early works. We felt all the more entitled to expect an honourable retraction as sociology was taking an ever more important place in state education.

The extent to which Durkheim was then modifying and expanding his notion of the subject and scope of sociological studies is known. In *Les Règles de la méthode*, sociology had been presented as a very special science, rigorously inductive and historical, independent of all philosophy. Eight years later it was being challenged about its ability to arrive at truly general laws, and was being reduced to the modest dimensions of a 'corpus of social sciences'. It was then to become the theory of collective understanding and to see itself called upon to resolve the very problems of the origin of knowledge.[34] What a good opportunity for revising hasty and imprudent solutions!

Did the study of 'religious phenomena' lead Durkheim to reject this hypothesis according to which the development of religions and their relations to society is merely a regression, as uninterrupted as it is inevitable? This is the question raised by the study of *Les Formes élémentaires* (disregarding all more specifically philosophical problems). Did Durkheim succeed (or think he had succeeded) in verifying his first conclusions? If not, was he an impartial critic of his own work?

II (ii)

The plan of the book is in itself instructive. The introduction declares that it is to be the study of a religion independent of the idea of God. The first book is an examination of positivist hypotheses of religion; the second is devoted to totemic beliefs; the third to ritual attitudes. Two chapters, however, of Book II deal with the twofold belief of primitive peoples in the soul and in God, almost as if they were secondary ideas. The conclusion is a theory about the relationship between religion and science, which is completed by the presentation of a theory of concepts which transforms itself into a critical revision of the main contemporary systems of knowledge—those of Lévy-Bruhl and Bergson. An effort was obviously made not to define the important distinguishing characteristics of religion but to reduce it to something which, in the eyes of the religious man, is no longer religion at all, and to abstract it from all religious experience worthy of the name. Contrary to the enlightened advice of James Darmesteter, the method formulated in the *Règles de la méthode* has been faithfully adhered to. But is it not the value of this method which is in dispute? Was it not precisely this which W. James had discredited in his book of worldwide interest on *The Varieties of Religious Experience*,[35] which Abauzit through his translation has put within the grasp of the French public?

The conclusions of *Les Formes élémentaires* does not retain the hypothesis of regression 'as uninterrupted as it is inevitable' without some modification. The unity of religion is divided into two. In it we have an intellectual element and an affective element. The intellectual element, which is belief, is open to variation and liable to decline. The affective element is permanent. A few pages are even dedicated to a brief examination of W. James's book—James being classified as an 'apologist for the faith' (p. 596). Durkheim recognizes that for the believer religion does not represent an enrichment of his knowledge but an increase in his power (ibid.). He concedes that 'this unanimous sentiment of believers all through history cannot be purely illusory'. This, however, is immediately followed by '*the objective, universal and eternal* [!] *cause of those* sui generis *sensations of which religious experience consists is society*', or that only society 'awakens the feeling of support, protection, and tutelary dependence which links the believer to his cult'.[36] In other words, the interior God which W. James disentangles from a multitude of impartially analysed experiences and testimonies, and which the psychologist attempts to reduce to a *subliminal* 'I', is replaced in the mind of the sociologist not by social man, the socialized individual, but by society exterior to man, of which a horde of black Australians, the Blackfellows, are deemed to be the best example!

I think we are entitled to ask ourselves whether, after seventeen years dedicated to the sociological study of religion (1895–1912), Durkheim succeeded in doing more than to elucidate the formula he had stated in his earlier works, namely, that it is a form of solidarity condemned to retrogression or disintegration by the very laws of its formation and development.

Let it be noted that for religion to retrogress slowly and steadily from one social type to another without at the same time disappearing, without being able to predict its total and future disappearance, there must be a permanent element in it as durable as man himself. There must also have been originally some major function that religion fulfilled. Otherwise, this indefinite regression which in the *Division du travail* corresponded to the continuous metamorphosis of the solidarity of resemblance, would take on the form of an unintelligible mystery.

If this is the case, it becomes evident that the sole object of *Les Formes élémentaires* is to acquaint us with both the permanent element which decreases towards a minimum below which it cannot fall and the original function which can be eroded by the very fact that it has been accomplished. The permanent element of religion is collective emotion. Its original function was to enable the human intelligence to progress beyond animal sensations (pp. 336–42). [See pp. 139–44 in this book.—W.S.F.P.] The function was therefore to make possible the first affirmations of collective understanding and then to allow the transition from empiricism to science, a transition which otherwise could not have taken place. There is no need to seek the unity of the two elements elsewhere than in the experience of social life. It alone can arouse collective emotion and give rise to its formation; it alone helps man to consider and comprehend the persistence of the relation between a progressive element, science which is the product of collective understanding, and a stable element, which is of an inferior nature, that is, collective emotion. How can an emotion, even a collective one, react so extensively on mental activity? There lies the true mystery of the theory. It is not a greater mystery than the gulf artificially created between human and animal intelligence, and even more artificially closed up by the call to sociability, as if man were the only sociable animal! Still, let us not ask any more awkward questions.

Religion appears to be explained through the eyes of someone who considers it without living it and who only sees it to be a purely exterior phenomenon. In actual fact it is stripped of everything peculiar to it and everything which distinguishes it from other modes of affective and intellectual life. In this way it is reduced to a primitive form of science, an embryonic science destined to be replaced by the many-sided and unrestricted science of today. Reduced to a system of collective emotions and ritual practices which have also been replaced to a great extent by our poetry and art, nothing remains to religion which would enable us to distinguish the religious man from the non-religious man, and one type of believer from another. Today, in the midst of our cosmopolitan civilization—our society of nations—what criterion can we adopt to distinguish one believer from another, the Christian from the Moslem, from the Buddhist; always assuming, and this is quite possible, that each of them has received the same scientific education as the other two? In our Western, or even national environment, how are we to distinguish the Catholic from the Protestant or Jew? This may appear to be a very trifling question yet it would seem that anyone who cannot answer it has nothing to tell us about the nature of religion. Do not the free thinker and the believer, the Christian and the Jew, have the same scientific background, and often the same collective emotions? Where then is the source of the variety of their religious experience to be found?

Here we can compare the work of Durkheim with that of the psychologists. Let us eliminate those he classifies as 'apologists for the faith' and consider only psychologists with positivist training and outlook. We observe in the case of these, notably Ribot, that the problem is to discover the specific character of the religious sentiment, that which, in the order of the emotions or the passions distinguishes it from other sentiments with which it is often associated such as the social, moral and aesthetic sentiments. Here we have, to be sure, work which is scientific and very fruitful in pedagogic or political applications.[37] Compared with theirs, Durkheim's work is conservative. It brings back the confusion dispelled by the analysis of the psychologists: a confusion authorized by history no more than by psychology, for if psychology sees in the social sentiment a simple transformation of the family sentiment, which cannot seriously be identified with religious sentiment, history shows us that too often religious sentiment has violated social sentiments, notably compassion, and even family sentiments by authorizing human sacrifice and even the sacrifice of children.

Aided by the convenient ambiguity which always and everywhere leads him to make the identification of the collective with the social, Durkheim assimilates the religious sentiment into every category of sentiments, however different they may be. For him, the characteristic of religious sentiment is exaltation. He does not for an instant consider discussing the opinion of James and Boutroux, who cite serenity and moral equilibrium as being the effects of religion. Durkheim sees religious man as an energumen—people must forgive the word. Religion cannot be distinguished from a dionysiac or orgiastic state which is incompatible with any moral *conscience* tempered by reflection, and it is very difficult to reconcile with that logical thought of which, according to the hypothesis, religion is the source.

The examples he quotes are such as to win sympathetic adherents to his thesis.[38]

> What essential difference is there between an assembly of
> Christians celebrating the main events of the life of Christ, or
> Jews keeping either the Exodus from Egypt or the promulgation
> of the Decalogue, or a gathering of citizens commemorating the
> institution of a new moral charter or some great event in the life
> of the nation?

To this question Durkheim seems to expect unanimous, affirmative replies. It is likely, however, that the psychologist and the historian will raise objections. 'There can be no society', says Durkheim, 'which does not feel the need at regular intervals to maintain and strengthen collective sentiments and ideas which constitute its unity and personality.'[39] Agreed, but this is no less true of a group of drinkers, gastronomes, race-goers, sportsmen, enthusiasts, and gamblers, as of an association of patriots or a community of believers. Everywhere, the act of gathering reinforces collective states without drawing a distinction between them. In all cases the law of psychological unison produces its effects. Each one of these groups could, accordingly, be a focus of religious emotion. As a result, we are faced with a veritable enigma.

What happens when the gathering is over? In so far as it is collective, it has ceased to exist. Does it not persist as a desire, an aspiration, a passion even? A gathering of music-lovers, lovers of painting and poetry, will feel a 'religious' emotion at a new exhibition or on the first performance of an opera, but when they have gone their separate ways their emotion and their pleasure will become purely aesthetic. Patriotism will change into a source of religious emotion in a crowd present at the unveiling of a monument to the dead and on hearing the official speeches, but when each individual returns to his home, the religion will be replaced by an inferior sort of emotion which is good enough for everyday life. This conclusion is the only one possible if religiosity implies contagion and exaltation.

This is not the only mystery. In the deserts of Central Australia, where a few scattered families occupy large territories,[40] the gathering together of a few men around a stone or tree is enough to arouse within them a collective emotion which at once takes on a religious character of the most definite kind. Imagine then the situation in our colossal cities with their closely packed populations where the masses gather so quickly. Think of all the centres of 'religious' emotion offered by all the cinemas, department stores, music halls, skating rinks, lecture halls, and labour exchanges! However, Durkheim gazes sadly at our collective religiosity. 'Today we may have difficulty in imagining what form feasts and ceremonies of the future might take.'[41] It is because 'we are passing through a period of transition and *moral mediocrity*'.[42] Really? Have we indeed fallen morally so far below those savages of Central Australia which Spencer and Gillen show us to be so quick off the mark when it is a question of vengeance, homicide and even infanticide?[43] The truth of the matter is that we lack enthusiasm.[44]

> The great things of the past, those which fired our fathers with enthusiasm, do not arouse in us the same fervour, either because they have passed into common usage to such a degree that we are no longer conscious of them, or because they do not meet our current aspirations.

We will accept the explanation however ambiguous it may be. Does it not assail every attempt to reduce the religious life to social life? Is it not the rule that all religious ritual is transformed into custom, and how could the intensification of the collective emotion so aroused continue to remain afterwards? Does not the clue to the riddle lie in the fact that there is an immeasurable distance between the triviality which every crowd brings in its wake and the sublime nature of the religious sentiment, which is truly and profoundly experienced by the individual? He who taught men the Lord's Prayer and who preached the Sermon on the Mount did not tell his listeners to assemble periodically in order to experience contagious emotions but to retire into solitude, to meditate, to stand in the presence of the Absolute and to pray from the heart.

> And when thou prayest, thou shalt not be as the hypocrites are: for they love to pray standing in the synagogues and in the corners of the streets, that they may be seen of men. Verily I say unto you, They have their reward. But thou, when thou prayest, enter into thy closet, and when thou hast shut thy door, pray to thy Father which is in secret; and thy Father which seeth in secret shall reward thee openly. (Matthew 6:5 ff.) [A.V.]

It must truly be said that the 'French' sociological school pays scant attention to the testimony of Jesus and even deems him incompetent in matters of religion.

Moreover, the critical history of religions, even written from an entirely positivist point of view, has not failed to join its protestations along with those of psychology. René Dussaud, editor of the well-known *Revue*, has expressed the most explicit reservations on the value of reducing religious sentiment to collective emotion. It was an easy task for him to demonstrate the major role played by recluses in the formation and transformation of religions. Even more striking, he was also able to observe this role already being played among primitive peoples. Let us quote his evidence which is not that of a systematic adversary of Durkheim.[45]

> In this development—and here we are looking at resources of energy—collectivity has played a considerable part, as a result of the enrichment of sentiments which Durkheim has so skilfully brought to light. The work of individual thought, however, has been no less decisive. In any case, these two extreme modes are theoretical; there has been constant interpenetration, notably in the elaboration of thought brought about by small groups of loyal listeners. On the whole, the individual probably occupied a relatively more important place in primitive society than he does in modern times. The role and influence of a specially gifted man are infinitely more marked where a lower state of intellectual activity is the norm. . . . If exaltation is a necessary precondition in nature for a man to feel something powerful and external to himself—a force or life principle—it should be noted that this

exaltation is achieved just as well by meditation and solitude as in the company of others. It is in this way that certain American tribes isolate the initiate in order to lead him to claim his guardian spirit or individual totem by himself. People are so familiar with the experience of exaltation in solitude that they generally represent prophets isolating themselves as a prelude to their mission.

Thus, either the author of *Les Formes élémentaires* passed over the most important facts of the religion of primitive peoples, or in restoring sentiment as the permanent element of religion, he removed from this very sentiment all its peculiar characteristics. In this respect, the restriction imposed by *Les Formes* on the first hypothesis can be taken as negligible.

II (iii)

This was not Durkheim's real object in writing the book which evoked world-wide interest. The theory of the religious sentiment is merely an episode in it. The main idea of his work is that religion is the primitive form of science, the first manifestation whereby collective understanding went beyond animal intelligence in differentiating concept from sensation. Totemic religion is the science of the primitive mind, a science worthy of the name and not, as Lévy-Bruhl would have us believe, a mystical way of thinking whose laws are foreign to our logic.[46] Does it not follow as a consequence of this that the first hypothesis, that of continuous regression, is in itself re-established? If religion is the science of primitive peoples, our science must be the equivalent of their religion.

It must be said that when he formulated his conclusion on the current relationship between religion and science, Durkheim found himself in a rather embarrassing position, somewhat akin it would seem to that of W. James. Many unwary readers have perhaps been caught out by this. He appears to be asking the religious man to make one concession only, which is to be granted in advance: it is that religion should claim no rights over the domain of science.[47]

There is but one point at issue between science and religion: it is not the right of religion to exist, it is its right to dogmatize about the nature of things, and the special competence religion claims for itself to know about man and the world.

Let us beware of being lulled to sleep by this moderate demand! We shall soon see that the very essence of religious thought is being brought ino question. *Religion will see the very right to its own conscience taken away from it.*

As a matter of fact, it does not know itself. It knows neither what it is made of, nor what needs it satisfies. Far from being able to dictate to science, it is itself the subject of scientific investigation! Again, apart from that reality which is the subject of scientific thought, there exists no proper object for religious speculation to be concerned with, and it is obvious that it will be unable to play the same role in the future as it did in the past.

And further:

Faith no longer exercises over the system of *représentations* which we can continue to call religious, the same hegemony as before. Confronting it stands a rival power, its offspring which will subject it to its own criticism and control. All the signs indicate that this control will continually increase and be ever more effective, while no limit can possibly be fixed on its future influence.[48]

It is now clear: religion is on the dissecting table awaiting vivisection; standing alongside is the operating surgeon, scalpel in hand. The logic of the system is stronger than all oratorical precautions destined to lull suspicion. Just as religious sentiment has no characteristic which enables it to be distinguished from all other collective emotions, so 'there exists no proper object for religious speculation to concern itself with'. If the most clearly defined religion which has the most social form, totemism, is the very science of primitive peoples, the intellectual equivalent of our religion is not our faith in God, it is our science, on condition that it is widened to include not only the group—mathematics, physics, biology—but the sociology of religion, including the theory of collective understanding.

I think we may venture to ask a question here. If 'apart from that reality which is the subject of scientific thought, there exists no proper object for religious speculation to be concerned with' (pp. 614–15), what becomes of the idea of God in religion and what is this idea worth? *Les Formes élémentaires* only provides an answer by omission but the paper on 'Jugements de valeur' is more explicit and is inseparable from it as much because of its date as because of the subject matter.

It is plain that the object of the essay is to re-establish the theory of collective understanding, much shaken by the contemporary philosophy of values which by the most profound operations of conscious thought demonstrates the irreducible part of individuality—of individual sentiment and action.

For as long as this 'axiology', to give it its most convenient name, remained an American or Austrian doctrine, Durkheim and his school ignored it. *L'Année sociologique* scarcely gave a half-page review to the work of Kreibig, Ehrenfels, Urban or Munsterberg. The theory of value judgment or value concept with its implications so favourable to a measured individualism was, however, gradually penetrating into France. Gabriel Tarde devoted the first volume of his *Psychologie économique* (1902) to it. Ribot examined it further in his *Logique des sentiments* (1905). The interest shown in a form of social psychology which was quite incompatible with the form exerted on sociological studies, coincided with the translation and resounding success of *L'Expérience religieuse [The Varieties of Religious Experience]* of William James (1906). It was necessary to offer a reply. The occasion for it was provided by an international philosophical congress. Durkheim used it as a platform to introduce the major work which was at that time in the course of publication.

The thesis is essentially the same, but the argument is quite different. The common point is that man, isolated from society, is merely an animal reduced to sensation and image. The individual therefore cannot make evaluations. The creation of value judgments belongs solely to the sphere of collective understanding. If we are to concede to the human individual the ability to evaluate, it would also be necessary to recognize it in the animal. We should then be incapable of explaining the possibility of the existence of a system of objective values recognized by all men, or at least by all men of the same civilization.[49] At this point the problem of values may be confused with the problem of religion and be resolved by opting for God or society.

Value is not a property of things. It only exists in a subject. This subject cannot be the conscious personality, for its sensibility is no different from that of the animal. If this subject is not society it can only be God. However, this reduction of the order of values to an inexplicable ideal presupposes a radical heterogeneity between the value judgment and the judgment of reality. Now, 'if the ideal does not depend on the real, the causes and conditions which make it intelligible cannot be found in the real. Outside the real, where can we find the necessary basis for any sort of explanation?'[50]

We must choose then between theology and sociology (or, to be more exact, the theory of collective understanding which makes society superior and heterogeneous to all its members). From that moment Durkheim thinks he has won the battle and can already see the philosophy of values integrated into the sociology of religion. What does God mean to him? God means the ideal, the system of values, but fixed, immobile, and withdrawn from the movement of collective life.[51]

When we hypostasize the ideal, we simultaneously immobilize it and remove all means of explaining its infinite variability. The ideal is in fact open to variation. Not only does it vary from one human group to another but it must by its nature vary. These variations have their foundation in the nature of things. How can it be explained if the ideal expresses one and at the same time unknowable reality? We should then have to admit that God too varies in space and time and what, in any case, would be the point of this surprising diversity? The divine changeability would only be intelligible if God himself had taken on the task of realizing an ideal outside himself and this would merely be shifting the problem.

Unfortunately one cannot set the ideal outside nature and science. A single solution is possible and it is the sociological solution. Since ideals vary with human groups, they must be collective. Society constitutes the reality that is sought. 'Indeed, society is the centre of an intense moral life whose power and originality has not always been recognized.'[52] Here Durkheim, in anticipating the exposition of the theory of religious sentiment which was soon to provide the conclusion of *Les Formes élémentaires*, shows us the[53]

transformation undergone by the individual caught up in a collective movement. He has the impression of being dominated by forces which he does not recognize as his own, and of being transported into a different world from the one in which he actually exists. Life is at one and the same time more intense and qualitatively different.

Here we already have the theory of religion based on exaltation and on orgiastic frenzy.

It can be clearly seen how impossible it is to separate the theory of values and the theory of religion in the work of Durkheim. It can equally clearly be seen how much the essay on 'Jugements' and *Les Formes élémentaires* are closely dependent on each other and must share the same fate. The essay demonstrates that not only does God not exist, but that he is inconceivable. In the language of the seventeenth century his essence is denied as much as his existence. It is not only the belief in the existence of God which would seem to be unjustifiable. It is the very idea of God himself which is set outside human consciousness and which is driven from the realm of the ideal as well as that of reality.

It becomes all the more necessary to show that where religion exercises the maximum influence on society, as among primitive peoples, it manages entirely without the idea of God. The essay on values gives us the last word on the religious philosophy of Durkheim but it is the task of *Les Formes élémentaires* to present the scientific proofs.

II (iv)

The preceding considerations are sufficient to show that after seventeen years of studying religion, Durkheim had confirmed his first views. From the strictly scientific point of view we do not seek to reproach him for having posed the problem in this way: he was the master of his hypothesis. However, this was all the more reason for giving grounds to justify the transformation that he was exerting on the very notion of religion. It is from this point of view that we must examine the contents of *Les Formes élémentaires*.

This is how the question is posed. The sociology of religion consists essentially in denying that religion has anything to distinguish it intellectually from the beginning of science and affectively from any other order of collective emotions. Is this a postulate which the sociologist will take as his point of departure, both in the choice of his observations and in the interpretation that he will give to them? Or, have we here a hypothesis which will be subjected to doubt, criticized and justified by proofs scientifically worthy of the name?

It must be noted that Durkheim did not even attempt to sketch out the history of religions. There is nothing in *Les Formes élémentaires* to recall *An Introduction to the History of Religion*, published by Byron Jevons in England, and later the works of Salomon Reinach and Dussaud in France. Durkheim, as his method no doubt required, does not seek to present the evolution of the higher religions or even their rites. In spite of the tendency which so often led him to incorporate history into sociology, he freely admits that his work is not historical in character. As far as he is concerned, it would serve no useful purpose. 'We are thus justified in hoping', he writes,[54]

> that the results we have reached are not peculiar to totemism alone but can help us to understand what religion is in general. The objection will be raised that a single religion, whatever its areas of influence may be, constitutes a limited basis on which to make such an inference. We do not fail to appreciate that extended examination can add authority to a theory. But it is no less true that when a law has been proved by one well-conducted experiment, such a proof is universally valid. Even in one single case, if a scientist succeeded in discovering the secret of life, be the instance that of the simplest protoplasmic being imaginable, the facts so obtained would apply to all living beings, even the most developed. If then in the very lowly societies which we have just studied, we have really succeeded in perceiving some of the elements which make up the most fundamental religious ideas, there is no reason for not extending the more general results of our research to other religions.

For Durkheim history is thus reduced to the hypothetical determination of a stage assumed to be primitive.[55] It is of little consequence to him that this primitive society is basically a society contemporaneous with our own. If we object that such research has nothing historical about it, he adopts an authority derived from the methods of biology. It would seem that biologists are unaware of the distinction between coelenterata and fossils of the earliest period.

Australian totemism will suffice then to reveal to the sociologist everything he needs to know of the essence of religion and of its relations to collective understanding. Durkheim is prepared to admit that totemism may not be universal. It matters little to him whether or not it is found outside the least of the three continents.[56] All that is required is that it should be considered to be primitive. Now there are two reasons for this, one which is admitted and the other which is implied. The first is stated in the opening lines of the book. Australian totemism is, at least in a relative sense, a primitive religion: it is the religion of the society which lives in the simplest conditions imaginable, and no other religion is thought to have existed before it.[57] Up to that time it was assumed in England that totemism had been viewed as a form of embryonic Christianity.[58] As currently taught in English[59] universities, totemism appeared to fit in with the providential mission of the Jews and the possibility of Christian revelation. It was in opposition to the animism of Spencer who made primitive religion, scarcely distinguishable from magic, a spontaneous product of the struggle for life and of a war unto death between the clans. Durkheim had to challenge at all costs this interpretation which was potentially dangerous to his system.

The sociology of religion, when fixing attention on the beliefs and rites of indigenous Australians, has the advantage that the evidence is homogeneous and somewhat limited. Its essential task is to interpret it faithfully without distorting and falsifying the meaning. Was this achieved? We should like to set out briefly our reasons for doubting it.

We must state these reasons but at the same time compare carefully the data to be found in the main sources investigated by Durkheim, together with the interpretation he made of them. This procedure is necessarily tedious but it is indispensable. Durkheim tells us[60] that he confined himself to four sources of information: (1) the *Native Tribes of Central Australia* by Baldwin Spencer and F. J. Gillen, (2) the *Northern Tribes of Central Australia* by the same authors, (3) the notes of the German missionary Strehlow (*Die Aranda- und Loritja-Staemme in Zentral-Australien*), (4) the *Native Tribes of South-East Australia* by Howitt. From the correct and prudent interpretation of such a small amount of data, it is perhaps difficult to draw a conclusion for the resolution of so fundamental a problem as that of the nature and social origin of religion. But if the interpretation is arbitrary—if it consists in constantly putting 'the witnesses to torture' in order to extract from them confessions contrary to their convictions—at least the issue will be presented before impartial judges.

An examination of the *Native Tribes of Central Australia* is quite suitable to our purpose, in that the authors of this book are much more imbued with the totemic system than Strehlow and Howitt.

Let us begin by noting the immediate violation of all the rules of historical method. In chapters VI and VII of Book II, Durkheim deals with totemic mana or the religious idea of force. The question is of the utmost importance since it is a matter of interpreting the supra-sensible reality which is the object of the faith of the people studied. The reader who allows himself to be guided by the text of *Les Formes élémentaires* is led to believe that this totemic mana has been noted by the only observers which Australian religion has so far found, Spencer, Gillen, Strehlow and Howitt. However, if reference is made to the first and chief source it is evident that this is not the case. In the last pages of the *Native Tribes* we find—(1) a lexicon (glossary of native terms used) and (2) an index: these two sources of information are of extreme importance. In vain we seek the term *mana* in the glossary and in the index. Is the fault to be laid at the door of the authors of the book who passed over this idea without appreciating its significance? Or is it Durkheim's fault for having imported mana into Australia during the course of an imaginary voyage undertaken more or less in the same manner as Xavier de Maistre travelling around his bedroom?[61]

If we want to solve the mystery, we only have to look at Codrington's book, *The Melanesians*, a book well known to all those concerned with the customs and beliefs of Oceanian peoples. The author lived for twenty years among the people he wrote about and in the book mana is studied in two comprehensive chapters, chapter VII (Religion) and chapter XII (Magic). We learn there that the idea of mana is widespread throughout the Pacific, among the Polynesians and the Melanesians, but there is no mention of the Australians.

Is this notion not known to the Australians, totemic or bound up with the system of beliefs and institutions that boil down to totemism? Durkheim sees Codrington as an adversary of his system[62]—a redoubtable adversary against whom he prudently refrains from matching himself. The fact is that Codrington was able to live for twenty years among two different groups of Melanesian clans, those of the New Hebrides and those of the Solomon Archipelago, without noting any authentic trace of totemism.[63] On the other hand he did observe[62] there a belief in disembodied spirits which were reputed to be superior to men,[63] a cult of ghosts,[64] a belief in the reincarnation of human souls in animals and plants.

Durkheim borrows from him his definition of mana, but he cannot incorporate it into his purely sociological notion of the totem without distorting the evidence.⁶⁴ One wonders whether such scientific conduct would have been condoned in anyone other than the founder of a school?

This reason for non-belief might suffice but hardly have we glanced through the introduction to the *Native Tribes* than we find there another reason, which is perhaps more decisive, because it does not in this instance refer to the differences between Melanesians and Australians but to the actual study of Australians.

On pages 34–5, it is the observers through whose eyes and intelligence Durkheim became familiar with the men whose beliefs he was studying, who warn us against the tendency to visualize an Australian people being homogeneous with regard to customs, institutions, beliefs and rites. We should like to reproduce the passage *in extenso*. Let us be content with this quotation:⁶⁵

> In many works on anthropology it is not unusual to see a particular custom which is practised in one or more tribes quoted in general terms as the custom of 'the Australian native'. It is, however, essential to bear in mind that whilst undoubtedly there is a certain amount in common as regards social organization and customs amongst the Australian tribes, yet, on the other hand there is great diversity. Some tribes, for example, count descent in the maternal line, others count it in the paternal line: indeed, it is not as yet possible to say which of these methods is the more widely practised in Australia. *In some tribes totems govern marriage, in others they have nothing to do with the question.* In some tribes a tooth is knocked out at the initiation rite, in others the knocking out of the tooth may be practised, but is not part of the initiation rite, and in others again the custom is not practised at all. In some tribes the initiation rite consists in circumcision and perhaps other forms of mutilation as well; in others this practice is quite unknown. *In some tribes there is a sex totem, in others there is no such thing; and in isolated cases we meet with an individual totem distinct from the totem common to a group of men and women.*

It is to be wondered whether Spencer and Gillen had foreseen the sociology of religion of the French school so that they could challenge the conclusions in advance.

From the very first, Durkheim's studies of Australian ritual showed a particular predilection for the Arunta, yet according to the evidence of Spencer and Gillen those Australians were precisely the ones in whose social life totemism played the least part.[66] Durkheim makes them the representatives *par excellence* of Australian totemism; he expects them to reveal the foundation of a primitive religion which to him is essentially social. What is the religion, we may ask? Can we, if we stick to the evidence, call it totemism? Here we find ourselves at the very heart of the matter.

Our impression, which doubtless will be shared by every attentive reader of the *Native Tribes* is that the Arunta, like their fellow tribes, believe in a demonology along with reincarnation. In other terms, the problems of God and the soul have presented themselves to their *conscience* in the same way as they have to ours, but the second problem more clearly than the first. Their fundamental belief rests in the myth of the Alcheringa. The Alcheringa represents genesis, the age which saw the emergence of the ancestors of which the men of today are the reincarnation. Every child who comes into the world is the reincarnation of an ancestor of the period of the Alcheringa. The *churinga,* which are sacred things, owe their character to the spirits of the ancestors who inhabit them.[67] Now these ancestors were neither animals nor men but intermediate beings, *inapertwa,* from whom men evolved. The Alcheringa, the Australian genesis, is itself subdivided into several mythological phases.[68]

If this is the case, whence the idea of totemism? Why is this Algonquin term applied to the elucidation of the beliefs of a race, or a part of a race, which has no affinity either of origin or habitat with Red Indians? What has happened to the critical mind? If one undertakes to construct a *représentation* of 'primitive peoples' according to knowledge about the Australians or of one of their offshoots, why not be bold enough to borrow terminology from the language of the people who are being studied? Why not talk about Alcheringism or inapertwism? People may well think that the term totemism is itself sacred. Surely the question is whether or not it is legitimately so. The advantage of retaining the term is not readily obvious: its inconvenience is evident, for it lies in the amalgamation of the observation of the Australians and the conclusions to be drawn from it, with conclusions about the natives of North America. Why bother with Australia at all if the language used is one that has only been applied to the oldest American societies?

It is here that Durkheim reveals his mania for systematization

from which he was never able to free himself. He is not studying the
Australians, or rather the Arunta, in order to arrive at a precise
notion of what they believe concerning the destiny of the soul and its
relations with the supernatural. *It is clear that their religion does not
interest him in itself, but only in so far as it can be reduced to the*
conscience *of their collective life.* That is why, instead of giving
prominence to reincarnation as do the observers, he gives it to the
study of ceremonies which they also call totemic by reason of
mental habit, a habit new in France but one already established in
England and in the English-speaking countries. His work was
intended to modify this very habit.

If religious belief proper can only reside in the *conscience* of
individuals, the religious ceremony is an essentially collective thing.
If the beliefs of the Arunta and their fellow tribes in demonology and
reincarnation take the form of ceremonies which observers can label
as totemic (intichiuma, engwura, etc.), the preconceived thesis will
assume an appearance of verification which will appear to be
adequate for a public not very exacting in such matters.

The problem is to know whether the ceremonies which might be
called totemic are the only ones which express the relationships of
the Australians with their ancestors. Essentially, they are: (1) a
propitiatory ceremony, the intichiuma, defined by the glossary as a
'sacred ceremony accomplished by the members of a local totemic
group and having as its object the increase in the number of totemic
animals and plants' (p. 690); (2) a ceremony of initiation, the
engwura. This is the part played by totemism if this term really has
the right to appear in any terminology which claims to be accurate.
This, however, is only a part of the ceremonial among these peoples,
when confronted by the elements of life which are everywhere the
most likely to arouse a truly religious emotion.

The Native Tribes of Central Australia contains a chapter
(chapter XIV) devoted to funeral ceremonies (customs relating to
burial and mourning). It is of the greatest interest to the reader
unacquainted with the mania for systematization, if he wants to
become familiar with the true beliefs of these peoples. The two
succeeding chapters on individual minds and spirits and on the
relation between magic and religion are in any case inseparable.
They succeed in justifying our doubts on the radical inadequacy of
the verification of the hypothesis which was guiding Durkheim.

Durkheim created a gap between the cult of the dead and the

totemism which he attributed to the Arunta and to other Australian tribes.[69] If we look at the *Native Tribes*, we find there the description of a cult of the dead which is as detailed as it is rigid, and is as socially important for those tribes as it is in most other races. The Australians, the Arunta included, practise inhumation. This gives rise to ceremonies as much directly related to the myth of Alcheringa as the so-called totemic ceremonies. The corpse is placed in the grave, in a position identical with that he was assumed to occupy among his ancestors of the Alcheringa whilst in spirit form.[70] After the burial, the dwelling of the dead man is burned. Everything it contained is destroyed. And henceforth it is forbidden to pronounce his name, at least for a period of mourning which lasts from twelve to eighteen months, because during that time the dead man is reputed to wander among the living in the form of an *ulthana* (ghost) and if the *ulthana* were to hear his name uttered, he would thereby conclude that his kin were neglecting to observe the mourning.[71] At the end of this period, the ceremony of urpmilchima is performed beside the grave.[72] It is a solemn occasion, carefully prepared by the women and only the details vary from one tribe to another. The widow plays the main role, but the whole family is obliged to take part. As is the case among many peoples, a rhythmic dance, accompanied by exclamations, constitutes the culminating point. It appears to be designed to enrol the spirit of the dead man as a witness to the fact that the mourning due to him was properly carried out for 'the spirit of the dead man was supposed to have been watching all these proceedings as he lay at the bottom of the grave'.[73]

In cases where the inhumed body is that of a woman, the ceremony shows even more remarkable characteristics, for it is accompanied by the simulation of a human sacrifice.[74] The mother of the dead woman tries to decapitate herself with a cutting instrument made of wood but the other women prevent this. Bloody scenes are re-enacted near the grave. The female relatives of the dead woman cut their bodies and whip themselves into a frenzy, even going to the extent of beating themselves with clubs, so much so that afterwards they are covered with scars, which in former times were wrongly attributed by Europeans to male brutality.[75]

Can the religious character of this ceremony be questioned? It is obviously derived from a belief in reincarnation, from that belief which leads every northern Australian to consider himself the reincarnation of an ancestor of the time of the Alcheringa, and to see in each one of his children another reincarnation.[76] The mutilations and bloody flagellations which accompany it denote its character. The voluntary shedding of blood is quite certainly just as religious as the act of sharing at a banquet the flesh of an animal. If in any case the contagion of an emotion in a human group is sufficient to confer on this emotion a religious character, how can it be denied to a ceremony where, according to observers, this contagion is carried to the extreme and by their own expression becomes a 'frenzy'.[77]

Durkheim extricates himself from the difficulty that this evidence presents to his system by his use of a word. This word is in itself enough to reveal the arbitrary nature of his method. These funeral ceremonies become for him 'piacular rites'. Here we have a term borrowed from Roman religion and which appears to contain a disastrous concession because this religion was based on the cult of the dead. Durkheim, however, makes haste to extend the sense of the term *piaculum*. A sentence of Pliny's enables him to do this. The *piaculum* is no longer, as it is in the *Aenead*,[78] the offering to the dead, it is simply a ceremony of *misfortune*. Now, every religion must have ceremonies for the misfortunes of existence, as it has for the happy side of life![79] That is how, yet once again, totemism wins the day, this time at the expense of Latin!

Within the system of interpretation adopted by Durkheim, everything in Australia that takes on the aspect of a belief in spirits is and can only be totemic, and everything which is totemic is social in origin and essence. However, if we refer back to the chief of his sources, we will find there is a chapter, chapter XV, which is entirely devoted to individual spirits. In this chapter, the authors set out to sum up the belief in spirits among Australians. Of these spirits some are reincarnated and others are not; the latter are the *arumburinga* and the *iruntarinia*. The Australian beliefs attribute great power to the *iruntarinia*. However, the reader who goes by the texts fails to notice the analogy with totems, in spite of the fact that they are the objects of ceremonies. They are in no way represented in the guise of animals or vegetables. 'In general appearance the *Iruntarinia* are supposed to resemble human beings, but they are always youthful looking, their faces are without hair, and their bodies are thin and shadowy!'[80] The natives see in them real and even benevolent beings.[81] Far from being to some extent created by the totemic ceremony, from being seen in relation to it, it is this ceremony which is dependent on them. It is by showing themselves in dreams to the

alatunja or the chiefs of the clan, that they warn them that the time
has come to celebrate the intichiuma.[82]

This fact alone would already be sufficient to make us doubt the
existence of collective thought and especially of rudimentary science
which to the Australians would be inseparable from the carrying out
of totemic ceremonies. We observe in these peoples the elements of a
priesthood and even the duality of the priest and the soothsayer. If
they do have a rudimentary science, it is the possession of the
individual not the group. The totemic group has a chief, the alatunja.
This chief calls it together: he himself is informed of the opportunity
for the assembly by personal revelation, a communication with the
spirits, a condition of his own *conscience*. Where in this do we see
anything of a collective understanding? Nowhere!

On the other hand, two chapters of the *Native Tribes* instruct us
on what the science of the Australians is: chapter XVI on the power
of the medicine men and different forms of magic, and chapter
XVIII on astronomical myths. Only a mania for systematization
could interpret these weak and vague data in the sense of identifying
Australian science with totemic beliefs. Reincarnation, the belief in
spirits who are reincarnated in multiple forms is, in our opinion, the
only link between the one and the other. Like so many other people,
it is by the action of the spirits that Australians explain the origin of
illness,[83] but it is by this action also that they explain eclipses. The
eclipse of the sun is attributed to the evil action of a spirit,
arungquiltha, which doubtless can assume the form of an animal but
which is not a totem.[84]

The natives have a very great dread of eclipses, they have
naturally no idea of the distance away of the sun, believing it
to be quite close to the earth, and the visible effects of
Arungquiltha so close at hand, and so patient, cause them great
fear. They believe that the eclipse is caused by the periodic visits
of the *Arungquiltha* who would like to take up his abode in the
sun, permanently obliterating its light, and that the evil spirit
is only dragged out by the medicine men who on occasion
withdraw the *atnongara* stones from their bodies and throw them
at the sun while singing magic chants—always with success.

By itself this major text proves to us that Australian science is
magic.

The eclipse is an illness of the sun caused in the same way as human illness; indeed like death itself caused by malevolent spirits which under certain conditions obey the magicians. This observation has nothing unexpected about it, but how can we judge it compatible with a system of interpretation which on the one hand opposes magic and totemic religion along with the individual and the social, and on the other identifies totemic religion with primitive science?

It must be said that the relation between magic and religion is the bane of Durkheim who has never reached a clear and satisfactory solution on this major point. If in Book I of *Les Formes élémentaires* he sets one over against the other from the social point of view (because there is not a magic church and the magician is an isolated individual),[85] in chapter II of Book III this is no longer the case. It is the magic principle of like producing like which represents the causality in totemic religion. Magic then proceeds from religion. I wonder if theology has ever set before its pupils more thorny problems than these?[86]

A last word on Australian science. The most elementary of scientific operations is doubtless numeration, and the key to all human science is the idea of number along with its relation to the idea of measurable size, notably the idea of time. The *Native Tribes* tells us about the subject of numeration among the Australians which is stated to be 'very deficient'.[87]

At Alice Springs they occasionally count, sometimes using their fingers in doing so, up to five, but frequently anything beyond four is indicated by the word *oknira*, meaning much or great. One is *nintha*, two *thrama* or *thera*, three *urapitcha*, four *therankathera*, five *theranka-thera-nintha*. Time is counted by 'sleeps' or 'moons' or phases of the moon, for which they have definite terms: longer periods they reckon by means of seasons, having names for summer and winter.

One must be very easy-going to associate this mathematics with totemism! Yet what happens to the system if we dissociate it from it?

To sum up, we can see how Durkheim imposed on the evidence brought to him by the principal observers of Central and North Australia, a preconceived system—a system which he had evolved over a long period of time and according to which 'men cannot represent to themselves the world at large other than in the terms of the small social world of which they are a part'[88]—a system which does not admit the conception of a religion distinct from a ritualism of nature, and of a social or rather collective origin. What we do not have is the faithful, exact and measured interpretation that one has the right to expect from every intelligent and conscientious historian in this field more than in any other. The best refutation of Durkheim's system is drawn from a study of his sources or at least of the main source.

II (v)

The hypothesis can only owe its value to its coherence—to its internal unity—since it does not even seek to account for the totality of religious phenomena and does not receive any confirmation from the evidence quoted in its support. Can we establish its coherence?

Les Formes élémentaires contains less a theory of religion than a theory of knowledge and of the origins of science, which in the mind of the author is expressly opposed to that of Bergson, to a lesser degree that of Lévy-Bruhl, and the theistic conclusions of the system of Octave Hamelin.[89] Durkheim's aim is to kill two birds with one stone. One, he wants to demonstrate the primitive identity of religion and science, where religion is the science of primitive man, the unification of his experience; and not his faith in a supernatural order, or his intuitions of a supra-sensible reality. Two, he attempts to show the fully social character of scientific thought—thought which once it has reached full maturity has on its own the ability to control social education.[90]

If we want to appreciate the coherence of the system, we find ourselves confronted with two problems which can be brought together. The first is the relation between the totem and the idea of God, the second the relation between the idea of God and the social origin of the concept. Durkheim was unable to put forward a solution that did not fall into contradictions such that his system becomes reduced to absurdity.

To answer the demands of a theory, it is necessary, first, that the totem should be an exclusively social thing; second, that it should be clearly distinguished from the idea of God. Now the result of the facts which Durkheim noted in particular (and which his sources would not permit him to deny) were, first, that the totem can be individual; second, that in Australia even the idea of God co-exists with the idea of the totem.

In the first place the totem is defined as an emblem, and then at the same time assimilated into the family name and the armorial bearings of the lineage. This is because the emblem is essential to collective life. *'The clan like every type of society can only live in and through the individual* consciences *composing it'* (p. 317). However (p. 329),

> individual *consciences* are cut off from each other; they can only communicate by means of signs, which translate all their interior states. In order that the communication established between them should end in communion, that is to say, in a fusion of all individual sentiments, it is necessary that the signs which are a manifestation of them should themselves come and merge into a single and unique product.

The emblem 'by expressing social unity in a material form makes it more perceptible to everyone'.

> This idea of the emblem must erupt spontaneously out of communal life; the emblem is not only a convenient method which clarifies the sentiment that society has of itself but it helps to produce this sentiment in itself as a constituting element [p. 329].

Agreed: the totem is the emblem of the clan. It pre-exists in a sense that of which it is an expression, which is to say, the collective sentiments which are epitomized in it. It modifies its own condition. Neither from the psychological point of view nor from the logical point of view is this very intelligible. What is more, it is necessary for us to see there the origins of religious sentiment, or the origins of the obscure transformation of social sentiment into religious sentiment, that the totem should always be a social emblem. Now Durkheim is the first to tell us that the Australian tribes are familiar with sexual and individual totems, along with the clan totems. All his efforts are bent on deriving them from collective totems.[91]

At this point we give up the attempt to understand him. We will let the sexual totem pass, for each one of the sexes could in certain conditions form a religious group on its own account. But if individual totems really exist, each one valid only for one single person, the essential thesis of the sociology of religion would seem to be precarious. *It cannot have a psycho-social law as its conclusion.* Inadequately formulated, the law meets the exception which proves it false. An individual totem can no longer be the emblem indispensable to the fusion of personal *consciences,* naturally cut off from each other. One must choose between two alternatives. Either the individual totem has religious value or it is foreign to what is defined as being the religion of the Australians. In the first case it is proved that, even among these primitive populations, religion can be a state of individual *conscience.* The individual, the human animal, according to Durkheim can become religious by his own efforts. In the other case, the sociologist is encouraged to interpret arbitrarily the observations submitted to him and to make them favour a preconceived system. In what respect, indeed, is the collective totem more religious than the individual totem, if this collective totem is represented as independent of the idea which seems to us to be the religious idea *par excellence,* namely divinity? The only reason is that collective life is religious as a consequence of the exaltation that it can communicate to certain sentiments. That, however, is precisely what we are questioning! The sociology of religion is here proclaiming its affinities with metaphysics, by using the ordinary method of metaphysics which is to transform the terms of a problem into a solution by means of verbal juggling.

From that moment we can only hope that at least it will be good metaphysics, that is to say, that it will refrain from exposing itself to a *reductio ad absurdem.*[92] This satisfaction is unfortunately denied us.

The very object of *Les Formes élémentaires* is to reduce the divine to the social, religious experience to that of the collective life by dissociating the two ideas which an infinitely long tradition has indissolubly united in our minds—the idea of religion and the idea of God. 'Religion extends beyond the idea of gods or spirits and consequently cannot be exclusively defined in terms of the latter' (p. 49). We are invited to travel to Australia to be convinced of this independence of belief or religious sentiment and the idea of God. Australian totemism must be, like Buddhism, indeed more than Buddhism, the prototype of a religion, or, if preferred, a system of ritual without gods.

For the thesis to be conclusive and the book to be really meaningful, it would be necessary to be able to go from one end to the other of indigènous Australia without ever finding the cult of gods but only that of individual or collective totems. Better still, if the idea of God emerges, it must be in the same guise as the Great Spirit of the Red Indians: one must be allowed to see there the echo of the preaching of the Christian missionaries. If not, it will be proved that the mind of an Australian, as much individually as collectively, can rise to the idea which has been generally considered as being the condition of religious belief proper, if not of every kind of ceremony. It will be proved that if the birth of the totem presupposed the idea of the emblem, the same Australian comprehension can both conceive of a god and create the emblem which symbolizes the union of his worshippers, which is the very contrary of the hypothesis, since it tends to give birth to belief regarding practice and not practice regarding belief.

We cannot, indeed, accept the ambiguity of a 'quasi-divine bond', an expression which comes from Durkheim's pen on several occasions. We can accept if needs be a cult which the community directs to itself or to its past. We can accept even more readily the cult of a supra-sensible reality. What we cannot accept is a quasi-god, the object of a quasi-cult. We should then be allowing ourselves to be thrown into complete arbitrariness or into complete illogicality.

Very loyally, Durkheim informs us that totemism is not[93]

the highest point of mythological formation to be found in Australia. There are at least a certain number of tribes which have attained the conception of a god who is supreme if not unique, to whom is attributed a pre-eminent place in relation to other religious entities.

He does not stop at the facile explanation, drawn from the influence of missionaries on the belief of the tribes which were the first to come into contact with Europeans, long before their fellow tribesmen of Central Australia. 'The ideas relative to the great tribal god are native in origin. They were observed at a time when the influence of missionaries had not had the opportunity to make itself felt.'[94]

These gods really are gods, according to the meaning usually given to that word by other people. The Australian god is not merely a 'good god', to quote the expression of Strehlow. 'He is an immortal and even an eternal being, *for he has his origin in no other*.'[95] 'He is acknowledged to have power over the stars. It is he who has regulated the paths of the sun and the moon; he gives them their orders. It is he who causes the lightning to flash from the clouds and who hurls down the thunderbolts.'[96] 'He is spoken of as a sort of creator: he is called the father of men and it is said that he made them.' [97]

Lang had explained these facts by the probable duality of Australian beliefs, of a totemism founded on the belief in spirits and destined to take the place of science, and of a spontaneous theism of a moral nature.[98]

By a sort of intuition, the nature of which no one seems to be able to explain, human intelligence appears to have succeeded in one operation in conceiving a unique god, the creator of the world, the legislator of the moral order.

To adopt Lang's interpretation is to abandon the preconceived thesis of the sociology of religion and along with it the hypothesis of collective understanding. Durkheim cannot resign himself to do this. It remains for him then to prove that the Australians are mistaken in the true nature of their belief in god. It is not true that the great tribal god has his origins in no other god: he must originate in the totem and he does originate there. We must admire the power of 'French sociology': it can even straighten out the *conscience* of savages which make up the sole object of its study! If it succeeds, is it not at the expense of its own cohesion?

What, in fact is a totem according to the definitions previously studied? First, it is an animal or vegetable species; second, an essentially collective emblem. How then can the *représentation* of a species be transformed into that of a unique being? How can an emblem be sublimated to the point of being 'capable of regulating the stars in their courses'? Durkheim remained too much of a logician not to perceive the weakness of his explanation, especially as he had rejected the opinions of Lévy-Bruhl on the illogicality of primitive thought (p. 1). He would notice the crumbling of his main thesis if he had not already transmuted the notion of the totem into that of strength, of the totemic mana. We know by what arbitrary process this Melanesian notion of mana had been introduced into the interpretation of Australian beliefs. Besides, how can an impersonal force become a divine personality? So the contradictions accumulate.

Without becoming unfaithful to his theory of collective understanding, could Durkheim thus reduce the idea of god to the system of concepts which characterizes totemism and makes an embryonic science of it as much as a primitive religion? Had he not excluded the possibility of such a reduction in advance?

Whatever value the synthesis of the Australian or American-Indian idea of the totem, or the Melanesian idea of mana may have, the totemic mana that Durkheim draws from it represents in his eyes the totality of values—the social idealities (*idéalités*)—that a rudimentary community can conceive. Otherwise, the sociology of religion expounded in *Les Formes élémentaires* no longer makes sense. We know from his article on 'Jugements' that the idea of God cannot symbolize social values. Therefore, either Durkheim and his school must abandon their theory of values, or they must refrain from trying to incorporate into totemism that idea of god which, on their own admission, Australian thought can aspire to.

For the credibility of the sociology of religion, each of these solutions is as disastrous as the other. Each one convinces us of the absurdity of the dogmatic atheism with which it was originally injected.

If we refrain from reducing the 'great gods' of the Australians—those immortal and fully independent beings—to a totem, we would be adopting the interpretation of Lang which leads straight to the possibility of what W. James calls religious experience. From then on Australian totemism, inseparable from demonology and magic, could if necessary be considered as a primitive form of science, but the origins of religion would have to be found elsewhere.

To abandon the theory of values is to sacrifice the other aspect of the sociology of religion, that which sets the origin of religious sentiment within social experience. The value of society and social things will continue but as a means, of instrumental value, as the axiologists say. The supreme values, truly ideal and completely adequate, if not formed can at least be measured in relation to a supreme ideal, the idea of divine perfection.

It can then be understood that the founder of the school, and up to now the school which has followed in his footsteps, have declined to resign themselves to such a painful option. But logic, if there is still such a thing in this world, will force it on them sooner or later.

Let us look at the contradiction Durkheim finds himself in as seen through the eyes of those who prefer to read him reflectively, rather than of those who view his works with the complacent admiration of a bigot, who venerates the holy book to the extent of never opening it.

According to the conclusion of *Les Formes élémentaires* the concept, a condition of science, is the work of collective understanding, whilst individual understanding can only form general but quite empirical ideas.[99] This distinction between the general idea and the concept is the great discovery which the theory of knowledge owes to the sociology of religion. Let us pass over the difficulty of accepting such a subtle differentiation, a difficulty aggravated by an unexpected definition of universality,[100] and look for the mark which distinguishes the creations of the collective understanding. We learn that[101]

> logical thought is only possible from the moment when, above the fugitive *représentations* which he owes to sentient experience, man has been able to conceive *a whole world of stable ideals, the commonplace of intelligence.* To think logically is always to some extent to think in an impersonal way; it is also to think *sub specie aeternitatis. Impersonality, stability, such are the two characteristics of truth.* To live as a logical being evidently presupposes that man knows, at least confusedly, that there is a truth distinct from sentient appearances. How has he arrived at this conception? In what experience was this sentiment founded? It was in the collective experience. It was in the form of collective thought, that impersonal thought has, for the first time, revealed itself to humanity.

However, we know from the article of 1911 that values are essentially fugitive *représentations*, that they vary and must vary, and that for this reason they can only be hypostasized as God.

If collective understanding determines what man thinks, moral values escape him. They must be restored to the individual *conscience* and with them those idealities (*idéalités*) which Durkheim makes the very object of sociology. On the other hand, the idea of God, characterized by stability, can be thought of as *sub specie aeternitatis.* The concept of a divinity is the epitome of a communicable concept.[102] Why then stretch the evidence which shows itself to be present even in the religious experience of the Australians? It is one of the essential theses of the sociology of religion which is crumbling.

If collective understanding does not determine what man thinks, what happens to the distinction between categories and general ideas, and along with the distinction, the criterion of the duality of collective understanding and individual understanding? What then is the second of the theses of the sociology of religion worth, the identification of the science of primitive peoples with their ritualism if not their religion?

Sooner or later, the logic so boldly called upon will get the better of such flagrant contradictions. Shall we not then regret having introduced the expression of them into the teaching of the state, regret the presentation of them to young defenceless minds as statements of fact which run the risk of clouding their moral ideas? It seems to us that people have relied on an eclipse of the idea of God, but Hamelin, courageously warning against official atheism less than twenty years ago said[103]

> Theism is not a fashionable doctrine. But fashion is fickle, and humanity, which has been made to see God as an obstacle to its most legitimate aspirations, or the object of absorbing a premature contemplation, will be capable of once again thinking of God when he is no longer an encumbrance.

Notes

1 *Journal officiel*, October 1920.
2 [See The Translations, p. x. *Sociologie religieuse* as used by Richard refers specifically to that sociology of religion developed by Durkheim.—W.S.F.P.]
3 This is the way Durkheim presented it to several of his collaborators, of whom I was one for some years.
4 [For passages from *Les Formes élémentaires* quoted by Richard, which correspond to translations given in this book, such translations made by J.R. and W.S.F.P. have been reproduced. To certain other references to *Les Formes élémentaires* have been added the corresponding pages in the English translation by J. W. Swain with the notation t.1915d.—W.S.F.P.]
5 'Since the world expressed by the total system of concepts is that which society represents to itself, society alone can supply us with the most general notions by which it must be represented. Only a subject which includes all particular subjects is capable of embracing such an object. In as much as the universe only exists to the degree that it is conceptualized, and in as much as it is totally conceptualized by society, it is seen to exist in society; it becomes an element of its interior life and thus it is in itself the total genus outside which nothing exists. The concept of totality is only the abstract form of the concept of society: it is the whole which includes everything; the supreme class which encloses all other classes. ... Basically, the concepts of totality, of society, of divinity, are probably only different aspects of a single, identical notion.' *Les Formes élementaires de la vie religieuse*, Conclusion, section IV, p. 630.
6 *Les Règles de la méthode sociologique*, Conclusion, pp. 172–3. [English translation, *The Rules of Sociological Method*, by S. A. Solovay and J. H. Mueller, 1938, pp. 141–2.—W.S.F.P.] The last lines are not italicized in the text. They are to be compared with the conclusion of *Les Formes élémentaires*.

7 [English translation, *The Division of Labor in Society*, by G. Simpson, New York, 1933.—W.S.F.P.]

8 *Quid Secundatus politicae scientiae instituendae contulerit.* Burdigalae, Extypis Gounouilhou, 1892.

9 [English translation, *Suicide*, by J. A. Spaulding and G. Simpson, New York, 1950.—W.S.F.P.]

10 Ibid., Caput I, *Quae sint conditiones institutioni politicae scientiae necessariae*, 11–21.

11 *Les Règles de la méthode sociologique*, p. 43.

12 Ibid., p. 42.

13 Ibid., p. 6.

14 [The reference here is to *De la Division du travail social.*—W.S.F.P.]

15 Ibid., p. 183. Our italics.

16 Ibid [Richard gives no plage number. It is in fact p. 186.—W.S.F.P.]

17 Ibid., p. 186.

18 *Le Suicide*, Bk III, ch. III, sections III and IV.

19 Ibid., ch. II and ch. III, section I.

20 Ibid., Bk II, *in extenso*.

21 Ibid., ch. IV, section I.

22 Ibid., section II.

23 Ibid., Bk II, ch. IV, p. 244.

24 Voluntary sacrifices.

25 Ibid., p. 245. Our italics.

26 Ibid., Bk II, ch. II, sections I and II.

27 Ibid., p. 157.

28 Ibid., p. 153.

29 The résumé is to be found in a pamphlet of P. Krose, *Der Einfluss der Konfession auf die Sittlichkeit*, Herdersche Verlagsbuchhandlung, Freiburg, 1900.

30 *Revue néo-scolastique*, vol. 14, no. 4, p. 8, Louvain, Institut supérieur de philosophie. This correspondence is to be found in the book published four years later by Deploige and reprinted in 1912 as *Le Conflit de la morale et de la sociologie*, Alcan. Appendix pp. 393–413. The whole work ought to be read.

31 *Le Suicide*, Bk III, ch. III, section II, pp. 430–1. Our italics.

32 *La Prohibition de l'inceste et ses origines*, 1898—*De la Définition des phénomènes religieux*, 1899—*Deux Lois de l'évolution pénale*, 1901—*Le Totémisme*, 1902—*L'Organisation matrimoniale des sociétés australiennes*, 1905—*De quelques formes primitives de classification* (in collaboration with M. Mauss(, 1903.

33 *Revue de métaphysique et de morale*, vol. 19, no. 4, July 1911. [Reproduced in *Sociologie et philosophie*, Paris 1924. English translation, *Sociology and Philosophy*, by D. F. Pocock, London, 1953.—W.S.F.P.]

34 Durkheim and Fauconnet, *Sociologie et sciences sociales, Revue philosophique*, vol. 55, May 1903. [This note does not have a reference number in the French text. It is thought that the note might refer to the sentence stated above in the text.—W.S.F.P.]

35 We have restored the exact title which was unsatisfactorily abridged in the French translation. It attracts immediate attention to the individuality of religious experience. [The French title was *L'Expérience religieuse*. See p. 252 in this book.—W.S.F.P.]

36 *Les Formes élémentaires*, p. 597.

37 Ribot devoted an important chapter to religious emotion in the second part of

his *Psychologie des sentiments*. His distinction between a religion of fear which is primitive and a religion of love which has evolved from it, is in certain respects sociological. His study of religious passions (mysticism, ascetism, proselytism and fanaticism) is much more precise. Their individual character cannot be challenged. *Essai sur les passions*, 1907, ch. III.

38 *Les Formes élémentaires*, p. 610.

39 Ibid., p. 610.

40 Spencer and Gillen, *Native Tribes of Central Australia*, Introduction, p. 9.

41 *Les Formes élémentaires*, p. 610.

42 Ibid., p. 610.

43 Spencer and Gillen, op. cit., pp. 51, 264, etc.

44 *Les Formes élémentaires*, p. 610.

45 René Dussaud, *Introduction à l'histoire des religions*, Paris, 1914, ch. III, p. 32.

46 *Les Formes élémentaires*, Bk II, ch. VII, section VI, pp. 336–42. It is in note 1 on p. 336, that Durkheim contrasts his interpretation with that of Lévy-Bruhl. [See pp. 170–3 in this book.—W.S.F.P.]

47 Ibid., Conclusion, section II, p. 614.

48 Ibid., Conclusion, section II, pp. 615–16. Our italics.

49 *Revue de métaphysique et de morale*, vol. 19, no. 4, p. 440. [English translation, op. cit., p. 84. See note 33 above.—W.S.F.P.]

50 Ibid., p. 445.

51 Ibid., p. 445.

52 Ibid., p. 447.

53 Ibid., p. 447.

54 *Les Formes élémentaires*, pp. 593–4.

55 Ibid., p. 4. [See pp. 104–5 in this book.—W.S.F.P.]

56 The question of knowing whether totemism was more or less widespread is of secondary importance in our eyes. The importance we attach to totemism is quite independent of the question of knowing whether or not it was universal. See *Les Formes élémentaires*, p. 134, footnote 1. [t.1915d:95—W.S.F.P.]

57 *Les Formes élémentaires*, p. 102 in this book.—W.S.F.P.]

58 Notably by Byron Jevons, *An Introduction to the History of Religion*, chs XXV and XXVI. 'But of all the great religions of the world it is the Christian Church alone which is so far heir of all the ages as to fulfil the dumb, dim expectation of mankind: in it alone the sacramental meal commemorates by ordinance of its founder the divine sacrifice which is a propitiation for the sins of all mankind' (p. 415).

59 [It is assumed there is a mistake in the French text. The words which appear are *les universités anglicanes*. Richard is obviously referring to English universities.—W.S.F.P.]

60 Pp. 128–31, especially note 2 on p. 128. [This refers to *Les Formes élémentaires*. See t.1915d:91–3—W.S.F.P.]

61 [Xavier de Maistre (1763–1852), *Voyage autour de ma chambre*.—W.S.F.P.]

62 *Les Formes élémentaires*, pp. 87–90. [t.1915d:62–4. Notes 62, 63 and 64 have double references according to the French text.—W.S.F.P.]

63 *The Melanesians*, ch. II, p. 32. [See note 62 above.—W.S.F.P.]

64 'The Melanesian mind is entirely possessed by the belief in a supernatural power or influence, called almost universally *mana*. This is what works to effect everything which is beyond the ordinary power of men, outside the common processes of nature; it is present in the atmosphere of life, attaches itself to persons and to things, and is manifested by results which can only be ascribed to its operation. . . . But this power, though itself impersonal, is always

connected with some person who directs it; all spirits have it, ghosts generally, some men.' (There is no allusion to the animals who might possess it.) *The Melanesians*, pp. 118–20. 'This again is the active force in all they do and believe to be done in magic, white or black. By means of this men are able to control and direct the forces of nature, to make rain or sunshine, etc.' Ibid., ch. XII, p. 191. [See note 62 above.—W.S.F.P.]

65 *Native Tribes of Central Australia*, Introduction, pp. 34–6.
66 Ibid., pp. 73, 121.
67 'We meet in tradition with unmistakable traces of the idea that the Churinga is the dwelling place of the spirit of the *Alcheringa* ancestors.' Ibid., p. 138.
68 Ibid., chs X and XI.
69 *Les Formes élémentaires*, especially pp. 90, 91. [t.1915d:64–5—W.S.F.P.]
70 *Native Tribes*, ch. XIV, p. 497.
71 Ibid., pp. 497 ff.
72 Ibid., p. 503.
73 Ibid., pp. 506–7.
74 Ibid., pp. 508 ff.
75 Ibid., pp. 42, 509.
76 Ibid., p. 123, etc.
77 Ibid., p. 510.
78 Notably in Bk VI where the Sybil makes known to Aeneas the obligation imposed on him by the death of Misenus. *Dus nigras pecudes: ea prima piacula sunto.*
79 *Les Formes élémentaires*, Bk III, ch. V, especially p. 557. 'Every misfortune, everything which bodes evil, everxthing which inspires sentiments of anxiety and fear requires a *piaculum* and in consequence is called a *piaculum*.' Durkheim is forgetting the original meaning of the verb *piare*, to appease.
80 *Native Tribes of Central Australia*, p. 516.
81 Ibid., p. 521.
82 Ibid., p. 519.
83 Ibid., pp. 522–37.
84 Ibid., p. 566.
85 *Les Formes élémentaires*, Bk I, ch. I, pp. 61–3. [See pp. 120–2 in this book.—W.S.F.P.]
86 Ibid., pp. 508 ff. [t.1915d:355 ff.—W.S.F.P.]
87 *Native Tribes of Central Australia*, Introduction, p. 25.
88 *Le Suicide*, p. 245.
89 *Les Formes élémentaires*, pp. 625 ff. [t.1915d:438 ff.—W.S.F.P.]
90 This practical conclusion of the sociology of religion is frankly advocated in a posthumous work of Durkheim's. *Éducation et sociologie*, published by Alcan and edited by Fauconnet. 'It is a matter of providing an education which is moral, secular and rationalist. This secularization of morality is commanded by the totality of historical development. Religious truths must be found again 'by projecting them onto the plane of secular thought'. Introduction. p. 14. [English translation, *Education and Sociology*, by S. D. Fox, New York, 1956, p. 40—W.S.F.P.]
91 *Les Formes élémentaires*, Bk II, ch. IV, pp. 223–38. [t.1915d:157–66—W.S.F.P.]
92 Good metaphysics is of the kind offered to Durkheim by the work of the great thinker whose testamentary executor he was. I am thinking of *Les Éléments principaux de la réprésentation* by Octave Hamelin. In ten pages we find there the theistic doctrines expounded as the only possible conclusion of every philosophy which bases reality on conscience (pp. 450–60, especially

p. 453). The impossibility of a sociological solution is demonstrated by the hand of a master. Some kind of challenge is thrown somewhat ironically, at the unknown spirit who might exempt us from opting between anthropocentrism and theism (p. 458). The god of Hamelin is not only the god of a philosophy, but the god of a religion, for he is not only *absolute thought* but *absolute goodness* and we must thank him for having the attribute of goodness (p. 460).

93 *Les Formes élémentaires*, p. 409.
94 Ibid., p. 415.
95 Ibid., p. 410. Our italics.
96 Ibid., p. 411.
97 Ibid., pp. 411, 414.
98 Ibid., pp. 336–42. [This reference is unclear: it does not contain the quotation. —W.S.F.P.]
99 Ibid., Conclusion, pp. 621 ff. [t.1915d:435 ff.—W.S.F.P.]
100 'This universality of the concept must not be confused with its generality: they are quite different things. What we call universality is the property the concept has of being communicated to a plurality of minds and even in principle to all minds: now, this communicability is quite independent of its degree of extension.' Ibid., p. 619, footnote 1.
101 *Les Formes élémentaires*, Conclusion, pp. 622–3. [t.1915d:436–7— W.S.F.P.]
102 Ibid., p. 619, footnote 1. [See note 100 above.—W.S.F.P.]
103 *Les Éléments de la représéntation*, p. 454.

16

W. E. H. Stanner   1967

'Reflections on Durkheim and aboriginal religion'

First published in M. Freedman (ed.), *Social Organization: Essays Presented to Raymond Firth*, Cass, London, pp. 217–40.

One of the first reviewers of *The Elementary Forms of the Religious Life* described it as the work of 'a veteran in Australian ethnology' (Goldenweiser, 1915, p. 719). He might better have said 'veteran at a distance'. Durkheim of course had never visited Australia, but apparently he had read every significant work about its ethnography; Lowie's observation (1937, p. 211) that he was 'saturated' with the technical literature was not an over-statement. It has been said that he 'could have chosen to write [the work] without more than passing reference to Australian or any other primitive peoples' (Seger, 1957, p. 20). In that case it would have made as little mark comparatively as, say, his posthumous *L'Éducation morale*. The imperious quality of *The Elementary Forms* came from the junction of revolutionary theses and apparent factual support at a particular time in the history of anthropology. A comment which Durkheim himself made on the French socialists—that 'the research was undertaken to establish the doctrine ... far from the doctrine resulting from the research' (Peyre, 1960, p. vii)—could justifiably be made concerning *The Elementary Forms*, but it would not detract from the masterly ethnographic feat, even though a detailed analysis would certainly show much wrestling and contrivance to make the facts fit the doctrine. In this paper I do not undertake to make a thorough assessment of this 'brilliant but unconvincing treatise on religion' (Goldenweiser, 1914, p. 288)[1] against the findings of modern Australian anthropology. To do so would be a very formidable task, and whether the work should be so assessed is perhaps itself a question. I wish, rather, to reflect on some particular questions that arose in my own fieldwork, which was much affected by Durkheim's approach. Was the Australian ethnographic material merely illustrative (Seger, 1957, p. 69) for Durkheim? Had it only an accidental role in the development of his ideas on religion to the point which they reached in *The Elementary Forms*? Is it the case, as Talcott Parsons seems to argue (1937, p. 410n), that no empirical fault is to be found with the contentions of fact involved in Durkheim's 'sacred' and 'profane' classes, and in the conception of sacred things as things of symbolic significance? To what extent did Durkheim succeed in his main purpose—'to go underneath the symbol to the reality which it represents and which gives it its meaning'?

Under Durkheim's editorship *L'Année sociologique* from the first showed a lively and critical interest in aboriginal society. He himself contributed original articles largely concerned with aboriginal culture—on the prohibition and origins of incest (vol. I), totemism (vol. V), and marriage systems (vol. VIII). He also wrote, with Mauss, on primitive forms of classification, one-third of the study having to do with aboriginal data (vol. VI). There is little to suggest that he thought personal unfamiliarity with aboriginal life a disadvantage. At more than a dozen places in *The Elementary Forms* he looked back approvingly at the early papers without evident wish to make significant changes in their approach or argument.

The studies mentioned fell within what Talcott Parsons (1937, p. 304) has called Durkheim's 'transitional' period following on the breakdown of the theoretical synthesis exemplified by *The Rules of Sociological Method* (1895) and *Suicide* (1897). It is more to my purpose to mention that they overlapped some primary contributions to the ethnography of Australia. The more important were R. H. Mathews's papers from 1894 on; the report of *The Horn Scientific Expedition to Central Australia* (1896); Roth's *Ethnological Studies among the North-West-Central Queensland*

Aborigines (1897); two major works by Spencer and Gillen: *The Native Tribes of Central Australia* (1899) and *The Northern Tribes of Central Australia* (1904); and Howitt's *The Native Tribes of South-east Australia* (1904). These were the product of the first more or less systematic researches. To some extent all were guided by theoretical ideas. We have now lost a full sense of the impact they made. Nothing since the explorers' journals had attracted such intellectual attention to Australia. According to one judgment of the day, armchair anthropologists capitalized the accounts 'with the daring, but not always with the success, of a Cortes or a Pizarro', so much so that 'the quiet non-combatant student is astonished to find himself in the theatre of war, and hardly knows where to seek a bomb-proof burrow that he may hide his head from the shells of their polemics' (Hartland, 1900, pp. 57–8).

Spencer and Gillen's work especially 'fascinated the anthropological world' (Elkin, 1964, p. 241). Frazer said that it had earned the gratitude of all future generations. He identified the central Australians as 'humanity in the chrysalis stage'; he assumed that this was one and the same as 'the totem stage'; and (though later he recanted) he pronounced the *intichiuma* ceremonies to be 'the actual observance of that totem sacrament which Robertson Smith, with the intuition of genius, divined years ago, but of which positive examples have hitherto been wanting' (Frazer, 1899, p. 838). Durkheim, feeling his way towards a new synthesis, was also clearly captivated by what seemed an extraordinary primitivity.

In the decade during which he developed the substance of *The Elementary Forms*, anthropology was still largely a prisoner of the cults of social evolution and historicism. Two assumptions in particular were yet scarcely questioned. One was that the nature of anything is entirely comprehended in its development, the other that the proper way to interpret the facts of human social life is by historical explanation. At this previsionary level, on which so much depends, there was not much to choose between any of the anthropologists writing around the turn of the century. For all their other differences, Frazer and Durkheim, to choose two natural opposites, were at one in accepting that the field of study was mankind at all times and in all places; that enquiry must begin with the most primitive and simple institutional forms; that the method must be the historical analysis of development; and that the data of aboriginal society were splendidly adapted to the purpose.

Durkheim, in spite of his already well-developed sociology of co-existent functions, did not break radically with the genetic-historic viewpoint. In the first sentence of the first article in the first volume of *L'Année* we find him saying: 'In order to understand a practice or an institution, a judicial or moral rule, it is necessary to trace it as nearly as possible to its origin; for between the form it now takes and what it has been, there is a rigorous relationship.' He tried to avoid the crudities of historicism, the 'tumultuous and summary comparisons' of the loose comparative method, and the 'cartesian' or dialectical approach to theory, but in what I have called the previsionary aspect he remained very much of his time. For example, in order to deal with 'origins' in 'a wholly relative sense', he substituted the idea of 'ever-present causes' for 'absolute beginnings', but went on to speak almost in the same breath, and without very clear discriminations, of 'genesis', 'prototypes', and 'stages', so that much of the effect of the caution was lost. The loose comparative method may have many guises, and to one of them he fell victim. His conceptions of totemism (Pater Schmidt's appellation 'pantotemism' was fully justified) and the clan-totem relation were essentially 'cartesian'—'a logical concept, a pure possibility, constructed simply by force of thought' (Durkheim, 1915, p. 4), although he believed them to be based concretely. The effect of the 'model' was to wrench varied facts from many particular contexts. It has sometimes been argued that, as with the thesis and the proof, the framework and the content of Durkheim's thought can and should be separated, and it may readily be agreed that it would be absurd to judge the worth, say, of his theory of social functions as essentially connected with his dogma of origins and causes. At the same time, to separate them in a study of *The Elementary Forms* requires something like an act of violence. It is this fact of organic connection which impels one to wonder if one is justified in reducing the Australian material to a merely illustrative place in the development of his thought.

A main proposition of *The Elementary Forms*—that 'religion is something eminently social'—was first formulated in *The Division of Labour* (1893). It may be found in the criticism of Fustel de Coulanges for having supposed the primitive family to be constituted on a religious basis, or, as Durkheim said, for having deduced 'social arrangements' from 'the religious idea'. Durkheim argued that 'on the contrary it is [the social arrangements] that explain the power and nature of the religious idea' (Durkheim, 1933b, p. 179). He had apparently read Frazer's first study of totemism (1887) while *The Division of Labour* was in a late stage of preparation as a doctoral dissertation (Alpert, 1939, p. 37), but had not yet conceived of totemism either as part of the social arrangements leading to religion or as the source of all religions. That inspiration evidently did not come until 1895 in circumstances that remain somewhat unclear. Certainly, it owed nothing to Frazer, who had had no theory of totemism at that time, though he was moving towards the first of three theories, and still regarded it simply as a two-sided phenomenon, religious and social. It may have drawn, but only in a very general way, on the thought of Spencer, Lubbock, Tylor, Caird, Jevons, and other English writers on the history of religion. But Durkheim was critical of all of them, and it is clear that his main dependence was on McLennan's pupil, Robertson Smith, to whose studies he appears to have turned when lecturing on religion at Bordeaux University in 1894–5 (Parsons, 1937, p. 409n; Alpert, 1939, p. 215). But somewhat oddly, this dependence was not avowed—and then only under challenge—until twelve years after the event. In 1907 he wrote (quoted by Alpert, 1939, pp. 67, 215):

it was only in 1895 that I had a clear understanding of the capital role played by religion in social life. It was in that year that, for the first time, I found the means of approaching the study of religion sociologically. It was a revelation to me. The course of 1895 marks a line of demarcation in the development of my thought; so much so that all previous researches had to be taken up again with renewed efforts in order to be placed in harmony with these new views.

It may be doubted if the 'new views' were yet wholly of one piece. Some observations made nearer the time of the 'revelation' suggest that he may not yet have cast the die for the primacy of society over religion. In 1897, when criticizing a materialist view of history, he wrote (ibid., p. 54):

sociologists and historians tend more and more to agree on this common affirmation: that religion is the most primitive of all social phenomena. It is out of it that there have come, by successive transformations, all the other manifestations of collective activity, law, morality, art, science, political forms, etc. In the beginning, all is religious.

In *Suicide*, published in the same year, the general thought of *The Elementary Forms* is adumbrated quite clearly. He may be read in several places (Durkheim, 1951a, pp. 170, 254, 312) to say that religious conceptions are the products of the social milieu (e.g. religion is the system of symbols by means of which a society becomes conscious of itself). Yet in others he seems to make religion the determining element (pp. 334, 374–5). This ambiguity never disappeared entirely. It is heavily concentrated in the propositions stated in *The Elementary Forms* that 'nearly all the great social institutions have been born in religion' (economic activity being tentatively excluded) and that 'society is the soul of religion'. In a simple sense the matter might be said to turn on a question of whether conceptual or chronological primacy is being asserted. But such a distinction would seem to strike at the heart of the Durkheimian thesis. If there is 'a rigorous relationship' between primordial and developed forms—'a continuous series of intermediaries'—as between pristine exogamy and contemporary codes of marriage, then the distinction cannot apply. Evidently one must reformulate the thesis as the price of a possible acceptance. Alpert has said (p. 55), it seems to me correctly, that what Durkheim was really stating was 'the *identity* of religious thought and of social thought and consequently the social character of thought in general' (my italics). Identity, not being a relation, does not require either primacies or causalities to be asserted. Fundamentally, it was the failure to break with historicism that prevented the proposition from emerging clearly as one of identity. In this connection it is interesting to note Parsons's suggestion (1937, p. 427) that the significant way of putting Durkheim's proposition is not 'religion is a social phenomenon' so much as 'society is a religious phenomenon'. But the conversion is not possible logically. The original proposition was not symmetrical—all R is S, but not all S is R, at least, on Durkheim's reasoning. At all events, it would seem that, up to 1897, in spite of the 'revelation', Durkheim had no systematic or final answer to three questions: the intimate but elusive relations between religion and social order; the place of religion in a sociological schema; and the status of religion as determined or determining.

Two things may be noted about the post-1897 period, during which Durkheim took up the sociology of religion in earnest. It was also the period of the great Australian ethnographic publications and, as well, the period in which his general sociology came under sharpest attack. Two of the more severe criticisms will serve as examples. I will take them from a single critic (Tosti, 1898, pp. 464–78). The central postulate, that society is a reality *sui generis*, had led the nominalist Tarde to accuse Durkheim, in Tosti's words, of 'reproducing in the field of sociology the ontological delusion of medieval realism, by conceiving society as an essence or a transcendental unity'. Tosti, from much the same position, said that

Durkheim completely overlooks the fact that a compound is explained both by the character of its elements and by the law of their interaction. He tries to explain the 'product' by the 'product' itself, thus overthrowing the scientific conception of cause. It is a startling error of logic, the more surprising in a logician of Durkheim's subtilty.

Durkheim replied that both critics had misunderstood him, and that surely was so. The statement 'a society is a reality *sui generis*' is equivalent to the statement 'there is such a thing as a social system'. The idea of a social system as a *relational* system, as Durkheim developed it, will not sustain the philosophical interpretation that Tarde (who incidentally was described by some of *his* critics as an ontologist) put upon it. His charge of 'social realism' (for that is what it amounted to) can readily be rebutted from Durkheim's writings. Nevertheless, there was some excuse for the criticism. On occasions, in trying to force an idea to precision, or to destroy a rival conception, Durkheim used an unfortunately realist language. There was less ground for Tosti's criticism. He did not do justice to Durkheim's conceptions of society and of causation. Durkheim sought to find causes *and* conditions (this, incidentally, was the title of Book II of *The Division of Labour*); he accepted the fact of multiple causes; he sought to extract causes from the intensive analysis of correlations; and he dealt with causes, conditions, and correlations within many-variable systems of functional interdependences. Tosti's charge of 'explaining the product by the product', if pressed radically, would make any study of the connections between social variables quite impossible. It would seem to require psychological and sociological study to be complete and simultaneous.

It was probably with these criticisms in mind that Durkheim wrote his next paper, 'Individual and Collective Representations', published in the *Revue de métaphysique et de morale* in May 1898. This was extremely important from the viewpoint of *The Elementary Forms*. It made a sustained attack on attempts to reduce sociology to a corollary of individual psychology, and to treat society as an epiphenomenon of individual life. In *The Division of Labour* and *Suicide*, Durkheim had proclaimed society as something external to the individual, endowed with a power of constraint on him and, therefore, not deriving from him. Now, dangerously, he introduced the idea of the social as the 'hyperspiritual', a distinct reality obeying laws of its own. 'Despite its metaphysical appearance,' he said,

> this word designates nothing more than a body of natural facts which are explained by natural causes. It does, however, warn us that the new world thus opened to science surpasses all others in complexity; it is not merely a lower field of study conceived in more ambitious terms, but one in which the laws may not be discovered by the methods of interior analysis alone.

There was one passage which is particularly interesting for its suggestion of something relatively *un*determined and potentially *beyond* institutional control in the cognitive and moral orders. While maintaining the social nature of religion, he admitted that many religious phenomena—e.g. myths, legends, theogonic systems, and popular cosmogonies—that grow out of religious thought are not directly related to particular features of social structure. They are 'social products of the second degree', or 'partially autonomous realities with their own way of life' which are 'relatively free of their matrix'. He compared these phenomena with images and conceptions, as distinct from sense-impressions, forming in the individual psyche, and said that 'a special branch of sociology, which does not yet exist, should be devoted to research into the laws of collective ideation'. He was referring to the derivatives rather than the concomitants of synthesis (Peristiany, 1953, p. xxiv). A hint to the same effect, not followed up as far as I am aware, was contained in *The Elementary Forms* in the apparent query whether religious beliefs depend on necessities as universal and permanent as do religious rites (p. 428). There were many such tantalizing asides.

The ethnographic papers followed. In the same year as 'Individual and Collective Representations' he wrote on incest (vol. I of *L'Année*). This paper, now much neglected, could be described as a first cast, rough but nevertheless recognizable, of the foundations of *The Elementary Forms*. Many of the leading conceptions are stated clearly—among them the diametric opposition of 'the sacred' and 'the profane', totemism as religious principle, the duality of religious ideas, the religious origin of exogamy, and the primordial connection of clan and totem. In vol. II he took up the question of the definition of religion—unsatisfactorily, according to a reference in *The Elementary Forms* (pp. 23n., 47n.)—the definition coming to seem to him too formal and too neglectful of the content of religious ideas. Its real weakness seems rather to have been that in defining religion by the obligatoriness of beliefs it did not provide any means of discriminating between beliefs of religion, morals, and science. It also had elements of circularity (Webb, 1916, p. 60n.).

Now, in the same year (1899), Frazer's second article on, and first theory of, totemism appeared in the *Fortnightly Review*. In its way it could have served as another 'line of demarcation' for Durkheim. Something may be said for a view that, in relation to his developing second synthesis, Frazer had begun to assume for Durkheim the role that Spencer had played in relation to the first synthesis. Spencer's individualism, utilitarianism, and nominalism were not more opposed to Durkheim's views of 1893 than were Frazer's views of religion, magic, and totemism to Durkheim's views of 1897–1904. Frazer had now begun to discount, and would soon pooh-pooh, the religious character and significance of totemism. By 1905 he would see in it only 'a few rudimentary germs of theology'; for the rest, magic; and under his guidance, Baldwin Spencer, who had come to be Durkheim's main factual authority, was now sailing with the same wind. Durkheim's paper on totemism, 1902, and his study, with Mauss, of primitive classification, 1903, reveal him as almost diametrically opposed to Frazer. The rather crude statement in the paper on incest that 'the totem is a god and totemism a cult' deepens. 'A totem, in short,' he says, 'is not a mere name but before all and above all . . . a religious principle . . . one and consubstantial with the person in whom it has its dwelling place; it forms part of his personality' (*L'Année*, vol. V, pp. 110–11). He saw it also of course as essentially social, but in a vastly different sense from Frazer's 'social'. His definition of religion was now also centrally in terms of sacredness, a concept which Frazer had used in a characteristically unanalysed way. (The papers, incidentally, make clear too that Durkheim had begun seriously to misunderstand Australian social organization, by making false distinctions between 'the totemic clan' and the local group or clan, and by depending too heavily on the central Australian material. 'The clan', he says, 'is an amorphous group, a floating mass, with no very defined individuality; its contours especially have made no material marks on the soil.') As to the essay on classification, it remains one of the cardinal documents for an understanding of the second subject of *The Elementary Forms*: an enquiry into the most fundamental categories of human thought. A single extract will sufficiently indicate its content and argument. 'Society was not simply a model which classificatory thought followed,' Durkheim and Mauss (1963, pp. 82f.) wrote,

> it was its own divisions which served as divisions for the system of classification. The first logical categories were social categories; the first classes of things were classes of men, into which these things were integrated. It was because men were grouped, and thought of themselves in the form of groups, that in their ideas they grouped other things, and in the beginning the two modes of groupings were merged to the point of being indistinct. Moieties were the first genera; clans, the first species. Things were thought to be integral parts of society, and it was their place in society which determined their place in nature.

It is interesting to note that this essay was explicitly contra-Frazer: 'Far from it being the case, as Frazer seems to think, that the social relations of men are based on logical relations between things, in reality it is the former which have provided the prototype for the latter' (ibid., p. 82).

One other paper should be referred to: *La Détermination du fait moral* (1906b). It was published at or about the time Durkheim was giving his second course on religion, this time at the Sorbonne. Presumably it reflected the ideas explored in those lectures and further developed for *The Elementary Forms*. It sketched the main structure of concepts and argument of that book. The dichotomy of 'the sacred' and 'the profane' was set out clearly. So were the ideas that morality begins with the membership of groups; that all moral systems are thus functions of social organizations and vary with the social structures of those who practise them; that each society has, in the main, the morality that suits it; that society is not only the source but also the end of all morality, since its end is the realization of society's ideal of itself; that there must be moral elements in religion and religious elements in morality; that morality would no longer be morality if it had no element of religion; that moral values necessarily take on sacredness; and that this is why no ethic has ever existed which did not have a religious character. Society, Durkheim now has it, commands us because it is exterior and superior to us; because the moral distance between it and us makes it an authority before which our will defers; and because, in deferring, we defer to a hyperspiritual reality from which flows everything that matters to us. In these terms he essayed to meet his chief theoretical problems: how to explain the essence of morality, and how to 'place' religion in society, that reality which transcends man while being immanent in him. 'In the world of experience,' he wrote,

> I know of only one being that possesses a richer and more com-
> plex moral reality than our own, and that is the collective being. I
> am mistaken; there is another being which could play the same
> part, and that is the Divinity. Between God and society lies the
> choice. I shall not examine here the reasons that may be advanced
> in favour of either solution, both of which are coherent. I can only
> add that I myself am quite indifferent to this choice, since I see in
> the Divinity only society transfigured and symbolically expressed.

It will be apparent from this notional sketch that by 1907 Durkheim had overcome, in principle, the schematic and conceptual difficulties standing in the way of his religious sociology. The essential instrument had been the rounding out of his theory of social control: the theory that in society people are constrained by a sense of an imperative duty, arising from the axiology of life, to obey rules which are necessarily objectified in religious and quasi-religious symbols. This approach allowed him to rectify one shortcoming—too formal a stress on pure obligation—which he had found in his first definition of religion. There remained the second shortcoming: a certain neglect of the content of religious ideas. In this respect the Australian material was so apt to his needs that on this ground alone one might well ask if it was more than the vehicle of his purpose. His general propositions were of such range that only history and ethnography could provide a persuasive content. He was entirely satisfied that aboriginal Australia would do so if studied with strict regard for scientific method. That given, there was 'no reason for not extending the most general results of our research to other religions'. But there was another difficulty—that of proof. A crucial experiment was the central ideal of his conception of positive science. It was here that the new Australian ethnography came into its own. The reports made possible, for the first time, something like a continental view of a whole people, an exhaustive account of the simplest known instance. 'We have not dreamed for a moment,' he wrote, 'of ignoring the fact that an extended verification may add to the authority of a theory, but it is equally true that when a law has been proved by one well-made experiment, this proof is valid universally.' *The Elementary Forms* was the 'well-made experiment'.

One need not oppose a contention that Durkheim's main impulse was to complete a theoretical system. The book itself, with its thirty or more references to all the preceding works, presses that conclusion on one. Nevertheless, the mating of the theoretical problems to Australian answers—let us not press the opposite possibility—was something more than a happy conjunction. To argue that without the aboriginal material the book could not have been written would be to go too far. Indeed, as I have tried to show, it had already been written in more general terms in the decade 1898–1907. It could not, however, have been the book that for all its faults remains indispensable to the philosophical, sociological, and—let us not fail to say—the ethnographic education of any anthropologist.

Durkheim at first intended to publish under the title *Elementary Forms of Thought and Religious Life*. In 1909 three parts appeared as articles with titles consonant with that intention. The introduction, plus a part omitted from the book, was printed in the *Revue de métaphysique et de morale* as 'Sociologie religieuse et théorie de la connaissance', and versions of the second and third chapters in the *Revue philosophique* as 'Examen critique des systèmes classiques sur les origines de la pensée religieuse'. I have not seen any explanation of the change of title, but the effect was to obscure the second though in no way secondary object of study: an attempt to 'renovate the theory of knowledge' by a new examination of the categories. This was unfortunate because the book's longer perspective went far beyond religion. It looked in the direction of a grander sociology based on what might be called a natural positivist epistemology—'natural' in the sense of being grounded on social reality, which to Durkheim's positivist mentality was the highest reality observable in the moral and intellectual orders. It was by means of this epistemology that in his view religion, morals, and science could be conciliated. The sociology of religion only mediated that longer vision. *The Elementary Forms of the Religious Life* was not the consummation of his thought: it was but antepenultimate.

Another curious change of title, again unexplained, was made in the English translation (1915) by Joseph Swain, and in the later reprinting (1926). The sub-title of the original French edition, *Le système totémique en Australie*, was dropped. It may be presumed that the author consented, but if so it is hard to suggest a motive. Was it from deference to the trend of opinion among anthropologists? (I have in mind Pater Schmidt's question—1931, pp. 115–16: how was it possible for Durkheim not merely to defend the religious character of totemism but to exalt it to the position of the source of all religion at a time when 'all other researchers were more and more definitely denying any connection between totemism and religion whatsoever'?) It seems unlikely. There had been a large deflation of totemism, not only of its religious significance, since Tylor's sceptical statement (1898, pp. 138–48) even though speculation still ballooned (Hartland, 1900, *loc. cit.*). But not to air his convictions would have been very unlike Durkheim. He took no great part (but see *Folklore*, June 1904, and Lang, 1905, pp.91–110) in the violent controversy which went on, in books and learned and literary journals, about and round totemism, culminating in the *Anthropos* colloquium of 1914–17; but an explanation is not hard to give. As Frazer had done after the criticisms of the first edition of *The Golden Bough*, he let the controversy for the most part pass him by while preparing a definitive answer. The language he then used shows how irked he had been by the spate of new theories following on those of the classical writers. Tylor, he said, had begged the question; Jevons's hypothesis left the problems inexplicable; Frazer's changing theories were inconceivable; Lang's explained nothing; Schmidt's did not interest him; and so on. Deference in the title would indeed have been odd when there was so little in the book.

It might be argued rather more convincingly that the change of title blazoned Durkheim's thesis that 'religion has a meaning and a reasonableness that the most intransigent rationalist cannot misunderstand'. The scepticism about totemism disturbed him less than the 'bleakly hostile' attitude to religion which had dominated anthropology and sociology (Evans-Pritchard, 1962, p. 29). There was no doubt whatever in his mind about the religious significance of totemism. 'We cannot repeat too frequently that the importance we attach to totemism is absolutely independent of whether it was universal or not.' If universal, all to the good; if not, no matter. What he sought to prove was the proposition that the believer is not deceived, that 'when the Australian is carried outside himself and feels a new life flowing within him whose intensity surprises him, he is not the dupe of an illusion . . .'. Totemism was but the vehicle or material of proof. The sharpest barbs in all his writings—'lying fictions', 'extraordinary dupery', 'vain fantasy', 'presupposition of a thoroughgoing idiocy'—were shot at the entailments of the illusionist theories.

A third aspect of the title invites comment. It lures a reader into reading the book in a deceptive light. The work substantially is a study of the sociology of totemism and of the social determination of categories. Whether totemism is the sort of entity Durkheim imagined it to be, and whether it can be identified with primitive religion or religion at all, are important questions, but they are not central if the view stated earlier—that the fundamental object was to establish the identity of religious and social thought and therefore the social character of all, including scientific, thought—is correct. From such a viewpoint there may come, for some at least, an impulse to turn back and to study again and again this inexhaustibly interesting scholar. There is a widespread view that everything of value which he wrote has long since been incorporated into the theory and practice of social anthropology. This does not seem to me true. On the other hand, two of his leading conceptions have notably helped the other influences (Horton, 1960, pp. 201–26) which have restricted the social anthropologist's approach to religion. I refer to the categorial use of 'the sacred' and 'the profane' and to the insistence on giving religious symbols an empirical reference only.

Historians of ideas will no doubt wish to say much about Durkheim's inclination to dichotomism and dualism. The sacred-profane division is one of the most pre-emptive. After 1899 it had a leading place in his thought. The static or timeless character of the conception contrasts with the dynamic character of his theory of value, on which it really depends.

One doubts if many anthropologists subscribe literally to the thesis of a 'bipartite division of the whole universe, known and knowable, into two classes which embrace all that exists, but which radically exclude each other'. Such was its established force, however, that in studying aboriginal religion I blamed myself for incompetence when the facts would not fit in. I might have saved myself much trouble by following up more quickly a hint given by van Gennep in *The Rites of Passage* (1960, p. 1), that an intermediate stage between sacred and profane is necessary. I will not concern myself with the many criticisms that have been made of the concept of 'the sacred'. I will argue not only that 'the profane' is the weaker of the two categories, but that the dichotomy itself is unusable except at the cost of undue interference with the facts of observation.

My criticism of the schema as such arose in the first place from the difficulty of finding a conceptual home for facts which, excluded from the first category, should have fallen within the second, but would not do so. I came to two conclusions: that even if we accept the categories as given, a third—which I shall call the mundane—is necessary, and Durkheim himself tacitly admitted the necessity; secondly, that there is an important class of facts, so far inadequately explained, which bring the worth of the schema, whether double- or triple-barrelled, into question.

Anyone may observe that the Australian aborigines in their religious rites use objects which in that context are not in any degree or sense sacred. They include natural objects (water, fire, earth, food) and manufactured objects (cosmetics, tools, weapons, musical instruments). All have utility and common value and some, in particular contexts, may have symbolic value. They are brought into direct association, even into physical contact, with sacred objects and persons without taking on sacredness and without having deleterious effect. Neither in the general sense of having to be kept *pro fanum*, nor in the more restrictive sense of having to be used guardedly because of some property or postulated quality inimical to sacred things or persons, can they be described as 'profane'. They are simply ordinary, common, or mundane things that happen to be useful. The matter is simple but not trivial.

Durkheim implicitly admitted a third category in referring, as he did frequently, to 'ordinary things', 'things of common use', 'the ordinary plane of life', 'reasons of temporal utility', and so on, but he suppressed it on the schematic plane in the interest of the dichotomy. His two classes can 'embrace all that exists' only at the cost of an ambiguous second class. Perhaps one may infer from his comment on the terms *sacré* and *profane*—that the two classes are only 'well enough translated' by them—that he sensed some difficulty. But one may doubt if he appreciated the act of suppression.

The aboriginal universe of 'all that exists' is not divided in fact, and therefore should not be divided in theory, into two classes. To use the dichotomy is to disregard what is the case. One may say so confidently in spite of the commonness of dual organizations in aboriginal society and dualistic tendencies in the intellectual culture. Not even the facts of these orders support Durkheim's thesis. The two moieties of a segmented tribe or group of tribes might be said to 'embrace all that exists' in that, between them, they include all persons in that universe. It might also be said that they 'radically exclude each other' in that no one person belongs to both. But the moieties do not exhibit 'absolute heterogeneity'; they are not 'profoundly differentiated'; they are not 'radically opposed' (1915, p. 38). They are interdependent. Groups which, say, paint each other but not themselves in order to celebrate joint religious rites do not form 'two worlds between which there is nothing in common' (p. 39). Again, the schedule of totems in some tribes may be said virtually to 'embrace all that exists' in making symbols from all significant things in the environment and in apportioning the symbols between groups which, within limits, 'radically exclude each other' in the sense stated. Sometimes a principle signifying opposition—as between light and dark, or land and sea—may be found to categorize each such group. But *all* the totems have meaning for *all* the groups as a condition of joint social and religious life. It is far from being the case that they 'cannot even approach each other and keep their own nature at the same time' (p. 40). The fact is that they intermix by system while preserving their identities. Similarly, Durkheim's dual categories have a different character from the dualism exhibited in aboriginal thought. The first is that of intractable hostility between unlike things that can never meet. The second is that of perennial struggle between couplets or complementary opposites, e.g. left hand and right hand. One could not say of these facts that 'in all the history of human thought there exists no other example of two categories of things so profoundly differentiated or so radically opposed to one another' (p. 38). How did we ever give credence to such an image of aboriginal life? Two domains of *life* that 'cannot even approach each other and keep their own nature at the same time': *both* domains being lived in by the *same* persons? Two categories of *thought* between which there is 'nothing in common': not even the practice of interdependence? Two classes of things and actions so 'absolutely heterogeneous' that there is between them a 'break of continuity' (p. 39) amounting to 'logical chasm' (p. 40): so that beliefs and practices could not have had *any* significance for the same persons in ordinary life? The approach simply will not do. It makes too many difficulties of classification and analysis, and the heuristic value is illusory. It appears to be due to following a false lead from divisions of the *noa-tabu* kind. From another point of view it is a typical congestion resulting from Durkheim's love of dualism and of realist or substantialist terms, a combination which did repeated disservice to his true theoretical outlook. The conception of a society as 'a system of active forces' is beyond question a relational theory. The criticism one would make of the way in which he developed it is that he hovered between an unrigorous statics and a covert dynamics. This remains an essential criticism of the functional-structural anthropology which he influenced.

When *The Elementary Forms* was published there was immediate criticism of, among much else, the concept of 'the sacred'. I am not aware that there was as much, or as continuous, examination of 'the profane'. In Durkheim's usage it connoted one or all of the following: commonness (work is 'an eminent form of profane activity'); minor sacredness (the less sacred is 'profane' in relation to the more sacred); non-sacredness (the two classes have 'nothing in common'); and anti-sacredness (profane things can 'destroy' sacredness). Things so disparate cannot form a class unless a class can be marked by a property, its absence, and its contrary. To retain the categorial usage is unjustifiable.

If we subtract from 'all that exists' *both* the sacred and the mundane, what is left is still too complex for simple appellation. On religious occasions the aborigines keep a number of things *pro fanum* for distinct reasons. Certain songs and dances would simply have no place in a liturgical formulary, but there is nothing 'ritually dangerous' about them. Much the same is the case with levity and quarrels. Their tone would be alien; they might possibly imply disrespect; but they would not be sacrilegious. Certain foods, on the other hand, are ruled out because it is supposed that they would endanger the lives or well-being of neophytes if eaten in other than a given order or from any but the hands of an elder. The danger is of impersonal, magical causation, though the food in itself is good. The same magical danger would arise from contact with female possessions or exuviae. On the other hand, the presence of a stranger or a woman at a sanctified place might be a provocative desecration without any necessary magical element. That is too great a load of distinct meanings even for a remaindered 'all that exists'. It is a fact that the aborigines take great care to protect sacred things, persons, occasions, and situations from anything—ritually dangerous things and acts, breaches of secrecy, disrespect—that may derogate from them. My own impression is that the care is exercised more against persons than against impure or dangerous things, and that malignant or careless human actions cause more upsets than magical effects. Human acts (trespass on the ritual ground, breach of secrecy) 'profane' the sacra but not in the same sense as magical effects. There is little point in trying to couple them under a single notion.

It seems then that although Durkheim's system requires, and implicity admits, a third category, not even three categories could suffice to represent the facts adequately in a dynamic analysis. The conceptual, to say nothing of the logical, difficulties of the system are too many to mention, but a few points may be noted in connection with the empirical difficulties. The dual categories, it will be remembered, were in the first place classes of things and, by extension, became classes of persons, ideas, situations, values, and other components of action. The theory of two 'worlds' or 'domains' was a further extension. It will be remembered too that Durkheim thought the 'incompatibility' between the 'propitiously sacred' and the 'unpropitiously sacred' just as 'all-exclusive as that between the sacred and the profane'. In a tantalizing aside he remarked that the incompatibility (ambiguity, bipolarity) 'is not peculiar to the idea of sacredness alone' (p. 414). Did he imply that 'the profane', like 'the sacred', also 'gravitate[s] about two contrary poles between which there is the same opposition as between the pure and the impure, the saint and the sacrilegious, the divine and the diabolic'? So that there would be a purifying and a defiling sacred, and an ennobling and a vulgarizing profane? What he actually wrote probably cannot be pressed that far, but some of the problems of the dichotomy would be easier to unravel if that had been his meaning. For example, it would then almost be possible to rephrase them in terms of two continua, one of positive and negative sacred values, and one of positive and negative secular values. But a problem would still remain: the insistence that the opposition between the categories is unlike any other in human thought, such that compared with it 'the traditional opposition of good and bad is nothing'. That appears to rule out a conversion of the categories to schedules of values in a scale along a continuum such that there is a positive stretch, a point of transition, and a negative stretch. That this evidently cannot be done is curious, because Durkheim insists that sacredness is not an intrinsic property of things. It is a quality attributed to or 'superposed' on them; a quality which, therefore, can change over time, be acquired and lost. If there are, as he says, 'eminent' values then there must be lesser values of the same order on the same scale. Negative values are also implied. Logically, the antithetical notions should also refer to qualities, not properties, and should respond to conceptualization in value-terms.

The difficulties may be expressed figuratively. Let a rectangle be the supposititious 'whole universe' divided into two 'domains' which 'exclude each other' and together exhaust 'all that exists'. S contains all that is sacred, P all that is profane. The uniformity of S does not properly convey the 'ambiguity' and 'polarity' of 'the sacred', and the shared boundary between S and P does not properly convey the 'sort of logical chasm' and 'break of continuity' asserted to lie between the two domains. We need another system of divisions, such that a cross-division is made within S to show $\bar{S}$ as the 'polar opposite' of S, with a domain O interposing between S–$\bar{S}$ and P. This is the only condition on which S–$\bar{S}$ and P can have 'nothing in common' except co-existence within the 'whole universe' of the rectangle. But what then of O? A 'dichotomous' universe of three necessary parts? A universe 'exhausted' by two parts but requiring a third in order to be possible? One part containing its own antithesis, the other(s) uniform? The complex part susceptible of being destroyed only from that part with which contact is 'impossible'? I can see no way of dealing with these and other such questions in the terms Durkheim used. On the other hand, the problems are at least eased if the implicit third category is made explicit. Then O becomes the domain of mundane things. The construction may be ready to say: sacred things may readily lose their sacredness and become commonplace, which is in line with empirical experience and would not contravene Durkheim's idea of sacredness. (Even in the aboriginal tradition the sacred bullroarer had a secular valuation as well, and when the tradition collapsed the secular value succeeded the sacred value.) But the construction also seems to say: sacred values must become commonplace before they can become profane, which does not sound Durkheimian, and is difficult to translate into empirical terms. The trouble obviously arises from the static categorial forms. While these are retained a trichotomy has no advantage over a dichotomy. The schema, plainly, is empirically inadequate while at the same time being caught up with conceptual and logical difficulties. It requires a conversion from the categorial plane to the plane of human interactions or, as I would prefer to say, operations and transactions about things of value. Actually, there are excellent bases in Durkheim's thought for so doing. His general theory of society as 'a system of active forces', his conception of symbolic relations, and his axiology (the theory of the ideals and values by which social persons direct their behaviour), would probably allow the conversion to be made.

It was in part in this sense that I remarked earlier that *The Elementary Forms* was but antepenultimate in the development of his thought. His untimely death left a large potential undeveloped. But as far as *The Elementary Forms* is concerned, the utility of one bequest—the strained, static categories—has long been used up.

The conclusion of *The Elementary Forms* rings with a conviction that, inexplicable and disconcerting as aboriginal religious symbols might seem at first, 'the mystery which appears to surround them is wholly superficial and disappears before a more painstaking observation' (p. 429). Durkheim was confident that he had demonstrated the referent of the symbols to be concrete and unmysterious. What in fact he had done was to use novel material, in an extraordinarily vivid way, to vindicate a postulate which permanently invested his thought: that there *cannot* be 'an aspect of reality which evades ordinary knowledge as well as science'. His was not the ordinary positivist dogma—that it is meaningless to set up a transempirical reality—but rather a profession of faith in the destiny of science to discover and identify the empirical reality which, since there could be no other, *must* be behind the distorting veil of mythological imagination. To keep his promise (p. 1) to proceed 'with all the exactness and fidelity that an ethnographer or an historian' could bring to the task, required at least an open mind towards the opaque symbols, in which aboriginal religion abounds, which no amount of 'painstaking observation' can interpret, and towards the multitude of others which, more transparent, appear to point to 'aspects of "reality" significant to human life and experience, yet outside the range of scientific observation and analysis' (Parsons, 1937, p. 421).

Part of the difficulty seems to have been due to a flaw in his analysis of symbolism. Parsons has suggested that it was a failure to appreciate the 'double incidence' of non-empirical symbols, and I consider the criticism a basic one. Take the word 'rainbow' in an aboriginal totemic universe. The 'double incidence' is (1) word——→event and (2) event——→totemic ancestor. In both cases the cognitive structures and functions are similar, but the organized sense-perceptions of the first are replaced in the second by ideas, only more or less organized, which refer to an imagined object. If the ideas constituting the symbolic relation (2) are to be intelligible there must be some sort of conceptualization of the object. Men, being the makers as well as the interpreters of symbols, must as makers produce operable symbols if as interpreters they are to make use of them. It may be for this reason that the conceptual imagery of religious symbol-making is drawn largely but by no means wholly from familiar situations of social life. The supposed properties of objects, it seems, are transposed to the symbols in terms that are *already* meaningful. But neither the imagery, nor the situations from which it is drawn, are themselves the referents: on the view here put forward, they are, or provide, only an idiom in which the referents are conceptualized. Durkheim did not make this particular error, but he short-circuited the analysis of the symbolizing process in another way, by imposing the philosophical postulate that non-empirical symbolic referents *must* be distorted representations of empirical reality. This led to two substantial errors. He assumed—to a modern student unjustifiably—that the aborigines were incapable (in part because of his belief that they had an 'insufficient aptitude for abstracting and generalizing') of objectifying in symbols a deeper view of life. He thus did not enquire seriously into the dimension of 'ultimate concern' exemplified, strongly if darkly, in their symbolism. Secondly, he did not perceive that there is a 'multiple' as well as a 'double incidence' in the symbols. By this is meant that there are cognitive aspects of the feelings, valuations, and aspirations which as well as the conceptualizations go with the symbols. Durkheim, as positivist, did not follow the analysis through to the realm which, as sociologist, he was magnificently equipped to study.

When *The Elementary Forms* was in preparation less was known than at present of the aboriginal myths, that great repository of religious cognition, but enough was known to make a modern reader wonder why it was that Durkheim did not see that his thesis was very depreciatory of man. It did not presuppose a 'thorough-going idiocy' as bad as that which he had found unacceptable in Frazer's account of the origin of totemism, but it did not credit primitive man with any capacity to form judgments of experience, to objectify in symbols determinants of social life more ultimate than any which arise from human association as such, or form an idealization of it. One cannot criticize Durkheim for pressing the view that the task of science is to go 'behind' the symbolisms. What cannot be accepted is the posture that he demonstrated the concrete collectivity to be the only possible referent.

If anything can be said with certainty of the belief-systems which have been studied it is that they do *not* symbolize the clan, or any other concrete social entity, or even idealizations of them, although these elements may colour or mediate what is symbolized. On the other hand, it seems incontestable that in a broad sense they *do* symbolize 'aspects of reality significant to human life and experience': we are not constrained to uphold Parson's further contention that such aspects are 'outside the range of scientific observation and analysis'. In my recent monograph *On Aboriginal Religion* I have tried to show that in fact some very perceptive truths about human experience, and about the condition of man's life, are expressed in aboriginal myths and rites. The expression is in a metaphorical idiom and it makes use of many vehicles of dramatic imagination. Here and there the reflective imagination breaks through to the plane of explicit statement. In a few places in *The Elementary Forms* one may sense that Durkheim was not unmindful of this aspect of aboriginal religious thought. It must of course remain an open question whether somewhat better information on the rites and beliefs would have led him to see that his philosophical presuppositions were preventing the facts from telling an essential

part of their story. On the whole, however, he was rather too imbued
with the notion of the primitivism of the aborigines to let us suppose
that he would have thought it a fruitful field of further enquiry, and
indeed the question scarcely came within the possibilities of his
study. One of the things which distinguishes his from the present
period is the extent to which the whole stance of anthropology, with
its emphasis on the historical-hierarchical viewpoint, forced on
enquiry a more or less systematic misrepresentation of the
experiential aspect of institutions, in particular of religion.

It would be unjust to include Durkheim among the scholars who
at the least were not displeased to see religion and science at each
other's throats (Evans-Pritchard, 1962). He inveighed against 'subtle
theologies', against 'theological and confessional prejudice', and
against the 'hegemony of faith' over religious thought, but he did not
deny religion, as he said, 'in principle'. How could he, since he saw it
as a necessary and thus eternal part of man's life and thought? He
denied only its right to dogmatize upon the nature of things and its
claim of special competence to know man and the world. It
might—indeed, by its nature must—essay to go beyond science. In
this way he seemed to leave open to it, rather surprisingly, a
legitimate field of metaphysical speculation. The only boundaries he
set were that it must not claim or deny things for which it had no
scientific authority. In this aspect his positivism was scarcely
Comtean. The tone of conscious superiority to illusion which had
characterized so many anthropological writers on religion cannot be
found in his work. He stood apart in other respects as well: for
example, in his dislike of historical materialism, and in the zeal with
which he sought to correct what he called the 'moral mediocrity' of
his time. He was not alone in considering all religions of equal value
and dignity, but as far as I am aware, no other scholar of such
eminence was prepared at the time to treat the cognitive elements of
primitive religion, including 'the crude cults of the Australian tribes',
with such seriousness. Here indeed was a change from his
predecessors. It was at once the penalty and tragedy of his approach
that for systematic reasons he could not accommodate the
postulational and experiential elements of aboriginal religion.

It has been said with much truth that *petitio principii* was a besetting
scholarly vice of Durkheim (Needham, in Durkheim and Mauss,
1963, p. xiv n.). Is it not strange that this was so? He had the

sharpest of eyes for question-begging. Note as an early illustration how he had dismissed—as a 'refusal of explanation', a posing rather than a resolution of a question—any attempt to account for exogamy and the prohibition of incest by an 'instinctive repulsion that man feels for consanguineous marriage'. This, as he pointed out, says only that man condemns incest because it appears condemnable to him. Yet from the very sentences (see the paper on incest) in which he made the objection he went on to state propositions, afterwards made into the anatomy of *The Elementary Forms*, which then and later were as much in need of proof as the vast conclusions drawn from them—the primordiality of clan and totem, the indissoluble link between them, totemism as religious principle. There is something like the hyperbole of question-begging in the whole suite of now familiar statements: the clan is the *fons et origo* of totemism; clan and totem mutually imply each other; the clan presupposes a totem; a totem has meaning only in and through the clan; to take away the totem makes the clan no longer representable; the group is possible only on the totem as condition. A single doubt—on the 'ism' of totemism, or that a non-totemic clan may not be 'an amorphous group, a floating mass, with no very defined individuality; its contours especially, have made no material marks on the soil'—if entertained, however briefly, might have toppled the edifice. Goldenweiser's incisive criticisms (1910) came too late, but why was it that Durkheim paid no attention whatever to the cautions of Tylor, 'whose lightest word carries with it all the weight that justly attaches to any utterance of one whom we all regard as the most eminent of anthropologists' (Jevons, 1901)? One has to look deeper than a mere nodding over matters of logic. Perhaps the explanation may be found in an absolute dedication to a single central vision. His sociocentric fixation was all-consuming. In this respect he was, in Sir Isaiah Berlin's terms, the arch-hedgehog.[2] The insistence that *all* relations run *from* the social order *to* the social order was a sort of theodicy justifying the worship of sociological science. There could be but one mould for everything: beliefs, rites, sentiments, social forms, categories of thought, schemes of classification, scientific concepts. It is this vision which explains the quality, a pervasive atmosphere of inevitability, that every reader of *The Elementary Forms* must have noticed. It produces a sense, which grows always stronger, that the earnest stress on scientific method, the painstaking empiricism, the textual care, the dazzling erudition, the sinewy argument are supererogatory, which is not in any way to say unauthentic, but merely that in the beginning was the end.

Durkheim's thought does not lend itself to apt summary or to an easy scrutiny of sequences. It courses like a vine covered with a profusion of laterals and spurs. The totality eludes an ordinary span of mind. *The Elementary Forms* is particularly difficult. How does one reach a unitary critical view of a work with two profound objects and half a dozen major theses? The difficulties, whether of focus or estimate, can in part be overcome by an ethnographic and theoretical annotation[3] of that third of the book (pp. 87–239) which shapes much of the Australian material for the culminating analysis.

One must resist the disposition of some commentators (e.g. Talcott Parsons, 1937, p. 411) to suggest that the ethnographic details are incidental to the general theoretical enquiry into the structure and principles of religion. I should be inclined to argue that to make the separation is a mistake with respect to any subject of the book. In the matter of aboriginal religion, the concern of this paper, the details are the very stuff of the 'crucial experiment'. Durkheim himself saw them as such. The experiment is crucial *to* the general theory. For this reason the theory stands or falls by those details until a test is made of some other set of materials. The critical literature reveals other dangers that flow from separation. At one extreme the student is offered what may be called 'sublimated Durkheim', e.g. Ginsberg's epitomization that the essence of the viewpoint is that 'religious ideas are collective ideas which represent collective realities' (1956, p. 231). At the other extreme the offer may be 'potted Durkheim', e.g. an impression that the function of religion is simply to be there, to support the structure and process of society as and when needed. From the first all that is provocative has gone; the second transforms a theory of transcended selves into a theory of public conveniences.

There is a chain of reasoning in six lines on p. 88 which shows, as well as any passage can, why it is essential to criticize *The Elementary Forms* ethnographically. Three propositions are stated: there should be a cult more fundamental and primitive than animism and naturism; there is such a cult; and that cult is totemism. One could say without logic-chopping that all the modes of *petitio principii* are there exemplified. The contentions were abstractly determined but not, I would say, established by the preceding pages, but pp. 87–239 transfer the inadequate certainties to what follows. The whole course of Durkheim's reasoning on religion required him to find empirical instances of fundamental and primitive social groups whose members were united, not by blood or common habitat, but solely by having the same name and emblem and by participating in the same cult. Sure enough, he found what he sought. A freakish, passing state of affairs in Australian ethnography gave some of the central Australian material the appearance of satisfying the requirement. In this respect the very merit of his approach—'concentration upon one clearly determined type'—was a prime cause of his undoing. He subdued a whole class of symbolized relations to the factitious importance of a sub-class which, as we now know, had been described inadequately.

The insistence on making religion—at least at the end of its historical course of 'rigorous relationships' with primordial causes—dependent on society inevitably put Durkheim at the mercy of his grasp of the society chosen for the crucial experiment. His insight from afar was in many ways brilliantly penetrating. He had a good sense of the factual shortcomings of the standing accounts and remarked on particular weaknesses, e.g. the poor studies of initiation rites. But, as I remarked earlier, nothing in the book suggests a feeling of being greatly handicapped. On the contrary, the tone was one of supreme confidence that enough was known to test and prove the thesis. The 'society' on which the argument turned was largely a figment to which, as Ginsberg has correctly said, Durkheim attributed 'powers and qualities as mysterious and baffling as any assigned to the gods by the religions of the world' (1956, p. 242).

Notes

1 [See References immediately below.—W.S.F.P.]
2 The reference is to a line from the Greek poet Archilochus: 'the fox knows many things but the hedgehog knows one big thing'. See Isaiah Berlin's *The Hedgehog and the Fox*. The description of Tolstoy—'by nature a fox, by belief a hedgehog'—in many ways fits Durkheim equally well.
3 Which I have prepared in part but here omitted.

References

[Most of the references in the article are found in the three bibliographies which follow on p. 305 below. References not in the bibliographies are given below.—W.S.F.P.]

ELKIN, A. P. 1964 A Landmark in Australian Aboriginal Anthropology: A Review', *Oceania*, 34, 4.

FRAZER, J. G. 1899 'The Origin of Totemism', *The Fortnightly Review*, April–May.

GENNEP, A. VAN 1960 *The Rites of Passage* (English translation M. B. Vizedom and G. L. Caffee), Routledge & Kegan Paul, London.

GOLDENWEISER, A. A. 1910 'Totemism, An Analytical Study', *Journal of American Folklore*, 23.

GOLDENWEISER, A. A. 1914 In W. Schmidt, 'Introduction' to 'Das Problem des Totemismus', *Anthropos*, 9.

HARTLAND, E. S. 1900 'Totemism and Some Recent Discoveries' (Presidential Address), *Folklore*, 11.

JEVONS, F. B. 1901 'The Place of Totemism in the Evolution of Religion', *Folklore*, 10.

LANG, A. 1905 *The Secret of the Totem*, Longmans, Green, London.

PERISTIANY, J. G. 1953 Introduction to E. Durkheim, *Sociology and Philosophy*, Routledge & Kegan Paul, London.

TOSTI, G. 1898 'Suicide in the Light of Recent Studies', *AJS*, 3.

TYLOR, E. B. 1898 'Remarks on Totemism, with Especial Reference to Some Modern Theories Concerning it', *Journal of the Royal Anthropological Institute*, 28 (n.s. 1).

Bibliography

1 Durkheim and Religion

A selection of books, articles and reviews written by Durkheim in which reference is made to religion. The dating-enumeration is that of Lukes (1973). Comments on items marked * are to be found in the section entitled Abstracts. Dates with the prefix t. refer to an English translation. References to reviews, the subject matter of which is marriage but which also mention religion, have been excluded, e.g. 1899a(iv)(19),(21), and (22). See section 2 of the Bibliography, Durkheim and Totemism.

1886a	Review. 'Herbert Spencer—*Ecclesiastical Institutions: being part VI of the Principles of Sociology*. London, 1885', *RP*, XXII, pp. 61–9.
t.1975	in this volume.
1887b	Review. 'Guyau—*L'Irréligion de l'avenir, étude de sociologie*. Alcan, 1887', *RP*, XXIII, pp. 299–311.
t.1975	in this volume.
*1887c	'La Science positive de la morale en Allemagne', *RP*, XXIV, pp. 33–58, 113–42, 275–84. (Wundt on religion, pp. 116–18.)
*1893b	*De la Division du travail social: étude sur l'organisation des sociétés supérieures*, Alcan, Paris.
t. 1933b	from 2nd ed. 1902b, with Introduction, by G. Simpson,

The *Division of Labor in Society*, Macmillan, New York.

*1895a   *Les Règles de la méthode sociologique*, Alcan, Paris.
t.1938b   by S. A. Solovay and J. H. Mueller, *The Rules of Sociological Method*. Edited, with an introduction by G. E. G. Catlin, University of Chicago Press, Chicago, and (1950) Free Press, Chicago.

*1897a   *Le Suicide: étude de sociologie*, Alcan, Paris.
t.1951a   by J. A. Spaulding and G. Simpson, *Suicide: A study in Sociology*. Edited, with an introduction by G. Simpson. Free Press, Chicago, and (1952) Routledge & Kegan Paul, London. (Bk II, ch. 2, included in this volume.)

*1897e   Review. 'Antonio Labriola—*Essais sur la conception matérialiste de l'histoire*', *RP*, XLIV, pp. 645–51.

*1898a(ii)   'La Prohibition de l'inceste et ses origines', *AS*, I, pp. 1–70.
t.1963a   with an introduction, by E. Sagarin, *Incest. The Nature and Origin of the Taboo by Émile Durkheim*, Lyle Stuart, New York.

*1898a(iii)(13) Review. 'Marcel Mauss—"La Religion et les origines du droit penal", deux articles parus dans la *Revue de l'histoire des religions*, 1897', *AS*, I, pp. 353–8.

1898b   'Représentations individuelles et représentations collectives', *RMM*, VI, pp. 273–303. (Reproduced in 1924a.) (This is concerned more with philosophical than religious issues.)
t.1953a   See 1924a

1898c   'L'Individualisme et les intellectuels', *RB*, 4th series, X, pp. 7–13.
t.1969d   by S. and J. Lukes, 'Individualism and the intellectuals', *Political Studies*, XVII, pp. 19–30. (Included in this volume.)
t.1973   by M. Traugott, 'Individualism and the intellectuals', in R. N. Bellah (ed.), *Émile Durkheim on Morality and Society*. University of Chicago Press, Chicago and London, pp. 43–57.

*1899a(i)   'Preface', *AS*, II, pp. i–iv.
t.1960c   by K. H. Wolff in K. H. Wolff (ed.), *Émile Durkheim 1858–1917: A Collection of Essays, with Translations and a Bibliography*, Ohio State University Press, Columbus, Ohio, pp. 347–53. (Republished in 1964 as *Essays in Sociology and Philosophy*, Harper & Row, New York.)

1899a(ii)   'De la Définition des phénomènes religieux'. *AS*, II, pp. 1–28.
t.1975   in this volume.

*1899d   Contribution to H. Dagan, *Enquête sur l'antisémitisme*, Stock, Paris, pp. 59–63.

*1900a(47)   Review. 'Ratzel (Friederich)—*Anthropogeographie, Erster Teil: Grundzüge der Anwendung der Erdkunde auf die Geschichte*, 2ᵉ éd., Engelhorn, Stuttgart, 1899', *AS*, III, pp. 550–8.

*1900c   'La Sociologia ed il suo dominio scientifico', *Rivista Italiana di Sociologia*, IV, pp. 127–48.
t.1960c   by K. H. Wolff, 'Sociology and its scientific field', in Wolff 1960. (See 1899a[i].)

*1901h   'Compte-rendu d'une conférence sur "Religion et libre pensée" devant les membres de la Fédération de la Jeunesse laïque, donnée 22 Mai 1901', *La Petite Gironde*, 24 May 1901. (A report of Durkheim's speech.)

*1903a(i)   (with M. Mauss) 'De Quelques formes primitives de classification. Contribution à l'étude des représentations collectives', *AS*, VI, pp. 1–72.
t.1963b   by R. Needham, *Primitive Classification*, with an introduction by R. Needham, Cohen & West, London.

*1903a(ii)(57)   Review. 'E. Fournier de Flaix—"Statistique et consistance des religions à la fin du XIXe siècle', *AS*, VI, pp. 550–1.

*1903c   With P. Fauconnet. 'Sociologie et sciences sociales', *RP*, LV, pp. 465–97.
t.1905d   'Sociology and the social sciences', *Sociological Papers*, 1, pp. 258–80 (pp. 473–84 omitted).

*1905a(ii)(2)   Review. 'Pellison (Maurice)—'La Sécularisation de la morale au XVIIIᵉ siècle', *La Révolution française*, No. 1903, pp. 385–408', *AS*, VIII, pp. 381–2.

*1905e   Contribution to discussion: 'Sur la séparation des églises et de l'état', *Libres entretiens*, 1st series, pp. 369–71, 496–500.

*1906a(6)   Review. 'Toniolo (Giuseppe)—*L'Ordierno problema sociologico*. Firenze, 1905', *AS*, IX, pp. 142–3.

1906b   'La Détermination du fait moral', *BSFP*, VI, pp. 169–212. (Reproduced in 1924a.)
t.1953a   See 1924a.

*1906e   Lecture on Religion and Morality delivered in the
                École des Hautes Études in the winter of 1905–6. Sum-
                mary by A. Lalande in 'Philosophy in France (1905)',
                PR, XV, pp. 255–7.

*1907a(17)   Review. 'Frazer (J. G.)—*Lectures on the Early History
                of Kingship*. Macmillan, London, 1905', *AS*, X, pp.
                411–15.

*1907b   'Lettres au Directeur de *La Revue néo-scolastique*',
                RNS, 14, pp. 606–7, 612–14. (First letter dated 20
                October 1907, second letter, 8 November 1907.)

*1907c   Contribution to: '*La Question religieuse: enquête inter-
                nationale*', *MF*, LXVII, p. 51. (Reprinted in a
                volume of the same title edited by F. Charpin, Paris,
                Société du Mercure de France, 1907, pp. 95–7.)

*1907f   'Cours de M. Émile Durkheim à la Sorbonne', *Revue
                de philosophie*, 7(5), pp. 528–39; 7(7), pp. 92–114;
                7(12), pp. 620–38. (A summary by P. Fontana of the
                1906–7 course of lectures on 'La Religion: origines'.)

*1909a(i)   Contribution to discussion: 'Science et religion', *BSFP*,
                IX, pp. 56–60.

*1909a(ii)   Contribution to discussion: 'L'efficacité des doctrines
                morales', *BSFP*, IX, pp. 219–31.

1909c   'Examen critique des systèmes classiques sur les origines
                de la pensée religieuse', *RP*, LXVII, pp. 1–28, 142–
                62. (This corresponds to chs II and III of 1912a.)

1909d   'Sociologie religieuse et théorie de la connaissance',
                RMM, XVII, pp. 733–58. (This corresponds to the
                Introduction of 1912a. Pp. 754–8 have been omitted.)

1910a(ii)(2)   Note. 'Systèmes religieux des sociétés inférieures', *AS*,
                XI, pp. 75–6. (Unsigned: probably by Durkheim.)
   t.1975   in this volume.

1911b   'Jugements de valeur et jugements de réalité', in *Atti
                del IV Congresso Internationale di Filosofia*, Bologna,
                1911, vol. I pp. 99–114. (Reproduced in *RMM* [1911],
                XIX, pp. 437–53, and in 1924a.)
   t.1953a   See 1924a.

1912a   *Les Formes élémentaires de la vie religieuse. Le
                système totémique en Australie*, Alcan, Paris.

t.1915d	by J. W. Swain, *The Elementary Forms of the Religious Life: A Study in Religious Sociology*. Allen & Unwin,
t.1975	London; Macmillan, New York.
1913a(i)(2)	Note. 'Systèmes religieux des sociétés inférieures', *AS*, XII, pp. 90–1 (Unsigned: probably by Durkheim.)
t.1975	in this volume.
1913a(ii)(6)&(7)	Review. 'Lévy-Bruhl—*Les Fonctions mentales dans les sociétés inférieures*. Paris, 1910', 'Durkheim (Émile)— *Les Formes élémentaires de la vie religieuse. Le système totémique en Australie*, Paris, 1912', *AS*, XII, pp. 33–7. Paris, 1912', *AS*, XII, pp. 33–7.
t.1972	by A. Giddens, *Émile Durkheim: Selected Writings*, C.U.P., pp. 246–9. (First paragraph and references omitted.)
t.1975	in this volume.
*1913a(ii)(9)	Review. 'Patten—*The Social Basis of Religion*. New York, 1911', *AS*, XII, pp. 79–80.
*1913a(ii)(10)	Review. 'Visscher (H.)—*Religion und soziales Leben bei den Naturvölkern*. 2 vols, Schergens, Bonn, 1911', *AS*, XII, pp. 83–8.
1913a(ii)(11)& (12)	Review with M. Mauss. 'Frazer—*Totemism and Exogamy*. vol. IV', and 'Durkheim—*Les Formes élémentaires de la vie religieuse. Le système totémique en Australie*', *AS*, XII, pp. 91–8.
t.1975	in this volume.
*1913a(ii)(15)	Review. 'Deploige, Simon—*Le Conflit de la morale et de la sociologie*. Louvain, 1911', *AS*, XII, pp. 326–8.
*1913b	Contribution to discussion: 'Le Problème religieux et la dualité de la nature humaine', *BSFP*, XIII, pp. 63– 75, 80–7, 90–100, 108–11.
*1914a	'Le Dualisme de la nature humaine et ses conditions sociales', *Scientia*, XV, pp. 206–21.
t.1960c	by C. Blend in Wolff (1960). (See 1899a[i].)

Published posthumously

*1918b	'Le "Contrat social" de Rousseau', *RMM*, XXV, pp. 1–23, 129–161.
t.1960b	by R. Manheim, *Montesquieu and Rousseau: Forerunners of Sociology*. Foreword by H. Peyre. 'Durkheim, Montesquieu, and Rousseau' by G. Davy. Note by A. Cuvillier. University of Michigan Press, Ann Arbor.

1919b   Contribution to discussion in F. Abauzit *et al.*, *Le
             Sentiment religieux à l'heure actuelle*, Vrin, Paris, pp.
             97–105, 142–3. Reproduced in *ASRel* (1969), 27, pp.
             73–7; (1971) 30, pp. 89–90.
t.1975   in this volume.

*1922a   *Education et sociologie.* Introduction by Paul Faucon-
             net. Alcan, Paris.
t.1956a   by S. D. Fox, *Education and Sociology.* Introduction
             by S. D. Fox and Foreword by T. Parsons. Free
             Press, Chicago.

*1924a   *Sociologie et philosophie.* Preface by C. Bouglé. Alcan,
             Paris. (Reproduces 1898b, 1906b and 1911b.)
t.1953a   by D. F. Pocock, *Sociology and Philosophy.* With an
             introduction by J. G. Peristiany, Cohen & West, London.

*1925a   *L'Éducation morale.* Introduction by Paul Fauconnet.
             Alcan, Paris.
t.1961a   by E. K. Wilson and H. Schnurer, *Moral Education.*
             Edited, with an introduction, by E. K. Wilson, Free Press,
             New York. (Chapter I included in this volume.)

*1928a   *Le Socialisme. Sa définition, ses debuts, la doctrine
             Saint-Simonienne.* Edited by M. Mauss, Alcan, Paris.
t.1958b   by C. Sattler, *Socialism and Saint-Simon.* Edited, with
             an introduction by A. W. Gouldner, Antioch Press, Yellow
             Springs, Ohio; and (1959) Routledge & Kegan Paul,
             London.

*1938a   *L'Évolution pédagogique en France.* 2 vols, Alcan,
             Paris. I. 'Des origines à la Renaissance' with an intro-
             duction by Maurice Halbwachs.
             II. 'De la Renaissance à nos jours'
             (*Lectures on Education,* transl. Peter Collins, Routledge
             & Kegan Paul, forthcoming.)

*1950a   *Leçons de sociologie: physique des moeurs et du droit.*
             Foreword by H. N. Kubali. Introduction by G. Davy.
             L'Université d'Istanbul, Istanbul, Presses Universitaires
             de France, Paris.
t.1957a   by C. Brookfield, *Professional Ethics and Civic Morals,*
             Routledge & Kegan Paul, London.

*1955a   *Pragmatisme et sociologie. Cours inédit prononcé à la
             Sorbonne en 1913–14 et restitué par Armand
             Cuvillier d'après des notes d'étudiants,* Vrin, Paris.
t.1960c   lectures 1–5, 13 and 14 by C. Blend in Wolff (1960).
             (See 1899a[i].)

2 Durkheim and Totemism

A selection of books, articles and reviews written by Durkheim in which reference is made to totemism. The dating-enumeration is that of Lukes (1973). The full details of some items have already been given in section 1 of the Bibliography, Durkheim and Religion. See Introduction, p. 9.

1898a(ii)   See section 1 of Bibliography.

1898a(iv)(1)   Review. 'Kohler, Professor J., *Zur Urgeschichte der Ehe. Totemismus, Gruppenehe, Mutterrecht.* Stuttgart', *AS*, I, pp. 306–19.

1900a(8)   Review. 'Spencer (Baldwin) et F.-J. Gillen—*The Native Tribes of Central Australia.* Macmillan, Londres, 1899', *AS*, III, pp. 330–6.

1902a(i)   'Sur le totémisme', *AS*, V, pp. 82–121.

1903a(i)   See section 1 of Bibliography.

1903d   Review. 'Andrew Lang, *Social Origins*, and J. J. Atkinson, *Primal Law*', *Folklore*, XIV pp. 421–5.

1904d   Correspondence. 'Response à M. Lang', *Folklore*, XV, pp. 215–16.

1905a(i)   'Sur l'organisation matrimoniale des sociétés australiennes', *AS*, VIII, pp. 118–47.

1906a(13)   Review. 'Merker (M.)—*Die Masai. Ethnographische Monographie eines ostafrikanischen Semitenvolkes.* Berlin, 1904', *AS*, IX, pp. 331–1.

1906a(19)   Review. 'Howitt (A. W.)—*The Native Tribes of South-East Australia.* Macmillan, Londres, 1904', *AS*, IX, pp. 355–68.

1906a(21)   Review. 'Kovalewsky (Maxime)—"Le Clan chez les tribus indigènes de la Russie." *Rev. intern. de sociol.* 1905, fev. pp. 81–101', *AS*, IX, p. 369.

1906a(22)   Review. 'Kovalewsky (Maxine)—"Le Clan chez les tribus et indigènes de la Russie." *Rev. intern. de sociol.* 1905, fev. ix, pp. 81–101', *AS*, IX, p. 369.

1907a(16)   Review. 'Lang, Andrew, *The Secret of the Totem.* London, 1905', *AS*, X, pp. 400–9.

1910a(ii)(2)   See section 1 of the Bibliography.

1910a(iii)(3)   Review with M. Mauss. 'C. Strehlow—*Die Aranda und Loritja-Staemme in Zentral-Australien*', *AS*, XI, pp. 76–81.

1910a(iii)(4)   Review. 'Marzan (de)—"Le Totémisme aux îles Fiji", *Anthropos*, 1907, pp. 715–21', *AS*, XI, pp. 105–6.

1910a(iii)(5)   Review. 'W. H. R. Rivers—"Totemism in Fiji", *Man*, 1908', *AS*, XI, pp. 105–6.

1910a(iii)(6)   Review. 'Seligman—"Note on totemism in New Guinea". *Man*, 1908', *AS*, XI, p. 106.

1910a(iii)(9)   Review. 'Thomas (Northcote W.)—"Kinship organisation and group marriage in Australia". Cambridge University Press', *AS*, XI, pp. 335–43.

1910a(iii)(14) Review. 'Kohler, J.—"Ueber Totemismus und Urehe". *Zeitschrift für vergleichende Rechtswissenschaft*, XIX, pp. 177–88', *AS*, XI, pp. 359–61.

1910a(iii)(15) Review. 'Kohler, J.—"Eskimo und Gruppenehe". *Zeitschrift für vergleichende Rechtswissenschaft*, XIX, pp. 423–32', *AS*, XI, pp. 359–61.

1910a(iii)(16) Review. 'Kohler, J.—"Nochmals ueber Gruppenehe und Totemismus". *Zeitschrift für vergleichende Rechtswissenschaft*, XXI, pp. 252–67', *AS*, XI, pp. 359–61.

1910a(iii)(17) Review. 'Crawley, A. E.—"Exogamy and the mating of cousins". *Mélanges Tylor*, pp. 51 ff.', *AS*, XI, pp. 361–2.

1910a(iii)(18) Review. 'Lang, A.—"Australian problems". *Mélanges Tylor*, pp. 203 ff.', *AS*, XI, pp. 361–2.

1912a   See section 1 of the Bibliography.

1913a(i)(2)   See section 1 of the Bibliography.

1913a(ii)(6)
&(7)   See section 1 of the Bibliography.

1913a(ii)(10) See section 1 of the Bibliography.

1913a(ii)(11)
&(12)   See section 1 of the Bibliography.

1913a(ii)(13) Review. 'Goldenweiser (A. A.)—"Totemism, an analytical study". *Journal of American Folk-Lore*, XXIII', *AS*, XII, pp. 100–1.

1913a(ii)(16)   Review. 'Fletcher (Alice C.) et La Flesche (Francis)—*The Omaha Tribe*. XXVIIth Annual Report of the Bureau of Amer. Ethnology, 1911, pp. 15–672', *AS*, XII, pp. 366–71.

1913a(ii)(17)   Review with M. Mauss. 'Endle (Sydney)—*The Kacharis* (with an introduction by J. D. Anderson). Macmillan, Londres, 1911', *AS*, XII, pp. 375–8.

1913a(ii)(30)   Review. 'Avebury (Lord)—*Marriage, Totemism and Exogamy. An Answer to Critics*. Londres, 1911', *AS*, XII, p. 429.

1913a(ii)(31)   Review. 'Frazer—*Totemism and Exogamy*. Macmillan, Londres, 1910, 4 vols', *AS*, XII, pp. 429–32.

1960c   'Letter to A. R. Radcliffe-Brown dated November 9, 1913' (see 1899a(i) in section 1).

3   On Durkheim and Religion

The following items have been written by authors other than Durkheim. They all make reference to Durkheim's analysis or theory of religion, or some aspect of his life and work which is related to religion. The list is by no means definitive.

ADAMS, G. P.   1916 'The interpretation of religion in Royce and Durkheim,' *PR*, 25, pp. 297–304.

ALPERT, H.   1938 'Durkheim's functional theory of ritual', *Sociology and Social Research*, 23, pp. 103–8. (Reproduced in R. A. Nisbet, 1965, *Émile Durkheim*. Prentice-Hall, Englewood Cliffs, New Jersey, pp. 137–41.)

ALPERT, H.   1939 *Émile Durkheim and his Sociology*, Columbia University Press, New York.

ALPERT, H.   1959 'Émile Durkheim, a perspective and appreciation', *ASR*, 24, pp. 462–5.

ANONYMOUS   1913 Review. '*Les Formes élémentaires de la vie religieuse. Le système totémique en Australie*', *RMM*, 21 (supplément), pp. 1–3.

ARON, R.   1967a *Les Étapes de la pensée sociologique*, Gallimard, Paris.

ARON, R.   1967b *Main Currents of Sociological Thought*, 2 vols. Translation of *Les Grandes Doctrines de sociologie historique*, Basic Books, New York. (1968 Weidenfeld & Nicolson, London.)

BARNES, H. E. and BECKER, H.   1938 *Social Thought from Lore to Science*, 2 vols, Heath, Boston.

BASTIDE, R.   1935 *Éléments de sociologie religieuse*, Colin, Paris.

BEATTIE, J.   1966 'Ritual and social change', *Man* (n.s.), 1, pp. 60–74.

BELLAH, R. N. 1959 'Durkheim and history', *ASR*, 24, pp. 447–61.
BELLAH, R. N. 1968 'Religion—II. The sociology of religion', *International Encyclopedia of the Social Sciences*, Macmillan and the Free Press, New York, vol. 13, pp. 406–14.
BELLAH, R. N. 1970 *Beyond Belief. Essays on Religion in a Post Traditional World*, Harper & Row, New York.
BELLAH, R. N. (ed.) 1973 *Émile Durkheim on Morality and Society*, Introduction by R. N. Bellah, University of Chicago Press, Chicago and London.
BELOT, G. 1900 'La Religion comme principe sociologique', *RP*, 49, pp. 288–99.
BELOT, G. 1913a 'Une Théorie nouvelle de la religion', *RP*, 75, pp. 329–79.
BELOT, G. 1913b 'L'Idée de Dieu et l'athéisme', *RMM*, 21, pp. 151–176.
BELOT, G. 1919 Contribution to discussion in F. Abauzit *et al.*, *Le Sentiment religieux à l'heure actuelle*, Vrin, Paris, pp. 105–34.
BENDIX, R. and ROTH, G. 1971 *Scholarship and Partisanship. Essays on Max Weber*, University of California Press, Berkeley, Los Angeles and London.
BENEDICT, R. 1934 'Ritual', *Encyclopedia of the Social Sciences*, Macmillan, New York, vol. 13, p. 396–7.
BENOIT-SMULLYAN, E. 1948 'The sociologism of Émile Durkheim and his school', in H. E. Barnes (ed.), *An Introduction to the History of Sociology*, University of Chicago Press, Chicago, pp. 499–537.
BESSE, DOM 1913 *Les Religions laïques. Un romantisme religieux*, Nouvelle Librairie Nationale, Paris.
BIERSTEDT, R. 1966 *Émile Durkheim*, Weidenfeld & Nicolson, London.
BIRNBAUM, N. and LENZER, G. 1969 Introduction to *Sociology and Religion: A Book of Readings*, Prentice-Hall, Englewood Cliffs, New Jersey.
BIROU, A. 1959a 'Religion e ideal en el pensamiento de Durkheim', *Revista mexicana de sociologia*, 21, no. 3, pp. 1001–40.
BIROU, A. 1959b *Sociologie et religion*, Les Editions Ouvrières, Paris.
BOCOCK, R. J. 1970 'Ritual: civic and religious', *BJS*, 21, pp. 285–98.
BOCOCK, R. J. 1974 *Ritual in Industrial Society*, Allen & Unwin, London.
BOUGLÉ, C. 1930 'Quelques souvenirs', in 'L'Oeuvre sociologique d'Émile Durkheim', *Europe*, 22, pp. 381–4.
BOURGIN, H. 1938 *De Jaurès à Léon Blum. L'École normale et la politique*, Fayard, Paris.
BUDD, S. 1973 *Sociologists and Religion*, Collier-Macmillan, London.
CAILLOIS, R. 1939 *L'Homme et le sacré*, Gallimard, Paris. (English translation by M. Barash, *Man and the Sacred*, Free Press, Chicago, 1959.)
CANTONI, R. 1963 'La Sociologia religiosa di Durkheim', *Quaderni sociologici*, 12, 3, pp. 239–71.

CAZENEUVE, J.   1971   *Sociologie du rite*, P.U.F., Paris.

CHATTERTON-HILL, G.   1912a   'L'Étude sociologique des religions', *Revue d'histoire et de littérature religieuses*, 3, pp. 1–42.

CHATTERTON-HILL, G.   1912b   *The Sociological Value of Christinaity*, A. & C. Black, London.

CLARK, T.N.   1973   *Prophets and Patrons*, Harvard University Press, Cambridge, Mass.

CUVILLIER, A.   1953   *Où va la sociologie française?*, Librairie Marcel Rivière, Paris.

DANSETTE, A.   1951   *Histoire religieuse de la France contemporaine*, 2 vols, Flammarion, Paris.

DAVY, G.   1911   *Émile Durkheim. Choix de textes*, Louis-Michaud, Paris.

DAVY, G.   1919   'Émile Durkheim: I. L'Homme', *RMM*, 26, pp. 181–98.

DAVY, G.   1920   'Durkheim: II. L'Oeuvre', *RMM*, 27, pp. 71–112.

DAVY, G.   1960   'Émile Durkheim', *Revue française de sociologle*, 1, pp. 3–24.

DEPLOIGE, S.   1905–7   'Le Conflit de la morale et de la sociologie', *RNS*, 12, pp. 405–17; 13, pp. 49–79, 135–63, 281–313; 14, pp. 329–54, 355–92.

DEPLOIGE, S.   1907   'Réponses aux lettres de M. Durkheim', *RNS*, 14, pp. 607–11, 614–21.

DEPLOIGE, S.   1911   *Le Conflit de la morale et de la sociologie*, Dewit, Bruxelles. (Reproduction of articles 1905–7.) (English translation *The Conflict between Ethics and Sociology*, Herder, St Louis and London, by C. C. Miltner, 1938.)

DESROCHE, H.   1968   *Sociologies religieuses*, P.U.F., Paris. (English translation by J. K. Savacool, *Jacob and the Angels: an Essay in Sociology of Religion*, with a Foreword by N. Birnbaum, University of Massachusetts Press, Amherst, Mass., 1973.)

DESROCHE, H.   1969   'Retour à Durkheim? D'un texte peu connu à quelques thèses méconnues', *ASRel*, 27, pp. 79–88.

DOUGLAS, J. D.   1967   *The Social Meaning of Suicide*, Princeton University Press, New Jersey.

DOUGLAS, M.   1966   *Purity and Danger. An Analysis of Concepts of Pollution and Taboo*, Routledge & Kegan Paul, London.

DOUGLAS, M.   1970   *Natural Symbols. Explorations in Cosmology*, Barrie & Rockliff, London.

DUNCAN, H. D.   1960   'The development of Durkheim's concept of ritual and the problem of social disrelationships', in K. H. Wolff (ed.), *Émile Durkheim 1858–1917*, Ohio State University Press, Columbus, Ohio, pp. 97–117.

DUNCAN, H. D.   1969   *Symbols and Social Theory*, O.U.P., New York.

DUVIGNAUD, J.   1965   *Durkheim, sa vie, son oeuvre*, P.U.F., Paris.

EVANS-PRITCHARD, E. E.   1956   *Nuer Religion*, Clarendon Press, Oxford.

EVANS-PRITCHARD, E. E.   1960   Introduction to the translation by R. and C. Needham of R. Hertz's *Death* and *The Right Hand*, Cohen &

West, London, pp. 9–24.

EVANS-PRITCHARD, E. E. 1962 *Essays in Social Anthropology*, Faber, London.

EVANS-PRITCHARD, E. E. 1965 *Theories of Primitive Religion*, Clarendon Press, Oxford.

FILLOUX, J.-C. 1970 Introduction and notes. Émile Durkheim, *La Science sociale et l'action*, P.U.F., Paris. (A selection of previously published articles by Durkheim.)

FORDE, D. 1958 *The Context of Belief: a Consideration of Fetishism among the Yakö*, Liverpool University Press, Liverpool.

FÜRER-HAIMENDORF, C. 1962 *The Apa Tanis and their Neighbours*, Routledge & Kegan Paul, London.

GEERTZ, C. 1968 'Religion—I. Anthropological study', *International Encyclopedia of the Social Sciences*, Macmillan and the Free Press, New York, vol. 13, pp. 398–406.

GELLNER, E. 1962 'Concepts and society', *Transaction of the Fifth World Congress of Sociology (Washington)*. Reproduced in I. C. Jarvie and J. Agassi (eds), 1973, *Cause and Meaning in the Social Sciences*, Routledge & Kegan Paul, London and Boston.

GENNEP, A. VAN See van Gennep, A.

GIDDENS, A. 1972 *Émile Durkheim: Selected Writings*, C.U.P., London.

GINSBERG, M. 1956 *On the Diversity of Morals*, vol. I, Heinemann, London, pp. 230–42.

GOBLET D'ALVIELLA, COMTE 'La Sociologie de M. Durkheim et l'histoire des religions', *Revue de l'histoire des religions*, 67, pp. 192–221.

GLUCKMAN, M. 1962 'Les Rites de Passage', in M. Gluckman (ed.), *Essays on the Ritual of Social Relations*, Manchester University Press, Manchester.

GOLDENWEISER, A. A. 1915 Review. '*Les Formes élémentaires de la vie religieuse*', *American Anthropologist*, 17, pp. 719–35. (Included in this volume.)

GOLDENWEISER, A. A. 1916 'The views of Andrew Lang and J. G. Frazer and Émile Durkheim on totemism', *Anthropos*, vols X–XI, pp. 948–70.

GOLDENWEISER, A. A. 1917 'Religion and society: a critique of Émile Durkheim's theory of the origin and nature of religion', *Journal of Philosophy, Psychology and Scientific Methods*, 14, pp. 113–24. (Reproduced in *History, Psychology and Culture*, Kegan Paul, London and Norwood, Mass., 1933, pp. 361–73.)

GOLDENWEISER, A. A. 1923 *Early Civilization: an Introduction to Anthropology*, Harrap, London.

GOODE, W. J. 1951 *Religion among the Primitives*, Free Press, Chicago.

GOODY, J. 1961 'Religion and ritual: the definitional problem', *BJS*, 12, pp. 142–64.

GRAFTON, H. G. 1945 'Religious origins and sociological theory', *ASR*, 10, pp. 726–39.

Bibliography 317

GRANET, M.   1930   'La Sociologie religieuse de Durkheim', in L'Oeuvre sociologique d'Émile Durkheim', *Europe*, 22, pp. 287–92.

GURVITCH, G.   1937   'La Science des faits moreaux et la morale théorique chez É. Durkheim', *Archives de philosophie du droit et sociologie juridique*, 7, pp. 18–44.

GURVITCH, G.   1938   *Essais de sociologie*, Recueil Sirey, Paris.

GURVITCH, G.   1950   *La Vocation actuelle de la sociologie vers une sociologie differentielle*, P.U.F., Paris. (3rd ed., 2 vols, 1957 and 1963.)

HALBWACHS, M.   1918   'La Doctrine d'Émile Durkheim', *RP*, 43, pp. 353–411.

HALBWACHS, M.   1925   *Les Origines du sentiment religieux*, Delamain, Boutelleau et Cie, Paris. (English translation by J. A. Spaulding, *Sources of Religious Sentiment*, Free Press, New York, 1962.)

HAMÈS, C.   1969   'Le Sentiment religieux à l'heure actuelle. Un texte peu connu de Durkheim. À propos de la parution des *Formes élémentaires de la vie religieuse*', *ASRel*, 27, pp. 71–2.

HAMNETT, I.   1973   'Sociology of religion and sociology of error', *Religion*, 3, pp. 1–12.

HARRISON, J. E.   1912   *Themis*, C.U.P., Cambridge.

HARTLAND, E. S.   1913   Review. 'Australia: totemism. *Les Formes élémentaires de la vie religieuse*', *Man*, 13, 6, pp. 91–6.

HARTLAND, E. S.   1914   *Ritual and Belief. Studies in the History of Religion*. Williams & Norgate, London.

HØFFDING, H.   1914   '*Les Formes élémentaires de la vie religieuse*', *RMM*, 22, pp. 828–48.

HONIGSHEIM, P.   1960   'The influence of Durkheim and his school on the study of religion', in K. H. Wolff (ed.), *Émile Durkheim 1858–1917*, Ohio State University Press, Columbus, Ohio, pp. 233–46.

HORTON, R.   1960   'A definition of religion and its uses', *Journal of the Royal Anthropological Institute*, 90, pp. 201–25.

HORTON, R.   1973   'Lévy-Bruhl, Durkheim and the scientific revolution', in R. Horton and R. Finnegan (eds), *Modes of Thought*, Faber, London, pp. 249–305.

HUGHES, H. S.   1958   *Consciousness and Society*, Vintage, New York.

ISAMBERT, F. A.   1969   'The early days of French sociology of religion', *Social Compass*, XVI/4, pp. 435–52.

KARADY, V.   1968   'Présentation de l'édition', in M. Mauss, *Oeuvres*, 3 vols, Les Éditions de Minuit, Paris, pp. i–liii.

KARDINER, A. and PREBLE, E.   1961   *They Studied Man*, Secker & Warburg, London.

KÖNIG, R.   1962   'Über die Religionssoziologie bei Émile Durkheim', in D. Goldschmidt and J. Matthes (eds), 'Probleme der Religionssoziologie', Kölner Zeitschrift für Soziologie und Sozialpsychologie, Köln und Opladen, West Deutscher Verlag, Sonderheft 6, pp. 36–49.

LACAPRA, D.   1972   *Emile Durkheim: Sociologist and Philosopher*, Cornell University Press, Ithaca and London.

LALANDE, A.   1906   'Philosophy in France (1905)', *PR*, 15, pp. 252–62.

LEACH, E. R. 1964 *Political Systems of Highland Burma*, Bell, London.

LE BRAS, G. 1960 Émile Durkheim et la sociologie des religions', *Annales de l'Université de Paris*, I, pp. 45–6.

LE BRAS, G. 1966 'Note sur la sociologie religieuse dans *l'Année sociologique*', *ASRel*, 21, pp. 47–53.

LECLERCQ, J. 1948 *Introduction á la sociologie*, Institut de recherches économiques et sociales de l'Université de Louvain.

LENOIR, R. 1918 'Emile Durkheim et la conscience moderne', *MF*, 127, pp. 577–95.

LEUBA, J. H. 1913 'Sociology and psychology: the conception of religion and magic and the place of psychology in sociological studies', *AJS*, 19, pp. 323–42.

LÉVI-STRAUSS, C. 1945 'French sociology', in G. Gurvitch and W. E. Moore (eds), *Twentieth Century Sociology*, The Philosophical Library, New York, pp. 503–37.

LÉVI-STRAUSS, C. 1960 'Ce que l'ethnologie doit à Durkheim', *Annales de l'Université de Paris*, I, pp. 47–52.

LÉVI-STRAUSS, C. 1962a *Le Totémisme aujourd'hui*, P.U.F., Paris. (English translation by R. Needham, *Totemism*, Beacon Press, Boston, Mass., 1963. Reprinted, Penguin, London, 1969.)

LÉVI-STRAUSS, C. 1962b *La pensée sauvage*, Librarie Plon, Paris. (English translation by R. Needham, *Totemism*, Beacon Press, Boston, Mass., 1963. Reprinted, Penguin, London, 1969.)

LIENHARDT, R. G. 1956 'Religion', in H. L. Shapiro (ed.), *Man, Culture and Society*, O.U.P., New York, ch. XIV.

LOISY, A. 1913 'Sociologie et religion' (a review of *Les Formes élémentaires de la vie religieuse*). *Revue d'histoire et de littérature religieuses*, 4, pp. 45–76.

LOWIE, R. H. 1925 *Primitive Religion*, George Routledge & Sons, London.

LOWIE, R. H. 1937 *The History of Ethnological Theory*, Harrap, London.

LUKES, S. 1968 'Émile Durkheim: an Intellectual Biography', D.Phil. thesis, Oxford University.

LUKES, S. 1973 *Émile Durkheim: his Life and Work*, Allen Lane, London.

LUPU, I. 1931 *Die Grundlagen der Gesellschaft, das Recht und die Religion in der Durkheimschule: Ihr besonderer Widenhall in der Jenenser Jerusalemschen Soziologie*, Viata Romacascâ, Iasi.

MCFARLAND, H. N. 1954 'Theories of the Social Origin of Religion in the Tradition of Émile Durkheim', unpublished Ph.D. thesis, Columbia University.

MALINOWSKI, B. 1913 Review. '*Les Formes élémentaires de la vie religieuse*', *Folklore*, 24, pp. 525–31.

MALINOWSKI, B. 1925 'Magic, science and religion', in J. D. Needham (ed.), *Science, Religion and Reality*, Sheldon Press, London. (Reproduced in B. Malinowski, 1948, *Magic, Science and Religion and other essays*, Free Press, Chicago.)

MARETT, R. R. 1909 *The Threshold of Religion*, Methuen, London.

MAUNIER, R. 1913 Review. '*Les Formes élémentaires de la vie religieuse*', *RIS*, 1913, p. 276.

MAUSS, M. 1925 'In memoriam, l'oeuvre inédite de Durkheim et de ses collaborateurs', *AS*, n.s., 1, pp. 7–29.

MAUSS, M. 1968 *Oeuvres*. 3 vols, edited by Victor Karady. Les Editions de Minuit, Paris.

MEHL, R. 1951 'Dans quelle mesure la sociologie peut-elle saisir la réalité de l'Église', *Revue d'histoire et de philosophie religieuses*, 21, pp. 429–38.

MEHL, R. 1965 *Traité de sociologie du protestantisme*, Delachaux et Niestlé, Neuchâtel. (English translation by J. H. Farley, *The Sociology of Protestantism*, S.C.M., London, 1970.)

NISBET, R. A. 1965 *Emile Durkheim* (with selected essays), Prentice Hall, Englewood Cliffs, New Jersey.

NISBET, R. A. 1974 *The Sociology of Émile Durkheim*, O.U.P., New York.

O'DEA, T. 1966 *Sociology of Religion*, Prentice-Hall, Englewood Cliffs, New Jersey.

OUY, M. 1939 'Les Sociologies et la sociologie,' *RIS*, 47, pp. 245–75, 463–91.

PARODI, D. 1913 'Le Problème religieux dans la pensée contemporaine', *RMM*, 21, pp. 511–25.

PARODI, D. 1919 *La Philosophie contemporaine en France. Essai de classification des doctrines*, Alcan, Paris.

PARSONS, T. 1937 *The Structure of Social Action*, Free Press, Chicago.

PARSONS, T. 1949 'The theoretical development of the sociology of religion', in *Essays in Sociological Theory, Pure and Applied*, Free Press, Chicago, pp. 52–66.

PARSONS, T. 1966 'Durkheim, Émile', *International Encyclopedia of Social Sciences*, Macmillan and the Free Press, New York, vol. 4, pp. 311–20.

PÉCAUT, F. 1918 'Émile Durkheim', *Revue pédagogique*, 72, pp. 1–20.

PERISTIANY, J. G. 1960 'Durkheim's letter to Radcliffe-Brown', in K. H. Wolff (ed.), *Émile Durkheim 1858–1917*, Ohio State University Press, Columbus, Ohio, pp. 317–24.

PEYRE, H. 1960 'Durkheim: the man, his time and his intellectual background', in K. H. Wolff (ed.), *Émile Durkheim 1858–1917*, Ohio State University Press, Columbus, Ohio, pp. 3–31.

PINARD DE LA BOULLAYE, H. 1922 *L'Étude comparée des religions*, vol. I, Beauchesne, Paris. 1925 Vol. II. 1931 Vol. III.

POGGI, G. 1971 'The place of religion in Durkheim's theory of institutions', *EJS*, pp. 229–66.

POOLE, R. C. 1969 Introduction, 'C. Lévi-Strauss, *Totemism*', Penguin, London.

POPE, W. 1973 'Classic on Classic: Parsons' Interpretation of Durkheim', *ASR*, 38, pp. 349–415.

RADCLIFFE-BROWN, A. R. 1952 *Structure and Function in Primitive*

Society, Cohen & West, London.

RADIN, P. 1938 *Primitive Religion: its Nature and Order*, Hamish Hamilton, London.

RICHARD, G. See bibliography on Richard in this volume (pp. 358–9).

RICHTER, M. 1960 'Durkheim's politics and political theory', in K. H. Wolff (ed.), *Émile Durkheim 1858–1917*, Ohio State University Press, Columbus, Ohio, pp. 170, 210.

ROBERTSON, R. 1970 *The Sociological Interpretation of Religion*, Blackwell, Oxford.

RUNCIMAN, W. G. 1969 'The sociological explanation of religious beliefs', *EJS*, 10, pp. 149–91.

SCHARF, B. R. 1970 'Durkheimian and Freudian theories of religion: the case of Judaism', *BJS*, 21, pp. 151–63.

SCHMIDT, W. 1931 *The Origin and Growth of Religion: Facts and Theories* (translated by H. J. Rose), Methuen, London.

SEGER, I. 1957 *Durkheim and his Critics on the Sociology of Religion*, Bureau of Applied Social Research, Columbia University, New York.

SPIRO, M. E. 1966 'Religion: problems of definition and explanation', in M. Banton (ed.), *Anthropological Approaches to the Study of Religion*, Tavistock, London, pp. 85–126.

STANNER, W. E. H. 1966 *On Aboriginal Religion*, Oceania Monograph 11, University of Sydney, Sydney.

STANNER, W. E. H. 1967 'Reflections on Durkheim and aboriginal religion', in M. Freedman (ed.), *Social Organization: Essays Presented to Raymond Firth*, Frank Cass, London, pp. 217–40. (Included in this volume.)

STEINER, F. 1956 *Taboo*, Cohen & West, London.

SUMPF, J. 1965 'Durkheim et le problème de l'étude sociologique de la religion', *ASRel*, 20, pp. 63–73.

SWANSON, G. E. 1960 *The Birth of the Gods: the Origin of Primitive Beliefs*, University of Michigan Press, Ann Arbor.

TAYLOR, S. 1963 'Some implications of the contribution of É. Durkheim to religious thought', *Philosophical and Phenomenological Research*, 24, pp. 125–34.

TIRYAKIAN, E. A. 1962 *Sociologism and Existentialism: Two Perspectives on the Individual and Society*, Prentice-Hall, Englewood Cliffs, New Jersey.

TOWLER, R. 1974 *Homo Religiosus: Sociological problems in the study of religion*, Constable, London.

VAN GENNEP, A. 1913 Review. 'Les Formes élémentaires de la vie religieuse', *MF*, 101, pp. 389–91. (Included in this volume.)

VAN GENNEP, A. 1920 *L'État actuel de problème totémique*, Leroux, Paris.

WALLIS, W. D. 1914 'Durkheim's view of religion', *Journal of Religious Psychology*, 7, pp. 252–67.

WALLWORK, E. 1972 *Durkheim: Morality and Milieu*, Harvard University Press, Cambridge, Mass.

WARNER, W. L.   1936   'The social configuration of magical behaviour: a study in the nature of magic', in R. H. Lowie (ed.), *Essays in Anthropology Presented to A. L. Kroeber in Celebration of his Sixtieth Birthday*, University of California Press, Berkeley, pp. 405–15.

WARNER, W. L.   1937   *A Black Civilization*, Harper, New York and London.

WEATHERLY, U. G.   1917   Review. '*The elementary forms of the religious life*', *AJS*, 22, pp. 561–3.

WEBB, C. C. J.   1916   *Group Theories of Religion and the Individual*, Allen & Unwin, London.

WEBSTER, H.   1913   Review. '*Les Formes élémentaires de la vie religieuse*', *AJS*, pp. 843–6.

WORMS, R.   1917   'Émile Durkheim', *RIS*, 25, pp. 561–8.

ZEITLIN, I. M.   1968   *Ideology and the Development of Sociological Theory*, Prentice-Hall, Englewood Cliffs, New Jersey.

Abstracts

Durkheim and Religion

The following abstracts consist of summaries of the references to religion in Durkheim's works. The items chosen are in books, articles or reviews which do not appear as complete translations in this volume. Since *The Elementary Forms of the Religious Life* is long, and since extracts are given in the translations no reference to it is made in these notes. For a résumé, see Durkheim 1913a(ii)(12). The full bibliographical details of each item are to be found in section 1 of the Bibliography, Durkheim and Religion. Numbers in the brackets refer in the first instance to pages in the items. Where there are two numbers, the second which is preceded by a t. refers to the corresponding page in the English translation. For example, in connection with *L'Education morale* 1925a, (19/t.21) means p. 19 in 1925a and p. 21 in 1961a, the translation by Wilson and Schnurer.

1887c   'La Science positive de la morale en Allemagne'

In this general review of a group of thinkers in Germany, among them Wundt, Schmoller, Schaeffle and Ihering, who were concerned with what was called the new science of morality, Durkheim's comments on Wundt are of particular interest because of his acknowledgment of having been influenced by Wundt (see 1907b). Wundt approached morality empirically and held that religion was one of its determining factors (116–18). In the beginning, law, morality and religion formed an indistinguishable synthesis: they later became dissociated from each other. However, religion and morality were always closely related and when they did become dissociated, religion turned towards morality and modified its own concepts accordingly. The gods project a moral ideal which is to be imitated by men. All religious *représentations* and sentiments which relate to an ideal existence conform to the wishes and desires of the human heart. The ideal varies with societies. It thus corresponds to a deeply rooted need in human nature. Wundt's position was strongly evolutionary as in his contention that the cult of natural forces was superseded by that of heroes, later giving rise to the idea of an incarnated god.

1893b   *De la Division du travail social*

In this, his first book, his doctoral thesis, Durkheim held that in societies characterized by mechanical solidarity, penal law is essentially religious in its origin (98–9/t.92–3). Religion exercises constraint over individuals and demands personal sacrifices of them. Sacrilege is very severely punished. In such societies people profess the same religion (144–5/t.135); schisms are unknown or not tolerated. Religion includes law, morality, and political institutions. By contrast with other religions, Christianity has idealistic beliefs (176–7/t.163–4). Through scholasticism there emerged free thought and the virtual disappearance of religious criminality. Durkheim rejects the notion that, scientifically speaking, religion is a belief in gods (182/t.168). Buddhism has no gods and many religious laws do not refer to gods—they are the product of the human imagination. 'Religion tends to embrace a smaller and smaller portion of social life' with the advance of history (183/t.169). Once it was co-terminous with social life, but political and economic functions have freed themselves from religious functions. Individuals are now less influenced by religion, although individuals are themselves becoming the object of religion (187/t.172). He criticizes Fustel de Coulanges for suggesting that religion explains the social:

rather, it is the social that determines religion (194/t.179). Philosophy emerged when religion, 'the eminent form of the collective *conscience*', lost its hold (316/t.285). Antagonism to religion emerges when new sciences appear. Believers find it repugnant that man is now studied as a natural being and moral facts as natural facts. As the collective *conscience* becomes weaker, as in societies characterized by organic solidarity, individual interpretations are given greater place (322/t.290). When God is held to be far away from man's actions, he is no longer seen to be omnipresent: nor does he possess such power as he once had. As soon as reflection is aroused, it is difficult to restrain it, as for example in the thinking about God. (This book shows early and important ideas which Durkheim had about religion, which he never revoked.)

1895a   *Les Règles de la méthode sociologique*

In his well-known essay on sociological method, Durkheim makes a few very brief but important references to religion. Religion is viewed as a social fact, that is, it is external to the believer who is presented with beliefs and practices already in existence at his birth: they are outside him and prior to him in time (6/t.1–2). In order to study social facts (e.g. religion) scientifically, one must not be emotionally committed to the subject matter. Durkheim quotes with disapproval the alleged requirement of religious experience for a historian of religions as suggested by James Darmesteter (42/t.33). The weakening of religious beliefs is normal in the type of society man now lives in (77 n. 3/t.62 n. 8). But the weakening of religion brings with it the need for knowledge along with a tendency to suicide (162/t.132). (See 1897a.) Man comes to know his dependence on society in *représentations* of it created by religion: he can also reach the same conclusion through science (150/t.123).

1897a   *Le Suicide*

Chapter 2 of Book II is included in this volume. Elsewhere Durkheim notes that insanity has been more frequent among Jews than those of other faiths, but between Catholics and Protestants the difference has only been slight (39/t.72). In the past, religion consoled the workers by making them content with their lot and

offering compensation in a world to come (shades of Marx!), masters
were remined that worldly goods were not to be man's highest
interest and that men were to be subject to moral norms (283/t.254).
But religion has now lost its power. Religion in the beginning was
not derived from feelings of fear and reverence (352/t.312). Man
worships society and society is but the gods hypostasized. Religion
is the system of symbols by which society becomes conscious of
itself—it is characteristic of thinking about collective existence
(ibid.). A historical outline of the relation of Church and state to
suicide is presented (370–6/t.327–32). Modern man may now be
said to worship himself, 'man has become a god for men' (379/t.
334), and so Durkheim argues that on such grounds suicide is
immoral, for to commit suicide is to kill God. His position logically
forces him to reject the notion that morality needs religion for a
foundation (359/t.318). Religion today is powerless to prevent
suicidogenetic currents (430–2/t.374–6). Roman Catholicism could
be more successful than Protestantism in this respect but its failure
to allow free criticism offends 'our dearest sentiments'. Thus
Catholicism fails despite its potential power and control through the
confessional. Homicide is more frequent in Catholic countries than
those dominated by Protestantism (403–4/t.353–4). The case of
altruistic suicide arising from a sense of duty is discussed with
reference to Hinduism, Buddhism, Jainism, and hence pantheism
(241–5/t.223–7). (The importance of this book in understanding
Durkheim's approach to religion is all too frequently overlooked.)

1897e   Review. 'Labriola—*Essais sur la conception matérialiste de l'histoire'*
A critical view of a Marxist writer who propounded a philosophy of
history based on economic factors. Durkheim states that the Marxist
hypothesis is not proved and is contrary to facts already established.
He also states that religion according to sociologists and historians
is the most primitive of all social phenomena, not economic action
(650). From religion have come other social activities—law,
morality, etc. In principle, everything is religious. An economy
probably depends more upon religion than religion on an economy.
(For references to the Reformers, see p. 646.)

1898a(ii)   'La Prohibition de l'inceste et ses origines'
This was the first article by Durkheim to appear in the first issue of

L'Année sociologique. He associates the incest taboo with exogamy and holds that the taboo is necessary to maintain exogamy. In analysing Australian totemism, Durkheim maintains that the totem is a god and therefore the cause of exogamy is to be found in the religious beliefs of lower societies (39/t.69). The incest taboo is similar to ritual taboos and is associated with the ritual importance of blood (47/t.81). The home is based on mutual love: it has today as in times past a religious character, even though the household gods have now disappeared (60/t.101).

1898a(iii)(13)   Review. 'Marcel Mauss—"La Religion et les origines du droit pénal" '

Some comments by Durkheim on two review articles by Mauss on Steinmetz's *Ethnologische Studien zur ersten Entwicklung der Strafe* (ethnographic studies of the primitive development of punishment), 1894. Durkheim disagrees with Steinmetz who held that the religious origin of blood revenge was located in the individual and the cult of the dead. Although there is a relation between religion and punishment in primitive societies, Durkheim holds that blood revenge relates to the collective sentiment of the clan and the religious sentiments *vis-à-vis* the nature of blood. Steinmetz is accused of failing to take into account the importance of ritual prohibitions and the concept of taboo.

1899a(i)   'Preface', *L'Année sociologique*, vol. II

In the second volume of *L'Année sociologique*, mainly devoted to the sociology of religion, it is argued that religious facts should be treated as other social facts. When they are explained or described they are to be related to their specific milieu. Religious phenomena constitute the germ from which all other phenomena are derived (iv). Religion has given rise to various forms of collective life; myths and legends have produced science and poetry; ritual has produced law and morals; from the notion of soul, life, came philosophy, etc. The only exception is *perhaps* economic organizations. Collective life emanates from religion (a point on which Durkheim was later ambivalent). A footnote (v) states that the views expressed do not imply that religion must play the same role today as it did in the past. It is to have a smaller role as new social forms emerge. But these new forms can only be understood in terms of their origin, that is, their religious roots.

1899d Contribution to H. Dagan, *Enquête sur l'anti-sémitisme*

In his contribution to a collected series of contributions by well-known writers such as Gide, Zola, Lombroso, Durkheim in the matter of four pages distinguishes between two types of anti-semitism; that of Germany and Russia which is traditional and lasting, and that of France which is characterized by acute crises owing to passing conditions, and which inspires violent passions and destruction. In France anti-semitism is due to a social malaise, and when a society suffers, as France did in 1848 and 1870, a wish to find a scapegoat usually emerges. Thus the Jews have been looked upon as being the cause of France's social and economic ills. However, Durkheim holds that Jews tended to lose their ethnic characteristics with extreme rapidity. The Jewish faith is no less alive than it was thirty years ago, but anti-semitism was not what it is now. Durkheim wants the situation 'cooled' by eliminating the causes of friction but avoiding any repressive measures. There should not be occasions for the satisfaction of anti-semitic feeling.

1900a(47) Review. 'Ratzel—*Anthropogeographie*'

Durkheim praises Ratzel for his *Anthropogeographie* but he is nevertheless critical of some of the associations Ratzel makes between natural (geographical) phenomena and social institutions. With regard to religion Durkheim states that the nature of the soil and climate has exerted an influence over collective *représentations*, such as myths and legends, but it is not the work of the sociology of religion to study them in this way (556). Also, geographical factors do not show the same power of influence at different times in history. They are weaker now that religion is becoming increasingly weaker. However, religious beliefs in primitive societies show the impact of the soil where they were formed (557).

1900c 'La Sociologia ed il suo dominico scientifico'

Here Durkheim makes further reference to social facts being

obligatory, especially religious, moral and legal beliefs and practices. 'Normally, they impose themselves by the veneration they inspire, by the obligation to respect them by which we feel ourselves held, and, whenever we tend to rebel, by the coercion they exercise in the form of sanctions' (t.365). This is particularly so in religion, the reality of which is seen to be derived from a source above the individual. 'The believer takes this symbolic manifestation literally and, quite logically, explains the religious or moral imperative by reference to the eminent nature of the divine personality' (t.366). However, for the scientist (t.366)

a question of this sort does not arise since the domain of science does not extend beyond the empirical world. Science does not ask whether some other reality might exist. What it considers certain is that there are simply manners of acting and thinking that are obligatory and are therefore different from all other forms of action and idea.

Durkheim makes his position clear that as a scientist studying religion he cannot accept that reality which believers maintain is the ground of their faith.

1901h   A summary of a talk on 'Religion and free thought'

In a short newspaper account Durkheim, as someone who said he approached the subject scientifically, foresaw the triumph of science over religion but at the same time it was necessary for science to supply the needs which religion had long satisfied. A common ground for peace could be found between science and religion in searching for moral ends such as justice and the good of others. Religious belief was contrasted to science; the first was obligatory and dogmatic, the second free and open to criticism.

1903a(i)   'De Quelques formes primitives de classification'

This essay constitutes an important introduction to those parts of *Les Formes élémentaires* which deal with symbolism and the sociology of knowledge. References to religion as such are not many. The authors state that metamorphoses, such as the materialization of spirits and spiritualization of material objects, are a component of religious thinking (3/t.5). From Chinese culture it can be deduced that within a system of divination there is at least implicitly a system of classification (63–5/t.77–9). Further, all myths, which are not scientific in character but religious, are classificatory. The gods in Indian, Chinese and Greek religion divide up nature into recognized spheres. Classification has helped to reduce a multiplicity of gods to one god, who absorbs all their attributes, and so polytheism becomes monotheism or pantheism. Among primitive people, a species of things does not relate just to knowledge but more to sentiment: in this, religious emotion plays a very significant part, especially in matters referring to the sacred and profane, the pure and the impure, and so on (70/t.85–6).

1903a(ii)(57)   Review. 'Fournier de Flaix—"Statistique et consistance des religions à la fin du XIXe siècle" '

Here Durkheim reviews a paper on religious statistics. He criticizes the treatment of Buddhist statistics and discusses the problem of using accurately statistics referring to religious categories. The writer tried to show the resilience of Paris as a 'religious' city in giving the numbers of baptisms, religious marriages and burials. Durkheim sees this as a poor indicator of religious belief. (Notice that Durkheim assumes belief to be more important than ritual.) He observes a decline in religious marriages from 85 per cent in 1875 to 70 per cent in 1885, with a corresponding fall of baptisms. The facts put forward by the author are held insufficient to support his thesis.

1903c   (With P. Fauconnet) 'Sociologie et sciences sociales'

In a general survey of sociological writers, beginning with Comte and extending to Simmel and Giddings, there are two small references to religion. One is to Müller and other writers such as Tylor, Lang and Smith who have collected many facts and created a comparative science of religions. The second criticizes religious studies, since thinkers look upon religious beliefs and practices as the product of sentiments which originate in the unconsciousness of the individual and are only social in form in their external expression (495).

1905a(ii)(2)   Review. 'Pellison— *La Sécularisation de la morale au XVIIIe siècle*'

Pellison stated that the way to the secularization of morality began to be opened during the period of the Renaissance. Later a reaction set in as preachers maintained that morality was inseparable from faith. Durkheim suggests that the events were more complex than Pellison described. The rationalist and non-religious (*laïque*) concept of morality was clearly enunciated by Descartes, though it was also apparent in La Rochefoucauld and Spinoza. The role of the eighteenth century was to extend to the moral world the work of rational analysis Descartes had undertaken earlier. The author in Durkheim's eyes failed to see that the religious aspirations of the French Revolution came from the collective effervescence of the times. It was religious in character and was neither retrogressive nor stemmed from the ideas of Rousseau.

1905e Contribution to discussion: 'Sur la séparation des églises et de l'état'

Durkheim spoke on two issues regarding the question of the separation of the Church from the state. It was generally felt that separation would bring about a revival in the Church by being lay in origin and probably democratic in spirit. The question then arose—how would this movement be related to the authoritarian, hierarchical component of the Church? Durkheim sees these forces entering into a conflict and doubts whether democratic changes could take place within the institution. The other question to which he makes reference is a short comment on the emergence of lay associations of Catholics. Surprisingly he said: 'L'Église, au point de vue sociologique, est un monstre' (369). This comment gave rise to considerable controversy then and subsequently (369 n. 1). Durkheim defended himself by pointing to the vast size of the Church as a homogeneity without differences, social, intellectual or moral.

1906a(6) Review. 'Toniolo—*L'Ordierno problema sociologico*'

Durkheim criticizes the book because it is an example of what might be called apologetic sociology. As always, such an approach belittles the natural sciences and emphasizes the spiritual character of certain sociological or moral theories. Something in social life, it is held, eludes scientific analysis. From there one quickly moves to faith. Durkheim states it is useless to refute this way of arguing.

Today there is a tendency to recognize the moral and historical role of religion and to treat religious facts with respect. The old positivist school saw religion as an aberration but the *Année* school denies it and views religion as a system of *représentations* expressing imperfectly something of reality. The outlook of the believer—the observer—has no place in such a methodological point of view. The author fails to understand Durkheim's theories which he uses and on which he relies.

1906e Lecture on religion and morality delivered in the École des Hautes Études, 1905–6

In a series of lectures on the non-theological teaching of morality organized by the School of Advanced Social Studies, Durkheim gave a lecture on the subject 'God is society'. He attempted to prove his thesis historically and practically. When society is conceived in positive terms it gives to morality all the support it gives to a revealed religion. The result is that in desiring God man only wishes to gain the highest realization of himself: in denying God man denies himself. In the contemporary cult of humanity, God does not disappear in humanity, rather humanity discovers God in itself and does not worship him any less fervently. Although changes have to be made in religion, moral principles ought not to be changed. Duty remains as it was for Kant, irreducible. Duty is also a good thing, to be loved, but it calls for sacrifice. (Lalande, who reported the lecture, noted that Durkheim wanted but changes in detail in the law.)

1907a(17) Review. 'Frazer—*Lectures on the Early History of Kingship*'

Much of the review is taken up with an exposition of Frazer's views. As was common at the time, Frazer held that in many societies royal personages were invested with religious powers, but he introduced the idea that the first kings had been magicians. Magical power later became royal power. For Frazer, magic was a pseudo-science, 'one great disastrous fallacy'. As it failed in its task, magic was forced to give way to religion, and so royalty itself took on sacerdotal characteristics. Kings became divinized. Durkheim disagrees with Frazer's general theory of magic as being a false science and an illusion. Hubert and Mauss have shown, he says, that from the beginning the magician was invested with religious characteristics like those of the priest or prophet, and possessed the quality of mana. The magician was not an acute charlatan. Nor are there good grounds for differentiating magician-kings from priest-kings. Frazer saw in totemism only magic, but Durkheim holds that the person who presides at the religious ceremonies of a totemic society can be assumed to be acting in a strictly religious way.

1907b 'Lettres au Directeur de *La Revue néo-scolastique*'

In a controversy with a neo-Thomist critic, Deploige, Durkheim was attacked for borrowing ideas, although carefully disguised, from German writers. In the first letter Durkheim replies that it was he who introduced the German writers to France. Such writers were not strictly sociological. He said he certainly owed a great deal to them as he did to Comte, but the German influence was different to that which Deploige suggested. In the second letter Durkheim states amongst other things that his religious ideas began to be crystallized in 1895 as a result of reading the historical studies of Robertson Smith and his school. In that year he said he underwent a virtual revelation in seeing religion as the matrix of social life and this allowed him to grapple with the sociological study of religion. The revelation he had received had nothing to do with Wundt's Ethik which he had read eight years before. (See Richard 1923.)

1907c Contribution to: *La Question religieuse: enquête internationale*

The *Mercure de France* invited scholars around the world to make short contributions about contemporary religion. Durkheim in about thirty lines speaks of the disintegration of a religious system which was founded in the Middle Ages and which began to crack in the sixteenth century. That religion has lost its power is demonstrated by the fact that it is now subject to scientific criticism. The future cannot be predicted but the new religious forms which will emerge will most likely be more rational than those of the present time.

1907f A course of lectures given in the Sorbonne, 1906–7, on 'Religion: its origins'

These reports of lectures given by Durkheim and compiled by

Fontana show that they relate in substance to *Les Formes
élémentaires* (1912a). They mark the first publication of his more
developed thought on religion. Subjects covered: definition of
religious phenomena; the most primitive forms of religion; animism;
naturism; totemism; the relation between religious sentiment and
thought; origin of the soul, spirit, demons; rites, positive and
negative; function and origin of ritual. This last topic is strenuously
described at the conclusion of the articles (637–8).

1909a(i)   Contribution to discussion: 'Science et religion'

Boutroux said that science dealt with established facts; religion with
action, with imprecise ends, with creating the new. While admitting
that the religion of the prophets has dynamic characteristics,
Durkheim holds that after a time religion crystallizes into dogmas
and rites. These can be studied by science, so can the dynamic stage
of religion. Religion is a fact, a reality which cannot be dissolved by
science. The sacred is continually coming into existence; for some,
democracy and progress are sacred. Only rigidly traditional
believers can reject a scientific approach to religion. Religion
performs two functions—one is speculative and relates to
knowledge about the universe, as such it is now in jeopardy—the
other is vital and practical, and for this science knows no substitute,
and because of this religion will continue. Science can claim no
privilege but religion does not have a science of itself. (A useful
summary of Durkheim's position regarding contemporary religion,
cf. 1919b.)

1909a(ii) Contribution to discussion: 'L'Efficacité des
doctrines morales'

The discussion, introduced by Delvolvé, centred on the problem of
imparting a secular morality, unsupported by the authority of a
religious or traditional foundation. Durkheim acknowledged the
strength of a religious morality, but against Delvolvé's solution,
which appeared vague and personalist, proposed as an ultimate
principle society—a reality which is concrete and transcendental
(228, 231). Morality is subject to change according to time and
society (221). No longer can it be said there is a single, unique
morality: there are as many moralities as there are social types. A

religious morality always opposes new moral ideas (222). Learning a secular morality demands an acceptance of the relative nature of morality, but also the adherence of the contemporary morality. The problem is acutely mirrored in the task of trying to 're-educate' an anarchist (230). Durkheim strongly rejected the notion that a false idea could be effective in society, even by means of skilful social engineering (227, 230).

1913a(ii)(9)   Review. 'Patten—*The Social Basis of Religion*'

Despite its name and author, the book is very inferior. The writer assumes that everything social is in fact economic. Sin is thus based on extreme poverty and man's struggle against sin is nothing more than a struggle against poverty. When life becomes difficult man becomes more religious both in faith and practice. This is what happened to Christianity after the death of Christ. But today industrialization has had the profound effect of transforming religion by bringing about a prosperous society. The religion of tomorrow will be a religion of liberty and joy, where enthusiasm will replace fear. Durkheim accuses Patten of relying upon a subjective approach.

1913a(ii)(10)   Review. 'Visscher—*Religion und soziales Leben bei den Naturvölkern*'

Durkheim criticizes Visscher for covering too many divergent subjects and showing confessional prejudices. There is similarity in his approach to that of Durkheim on one or two points but in the end there is little unanimity. Visscher held that all religions contain the notion of the divine, which is given by God to man. Society is only possible when there exists a moral unity between men, which comes from a common fatherhood derived from God. Religion thus sustains society. Visscher posited a biblical genesis of society, together with the idea of a fall. The practice of religion is identified with animism and the cult of the dead. However, there is an abyss between primitive religions and advanced religions in giving a unique place to individual personality as in Christianity. Although Visscher gave prominent place to the social component of religion, Durkheim is critical and suggests himself that in the end everything is religious and religion naturally expresses society. (A long, even wearisome review!)

1913a(ii)(15)   Review. 'Deploige—*Le Conflit de la morale et de la sociologie'*

The review is interesting because of its connection with the controversy Durkheim had with Deploige and the consequent confession that he had been crucially influenced by Robertson Smith (see 1907b). Durkheim again denies he borrowed his ideas from German thinkers. It is known that religion has a prominent part in his research and that 'the science of religion is essentially English and American'. He accuses Deploige of misquoting him and claims that, contrary to the title of the book, he sees no conflict between morality and sociology, for morality must be preceded by the scientific pursuit of establishing what moral facts are. The book is an apologetic 'pamphlet' for a return to Thomism.

1913b   Contribution to discussion: 'Le Problème religieux et la dualité de la nature humaine'

This important report of the proceedings of the Societé Française de Philosophie gives an account of the discussion Durkheim had which was centred on his then recently published book, *Les Formes élémentaires* (1912a). He introduced the discussion by concentrating on two themes—the function of religion in raising man above himself, in giving him confidence and power: and the notion of man as the possessor of two components or beings within himself, body/soul, sacred/profane, egoistic appetites/moral action, and so on. This second theme (not given a major place in *Les Formes*) was not as extensively criticized by the four participants, Delacroix, Darlu, Le Roy, Lachelier, as was his theory of religion expounded broadly on pp. 66–9. The social origin of religion and the alleged analysis of religion as an illusion were topics heavily criticized. Other subjects raised were animism, naturism, reductionism, the role of sociology, the scientific study of religion, the role of primitive forms, the concept of religious force, religion in its individual or solitary dimension, the religion of the prophets, the concept of society. (Admittedly not a great deal that is new emerges, except Durkheim's concept of human duality, and some of the dialogue is entwined and repetitive. There are, however, some very worthwhile statements by Durkheim particularly in connection with the problem of reality and illusion in religion.)

1914a 'Le dualisme de la nature humaine et ses conditions sociales'

A succinct account of Durkheim's doctrine of man written at much the same time as 1913b. Starting with a classical dualism of man—body and soul—he accepts the notion of man as homoduplex, of which one particular example is a division of things into sacred and profane. Collective ideals become fixed on material objects which themselves become sacred things. (Very similar to sections of 1913b but more systematically argued.)

1918b 'Le *Contrat social* de Rousseau'

In these posthumously published lectures, originally given in 1901–2 in Bordeaux, Durkheim makes two references to Rousseau's thought on religion. Law is religious in character (148/t.119). Secondly, in the past, religion was the basis of social order and cohesion (158–9/t.132–4. Each society had its own religion, practised by every member, as a reason for carrying out his social duties. Christianity broke the unity between the temporal and the spiritual. Today, the citizen must still have a religious base for his morality. The state should impose necessary dogmas to this end: other beliefs would be optional. A basic creed is outlined. (Although Durkheim does little more than expound Rousseau's ideas, they bear some similarity to his own—see Lukes 1973: 282 ff.)

1922a *Education et sociologie*

The book is made up of four articles and lectures on education. Those which contain brief and not very significant references to religion are the first two, published in 1911 for Buisson's *Nouveau Dictionnaire de pédagogie et d'instruction primaire*. In every society there is a common religion, no matter how the society is divided socially. A caste may have its own gods, but there exist gods which transcend the castes and are recognized by everyone. These gods symbolize and personify ways of looking at life. Even if there are no religious symbols, every society establishes ideas about man, society, duty, and so on. Education is concerned with these ideas (39–40/t.69–70). Science, which assumes the co-operation of scientists and is a collective work, has become heir to religion, itself a social institution. Every mythology posits conceptions of man and the universe (46/t.77). In some societies, as in India and Egypt, education was not diffused but is in the hands of priests. Among the priests there appeared the first kinds of science, for example, astronomy, mathematics. This was noted by Comte. Scientific knowledge had thus a sacred quality, since it originally stood at the heart of religion. In Greek and Latin cities there was no priestly caste and the state was responsible for religion: in these cases science and education were lay in character (64–5/t.96–7).

1924a *Sociologie et philosophie*

The book consists of three previously published but important essays, which cover such subjects as mind, memory, sensation, *représentations*, moral facts, values, but there are also references to religion, often overlooked. In the 1898b essay, morphological factors, such as clan and family life are held to be necessary in understanding the development of religion, such as that of Greece and Rome. However, the growth of myths, which emerge from religious thought, is not directly attributed to such factors but rather to a synthesis of ideas—to the birth of new *représentations* (43–44/t. 31). In the second essay (1906b) the sacred is seen as having two quasi-ambivalent components (like morality) consisting of the forbidden, the set apart, that which commands respect, even fear (duty); and the good, the object of love and aspiration (desirable) (51/t.36, 68/t.48; 103/t.70). The sacred is rigidly separated from the profane (103/t.70) but reason has never abandoned its rights over sacredness in morality, though not in theology (104/t.71; 70/t. 49). Morality is closely linked with religion and the first can never be completely dissociated from the second (68/t.48; 101/t.69). Therefore a present need exists to express the religious and the sacred in morality in secular terms (101/t.69; 103/t.71). The human personality has the qualities of the sacred and hence has a key place in the realm of the moral (51/t.37; 68/t.48; 105/t.72). But morality demands an end higher than the individual: the alternatives are God or society, but the divinity is society symbolically expressed (74–5/t.51–2). Although Durkheim alludes to a Kantian form of argument, he denied the notion that the categorical imperative is to be associated with the sacred (102/t.70). A theological basis for morality is rejected again (in 1911b) because

God appears to man in so many different forms that he must therefore be seen to vary with space and time (129–30/t.88–9). New kinds of psychic life emerge in group activity, as men feel themselves dominated by outside forces, and in such moments of ferment, great religious and other ideals are born (133–5/t.91–2. The ferment subsides but the ideals need to be periodically revived through rituals.

1925a   *l'Éducation morale*

The book covers the bulk of a lecture course given in the Sorbonne in 1902–3 and subsequently. (The Introduction is included in this volume.) As he proceeds, Durkheim states the need for a completely rational morality in education which excludes all principles derived from religion (21 ff./t.19 ff.). This cannot be achieved by simply eliminating from moral reality all references to religion, because in the past religion and morality have been inextricably intermingled. A radical expulsion of religious elements might also eliminate essential moral ideas. There is the need to rediscover basic moral forces in which spiritual power resides (46/t.41). Today, man who 'merits the respect that the faithful of all religions reserve for their gods' (123/t.107) has become sacred. The idea of humanity is an end which some nations pursue. God in the past was seen to be both a law-maker and an ideal to which the individual strove: today the individual attempts to realize society in himself and men revere 'God' in other people (119/t.104). This means that man worships society. A sense of duty comes from a being superior to man, which is not God but society (101–2/t.89–90). Conscience is thus society speaking in us. Durkheim states that all religious ideas are social in origin and that today they still remain pre-eminent in public and private thought, though for intellectuals science has replaced religion (79 ff./t.69 ff.). Science is the heir of religion and the work of society. Discipline is necessary to morality: some religions have preached a discipline of the flesh, however the need for discipline should be rationally seen as being demanded from nature itself (57–8/t.50–1). Reminiscent of *Suicide* (1897a) Durkheim speaks of a minority church having a strong sense of cohesion and providing mutual aid and comfort for its members (274/t.239–40).

1928a *Le Socialisme*

In analysing the work of Saint-Simon (1760–1825) and his school in lectures given in 1895–6, Durkheim devotes chapter IX to 'Internationalism and Religion', which includes (262–79/t.181–92) an exposition of Saint-Simon's last and unfinished book, *Nouveau Christianisme* (1824). According to Saint-Simon Christianity has lost its influence: there no longer exists a common faith sufficient to unite all men. However, against Condorcet (religion is an obstacle to human happiness), he held it had had an essential role in the development of the human spirit (144/t.101). He hopes that a new religion will be established which will embrace Europe, but its contents he did not describe. However, he placed great emphasis on morality and on the freedom of the individual. Durkheim holds that his religious ideas are pantheistic—'physics and morality have equal dignity'—'everything in nature participates in the divine'—(276/t.190). He is critical of the failure of Saint-Simon to introduce into morality any force of constraint over man's appetites (287/t.201). Durkheim also expounds and criticizes the ideas of Bazard, a disciple of Saint-Simon (see chapter XII, especially 325 ff./t.223 ff.). Bazard extended Saint-Simon's view of history and his pantheism, and proposed a materialistic theocratic form of society based on science and materialism but controlled by priests. (The references to religion offer another useful vignette of Durkheim's attitude to contemporary religion. Some of the points he makes about Saint-Simon's general concern for religion apply to himself.)

1938a *L'Évolution pédagogique en France*

The book, perhaps Durkheim's most serious attempt to deal with a historical subject, consists of a series of lectures first given in 1904–5, in Paris, and thereafter each year to 1913. They were intended for *aggrégation* students and dealt with the development of secondary education in France, especially volume II. Beginning with the early Church, Durkheim shows the important role Christianity played in the development of teaching both in terms of doctrine and pedagogical institutions, which extended until recent times. Christianity, over against paganism, is to be seen as a spiritual religion rooted in man's soul, his total personality. In the Carolingian period, which gave rise to scholasticism, grammar, logic and science began to be integrated with religious thought. In addition to references to monastic houses and universities, he notes the great importance the Jesuits gave to education with their emphasis on humanism and the classics, and methodologically on personal supervision and competition. He notes in a later period the links between Protestantism and science. Durkheim's aims are to show the development of ideals in pedagogy and corresponding concepts of man. (It is an important book not least for an understanding of Durkheim's approach to history, but it is history in the wide sweep, and he wished to be both empirical and normative. It is virtually impossible to offer a brief summary. See Wallwork 1972: 130–46. As a contribution to the history of pedagogy and intellectual ideas, the book deserves careful study.)

1950a   *Leçons de sociologie: physique des mœurs et du droit*

This consists of a course of lectures twice given in Bordeaux between 1896 and 1900 and subsequently in Paris. Mauss states the definitive draft of the lectures was made in 1898–1900 (Lukes 1973: 255). Durkheim deals with basic moral and legal problems sociologically, in particular emphasizing the role of professional groups. But the book has several references to religion. It is an early example of Durkheim's development of the notion of the sacred (68/t. 55; 170–1/t.143–4) and its relationship to property (177–8/t.149– 52). The word sacred is derived from the Latin *sacer* which means that which is distinct from the common. He relates *sacer* with the Polynesian *taboo* and suggests the concepts are very close. He refers to burial places being sacred and to the studies of Fustel de Coulanges (181–3/t.153–4). Certain types of property, e.g. the field, are related to the sacred (178–87/t.150–8). Religion is not an illusion: it interprets social needs symbolically (189/t.160). The gods are collective forces personified and hypostasized in material form (190–1/t.161–2; 195/t.229) and divinity is a symbolic form of society (229/t.195). Here is an early and important summary of Durkheim's main theories of religion. Other subjects covered: destiny of state bound up with the fate of gods (68/t.55); Christianity an inward religion (72/t.58); the modern cult of the individual now replacing the religious cult (84/t.69; 202/t.172); the gods man worships always demand sacrifices (139/t.116); blood covenant (211–15/t.180–3); religion and contract (ch. 16) where Durkheim states that religious formalities tend to become less important as life becomes busier (227/t.193).

1955a   *Pragmatisme et sociologie*

In these lectures given in 1913–14, compiled from students' notes, one lecture (12) is devoted to pragmatism and religion. In it Durkheim outlines basic ideas in *The Varieties of Religious Experience* (1902) by William James and translated by F. Abauzit into French in 1906. James is accused of neglecting the social institutions of religion, such as churches, and holding that the value of religion is to be found in the interior life. For him the truth of religion is to be judged by its results—its fruits. Durkheim considers three prominent elements in James's work—holiness, mysticism, polytheism including the idea of God. He notes that James is not interested in theological ideas or whether God exists but whether belief in God can be reconciled with the facts of science. Durkheim's criticism is a general one—pragmatism is impatient with every rigorous intellectual discipline; it is more an exercise against theoretical speculation than an enterprise favourable to action.

A note on the life of Gaston Richard and certain aspects of his work

I

Gaston Richard and Émile Durkheim were contemporaries. Antoine François Gaston Michel Richard, to give him his full names, was born in 1860 in Paris, two years later than Durkheim.[1] However, he considerably outlived his early mentor; he died on 9 June 1945 at the age of eighty-four. He entered the École Normale Supérieure two years after Durkheim and it was there that he came to know the fellow student who in his early years exerted considerable influence over him. From an early wish to teach history, Richard turned to philosophy, and from 1883 to 1902 taught the subject in various lycées, including Lons-le-Saunier, Vendôme, Coutances and Le Havre. In 1902 with strong backing from Louis Liard, Directeur de l'Enseignement Supérieur, he followed in the footsteps of Durkheim at the University of Bordeaux in being responsible for lectures in social science (Clark 1973: 59). Three years later he was made professor of philosophy in the same faculty, the Faculty of Letters, and the year following the title was changed to professor of social sciences at his request. About this time, he was lecturing three times a week to about fifteen students. He retired in 1930 when he was seventy years old, though he continued to write and serve on professional bodies, and in 1939 he was temporarily recalled to lecture in the university. He remained in Bordeaux until his death. In 1890 he married Jeanne Louise Kienné, four years younger than himself, who was born in Neufchateau in the Vosges. She died in 1942. There were two children by the marriage—one daughter who later married, and a son, killed in World War I, who was a promising student in zoology.

On the basis of these brief external facts, several biographical parallels with the life of Émile Durkheim become immediately obvious, but they could be extended. Both men were very much establishment figures in French university life—middle-class, hardworking, loyal to certain dominant ideals of contemporary France, and at the same time enjoying quiet, warm, undramatic domestic lives. But apart from these parallel personal facts, there was in the beginning a deep connection. It is evident that from their early acquaintance, Durkheim and Richard each had a high regard for the other's abilities. When Durkheim came to found *L'Année sociologique* in 1896 he asked Richard to be one of the team and his name was frequently placed at the top of the list of collaborators printed on the first page of the journal. Although he wrote one monograph for *L'Année sociologique*, 'Les Crises sociales et la criminalité' (1900), Richard's main contribution was in reviewing books in sections on criminal sociology and social statistics. He also contributed reviews in other sections. (A separate Richard bibliography appears after this Note, on p. 358.) He continued to work for the journal up to and including volume X, which was published in 1907. That Richard was highly esteemed by Durkheim seems to be beyond all doubt. When Durkheim moved to Paris from Bordeaux in 1902 his mantle fell on Richard. Instinctively one feels that Durkheim must have had some official or more likely unofficial influence in the appointment of his successor. The appointment was an important one for the future of sociology in France and more particularly for Durkheimian sociology. It was in Bordeaux that the first academic appointment in sociology had been made in 1887 when Durkheim was appointed as *chargé de cours* in social science and pedagogy and it was in 1895 that he became professor of social science. Of the many disciples Durkheim had gathered around him it seems that he thought that Richard was the best qualified to be his successor. Certainly Richard had obtained his Doctorat d'État which was necessary qualification to be a university professor.

Up to this point the interests of the two men and the paths they were treading appeared to be similar. They had been to the same college and as *normaliens* they had both been influenced by Fustel de Coulanges and Boutroux (Richard 1935a: 13 and 29). Richard's early academic concerns were centred on the sociological implications of economics and on social solidarity, together with criminology. When he reached Bordeaux two books of his were already before the public, *Essai sur l'origine de l'idée de droit* (1892) and *Le Socialisme et la science sociale* (1897) which by 1909 had gone through three editions. Then, in 1903, three further books appeared, *Notions élémentaires de sociologie, Manuel de morale, suivi de notions de sociologie* and *L'Idée d'évolution dans la nature et dans l'histoire*. The last book was given a national award, the Prix Crouzet. Not without point is the fact that some of the books that Richard published up to this time were produced by Félix Alcan who published Durkheim's works and those of the *Année* school.

And then came the rift. It occurred around 1907 after ten years of collaboration. Richard's later writings showed that there were many points of contention but they might be summed up by saying that Richard felt that Durkheim's sociology had exceeded its legitimate boundaries. Two particular issues had pre-eminence: the limited place given by Durkheim to the individual and his theory of religion. Difficulties had been growing for some time and it would seem that it was Richard who took the initiative and cut his links with Durkheim. It was a brave move to make since Richard would be an outcast of a school of sociology which by its very creativity, energy and discipline was beginning to dominate the sociological world in France and to be influential beyond its borders. Richard had to set out on his own professional path. From then on he would be counted among other isolated individuals or groups excluded from Durkheim's court, such as van Gennep, Worms and remnants of the followers of Le Play. Richard faced the prospect of entering a professional wilderness. However, by degrees, he began to find a niche in the Institut International de Sociologie and its journal, the *Revue internationale de sociologie (RIS)*, both organized by René Worms in Paris (see Clark 1973: 147 ff.). Through his involvement in the government during World War I, Worms was moved to Bordeaux when the Council of State went there at the end of 1914. Here a firm friendship was established between Richard and Worms from about 1916 onwards (Richard 1935: 32). When Worms died in 1925, a former close colleague of Worms, Achille Ouy, asked Richard, then sixty-six years old, if he would take over the Institut and the *Revue*. This Richard agreed to do but resigned in 1934 when Émile Lasbax, a considerably younger man, succeeded him.

The *RIS* ceased publication in 1939, having been founded in 1893 by Worms. Clark denigrates the journal on the grounds that its research efforts were 'fragmented, superficial, and noncumulative' (1973: 246). Certainly it did not command the uniformly high quality of work that is to be found in *L'Année sociologique* under Durkheim's editorship. But it was regularly published between the wars, in fact, every two months, and in this sense was unchallenged by the new series of *L'Année sociologique* which only managed to produce two issues which appeared in 1925 and 1926 and by the later *Annales sociologiques* (1934–42). Further, the intention of the *RIS* was to be international in character, despite the inherent weaknesses of such a policy. It drew on a large number of collaborators, such as Sorokin, Sée, Tylor, von Wiese, and in this way it was able to influence sociologists in France in a way that perhaps *L'Année sociologique* did not.

Richard died a little-known figure. It is true that he wrote extensively and indeed published far more books than Durkheim, but his influence began to wane after World War I. Just before the outbreak of hostilities he trained two able men, Daniel Essertier and Émile Lasbax, but although he continued to teach in Bordeaux and although he became associated with the *RIS*, he was no longer a rising or effulgent star. He was at his peak during the two decades preceding the war. He is to be remembered best as a collaborator of Durkheim and then his most searching critic. Nor must it be forgotten that in 1918 he was fifty-eight years old. As Durkheimian sociology began to go into a decline in the 1920s and 1930s, so on the whole did Richard's contribution to the discipline.

II

As far as can be ascertained, and as we have just noted, the collaboration between Durkheim and Richard finally broke down around 1907. At that time Richard had been five years in Bordeaux and two years as professor. No correspondence between the two men is known to exist: nor do we possess any personal accounts of the events that finally led to the break. It is true that in 1911 Richard published four articles under the general heading of 'Sociologie et métaphysique' in *Foi et vie*, a Protestant journal, in which he attacked Durkheim's sociology, and particularly his sociology of religion. It is also true that he displayed strong disagreements with Durkheim in his *La Sociologie générale et les lois sociologiques* (1912) which is one of Richard's most important works. More specifically, he launched a devastating broadside on Durkheim's sociology of religion in 'L'Athéisme en sociologie religieuse' which appeared in 1923 as a long article, the tone of which at times approaches the vitriolic (see p. 228). He reiterated his criticisms and developed others in two articles in 1925 (see 1925a(i) and 1925a(ii)). Shortly before he died he again dwelt on the inherent weaknesses of Durkheim's sociology of religion. This time it was in a book, *Sociologie et théodicée* (1943). This, his only book on the sociology of religion, portrays Richard's work at its best and is a book which should be more widely known. It was very much his 'testament philosophique' (Moreau 1944: 375). In the early days, Richard's criticism of Durkheim was seldom voiced but, after he had parted company with the *chef d'école*, he began to be openly critical. However, after the death of Durkheim and perhaps on account of his fear that Durkheim's sociology would become deified (1923: 125–6/t.228–9) he became a much more outspoken critic. It is not for nothing that he still frequently referred to as 'le vieil adversaire de Durkheim'.

In order to lay bare some of the issues on which the two men were divided it is necessary to refer briefly to Richard's early writings. The main thesis for his doctorate was presented in 1892, a few months before Durkheim's thesis, with the title *L'Origine de l'idée du droit*. Although accepted, it was criticized on account of its alleged socialistic leanings. Richard focused attention on economic competition and whether competition was compatible with social solidarity. This raised issues about positivism and evolutionism and whether as such they were in accord with ethical idealism. Further, he asked, in what sense was it possible to speak of sociology as a science?—an issue that was to remain with him to his dying days. For Richard social solidarity was a key concept in understanding society. In 1905 he wrote an article for the *Revue philosophique*, 'Les Lois de la solidarité', which brought a sharp retort from Durkheim who reviewed it in *L'Année sociologique*

(1907a(9)). Richard attempted to wrestle with the problem of the relations between the individual and society—a problem also central to Durkheim's thought. Richard feared that in attempting to formulate laws of society and their influence over individuals, the freedom of the individual was imperilled unless the nature of those laws was very carefully enunciated. In the 1905 article, with scant reference to Durkheim by name, he underlined the importance of the individual, seen as a person having moral rights and being the valid object of study by the social sciences. In this he was probably influenced by his, and Durkheim's, teacher at the École Normale, Renouvier. Richard was convinced that in much sociological thought the individual was seen to be completely subjected to social laws—to an 'entirely mechanical (*automatique*) sociality' (1905: 471). In such thinking morality thus becomes equated with sociality and as such virtually disappears. Elsewhere Richard agrees with Durkheim that social solidarity raises two basic questions—one of fact and the other of value. With Durkheim he also agrees, for they were both united in the early days on the value of the concept of solidarity, that Durkheim's theory of solidarity, as it was expounded in the *Division of Labour* (1893b), needed to be made more precise by a study of historical detail and by statistics: there was also the need to establish a number of variables. But it was on the second basic question—the metaphysical one, that of value—that Richard was critical of Durkheim's approach in attempting to absorb the moral conscience into the collective. He said later that Durkheim recognized only one type of causality, a mechanical causality (1935a: 21). Was it not therefore a fact that Durkheim had adopted that crude positivism which he claimed to reject, but which denied the freedom of human action? In a later article Richard observed that Montesquieu had had more success in dealing with the problem of personal freedom and social laws than had Durkheim (1935a: 14). Richard held that social life was basically a social system of voluntary relations between individuals free to enter such relations.

Some of the charges levelled against Durkheim were convincingly denied by him in his 1907 review. He saw Richard's article as a direct attack against his own position, if not against himself. Durkheim's defence was that Richard made the common mistake of confusing an 'ought' with an 'is'. It is necessary in sociology to begin by observing what happens, not with philosophical presuppositions about man and his moral behaviour. Simply stated, Richard's charge is little more than, in grappling dialectically with the relation of the individual to society and vice versa, he, Durkheim, had not given enough place to the individual: his emphasis was on the power and the influence of the collective.

In the eyes of Richard, and indeed many others subsequently, Durkheim changed his point of focus in sociological analysis over the the course of time. In his early days Durkheim's sociology was morphological, that is, it was a sociology focused on the importance in explanation of notions of social density, population, secondary groups, and so on. Such a position, Richard said, was based on a 'naturalistic and materialistic conception of history' (1912: 50). This charge Durkheim frequently refuted. But Richard's point was that neither Durkheim nor his school could continue to uphold the morphological position for long. The second period was marked by a switch to factors centred on *représentations collectives* and away from those based on morphology. Such a change, made at the turn of the century, meant a denial of the historical approach and the rejection of the value of mechanical and organic solidarity. Durkheim's interest from then onwards was focused on thought and concepts, *représentations*, as the key to understanding society (see Parsons 1937: 445, n. 4 on Richard). One practical implication was that religion, which formerly had been peripheral to explanation, began to assume greater importance: indeed, religion was at the heart of social understanding. When *Les Formes élémentaires* was published in 1912, after Durkheim and Richard had parted, Richard's fears seemed fully justified that religion had taken the key place in Durkheim's science. To Richard this was to make matters worse than they were before the change took place. The work that Durkheim was now doing was no longer science: it bordered on metaphysical speculation akin to that of Hegel and Schelling. It was Durkheim's early conviction that sociology should be free of philosophical doctrine (*Les Règles*, 1895a/t. 1938b: 141). On Richard's own confession he was critical of Durkheim on a large number of points before he went to Bordeaux in 1902 to lecture in the social sciences in the place of Durkheim. Each book that Durkheim had published up to that time Richard took exception to (1935a: 19 ff.). Above all in *Les Règles*, which had so much to commend it, the notion of the normal and pathological was severely condemned (Richard 1911a[iii]). One general point might be noted and it is that even in the early period, say from the time *L'Année sociologique* began to develop, and perhaps even before, there were areas of disagreement between the two men. There is probably little reason to doubt Richard's early admiration of Durkheim and he seems to have been closest to him in the very early days, but Richard did not have that unquestioning loyalty to the chief evidenced in other collaborators. What makes a study of Richard so interesting is that he is the only example known of a senior and important member of the team who later withdrew. Of course there might be those who would argue that the early differences were subsequently exaggerated and it is true from publications that criticisms of Durkheim become prominent only after Richard had left the *Année* school. Might it not be argued in retrospect that the criticisms were painted in more vivid colours in later years? One recalls the common phenomenon of a religious convert who describes his past in the darkest of terms. Whether Richard succumbed to this must remain an open question: only research will provide the answer or offer clues if a definitive answer turns out to be impossible. Besides, there is no evidence that Richard underwent anything approaching a sudden conversion.

As Benoit-Smullyan has noted (1948: 525) there can be no doubt that the final act of severance between the two men turned on Durkheim's approach to religion, and this decision, as we have just said, was taken before the publication of *The Elementary Forms.*

Perhaps it should be recalled that Durkheim was a non-believing Jew, a rationalist, an anti-clerical, though very sympathetic towards religion. So far as is known, all the members of his *équipe*, whether of Jewish origin or not, were agnostic, although none seems to have been as personally enthusiastic over religion as was Durkheim. Nor was any known to have had a strong Catholic background. By contrast, Richard as a member of the *Année* school was the one exception. He was brought up a Roman Catholic but, as a result of reading Renouvier, became a Protestant and a member of the Église Reformée at about the age of twenty, just before he entered the École Normale Supérieure, or just after he arrived. Richard remained a faithful, intellectually oriented Protestant to the end of his days although he did not attend public worship frequently, nor hold office in the local church: he contributed to Protestant journals, and a year or so before he died he began a biography of Raoul Allier, the theologian, missionary and philosopher of religion. The book was completed by a colleague and published posthumously in 1948. In taking the stand he did against Durkheim, he was acknowledged as being as much a spokesman for Catholics as for Protestants.[2]

Because of his beliefs, Richard was probably very sensitive to the fact that Durkheim's approach to Protestantism was somewhat negative. When Richard reviewed his *Suicide* (1897a) in *L'Année sociologique* (1898) he did not take issue over Durkheim's statements on the relatively high level of suicide among Protestants, their individualism, and lack of social coherence. Durkheim held that religion, and he implied especially Protestantism, was incapable of checking increases in suicide in modern times. If Richard was silent on these matters in the review, this was no longer the case in the articles of 1911, nor in 1923 when he bitterly attacked Durkheim for belittling and being inconsistent in his attitude towards religion.

The points Richard chose to raise were much more than confessional ones. The particular issues over Protestantism as such were disregarded in the face of more fundamental matters. Richard's attack centred on the legitimate place of sociology within the study of religion. What are the aims, methods, and legitimate conclusions to be derived from a sociological study of religion? In Richard's eyes Durkheim had failed at all these points because, in brief, he had gone beyond the permissible boundaries of the discipline in searching for a sociological explanation of the religious sentiment. Durkheim had created a path in this direction by reducing religion to a purely social phenomenon and defining it so as to exclude all references to mysticism, to God, and to the individual component. The opening up of such a path must have been apparent to Richard at the turn of the century in the essay on defining religious phenomena (1899a(ii)), where Durkheim first began a systematic treatment of religion. One feels that from this point, or perhaps from 1895 onwards when Durkheim began to pay greater attention to religion, Richard must have had increased searchings of heart. As in his general sociology, but now particularly in his sociology of religion, Richard was convinced that Durkheim gave far too little place to the individual, almost to the point of excluding him. To most Protestants and nineteenth-century religious thinkers influenced by liberalism—and one calls to mind Paul Sabatier, William James, and Renouvier—it is the individual, his faith and practice, which constitutes the focal point of religion. To understand religion one had to understand how individuals viewed it themselves. Richard, however, admitted that some form of sociological explanation of the religious sentiment was legitimate, for clearly there was a social component to religion; but Durkheim's explanation in giving, for example, the sociological account of the idea of God, was totally unacceptable by reason of its alleged positivism but above all because of its reductionism. Further, Richard's emphasis on individual faith as being the essence of religion caused him to question very seriously the notion of secularization held by Durkheim (1923: 133/t.236). Despite the alleged decline of the institutions of Christian faith—the churches—there is no evidence to show that individual faith has in any measure diminished.

Neither Durkheim's limited assessment of contemporary religion, nor his more penetrating analysis of primitive religion, satisfied Richard. He called Durkheim's theory of religion 'the daughter of Comte's religion of humanity'—a fact that Durkheim would have denied (Durkheim 1912a: 611/t.156)—which despite its pretensions did not by sociological induction explain the formation of the idea of God (1935a: 19). Again, he held that Durkheim's sociology of religion was a direct outcome of the works of English anthropologists, such as Frazer, Marett and Jevons, who showed considerably more caution than he did, and Frazer himself tended to veer away from those earlier extravagances about totemism which Durkheim continued to accept. Also, the Durkheimian school played down the importance of the cult of the dead unlike such scholars as Fustel de Coulanges, Tylor and Spencer (1935a: 22). For a full account of Richard's attack on Durkheim's sociology of religion the reader is referred to the 1923 article, 'L'Athéisme dogmatique en sociologie religieuse', which is translated in this volume. But two issues might finally be mentioned. Richard stood strongly opposed to Durkheim's formula, crudely stated, that God is Society. Durkheim had often mentioned it but in 1905 he gave an open lecture on religion and morality in the Hautes Études where the formula received prominence. He said that man in seeking God was but seeking the highest realization of himself (Durkheim 1906e). In 1907 he began a series of lectures in the Sorbonne which formed the basis of *The Elementary Forms*. A summary of the lectures was published in the *Revue de philosophie* (1907f) and it was here in these lectures that it was obvious that Durkheim was beginning to integrate his theories of religion with Australian totemism. More likely than not Richard was aware of these articles but he points to the fact that in 1909 in the *Revue de métaphysique et de morale* the official introduction to his forthcoming study on the sociology of religion was announced (Durkheim 1909d. See Richard 1911a(ii)). The other point is that Richard objected most strongly to the implication of Durkheim that primitive religion could be equated with religion of a more developed type such as Christianity (1923: 243/t.255).

In reviewing the areas of disagreement between the two men, it is apparent from the evidence we have that the break was not something that suddenly occurred and for this reason it is very difficult to give a precise date to the point of departure. Although Richard called himself a disciple of Durkheim (1911a(i)), the longer he worked in collaboration with him the more dissatisfied Richard grew with Durkheim's thought. Thus when the break took place around 1907 it was not the case of an immediate and unheralded 'conversion'. In this respect one is reminded of what happened to John Henry Newman whose conversion to the Roman Catholic Church in 1845 came as the result of a relatively long period of dissatisfaction with the theology and practice of the Church of England. And like Newman, too, when the point of decision came the result was rejection from the parent body and ostracism.

III

Of Richard's distinctive contribution to sociology we make no reference except in the area of the sociology of religion, and then only briefly.

In 1935 he admitted that his teaching and research interests were in the relations of sociology to ethics, to the science of education and to the history of social philosophy (1935a: 25). What he failed to mention—and perhaps he could not have foreseen it—was a growing interest in the sociology of religion. And here again, by a strange turn of fate, he resembles Durkheim, for the last book he wrote was on the sociology of religion, with the title *Sociologie et théodicée. Leur conflit et leur accord*. It seems it was published at his own expense in 1943 and was dedicated to his wife who had just died. However, Richard undertook no detailed studies in the religion of any one society, as Durkheim did in *The Elementary Forms*. He lacked Durkheim's extensive anthropological knowledge and probably the master's wide knowledge of religion in general. Nor did his learning in this field approach that of Mauss. He held that the best method to study religion was the comparative method, almost in the tradition of Spencer (1935a: 21). Comparison was sought on a historical basis *vis-à-vis* religious institutions. But to go beyond that had the potential danger of reducing the religious sentiment to social sentiments—a stick with which to beat Durkheim. He says at one point that the object of the sociology of religion was to pose and solve two problems: the relation between the religious sentiment and social sentiments; and the proper characteristics of specifically religious societies, or in other terms ways of differentiating the church, the family, and the state (1935a: 23).

Sociologie et théodicée is of particular interest because he selected a subject which has received little or no sociological attention. His main thesis is that sociology has no right to oppose a transcendental theology. He refers to theodicy in the writings of Leibniz and Kant, and refers to the work of Lammenais, Cournot and Boutroux. He confessed that his interest in the problem of evil occurred in the early days of working for *L'Année sociologique*, when he was made responsible for reviewing sections on criminology. It was as a result of a careful study of criminal statistics and behaviour that he was convinced of the reality of moral evil, which was to be found even in the most civilized and well ordered of societies (1935a : 19). He first began to point to the crucial role of the problem of evil as being central to the sociology of religion in 1905 in his article 'Les Lois de la solidarité'. He postulated that every religion offers a solution to the problem of evil (1905: 468). The issues are seen first in the concept of taboo which is an early manifestation of solidarity: when the taboo is broken society is polluted and as a result expiation is demanded. Similar components are to be seen in the theology of Brahmanism, Mazdaism and Judaism. A consciousness of evil arises from an intellectual reflection of the disharmony and disorder that is to be seen in the world. Religion is an early form of the consciousness of moral evil inherent in society—of common sin for which sacrifice or expiation has to be made. At a later stage of history, social solidarity, while it stands opposed to evil, moves into the civil dimension, into penal institutions and schools. The notion of moral worth, even in the individual, rests on the *conscience* of social evil.

IV

Richard was a prolific writer in terms of books, articles and reviews (see the short bibliography that follows). He produced more books than Durkheim, even for the period that Durkheim was alive. Substantively, he covered such subjects as the place of women in society, experimental education, socialism, communism, imperialism, and Rumanian culture. He was a good classical scholar: from 1905 he reviewed books for *La Revue des études anciennes* and contributed two articles (1935b, 1940). His earlier volumes proved to be very popular and quickly ran into several editions, for example *Le Socialisme et la science sociale* (1897), and *Notions élémentaires de sociologie* (1903a). Although his books seemed to sell extensively in the period up to World War I, none has so far proved to be a classic, for unlike Durkheim's works, none has weathered the test of time.

Richard's sociology was basically eclectic—a fact he readily admitted (1935a: 17). Parodi saw nothing of a unitary system in his writing and Richard was happy to let the criticism stand (1935a: 11). Philosophically he was opposed to anything that created unity based on a system. He was pleased to list thinkers from France, Germany, England, the USA who had in some way influenced him. However he gives Le Play a special place. His eclecticism admirably corresponded to that of the *Revue internationale de sociologie* with which he was later associated. He undertook relatively little empirical research and produced no book comparable with, say, Durkheim's *Suicide* nor, as we have noted, did he use a great deal of anthropological data. Indeed, he was very much opposed to what might loosely be called a crude empirical approach. He approved of no sociology that could be called materialistic or was based on biology (Barnes and Becker 1938: 861). Similarly, he was much opposed to theories of social evolution which were in any way unilinear: not surprisingly he was critical of Spencer.

Professionally Richard ploughed a somewhat lonely furrow. He did not create any school of sociology as did Durkheim and indeed his sociology by and large contained little that was generally outstanding. He said of himself that he was 'a craftsman much more than an architect' (1935a: 11). He readily turned his hand to many subjects within the general area of sociology. He was first and foremost a commentator and critic who like a circus rider straddled two horses, one philosophy and the other sociology. It was his ability in applying logic that made him so powerful in the analysis of other people's ideas. Clark is right in saying that his eclecticism provided him with a base for being 'one of the clearest critics of Durkheim' (1973: 224).

Finally, a word about Richard as a person. While he was a professor at the lycée at Coutances, he was accused by an academic inspector of being 'very dogmatic' and raising 'controversial questions' in a strongly Catholic area (Dossier). Perhaps unknown to the inspector was the fact that Richard had been brought up a Catholic! But he was given the compliment of being an excellent teacher and of encouraging students: he was also described as a 'very cultured man'! All his professional life he appeared to be a lecturer and teacher of a high order.

According to such evidence as we have, Durkheim showed more external friendliness towards Richard, than Richard to Durkheim and his disciples. His reviews of Richard's books were sometimes favourable, for example that of *La Femme dans l'histoire* (Durkheim 1910a(iii)(20)), which Richard published in 1909, after the two had parted company. But nowhere does Durkheim write publicly with that level of hostility seen in Richard's attack on Durkheim in the articles of 1911, or later in his more vigorous essay of 1923. The critics of Durkheim were verbally more aggressive in opposing the teaching of the most prominent sociologist of the day—and here one thinks of van Gennep as well as Richard—than he was towards them, except perhaps in the controversy he had with Tarde. By and large, Durkheim seems to have treated his opponents calmly, even to the point of ignoring them. Sometimes he responded to Richard by saying quite simply that he had misunderstood him (for example, Durkheim 1913a(ii)(1)).

Some of the ill feeling against Durkheim was directed at his dogmatism and that of his followers. The intolerance that he showed is virtually forgotten today as the writings of the master now flourish in a period of revived popularity, and as his opponents have largely been forgotten. Part of the dogmatism with which Durkheim was charged centred on intellectual matters, such as those raised by Richard, but far more was it focused on institutional dogmatism—propagated within the university, within the profession (see Lukes 1973: 363 ff.). Durkheim's control of academic appointments ensured that only those trained by him had any hope of securing key posts in the universities, and all other candidates were thereby excluded. While undoubtedly Durkheim helped Richard gain the chair in Bordeaux, it is clear that the intellectual ostracism that descended on Richard after he broke with Durkheim showed itself in the 'general' preventing his former 'lieutenant' having a chair in Paris, the centre of French learning. But Richard was aware of another form of intolerance which arose at the end of Durkheim's life and carried on afterwards, namely, that the official sociology taught in teacher training colleges and elsewhere was Durkheim's own brand, or a similar kind, for example that of Lévy-Bruhl. Alternatives were not allowed (Richard 1923: 125–6/t. 228). Such papal rigidity and denial of openness aroused Richard's anger. However, in retrospect, there are those today who are prepared to support Durkheim's stand and argue that, to establish an academic profession or school of thought, a high degree of social integration is necessary, which means discipline, rigour and intolerance (Clark 1973: 245).

Apart from his righteous indignation, Richard was generally acclaimed as a warm and generous person. He was affectionately thought of by the inner circle of the *RIS* and by his colleagues at Bordeaux. Lasbax said he scorned the vain searching for fame (1935: 38). He bore disappointments nobly. To the last, he remained absorbed in work, though in his final years he was isolated and cut off, without wife or child around him, and with France occupied by the Germans (Moreau 1944: 375). He was inspired by a deep humanism, itself infused by devoted and disinterested study. He sought justice for man and lived out his ideals, not least by his kindness. Indeed, he epitomized at its very best the nineteenth-century liberal scholar. More particularly, he wanted to see social science in the form of knowledge derived from sociology contribute to the greater education of man.

Notes

1 For these and other personal details, material has been drawn from Richard's dossier in the Archives Nationales, and also from information kindly given by Professors Chateau and Moreau of the University of Bordeaux, who knew Richard, and Mme Y. D. Miroglio.
2 I am grateful to Professor Moreau for this point.

Gaston Richard: Bibliography and References

Only those books and articles have been included which are relatively more important or which relate to Durkheim and the sociology of religion. No complete bibliography of Richard's works is known to exist. Even the special supplement of the *RIS* dedicated to Richard and published in 1935, contains no comprehensive bibliography up to that time.

1892   *Essai sur l'origine de l'idée de droit*, Thorin, Paris.
1897   *Le Socialisme et la science sociale*, Alcan, Paris.
1898a   'Avertissement à quatrième section. Sociologie Criminelle', *AS*, I,
          pp. 392–4.
1898b   Review. 'Émile Durkheim—*Le Suicide. Étude de sociologie*',
          AS, I, pp. 397–406.
1900   'Les Crises sociales et la criminalité', *AS*, III, pp. 15–42.
1903a   *Notions élémentaires de sociologie*, Delagrave, Paris.
1903b   *Manuel de morale, suivi de notions de sociologie*, Delagrave,
          Paris.
1903c   *L'Idée d'évolution dans la nature et dans l'histoire*, Alcan,
          Paris.
1905   'Les Lois de la solidarité', *RP*, 60, pp. 441–71.
1909   *La Femme dans l'histoire. Étude sur l'évolution de la condition
          sociale de la femme*, Doin, Paris.
1911a   'Sociologie et métaphysique', four articles, *Foi et vie*, June–
          July, 1911.
          (i) 'À propos de M. Durkheim' (1 June 1911)
          (ii) 'Brève Histoire des variations de M. Durkheim' (16 June
          1911)
          (iii) 'La Distinction sociologique du bien et du mal chez M.
          Durkheim' (1 July 1911)
          (iv) 'La Sociologie religieuse de M. Durkheim et le problème des
          valeurs' (16 July 1911)
1911b   *Pédagogie expérimentale*, Doin, Paris.
1912   *La Sociologie générale et les lois sociologiques*, Doin, Paris.
1914   *La Question sociale et le mouvement philosophique au
          XIXe siècle*, Colin, Paris.
1916   *Le Conflit de l'autonomie nationale et de l'impérialisme*,
          Giard, Paris.
1923   'L'Athéisme dogmatique en sociologie religieuse', *RHPR*, 1923,
          pp. 125–37, 229–61. (Translated here pp. 228–76.)
1925a(i) 'Sociologie religieuse et morale sociologique. La théorie
          solidariste de l'obligation', *RHPR*, 1925, pp. 244–61.
1925a(ii) 'La Morale sociologique et la pathologie de la société',
          RHPR, 1925, pp. 346–68.
1925b   *L'Évolution des mœurs*, Doin, Paris.
1928   'Nouvelles Tendances sociologiques en France et en Allemagne',
          RIS, 36, pp. 647–69.
1930a   'La Notion de société simple et primitive dans l'explication des

1930b faits sociaux', Arhiva pentru Reforma Sociala, Bucarest. (Partly reproduced in *RIS*, 43 (supplément), pp. 111–15.)
1930b 'La Pathologie sociale d'Émile Durkheim', *RIS*, 38, pp. 113–26.
1932   Notes and discussions. 'Auguste Comte et Émile Durkheim selon M. G.-L. Duprat 1932', *RIS*, 40, pp. 603–12.
1934   'Le Droit natural et la philosophie des valeurs', *Archives de philosophie du droit et de sociologie juridique*, 4, pp. 7–24.
1935a 'Avant-propos inédit', *RIS*, 43 (supplément), pp. 9–33.
1935b 'L'Impurété contagieuse et la magie dans la tragédie grecque', *Revue des études anciennes*, 37, pp. 301–21.
1937a *La Conscience morale et l'expérience morale*, Hermann, Paris.
1937b *La Loi morale. Les lois naturelles et les lois sociales*, Hermann, Paris.
1940   'Les Obstacles à la liberté de conscience au IVe siècle de l'ere chrétienne', *Revue des études anciennes*, 42, pp. 498–507.
1943   *Sociologie et théodicée. Leur conflit et leur accord*, Les Presses Continentales, Paris.

Published posthumously

1948   *La Vie et l'œuvre de Raoul Allier*, Editions Berger-Levrault, Paris.

The following is a selection of books and articles in which reference is made to Richard's life and work.

BARNES, H. E. and BECKER, H. 1938 *Social Thought from Lore to Science*, Heath, Boston.
BENOIT-SMULLYAN, E. 1948 'The Sociologism of Émile Durkheim and his school', in H. E. Barnes (ed.), *An Introduction to the History of Sociology*, University of Chicago Press, Chicago, pp. 499–537.
CLARK, T. N. 1969 Introduction, *Gabriel Tarde: On Communication and Social Influence: Selected Papers*, University of Chicago Press, Chicago and London.
CLARK, T. N. 1973 *Prophets and Patrons*, Harvard University Press, Cambridge, Mass.
DURKHÉIM, É. 1907a(9) Review. 'G. Richard—"Les Lois de la solidarité morale", *Revue philosophique*, Nov. 1905', *AS*, X, pp. 382–3.
DURKHEIM, É. 1910a(iii)(20) Review. 'Richard—"La Femme dans l'histoire" ', *AS*, XI, pp. 369–71.
DURKHEIM, É. 1913a(ii)(1) Review. 'Richard—*La Sociologie générale et les lois sociologiques*', *AS*, XII, pp. 1–3.
LASBAX, E. 1935 'L'Œuvre de M. Gaston Richard', *RIS*, 43 (supplement), pp. 37–40.
MOREAU, J. 1944 'Chronique des études anciennes. Gaston Richard', *Revue des études anciennes*, 46, pp. 375–6.

Name index

(Excluding names in the Bibliographies)

362   **Name index**

Subject index

(Where recognized translations have been made, Durkheim's books, articles and reviews are given according to the English title. In the Abstracts only the major titles as such are included, although the substantive matter is indexed. The bibliographies have not been indexed.)